The Diversity Challenge

The Diversity Challenge

Social Identity and Intergroup
Relations on the College Campus

Jim Sidanius, Shana Levin, Colette van Laar,
and David O. Sears

Russell Sage Foundation • New York

The Russell Sage Foundation

The Russell Sage Foundation, one of the oldest of America's general purpose foundations, was established in 1907 by Mrs. Margaret Olivia Sage for "the improvement of social and living conditions in the United States." The Foundation seeks to fulfill this mandate by fostering the development and dissemination of knowledge about the country's political, social, and economic problems. While the Foundation endeavors to assure the accuracy and objectivity of each book it publishes, the conclusions and interpretations in Russell Sage Foundation publications are those of the authors and not of the Foundation, its Trustees, or its staff. Publication by Russell Sage, therefore, does not imply Foundation endorsement.

Library of Congress Cataloging-in-Publication Data

The diversity challenge : social identity and intergroup relations on the college campus / Jim Sidanius . . . (et al.).
    p.   cm.
  Includes bibliographical references and index.
  ISBN 978-0-87154-793-4
  1. Education, Higher—Social aspects—United States.   2. School environment—United States.   3. Group identity—United States.   I. Sidanius, Jim.
LC191.94.D58 2008
378'.0170973—dc22   2008020352

Text design by Angela Gloria.

RUSSELL SAGE FOUNDATION
112 East 64th Street, New York, New York 10065
10 9 8 7 6 5 4 3 2 1

*We dedicate this book to the students
whose stories fill its pages.*

Contents

Contents

About the Authors

Jim Sidanius is professor of psychology and African and African American studies at Harvard University.

Shana Levin is associate professor of psychology at Claremont McKenna College.

Colette van Laar is professor of social psychology at Leiden University, The Netherlands.

David O. Sears is Distinguished Professor of Psychology and Political Science at the University of California, Los Angeles.

Kerra Bui is a graduate student in the Department of Psychology at Yale University.

Winona Foote is a graduate student in the School of Behavioral and Organizational Sciences at Claremont Graduate University.

Ming-Ying Fu is a methodologist at Honda R&D Americas, Inc.

Hillary Haley works as a private consultant in Los Angeles.

P. J. Henry is assistant professor of psychology at DePaul University.

Jeffrey R. Huntsinger is a lecturer at Loyola University, Chicago.

Stacey Sinclair is associate professor of psychology and African American studies at Princeton University.

Acknowledgments

This research was supported by grants from the Russell Sage Foundation, the UCLA Office of the Chancellor, and the National Science Foundation (Award No. BCS-9808686). The authors thank Marilynn B. Brewer for her valuable comments during the course of this project, Michael Greenwell for his efforts in data collection, and Miriam Matthews for her expert editorial assistance.

PART I

THEORETICAL BACKGROUND AND OVERVIEW OF THE STUDY

Chapter 1

Introduction

E thnic diversity in the United States has increased substantially in recent years as a result of immigration from abroad and differential birthrates across ethnic groups within the United States. The management of diversity and the assurance of equal opportunity for all Americans across political, educational, and judicial sectors remain hotly debated issues in contemporary American society. While in decades past equality of opportunity at lower levels of education aroused the most debate, in the past twenty years the focus has shifted to diversity in higher education. Attempts to achieve greater ethnic diversity on college and university campuses began in the mid-nineteenth century with the goal of increasing knowledge, understanding, and harmony among people of different groups and backgrounds (Rudenstine 2001). Although these efforts granted entry to small numbers of new immigrants and some African Americans, significant increases in the diversity of student bodies did not occur until the end of World War II, with the passage of the GI Bill in 1944. Unfortunately, although the bill was successful in increasing access to higher education for many returning veterans, this access was limited primarily to whites and to blacks outside the South. Black veterans in the South still faced significant barriers as a result of discriminatory policies that remained in place at many traditionally white colleges and universities.

The Civil Rights Act of 1964 effectively removed explicitly discriminatory policies in admissions to institutions of higher education that received federal funding. The removal of explicit barriers, however, did not remove all barriers to equal opportunity for underrepresented ethnic minorities. To remedy this situation, legislators developed active programs, such as affirmative action, to stimulate the participation of ethnic minority groups, especially African Americans, in higher education. Many of these affirmative action programs, originating in the 1960s and 1970s, were subsequently challenged in courts of law and by public opinion.

In 1978 the affirmative action program at the Medical School of the University of California at Davis was reviewed by the U.S. Supreme Court in *Regents of the University of California v. Bakke*. This case presented a challenge to the special admissions program of the UC Davis Medical School, which was designed to ensure the admission of a specified number of students from particular minority groups. In this landmark case, the Supreme Court ruled that race might be taken into account as one factor among many in university admission decisions if necessary to promote a "substantial interest," but it prohibited the setting aside of minority places and the use of differential cutoff points for admission. Therefore, although the judgment invalidated the medical school's special admissions affirmative action program, it also allowed race to be taken into account as a factor in future admissions decisions. As such, the benefits of exposing students to diverse experiences and ideas—and the necessity of a critical mass of students from any group to achieve these benefits—were acknowledged.

It was on the basis of the *Bakke* decision that colleges and universities continued to consider race in college admissions. Many of these efforts focused on the inclusion of African American students rather than on other minorities. It was not until the mid-1980s that increases in immigration changed the focus from a singular focus on the inclusion of African Americans to a focus on the underrepresentation of ethnic minorities in higher education more generally. One result of this shift was a change in focus from the specific issues faced by black students to a more general focus on the issues faced by underrepresented minorities in general.

Although increases in minority admissions stagnated during the economic downturns of the mid-1970s to the 1980s, a resurgence of minority recruitment followed in the latter half of the 1980s. By this time, African American students were competing with large numbers of Asian and Latino American students for university admission. As a result, the percentages of black college students in two- and four-year colleges have remained relatively stable over the last two decades, while those of Asian and Latino students have increased. For example, excluding nonresident aliens, minority enrollments at two- and four-year colleges increased from 17 percent of all undergraduate students in 1976 to 26 percent by the fall of 1995 (National Center for Education Statistics 2001). This rise was due primarily to the increased enrollment of Asian/Pacific Islander and Latino students. In the fall of 1976, African Americans accounted for 10 percent of undergraduate enrollments, including 2 percent at historically black colleges (HBCs); Latinos made up 5 percent, Asians/Pacific Islanders 2 percent, and American Indians/Alaskan Natives 1 percent. By 1995 African American undergraduate enrollment had increased to only 11 percent (including 1.7 percent at HBCs), American Indian/Alaskan Native enrollment remained at 1 percent, and undergraduate enrollment for Latinos and Asians/Pacific Islanders each increased by 4 percent (National Center for Education Statistics 2001).

These changing demographic patterns, combined with the concerns of minority students and their parents for cultural inclusiveness in college structures and curricula, have convinced many colleges and universities to develop forms of education that are pluralistic in orientation and positively embrace multiethnic and multicultural perspectives (Modgil et al. 1986). This multicultural education is designed not only to broaden students' educational base, but also to foster self-esteem and positive intergroup relations by emphasizing multicultural ideals and respect for people from different ethnic traditions (McHugh, Nethers, and Gottfredson 1993). The fundamental assumption of multicultural education—an assumption we hope to test empirically in the pages of this book—is that increased intergroup contact, combined with increasing knowledge about other groups' histories and cultures, leads to more cooperative intergroup relations.

The degree to which this assumption is actually correct has been hotly debated, with opponents of the multicultural perspective insisting that such emphasis on multiculturalism merely creates educational and societal balkanization (D'Souza 1991; Ravitch 1990; Schlesinger 1998; Shivani 2002). In contrast, proponents of the multicultural perspective claim that the only way to move forward in a multiethnic society is, in fact, by moving toward greater cultural inclusiveness (Banks 1986; Glazer 1997). Thus, one of the most urgent questions we address here is this: does a multicultural educational experience contribute to increased or reduced intergroup tension?

This question mirrors crucial theoretical concerns within the very active domain of intergroup relations research. A major theoretical concern is whether ingroup identification and attachment necessarily result in outgroup denigration and the consequent undermining of wider community attachment (see, for example, Turner 1999). These are examples of both theoretical and practical concerns that the research presented in this volume is designed to address.

Overview of the Book

The chapters in this book represent the cumulative effort of a large team of scholars whose original core members were Marilynn Brewer, Shana Levin, David O. Sears, Jim Sidanius, Stacey Sinclair, Pamela Taylor, and Colette van Laar. In the summer of 1996, we began a large-scale longitudinal study of the entering freshman class at the University of California at Los Angeles (UCLA). We surveyed these students every year until most of them graduated four or five years later. The theoretical approaches we use to examine this rich data set draw on several different paradigms, depending on the fit between the question being examined and the theoretical perspective. The theoretical frameworks guiding most of our work are contact theory, symbolic politics theory, social identity theory, and social dominance theory.

The chapters of the book are divided into four broad parts. Part I comprises the first three chapters, which frame and set up the substantive material that follows. Chapter 1 provides the overall rationale for the project and gives a brief overview of the book. Chapter 2 introduces the four major themes explored in the book and gives an overview of the major theoretical perspectives within the intergroup relations literature that have informed much of the research discussed here. Chapter 3 sketches the historical and political context in which this research was done, details the methodology employed (for example, the size and composition of the sample, the sampling procedures), and briefly describes the variables used and the manner in which these variables were operationalized.

The four chapters that make up part II begin the first substantive discussion of the major themes raised in the book. This discussion addresses the general questions of the crystallization of students' sociopolitical attitudes—specifically, the degree to which students enter college with adult-like political identities and political ideologies and how these initial ideologies and identities vary by ethnic group (chapter 4); the degree to which these initial political ideologies change during college for members of different ethnic groups (chapter 5); and the degree to which the ethnic identities of students from the "new-immigrant" groups (recent immigrants to the United States) are initially defined and subsequently change over the course of university exposure (chapter 6).

While chapters 4, 5, and 6 address the issues of ethnicity and multiculturalism largely through the analytic prism of symbolic politics theory, chapter 7 explores the issue of multiculturalism within the framework of social dominance theory. Social dominance theorists have argued that when there are power and status differences between ethnic and racial groups in societies such as the United States, members of dominant ethnic groups (for example, white Americans) feel a greater sense of ownership of, and attachment to, the nation-state than do members of subordinate groups (such as Latino, and African Americans). This also implies that there is a more positive relationship between ethnic and national identification among members of dominant groups than among members of subordinate groups (see Sidanius et al. 1997; Sidanius and Petrocik 2001). For example, ethnic and American identification are more positively related among whites than among Latinos and blacks in the United States. However, if the welcoming and multicultural environment of UCLA is operating as expected, there should be none of the asymmetry found in the relationship between university and ethnic identification across different ethnic groups that we find in the relationship between national and ethnic identification. That is, members of all ethnic groups should feel equal attachment to the university, and this identification with the university should relate to ethnic identification in similar ways for members of all ethnic groups.

The four chapters of part III address themes and issues that have been part of the multiculturalism and intergroup contact debates on American campuses for some time. Perhaps the most central issue here concerns the degree to which different forms of contact between various ethnic-racial groups actually improve intergroup relations or merely reflect initially positive attitudes between groups (chapters 8 and 9). A related—and up to this point poorly studied—issue within the broader multiculturalism debate is whether ethnically oriented and largely segregated student organizations help to alleviate ethnic and racial tension on campus or only aggravate it (chapter 10). Chapter 11 takes a closer look at some of the special problems and barriers facing students from underrepresented minority groups when they try to adjust to the challenges of academic and social life within the context of a multiethnic educational environment. As many other studies have shown (Pascarella and Terenzini 1991; Sedlacek 1989; Tracey and Sedlacek 1985), students from the two most stigmatized ethnic groups in the United States—Latinos and African Americans (see Smith 1991)—enter the university with generally lower levels of academic preparation, obtain generally lower grade point averages in college, take longer to graduate, and have lower graduation rates than their white and Asian American counterparts. Although academic preparation is related to academic success in college for members of all ethnic groups, the major thrust of chapter 11 is an examination of the non-academic factors associated with academic success for students from stigmatized versus nonstigmatized groups.

Finally, in part IV (chapter 12), we review the major themes addressed throughout the book, summarize the nature of the findings with respect to each of those themes, and integrate these findings into several overall conclusions. In exploring the analyses contained in this book, we hope not only to provide the reader with an up-to-date snapshot of the dynamics of intergroup relations as played out on the modern, multiethnic American campus but to deepen the reader's theoretical understanding of the dynamics of intergroup relations in general and practical understanding of the specific ways in which relations among ethnic and racial groups might be improved.

Chapter 2

Theoretical Orientations and Major Themes

Most research on the impact of higher education has focused on outcomes such as academic achievement, long-term earnings, and academic self-esteem; relatively few studies have focused on intergroup relations (for a review of the college impact literature, see Bowen and Bok 1998; Pascarella and Terenzini 1991). The few studies that have examined intergroup attitudes and behavior have generally found that increasing educational and intellectual sophistication appears to be correlated with decreasing levels of ethnocentrism and increasing ethnic tolerance (see Campbell 1971; Greeley and Sheatsley 1971; Schuman, Bobo, and Krysan 1992; Sidanius et al. 1991).

However, there are several problems with much of this earlier research. First, the bulk of the studies have used cross-sectional designs. These designs make it difficult to conclude whether differences in the level of ethnocentrism between people of different educational levels are a function of educational experiences, normal maturational effects, or simple time period effects. These time period effects can manifest themselves when the general level of ethnic tolerance in the society at large changes from one time period to another.

Second, much of the traditional literature has focused on variables that are likely to show only the positive effects of increased ethnic diversity on the quality of intergroup relations on the multiethnic campus. In this longitudinal project, we expand the list of variables in order to explore more seriously whether an emphasis on diversity might have both positive and negative effects on the quality of intergroup relations.

Third, an important shortcoming of the earlier college impact research is its almost exclusive focus on relations between African American and non-Hispanic white students (Loo and Rolison 1986). Even though relations between black and white students remain central to college campus life (indeed, much of the racial strife on campuses across the nation is between black and white students), the increasing diversity on many college campuses has broadened intergroup relations to include relations among several different ethnic communities.

Fourth, a major problem with the education–ethnic tolerance literature is the issue of "process." Even if we could conclude that the effect of education on attenuated ethnic tolerance is real rather than an artifact, it is not at all clear what processes underlie this causal relationship. Is the link a function of improved information processing, increased self-esteem, changes in basic values (some type of socialization), or a combination of all three? It appears to us that the process of educational socialization may be one of the least systematically studied, yet most fundamental, issues in the education–ethnic tolerance field. If we could obtain a satisfactory understanding of how the educational experience influences intergroup attitudes and behaviors, we would have an answer to the more general question of whether a multicultural educational experience facilitates or ameliorates intergroup tension.

Fifth, and finally, the majority of the college impact research relies almost exclusively on attitudinal measures of ethnocentrism and intergroup tolerance and does not explore the possible direct links between changes in attitudes and changes in behavior. The widely reported physical and verbal racial strife on college campuses across the United States in the 1980s (Elfin and Burke 1993; Phillips 1994) calls into question research findings stating that increased exposure to education necessarily leads to decreased levels of prejudice and ethnocentrism and indicates the need to explore both attitudinal and behavioral measures (Weil 1985).

The research reported in this book therefore attempts to provide a process-oriented understanding of the development of intergroup attitudes and behavior across the college years. In addition, it attempts to provide an understanding of the development of relations among students of color as well as between white and nonwhite students. In exploring these general questions, the chapters of this book discuss four

10

general themes: the crystallization of ethnic, racial, and political attitudes in college; the effects of a multiethnic educational environment on attitudes and behaviors and social and academic adjustment in college; the effects of intergroup contact on students' attitudes and behaviors; and the dynamics of ethnic and racial identity on campus. These themes are explored primarily within the context of four theories of intergroup relations: symbolic politics theory, contact theory, social identity theory, and social dominance theory. We first briefly describe these theoretical models and then discuss the four major themes.

Theories of Intergroup Relations

While there are dozens of theories dealing with intergroup relations, ethnic and racial discrimination, the four models below have been particularly influential for the analyses discussed in this book.

Symbolic Politics Theory

Symbolic politics theory is a sociocultural learning theory designed to explain the development and influence of central political predispositions, including inter alia those that deal directly with ethnic and racial groups (Sears 1983, 1993; Sears and Valentino 1997). It starts from the observation that attitudes vary considerably in strength. The strongest are described as "symbolic predispositions," such as the intense ethnic and religious identities and anti-outgroup prejudices in places of fierce intergroup conflict, such as the Balkans or the Middle East. The weakest have been aptly described as "non-attitudes" (Converse 1970), so named because they are neither stable nor very meaningful.

Symbolic politics theory builds in part from research on life-span political socialization. As a result, it takes a life-course approach to analysis of attitude acquisition, describing it as a process of learning over time. Any given attitude therefore exhibits a rising learning curve as it becomes stronger, attaining an asymptote at mature levels of acquisition. The life stage at which any given attitude reaches asymptote depends on a variety of factors. Notable factors include the intensity of the relevant information flow to which individuals are exposed from their social environment and the media, the homogeneity of an individual's information environment, and the opportunity to practice the attitude (Sears 1983; Valentino and Sears 1998). For example, a student attending a highly religious college that requires daily attendance at religious services is likely to be exposed to a strong and homogeneous information flow about religion, to be surrounded by an environment of like-minded people, to practice his or her beliefs daily, and thus to emerge from college with unusually strong religious attitudes.

Persistence   The roots of symbolic politics theory lie partly in research on pre-adult political socialization. One of the theory's most important foci is therefore on the lasting persistence of some early-acquired symbolic predispositions into and through adulthood. The persistence model claims that attitudes acquired in pre-adult life, often on the basis of minimal information, can last far into adulthood and influence political behavior decades later. There is a fair amount of evidence that some key sociopolitical attitudes, once they have initially become crystallized, persist quite strongly across time (Green, Palmquist, and Schickler 2002; Sears and Levy 2003). For example, Theodore Newcomb's classic study of Bennington alumnae revealed remarkable stability of their sociopolitical views over the fifty years after their graduation (Alwin, Cohen, and Newcomb 1991).

Impressionable Years Model   The impressionable years model offers an alternative, suggesting that the acquisition of significant sociopolitical attitudes can extend into and through young adulthood. In this view, young adults often have weaker attitudes than do older adults and are therefore especially vulnerable to influence. Late adolescence and early adulthood is also a critical time for identity development, and acquisition and shifting of personal values and ideologies is to be expected during this period. As a result, young adulthood is a life stage with much potential for change (see, for example, Jennings and Markus 1984; Jennings and Stoker 1999; for a review, see Sears and Levy 2003). For our purposes, the central assertion of the impressionable years model is that individuals' experiences in young adulthood may be crucial to their ultimate development. Although some sociopolitical socialization may have occurred before young people enter college, it may not reach adult levels until later in their early adulthood. In this model, the life stage we focus on in this book—the college years—also plays a unique and central role. Again, Newcomb's Bennington College study (Newcomb 1943; see also Alwin, Cohen, and Newcomb 1991) offers a familiar example of substantial and lasting political change during the col-

lege years. Moreover, the alumnae were also vulnerable to change immediately after college, when most married and began to develop new adult
friendships.

According to symbolic politics theory, the life stage at which people finally acquire strong and meaningful attitudes depends on the information flow reaching them at each point in life and is therefore partly a
matter of context. Among other things, vivid events can catalyze political socialization, and the absence of such events can delay it. For example, individuals are more likely to acquire strong partisan attitudes during a presidential election campaign than during the usually quieter
periods between campaigns (Sears and Valentino 1997). Similarly, students engaging in a hunger strike to force the establishment of an ethnic
studies department may be the talk of the campus, helping to
strengthen many other students' attitudes about race and ethnicity.

Two Exemplars: Party Identification and Symbolic Racism

On average, some attitudes show considerably more persistence through
adulthood than others do and may therefore be assumed to have approached complete acquisition earlier in life. The gold standard for the
persistence of sociopolitical attitudes, at least for American adults in the
past half-century, is political party identification, which is almost per-
fectly stable over time for most adults of all ages (see, for example, Converse and Markus 1979; Green, Palmquist, and Schickler 2002). Basic
racial attitudes and fundamental moral values also show relatively high
levels of stability (Henry and Sears 2002; Kinder and Sanders 1996). By
contrast, numerous other attitudes often show considerable temporal
instability, particularly those toward policy proposals that are much debated among elites but have little visibility with the mass public (Converse and Markus 1979; Jennings and Stoker 1999; Sears 1983). While
there are several explanations for why some attitudes are more stable
than others, symbolic politics theory suggests that stability is contingent upon the degree to which attitudes have been informed, contem-
plated, discussed, or behaviorally enacted (Sears 1983). Presumably, the
superior stability of party identification is partly due to the especially intense and frequent level of public communication about partisan attitude objects during election campaigns.

A companion dimension, central to this volume's primary focus on
cultural diversity, is racial prejudice. The strongest form of prejudice explicitly targeting racial or ethnic groups today in America is symbolic

13

racism (Kinder and Sanders 1996; Sears and Henry 2005). The theory of symbolic racism proposes that the old-fashioned racism of Jim Crow days, emphasizing blacks' inherent biological inferiority, support for racial segregation, and formal discrimination, has gradually been replaced by a more contemporary symbolic racism. Symbolic racism is manifested in beliefs that blacks no longer face much discrimination but are unwilling to work hard enough and that they make too many demands and receive too many undeserved favors. The origins of these beliefs lie in a blend of early-socialized racial antipathy and traditional conservative values, such as individualism. The concept of symbolic racism grew out of the broader theory of symbolic politics, with which it shares the proposition that much adult political behavior is influenced by symbolic predispositions acquired before mature adulthood. Symbolic racism theory suggests that racism, though now perhaps more subtle and difficult to detect, still has significant effects in American society. For example, much of the continuing white opposition to affirmative action in university admissions policies can be traced to symbolic racism (Sears and Henry 2005).

In sum, symbolic politics theory leads us to examine the extent to which political socialization is already complete at college entry, how much it continues to evolve through the college years, and how complete it is at college exit. We are particularly interested in comparing Asian and Latino students with white students. Almost all of the Asian and Latino students in our sample are products of relatively recent immigration and are possibly in the midst of sociopolitical incorporation into American society. We focus especially on three basic predispositions. One is general left-right political orientation, because it is so central to political decisions and so much is known about it from other research. The others are symbolic racism and ethnic identity, because they are central to students' responses to ethnic diversity.

Contact Theory

Contact theory is one of the oldest and most influential models of intergroup relations and lies at the heart of much of the work of this project. Beginning with the work of R. M. Williams Jr. (1947), contact theory was refined by Gordon Allport (1954) and has since become a major tool in our efforts to improve intergroup relations. Allport proposed that four features of intergroup contact are necessary for the improvement of intergroup relations: the contact situation needs to be characterized by equal status between groups; the groups must cooperate on a common task; the groups must perceive that they are pursuing a common goal; and the intergroup contact needs to be perceived as positively sanctioned by institutional authorities (see also Pettigrew 1998b). Since Allport's formulation of contact theory, a wealth of research supporting its basic contentions has been amassed. The positive effects of contact have been shown in numerous countries (including the United States, South Africa, Germany, and Australia) and across a wide range of target groups (for example, ethnic groups, the elderly, the physically disabled, gays and lesbians, and AIDS sufferers; see Pettigrew 1998b). Furthermore, the more systematic the research, the larger the positive effects of contact are found to be (Pettigrew and Tropp 2006). Finally, intergroup contact in situations that fulfill the four conditions outlined by Allport tends to lead to the largest positive effects. This is especially true for intergroup friendships, because they fulfill the four conditions and tend to be long-term and to occur across a wide variety of social settings (for a review, see Pettigrew and Tropp 2006). In sum, as Thomas Pettigrew and Linda Tropp (2006; see also Pettigrew and Tropp 2000) conclude, intergroup contact typically reduces prejudice. Recent research has sought to explore more specifically three issues: why does contact reduce prejudice (that is, what are the psychological mechanisms underlying contact's positive effects)?; how can the contact's effects be generalized—that is, how can positive attitudes toward outgroup members within the contact situation be translated into positive attitudes toward outgroups in general and even toward outgroups not present in the original contact situation?; and how important are cross-group friendships in reducing prejudice?

The Psychological Processes Underlying Contact

Why does contact work? The original contact hypothesis suggested that the four facilitative conditions were required to reduce tensions between groups, but it did little to explain the psychological processes triggered by contact that reduce prejudice (Pettigrew 1998a). Recent research has sought to determine what these processes are and how they improve intergroup attitudes. Three such processes are acquisition of new information, anxiety reduction, and development of a common ingroup identity.

First, optimal contact situations appear to allow for the learning of new information about outgroups (Pettigrew 1998a, 1998b). This increased knowledge about members of outgroups, especially when it is stereotype-disconfirming, allows for more individuated impressions of outgroup members and can lead to an increased sense of efficacy when interacting with members of the outgroup and, in some cases, reduced negativity toward the outgroup by helping the individual gain insights about past injustices endured by the outgroup (Dovidio, Gaertner, and Kawakami 2003). Second, contact improves intergroup relations by reducing the anxiety associated with intergroup interactions. The anxiety that often characterizes interactions between groups can heighten tensions and lead to increased stereotyping of outgroup members because anxiety reduces cognitive functioning (Wilder and Simon 2001). Through repeated interactions with members of the outgroup, the initial anxiety is reduced. Finally, contact improves intergroup attitudes when it inspires the development of a common ingroup identity (Gaertner and Dovidio 1986a, 1986b, 2000). Individuals often favor the ingroup over the outgroup when group distinctions are made (see, for example, Turner 1975). However, if members of different groups who come into contact start to think of themselves more as members of a single, more inclusive ingroup, former outgroup members are recategorized as members of the common ingroup and thus are viewed more positively.

The Generalization of Contact Effects   Although the reasons for contact's positive effects on intergroup attitudes are becoming more clear, a vexing problem for many researchers has been determining exactly what factors contribute to the generalization of these positive effects to new situations, new outgroup members, and even new outgroups (Pettigrew 1998a). This question is essential to any lasting improvement in intergroup relations. There are two main positions on how to translate contact into lasting positive changes. The first is called the personalization or decategorization model (Brewer and Gaertner 2000; Pettigrew 1998a). Norman Miller and Marilynn Brewer (1986), advocates of this position, have suggested that the intergroup situation should be structured such that the salience of social categories is reduced or eliminated. Participants in the contact situation would thus be able to interact with outgroup members in an individualized or personalized fashion, getting to know one another in terms of personal qualities rather than group identities. Over time and across situations, this approach is believed to reduce bias by reducing the meaning of social categorization and thus the negative attitudes attached to particular category labels.

The second position takes the opposite view: the salience of social categories should remain high during the contact situation in order for the effects of contact to generalize to other outgroup members. Advocates of this position argue that if the group context fades during the contact situation, it is no longer an intergroup encounter but rather an interpersonal encounter from which no intergroup effects will emerge (Hewstone and Brown 1986). Moreover, as Lucy Johnston and Miles Hewstone (1992) suggest, the positive effects of contact tend to generalize to other outgroup members when contact involves typical outgroup members precisely because it is these typical outgroup members who make group membership so salient within the contact situation.

These two approaches would structure the contact situation in completely opposite ways in order to promote generalization. However, if they are viewed as sequential rather than competing strategies for structuring the contact situation, using both together might lead to more generalization (Pettigrew 1998a). That is, it might be ideal to reduce the salience of social categories in the early stages of contact between groups to reduce anxiety and develop personalized impressions of outgroup members. As the contact situation progresses, however, it might be advisable to reintroduce the intergroup context in order for the effects of contact to translate into improved attitudes toward all members of the outgroup (see Pettigrew 1998a, 1998b). Finally, given enough time and interaction between groups, it might be fruitful to have individuals begin to recategorize themselves in terms of a more inclusive, common ingroup identity (Gaertner and Dovidio 2000). As mentioned previously, the common ingroup identity approach finds that intergroup attitudes are improved by recategorization. Recategorization leads an individual to categorize former members of the outgroup as members of the ingroup, thus allowing former outgroup members to benefit from the glow of ingroup favoritism.

Intergroup Friendships   A final important emphasis of recent research on the effect of contact has been on the role of intergroup friendships in reducing negative attitudes about other groups. Pettigrew and Tropp (Pettigrew 1998a; Pettigrew and Tropp 2000, 2006) have found that intergroup friendships are important for creating positive intergroup attitudes, for having these attitudes generalize to other members

17

of outgroups, and even for having these attitudes generalize to members of outgroups not involved in the contact interaction. As mentioned earlier, intergroup friendships have great potential for creating more positive intergroup attitudes because friendship situations tend to meet all of Allport's (1954) original conditions necessary for contact to succeed. In fact, in a review of the contact literature, Pettigrew and Tropp (2006) find that having friends from other racial or ethnic groups is strongly associated with decreased levels of prejudice. The effects of intergroup friendships are so robust that, in what is called the "extended contact effect," simply learning that one's friends have friends from other groups reduces prejudice (Wright et al. 1997).

Social Identity Theory

A third major model of intergroup relations that has inspired much of the work in this book is social identity theory. Henri Tajfel and his colleagues (Tajfel 1972; Tajfel et al. 1971; Turner 1975) developed social identity theory in an attempt to explain the finding that, once people are divided into social groups, they tend to favor their own group over another group. This occurs even if those groups are created arbitrarily (for example, by a flip of a coin) and there is no interaction between group members and no group competition. Social identity theorists proposed that social identity, the part of an individual's self-concept that is based on his or her group memberships, is a central ingredient in ingroup favoritism. That is, just as we seek a positive sense of self as individuals (a positive self-esteem), we also seek a positive sense of self as members of certain groups (a positive group-esteem). One means of creating or maintaining positive social identity is to perceive the ingroup as better than relevant outgroups (Hogg and Abrams 1990). This tendency to seek positive group esteem through expression of ingroup favoritism has been labeled the self-esteem hypothesis and conceptualized in two ways that lead to two distinct predictions: successful ingroup favoritism enhances self-esteem, and threatened or low group-esteem motivates ingroup favoritism (Hewstone, Rubin, and Willis 2002; Hogg and Abrams 1990). Although there is general support for the first prediction, there is scant support for the second (Aberson et al. 2000; Long and Spears 1997; Rubin and Hewstone 1998; Turner and Reynolds 2000).

Several factors influence the amount of ingroup favoritism a person expresses in intergroup contexts (for a review, see Hewstone, Rubin, and

Willis 2002). One key factor appears to be the status of one's group: higher-status groups express greater ingroup favoritism than those of lower status (Brewer and Brown 1998). The perceived legitimacy of status differences between groups appears to moderate the effects of group status on ingroup favoritism, with high-status groups expressing ingroup bias regardless of perceived legitimacy and low-status groups only expressing ingroup bias when they perceive the status differences to be illegitimate (Bettencourt et al. 2001). The stability of the social system also appears to moderate these effects. When the social system is perceived to be stable, high-status groups tend to express more ingroup favoritism than do low-status groups; however, when the social system is perceived to be unstable, this difference is less marked (Bettencourt et al. 2001). Threat appears to be an important factor as well. For instance, threats deriving from heightened similarity between one's group and a relevant outgroup (threats to group distinctiveness) lead to greater ingroup favoritism, apparently as a means of differentiating one's group from the threatening outgroup (Jetten, Spears, and Manstead 1996).

Finally, group identification appears to enhance the expression of ingroup favoritism, with those more highly identified with the group expressing greater ingroup favoritism than those less identified with the group (Branscombe and Wann 1994). It has long been argued and demonstrated that while the degree of identification with one's ingroup is associated with ingroup positivity and favoritism, this identification need not be associated with outgroup derogation, hostility, or conflict (see, for example, Brewer 1979). Furthermore, according to John Turner (1999, 20–22), rather than there being an automatic association between ingroup identification and any form of ingroup bias, this association is contingent on a number of limiting conditions. These conditions include the degree to which: one's group identity is defined in terms of "readiness" to categorize the self in terms of some group membership; one's social identity is made salient in relation to the specific comparative judgment to be made; ingroups and outgroups are perceived to be interrelated within an overall social structure; the comparative dimension is relevant to the intergroup status relationships; and the outgroup is actually relevant to the particular comparative judgments to be made. However, given that these are all conditions that are likely to be found on the multiethnic American college campus, there is reason to suspect not only that students' ethnic identities will be heightened and politicized during their college years, but that these politicized ethnic identities will be associated with various forms of intergroup bias, including both ingroup favoritism and outgroup denigration. Thus, for example, the degree to which membership in ethnically oriented student organizations increases the strength and "politicization" of one's ethnic identity is the degree to which such membership might also be associated with perceived intergroup tension and conflict on campus.

Social Dominance Theory

The fourth and last theoretical model inspiring much of the work in this book is social dominance theory, which starts with the observation that human social systems tend to be organized as group-based social hierarchies, with one social group at the top of the social system and one or a number of social groups in the middle and at the bottom of the social system (Pratto 1999; Sidanius 1993; Sidanius and Pratto 1999). Given this basic observation, the theory then assumes that human societies are predisposed to structure themselves as group-based social hierarchies and that the major forms of group oppression, prejudice and discrimination (for example, racism, sexism, nationalism, religious intolerance), are simply specific expressions of this general tendency toward the formation and maintenance of group-based social inequality. The theory attempts to uncover the many interlocking processes responsible for the creation, maintenance, and re-creation of group-based hierarchy at multiple levels of analysis—for example, in terms of individual differences, behavioral differences between social groups, the relative power of hierarchy-enhancing and hierarchy-attenuating social ideologies and social institutions, and the interactive psychologies of males and females.

At the level of individual differences, the theory posits the existence of a general orientation called social dominance orientation (SDO), which is defined as a "general desire for unequal relations among social groups, regardless of whether this means ingroup domination or ingroup subordination" (Pratto, Sidanius, and Levin 2006, 282). A consistent body of research has shown SDO to be strongly related to generalized measures of prejudice across a wide number of cultures, yet also to be empirically and conceptually distinct from a number of related constructs such as symbolic racism, political conservatism, right wing authoritarianism, and interpersonal dominance

(Altemeyer 1998; McFarland 1999; Pratto et al. 1994; Sidanius and Pratto 1999).

Within social dominance theory, it is also argued that a person's level of SDO is related to his or her endorsement of specific social ideologies and social institutions that either attenuate or enhance group-based hierarchy within society. Specifically, these theorists maintain that those high in SDO are relatively likely to support social ideologies and social institutions that support the existing hierarchy (called hierarchy-enhancing legitimizing myths or social institutions) and that those low in SDO are relatively likely to support social ideologies and social institutions that reduce the existing level of hierarchy (hierarchy-attenuating legitimizing myths or social institutions). Examples of hierarchy-enhancing legitimizing myths include racism, sexism, political conservatism, social stereotypes, minimization of racial discrimination, and attributions of poverty to the internal inadequacies of poor people themselves. In contrast, hierarchy-attenuating legitimizing myths include political liberalism, recognition of racial discrimination, attributions of poverty to the external nature of structural relations in society, and egalitarian principles of resource allocation (such as equity and socialism). Whatever their "objective" truth value, these social ideologies justify the social practices, social policy support, and social judgment of the individuals who endorse them. That is, persons who are high in SDO could justify their opposition to affirmative action, a hierarchy-attenuating policy, by recruiting their belief that racial discrimination, in fact, does not exist. The opposite would be true for those who are low in SDO, who would use their belief in enduring racial discrimination as a justification for the continued need for affirmative action and thus would support its continued use.

Primary Themes

Using these four theories of intergroup relations as our primary interpretative frameworks, this book explores four themes: the crystallization of ethnic, racial, and political attitudes in college; the effects of a multiethnic educational environment on intergroup attitudes and behaviors and social and academic adjustment in college; the effects of intergroup contact on students' attitudes and behaviors; and the dynamics of ethnic and racial identity on campus.

Theme 1: The Crystallization of Attitudes

We begin by asking at what life stage the acquisition of major sociopolitical attitudes is complete (the topic of chapter 4). Have students accomplished the basic life task of acquiring an adult-like political identity by college entry, or does it require the college experience or even substantial further experience after college? Symbolic politics theory principally guides this line of inquiry. The persistence model suggests that most students already have acquired fairly stable political and racial attitudes by college entry and are not open to a great deal of change in college. The impressionable years model suggests instead that students' key political and racial attitudes are still incompletely socialized at college entry and that the college experience supplies the additional learning required to place their attitude acquisition close to adult levels by college exit.

But how do we define completeness in the acquisition of sociopolitical attitudes? Two quite different criteria may be used. The traditional approach suggests that political socialization is complete when the individual has fully incorporated the conventional norms of his or her social environment. In the context of a college education, this criterion would suggest, by analogy to Newcomb's (1943) Bennington study, that many students enter college holding their family's conventionally conservative attitudes and then become more liberal as they progress through college, internalizing the progressive campus norms. They would then leave college as the "politically correct" liberals so often decried by conservatives.

An alternative criterion for completeness would be students' replacement of their weak and hesitant youthful attitudes with a more fully crystallized adult belief system, regardless of the content of their attitudes. More crystallized attitudes, within the framework of symbolic politics theory, are those whose learning has reached asymptote in attitude strength. Therefore, they are internally consistent, resistant to change, embedded in a network of other values and attitudes, and capable of influencing other attitudes (Sears 1983; see also Petty and Krosnick 1995). We believe that examining the crystallization of our entering students' attitudes and tracking it through college, using direct measures of crystallization of key political and racial attitudes, is one of the most innovative aspects of our analysis.

The first broad question we address with these tools grows out of the life-stage approach of symbolic politics theory. It assesses the meaningfulness of students' sociopolitical attitudes at college entry and then again at college exit to determine the impact of the college experience on them. A multicultural campus like UCLA is particularly devoted to conveying a message of tolerance to its students and easing the divisions between racial and ethnic groups. Students potentially have much to learn from such a college environment, given the nature of a liberal arts education, multicultural curricula, and the possibilities of multicultural living experiences. To do so, however, the college experience might need to counter such contrary sociopolitical attitudes as strong ethnic identities and racial prejudices. Do most entering college freshmen already have such crystallized sociopolitical attitudes that they are not very open to change during college? If those attitudes are firmly in place at the outset, highly crystallized and resistant to change, perhaps students' experiences with diversity are doomed to produce increased conflict and polarization through the college years.

Another broad question concerns ethnic differences in the crystallization of sociopolitical attitudes at college entry and through the college years. Whites have been the main subjects of political socialization research in the past. Have white students attained adult levels of key partisan and racial predispositions—in terms of both preference and crystallization—at college entry? Or is that a task that remains to be accomplished during the college experience or even after graduation? In fact, the students in our sample were initially more politically and racially liberal, not more conservative, than most Bennington students were as freshmen. That is fortunate for the campus goal of producing tolerant white students for tomorrow's multicultural society. Although the white students become somewhat more politically and racially liberal through the college years, we repeatedly see evidence in this book of only modest response to specific forces for change. Perhaps the reason is that their central sociopolitical attitudes also show adult levels of crystallization at college entry and show little change through college, consistent with the persistence model. At least this pattern of responses would indicate that the college experience does not exacerbate white students' antagonisms toward racial and ethnic minorities, contrary to the reports of campus conflict often seen in the media.

Turning to the ethnic minority groups, symbolic politics theory and the concept of crystallization lead us to focus on the incorporation of students from the "new-immigrant" groups—Asians and Latinos—into the American sociopolitical system. The majority of the Asians and Latinos in our study were either first-generation Americans born in another country or second-generation Americans who were born in the United States but whose parents had been born in another country and often were not yet fluent in English. As such, these second-generation Americans were not likely to have been exposed to very much information about American politics and society in adolescence. In fact, their parents as well as their peers in high school were often newly immigrated themselves who had little involvement or background in the broader American society and were often noncitizens and nonvoting, so we might expect the students' sociopolitical attitudes to have been relatively weakly socialized prior to college. Indeed, the data show that Asian and Latino students have lower levels of crystallization than whites at college entry, and so they initially do not seem to be fully incorporated into the American sociopolitical system. Some, but not all, of that gap is closed as a result of the college experience, indicating that, in the realms of politics and race, college plays an especially important socializing role for Asians and Latinos.

Finally, we also focus directly on the experience of recent immigration itself as a potential obstacle to sociopolitical incorporation into the broader society, as indexed by the crystallization of key partisan and racial attitudes. Asian and Latino students at UCLA are overwhelmingly the products of the large recent flows of immigration to the United States, and some of the gap in crystallization between whites and the new-immigrant groups may be due to this recency of immigration. Indeed, the data show that even the U.S.-born, English-fluent Asians and Latinos showed lower levels of attitude crystallization at college entry than did white students. Not surprisingly, those who were the products of the most recent immigration had considerably lower levels of crystallization. The college experience almost entirely closed the crystallization gap between whites, Asians, and Latinos who had been in the United States for a longer period of time. Even the immigrants themselves increased in crystallization, though their levels of crystallization did not reach those with longer time in the United States.

Theme 2: The Multiethnic Educational Environment

The second major theme running throughout this volume (largely the subject of chapters 5 and 11) concerns the effects of a multiethnic edu-

cational environment on students' political and ethnic attitudes and behaviors and their social and academic adjustment in college. For example, in chapter 11 we explore how perceptions of stereotyping and prejudice within a multiethnic educational environment affect members of
stigmatized groups. In this chapter, we are particularly interested in two
questions. First, do perceptions of stereotyping and prejudice affect the
feelings that members of stigmatized groups have about themselves and
their group memberships (for example, their self-esteem)? It has been
assumed that negative stereotypes and prejudices directed at stigmatized groups inevitably lead to lowered self-esteem and group-esteem
(Allport 1954; Cartwright 1950), but as we will see, this assumption may
not be accurate (see Crocker and Major 1989). Second, do perceptions of
stereotypes and prejudice affect the academic functioning of members
of stigmatized groups? It has been known for some time that members
of certain stigmatized groups (for example, women and African Americans) sometimes underperform in comparison to those from nonstigmatized groups (in this case, men and whites) within certain academic
domains (women in math and African Americans in academics generally). With these two questions as a starting point, we address how perceptions of stereotypes and prejudice may contribute to both individuals' sense of self-worth and their academic performance. The research
suggests that the negative influence of stereotypes and prejudice in
these domains is neither inevitable nor ubiquitous. Rather, the potential
for stereotypes and prejudice to undermine the self-esteem and academic performance of members of stigmatized groups is tied to specific
situational forces and particular social environments.

Theme 3: The Effects of Intergroup Contact

The issue of the beneficial, or perhaps even detrimental, effects of intergroup contact on the attitudes and behaviors of students within a multiethnic university is arguably the most central and critical theme of this
book (see chapters 8, 9, and 10). As already mentioned in our review of
contact theory, there has been a great deal of work generally supporting
the expectations of the contact hypothesis. Much of this work, however,
is not without its limitations. Even though these previous studies have
been able to show that intergroup contact is associated with reductions
in prejudice, the cross-sectional nature of most of this previous research
has not allowed us to establish definitively the causal direction of the re-

lationship between contact and prejudice (Pettigrew 1998a). It may be the case that intergroup contact reduces prejudice, as contact theory predicts, or conversely, it may be that individuals who are low in prejudice selectively engage in more intergroup contact. The best way to establish causality is through experimental and longitudinal research designs, which we were able to employ in our study.

Another limitation of previous research on the contact hypothesis is that it has tended to restrict its focus to contact between only two groups. This restricted focus has the advantage of simplifying the study of contact so that contact effects can be isolated and carefully examined, but such a simplification can also restrict the generalizability of contact effects, since contact in the real world often involves contact between multiple groups. Examination of contact between multiple groups raises at least three research questions worthy of further investigation. First, do the characteristics of the various groups engaged in contact influence the outcome of this contact? The limited research available on this question suggests that individuals' group memberships and the group memberships of the people they come into contact with may influence the extent to which contact reduces prejudice. For example, Pettigrew and Tropp (2000) find that contact has stronger effects on the intergroup attitudes of members of high-status majority groups than on the attitudes of members of low-status minority groups (see also Tropp 2006).

Second, do the beneficial effects of contact with members of one outgroup generalize to other outgroups? Again, the limited research available to answer this question suggests that such generalization is possible (Pettigrew and Tropp 2000). For example, Pettigrew (1997) has found that people who report having more outgroup friends exhibit less prejudice both toward the ethnic groups with whom they are likely to interact (those found in their country) and toward the ethnic groups with whom they are unlikely to interact (those not found in their country). This finding supports the notion that the positive effects of contact do indeed generalize from some outgroups (in this case, local outgroups) to other outgroups (in this case, distant outgroups).

Third, and finally, does contact with ingroup members actually increase prejudice? This is a particularly important question, since the positive effects of outgroup contact may be due to reduced ingroup contact rather than to increased outgroup contact per se. In ethnically heterogeneous contexts, extended contact with ingroup members may decrease opportunities for interaction with outgroup members, and vice versa. In addition to limiting contact with outgroup members, contact with fellow ingroup members may also reinforce biased ingroup norms (Blanchard, Lilly, and Vaughan 1991; Turner 1991).

Theme 4: The Dynamics of Racial and Ethnic Identity on Campus

The fourth and last major theme of this volume concerns the ways in which ethnic and racial identities both affect and are affected by various aspects of the college experience. In exploring the general issue of identity on campus, we concentrate on three kinds of questions. The first concerns the overlap between a student's ethnic identity, on the one hand, and his or her more superordinate and inclusive social identities, on the other hand (for example, identity as a UCLA student or as an American citizen; see chapter 7). Second, we consider the effects of membership in ethnic student organizations on the quality of relationships between different ethnic groups (chapter 10). Third, we examine the degree to which pan-ethnic categories in the United States (such as white, black, Latino, and Asian) are equally compelling and salient for whites and blacks, on the one hand (members of the "old-immigrant" groups), and Latinos and Asians, on the other hand (members of the new-immigrant groups; see chapter 6).

The Interface Between Subordinate and Superordinate Social Identities   In considering the issue of identity within a multiethnic-multiracial context, we have at least four conceptual lenses available to us: the classic melting-pot model; the multiculturalism perspective and its common ingroup identity variation; a more recent black exceptionalism approach; and the social dominance approach.

The classic melting-pot approach is based on the widespread assimilation into the United States of past European immigrants whose receding memories of earlier immigration promoted a gradual transition from ethnic to American identity. This assimilation prototype has become a dominant model of intergroup relations in the United States and is often described as part of the "dominant ideology" of American life (see, for example, Alba 1990; Alba and Nee 2003; Gordon 1964; Huber and Form 1973; Perlmann and Waldinger 1996). Just as their European counterparts did before them, the recent Asian and Latino immigrants have almost all immigrated to the United States voluntarily, drawn by economic opportunity or pushed by political expulsion. As such, the melting-pot perspective would expect these assimilationist trends to apply not only to immigrants from Europe but to the new immigrants from Latin America and Asia as well.

A second manner of thinking about the issue of identity within the context of multiethnic and multiracial environments is the multicultural perspective (see, for example, Berry 1984; Triandis 1977) and its major variations (see Gaertner and Dovidio 2000). The multicultural perspective stands in contrast to the melting-pot view that people from various ethnic and racial groups (including African Americans) exchange their highly salient and distinct definitions of social self for a superordinate and more encompassing definition of social self (for example, as American). Instead, the multicultural approach argues, it is possible, and even desirable, for people to maintain their distinct and salient subordinate definitions of social self (for example, as Japanese, Mexican, or African American) and simultaneously to embrace a broader and more inclusive understanding of the social self (for example, as a UCLA student or as an American).

Yet another contrast to the classic American assimilationist model is the relatively new black exceptionalism theory (see Sears et al. 1999; Sears et al. 2003; Sears and Savalei 2006). This theory argues that, while the trajectory of most immigrants and minorities in the United States follows a traditional assimilationist trajectory, African Americans are an exception to this pattern and thus represent a unique case. In contrast to other minority groups in the United States, African Americans were subjected first to slavery and later to the Jim Crow system before finally being given equal formal status in the 1960s. As a result of this unique history and historical inertia, blacks have not been able to integrate into the mainstream of American society in the same way and at the same pace as the European immigrants, neither in terms of socioeconomic convergence nor in social integration. According to the black exceptionalism model, one of the consequences of continued discrimination against and isolation of African Americans is a salient sense of racial identity that is distinct from simply being "American."

Social dominance theory is yet another approach that can be used to understand the relationship between subordinate and superordinate identities. However, it stands in contrast to the black exceptionalism thesis. Rather than regard black Americans as a unique case, social dom-

28

inance theory would simply regard black Americans as occupying a more extreme low-status position along a continuum of social status in which European Americans occupy the position of highest social status and the new immigrants occupy intermediate social status positions. As a result of their severe exclusion from the circle of concern and the rights of citizenship over most of American history, social dominance theory would expect African Americans to be somewhat less strongly identified with the superordinate American identity than members of other ethnic groups. However, to the extent that African Americans and members of other minority ethnic groups are treated fairly within the relatively hierarchy-attenuating university system, social dominance theory would expect members of all ethnic groups to be equally identified with the superordinate university identity. Thus, one of the interesting questions to be addressed in this book—and one rarely if ever posed—is the degree to which exposure to a multicultural educational environment increases or attenuates a sense of common superordinate identity for members of all ethnic groups over the course of their exposure to the university.

Membership in Ethnic Student Organizations Besides exploring the connection between students' ethnic and superordinate identities (as either UCLA students or Americans), yet another important question we explore is the manner in which students' ethnic identities affect and are affected by their membership in ethnically oriented student organizations on campus—for example, the Korean American Student Alliance, the Mexican American Student Collective, or the African American Student Association. Ethnically oriented student organizations have become a somewhat controversial and common feature of most American universities since the mid- to late 1960s. On the one hand, a number of critics have argued that such organizations are generally destructive to the creation of a common identity and merely maintain and even aggravate both ethnic tensions and the alienation of minority groups on campus (see, for example, D'Souza 1991). On the other hand, and using a multicultural frame of reference, others have argued that ethnically oriented student organizations provide minority students with a safe harbor and social support system from which to reach out to the larger campus community and form friendships with students from other ethnic communities (see, for example, Treviño 1992).

Despite the obvious importance of this issue, surprisingly little theoretical or empirical work has been devoted to uncovering the net effects of ethnically oriented student organizations on multiethnic campuses. Though rarely applied to the study of the effects of ethnic organizations on college campuses, modern theories of intergroup relations, such as social identity theory (Tajfel and Turner 1986), should be able to suggest what effects these would be. Namely, the greater the degree to which one's ethnic identity becomes "politicized," the more likely one should be to observe various forms of ingroup bias. Thus, there is at least some theoretical reason to suspect that the degree to which membership in ethnically oriented student organizations increases the political salience and importance of one's ethnic identity is the degree to which membership in these organizations also stimulates increased intergroup hostility and conflict.

Pan-Ethnic Identities   Finally, much of the contemporary social psychology literature on race and ethnicity in the United States goes no further than categorizing individuals into four large pan-ethnic groups, principally whites, blacks, Asians, and Latinos. This practice overlooks two possibilities: that these large categorizations may not correspond to the social identities preferred by these individuals, and that it may obscure important differences among distinctive ethnic groups that are usually collapsed together in larger pan-ethnic groups.

On the first point, at the beginning of each wave of data collection— before they had been primed to think in terms of pan-ethnic groups— we asked the students in our sample which ethnic or racial group they most closely identified with. The findings were quite revealing, as we see in chapter 6. The students in the two ethnic groups that were largely composed of native-born Americans, whites and blacks, almost all selected pan-ethnic labels. But large numbers of those in the new-immigrant groups preferred nationality-based categories, such as Chinese or Korean. In fact, well over half of the Asian students rejected the pan-ethnic terms, and about half of the Latinos did as well. This substantial preference for national rather than pan-ethnic identities did not change materially through college. This represents a cautionary note for the study of social identities in the United States. Specifically, the identities that social psychologists ask people about may not be the same identities people use to describe themselves.

A second point is that important differences may exist between subgroups routinely clustered within large pan-ethnic categories. For example, the Asian students came from a variety of different countries, and about half of them were immigrants. As such, at college entry, their nation of origin was probably still fresh in their minds, yet we normally collapsed them all together as "Asian" or "Asian American." But they differed quite substantially. Korean students, for example, tended to be overwhelmingly Protestant and highly religious. The Chinese, on the other hand, did not tend to be very religious. The Filipinos tended to be quite religious, but Catholic. The importance of such differences is that, for some Asians, religiosity makes a significant contribution to conservative political orientations, just as it does for whites. Indeed, religiosity was one of the strongest correlates of political orientation among Koreans, and this association increased substantially through college. However, religiosity had very little connection to political orientation for Filipinos.

A related point is that important differences also emerged between the most recent Asian and Latino immigrants and those Asians and Latinos whose families had been in the United States for longer periods of time. For example, the newly immigrated students had considerably less crystallized sociopolitical attitudes at college entry, especially concerning symbolic racism. By the end of college, the levels of crystallization among the more recently immigrated had all but reached those of their longer-resident counterparts. As such, the college experience played a considerably more important socialization role for the most recently immigrated students than it did for the white students or even the longer-resident Asians and Latinos.

Now that we have outlined the broad themes running through the pages of this book, chapter 3 presents the overall method of data collection, provides a detailed overview of the survey instrument used, and situates the collection of the empirical data within the sociopolitical context of the time. Chapters 4 through 11 then explore the important issues briefly reviewed here in greater detail, and chapter 12 provides a summary and theoretical integration of the empirical work.

Chapter 3

The Site and the Study

Any study in the social sciences is set within a particular historical, political, geographic, and social context. One broad societal context for our study consists of the major changes that were triggered in the 1960s as a consequence of the civil rights movement. The system of formal segregation and discrimination imposed on African Americans from the beginning of European settlement in North America was largely dismantled by that point. The attack on formal inequality soon spread to other ethnic groups, as well as to women, children, the disabled, gays and lesbians, and numerous other groups. These movements affected many domains of American life, including the domain with which we are concerned here—higher education.

Despite much tangible progress in reducing racial inequality in the aftermath of the civil rights era, forward movement seems to have stalled in certain respects in the last two decades. During the 1990s, for example, the overall educational attainment of blacks increased somewhat. The black-white gap did not close, however, and blacks' college enrollment rates actually fell. In addition, the racial gaps in both family income and proportion of families beneath the poverty line did not diminish through the economic expansion of the 1990s, and the racial gap in net worth actually expanded (Stoll 2005).

The second broad societal context for our study is the massive growth in immigration to the United States that has occurred since liberalizing federal legislation was passed in 1965. In 1970 about 4 percent of the

American population was foreign-born, but by 2002 this percentage had risen to 11.5 percent and was accelerating rapidly. Unlike earlier waves of immigration to the United States, the current wave comes most heavily from Mexico and Asia. In the 1990s, 60 percent of immigrants came from these two regions and only 15 percent from Europe and Canada, the main traditional sources of immigration (Kritz and Gurak 2005, 269–70). This rapid growth of immigration is not unique to the United States. It has occurred throughout most of the First World, though areas outside of the United States have not had the special ingredient of the relatively recently discredited and abandoned Jim Crow system of formal racial discrimination.

California and Los Angeles

Beyond the broad national and historical context in which our research is based, its regional context also deserves comment—namely, the fact that our research was conducted in California and in Los Angeles. California is distinctive in several relevant ways. First, it is relatively new. Its major population and economic growth occurred only within the last half-century. For this reason, it does not have the long history and traditions of the Deep South or the East Coast. Its history avoided both the lasting imprint of slavery and Jim Crow that characterized the Old South and the class conflicts caused by the influx of masses of European immigrants in the East and Midwest a century ago.

The absence of a history of slavery, Jim Crow, and class conflicts clearly does not mean that California has been free of inequality and discrimination. The decimation of the local Native American populations was no less harsh than elsewhere. Conflicts between white Californians and Chinese led to the Chinese Exclusion Act of 1882. Prejudice against Japanese Americans, who primarily lived in California, essentially ended their immigration to the United States with the so-called Gentleman's Agreement of 1907–1908, the Immigration Act of 1924, and later the internment of thousands of American citizens of Japanese ancestry during World War II. The Great Depression in the 1930s led both to the persecution of white refugees to California from the Dust Bowl, as immortalized in John Steinbeck's *Grapes of Wrath*, and to the forcible deportation of thousands of Mexican farmworkers. African Americans widely viewed prejudice and discrimination against their group as central factors behind the ghetto riots in Los Angeles in 1965 and 1992

(Sears 1994). Nonetheless, California has become one of the most ethnically diverse states. Its Latino and Asian populations grew rapidly in the 1990s, by 33 percent and 43 percent, respectively. By 2000, non-Hispanic whites were no longer the majority ethnic group (Alba and Nee 2003, 9). As such, California serves as a beacon of both the benefits and perils of an ethnically diverse society.

Second, California is big. Its economy is as large as those of all but a few of the most economically powerful industrialized nations. Its population is by far the largest in the United States, almost double that of the next largest states, Texas and New York. As a result, the state is able to afford a university system of unique size and quality. And it has a long history of commitment to public education. Although there are private universities in California, they have long drawn relatively few students compared to the public systems of higher education, and only a handful have the high status of the premier private colleges and universities of the East. There are private schools at the K through 12 level as well, but as we will see, they play a relatively minor role in preparing students for college. California's educational system is dominated by public education at all levels.

An important starting point for the discussion of cultural diversity in Los Angeles is the history of the city's race relations. A basic question concerns the relative sizes of the black and white populations. At the climactic moment when federal civil rights legislation was passed in 1965, Los Angeles was an overwhelmingly white city in an overwhelmingly white metropolitan area, with a relatively small black population. In the 1960 census, blacks constituted only 14 percent of the population of the city of Los Angeles and only 8 percent of the population of Los Angeles County. By 2000 the black proportion of the city of Los Angeles had actually fallen to 11 percent, though it remained at 8 percent of the metropolitan region as a whole.

Three decades ago, Los Angeles could have been described as having an overwhelmingly white majority. By 2000, however, non-Hispanic whites constituted only 30 percent of the city and 39 percent of the Los Angeles metropolitan area. The new-immigrant groups, Latinos and Asians, have expanded rapidly. Latinos now represent 47 percent of the city of Los Angeles and 40 percent of the Los Angeles metropolitan area, and Asians represent 11 percent of both. Indeed, Asians now constitute about the same proportion of the city as do blacks, and a substantially greater proportion of the Los Angeles metropolitan area as a whole. Los

Angeles is second only to Miami in the percentage of residents who are foreign-born (36 percent and 53 percent in 2000, respectively; see Kritz and Gurak 2005, 278).

Racialized Politics

Los Angeles, then, does not have numerically equivalent and highly competitive black and white populations, as does Chicago, nor does it have an outnumbered white minority trying to hang on to power, as do Atlanta and Detroit. Nevertheless, politics in Los Angeles has been recurrently racialized throughout the last four decades. By "racialized" we refer both to the polarization of the races in evaluating political events and to the strong role that racial prejudice plays in generating cleavages in whites' opinions about these events. Perhaps the most dramatic and shocking early event was the Watts Riot in August 1965, the most destructive race rioting that postwar America had seen up to that point. In most respects, the responses to the riots were highly polarized by race. Blacks were highly critical of the authorities' actions, attributing the rioting to such politically meaningful causes as pent-up black hostility, racial discrimination, and police mistreatment of blacks, and they were optimistic that the riot had sent an important message. By contrast, whites supported the authorities' actions and were inclined to dismiss any such sympathetic broader political interpretation of the rioting because they thought it would damage the civil rights cause. Moreover, whites' divisions of opinion about the rioting were significantly associated with conventional indicators of traditional racism (Cohen 1970; Sears and McConahay 1973).

The next two decades saw numerous examples of racialization in conventional politics. The conservative white mayor of Los Angeles, Sam Yorty, was a vigorous critic of blacks during the 1965 rioting. He was soon challenged by the first major black candidate in city history, Tom Bradley, in a strongly racialized campaign. Yorty won, but the vote was strongly polarized by race (Sonenshein 1993), and white voters split quite sharply depending on their levels of racial prejudice (Kinder and Sears 1981; Sears and Kinder 1971). Busing was also a strongly racialized issue in Los Angeles. When the Los Angeles Unified School District was sued over policies said to be responsible for its high level of racial segregation, the school board put a mandatory busing plan into effect to promote greater racial integration in the schools. In response, an antibusing organization quickly instigated the recall of school board members who had supported the busing plan and placed their own majority on the board. A statewide referendum soon amended the state constitution to void the legal basis for the busing order. Blacks and whites were strongly polarized over this issue, and racial prejudice was by far the strongest predictor of whites' opposition to busing, as shown in both local (Sears and Allen 1984) and national (Sears, Hensler, and Speer 1979) surveys.

Finally, in the 1990s, affirmative action became a powerfully racialized issue throughout the state. In 1995 the University of California Board of Regents made a controversial decision to end affirmative action in university admissions. Proposition 209 was then placed on the 1996 statewide ballot, seeking to eliminate all state and local programs that gave preferences to women and minorities. Ward Connerly, a black member of the UC Board of Regents and co-chair of the pro-209 campaign, further racialized the issue by relying heavily on quotes about a "color-blind" society from Martin Luther King Jr. Proposition 209 passed with 54 percent of the vote. Again the races were quite polarized, and racial prejudice had a central role in whites' support for it (Sears and van Laar 1999).

Since the mid-1960s, racialized politics has been a recurrent theme in Los Angeles specifically, and in California more generally. It has arisen in all the usual contexts: race riots, elections pitting black against white candidates, and ballot propositions, some directly and some only indirectly relevant to race. In all these cases, black and white Californians have been sharply polarized and racial prejudice has sharply divided whites. This is one side of the larger political context in which our students encountered cultural diversity in the 1990s.

That said, it is important to note a positive side of this political context as well. First, despite there being a relatively small minority of blacks in Los Angeles and California, they have enjoyed considerable political success. In 1973 Tom Bradley won a rematch with the white mayor Sam Yorty, and in the next three mayoral elections he handily eliminated both conservative white and black opponents, usually in the primary round. Of the largest twenty cities in the country, only Detroit had a black mayor as early as did Los Angeles, and almost all other cities with black mayors overlapping with Bradley's tenure had far larger black populations.

Second, although the racialized political context of California and Los

Angeles occasionally triggered racial violence—as in the Los Angeles riots in 1965 and 1992—it more often did not. In fact, there were quite a few other public events in Los Angeles in this era that could have been portrayed as significant and direct expressions of whites' disrespect of blacks and as such had great potential for triggering racial violence. Prominent among them were the elections in which white voters defeated the favored black mayoral candidate and passed the ballot proposition that eliminated affirmative action, a program expressly designed to reduce racial inequality. Each of these outcomes could easily have been interpreted as a collective insult by whites to the black community. But none in fact led to civil unrest. In short, racial violence in Los Angeles could have been much worse than it actually was.

The New Immigrants

We have said that the two crucial societal contexts for our study are the racial inequalities and tensions that persist in the aftermath of the civil rights era and the rapid influx of new immigrants to the United States, among whom Latinos and Asians are numerically dominant. To be sure, in the past voluntary immigrant groups might have been regarded, like the involuntary immigrants from Africa, as coming from a different "race" than Europeans. Asians and Mexican Indians often have been regarded as such. But there is an important difference between the political history of the black population, on the one hand, and the history of today's Latino and Asian populations in Los Angeles, on the other. Today's blacks are almost all descendants of the slaves brought to North America in the seventeenth and eighteenth centuries. They and their ancestors have been living in the United States as a stigmatized lower caste for centuries. In contrast, the Latinos and Asians in Los Angeles today are not, for the most part, descendants of hyphenated Americans who had been confronting discrimination and mistreatment for generations. Rather, most are recent voluntary immigrants with little experience with, or often knowledge of, the American past. In 1990 nearly three-fourths of the Asians and over half of the Latinos in the Los Angeles region were foreign-born (Farley 2001, 39).

In recent years, the new-immigrant groups have also been subject to similar kinds of electoral defeats at the hands of the white electorate, and so they too may be thought to have the potential for clashing with the white majority. The "official English" movement, which began in the

1980s, aimed to declare English as the official language (Citrin et al. 1990). The initial impetus was the development of bilingual education policies in the 1960s and 1970s, but the rapid growth in immigration, especially from Mexico, has been a catalyst as well. Many of these efforts have been successful. In California, two relevant ballot measures were both successful: Proposition 63 in 1986, declaring English as the official state language; and Proposition 227 in 2000, outlawing bilingual education in California. In truth, however, they have been mostly symbolic, with little practical effect.

A more draconian measure was Proposition 187; placed on the state ballot in 1994, it intended to prevent undocumented immigrants ("illegal aliens") from benefiting from state and local public services. Perhaps the most publicized provision was that the children of such immigrants would not be allowed to attend public schools. The proposition passed with strong majority support from whites. It was later overturned by the courts. But it is widely believed to have driven Latinos out of the Republican Party and into the hands of the Democrats, ensuring that California would remain a strongly Democratic state for more than a decade thereafter. Despite the differences between black Americans, longtime residents of the United States, and Asians and Latinos, many of whom are relatively recent immigrants, all faced, and lost, racialized political conflicts in Los Angeles and California over the past few decades.

The University of California at Los Angeles

Beyond being situated in California and Los Angeles, our study was conducted in the local context of undergraduate students at UCLA. It has long been known that the college experience can be pivotal in sculpting social and political attitudes. Such attitudes are formed and re-formed throughout the life span, but the college years in particular are believed to provide people with relatively extensive exposure to novel ideas and information and, just as importantly, with (their sometimes first) experiences interacting on an equal footing with members of various social, economic, and ethnic groups. As a result, important social and political views are thought to "take hold" in college. If the underpinnings of people's diversity-related attitudes—their causes, correlates, and consequences—are to be better understood, then college students seem to be an ideal population to study.

The History of UCLA

The University of California was founded in 1868 with a single campus at Berkeley. In the late 1950s, the state's "Master Plan for Higher Education" divided responsibility among three tiers of higher education: the University of California, which was limited to the top 12.5 percent of high school graduates and was to be solely responsible for advanced postgraduate education; the state college system (now state university), which was limited to the top 33 percent of high school graduates; and the junior college (now community college) system, which was open to any high school graduate. To accommodate "late bloomers," transfer access upward through these tiers was intended to be fairly open, and that has proven to be true in practice. For example, about 40 percent of the new undergraduates at UCLA each year transfer from other colleges, mostly after their sophomore years, and over 90 percent of these transfers are from community colleges.

UCLA opened in 1919 near downtown Los Angeles. In 1929 the university moved to a large tract of undeveloped land known as Westwood Village, between Beverly Hills and Santa Monica, a few miles from the Pacific Ocean. It began as a relatively small undergraduate institution and offered extensive doctoral and professional programs only after World War II. Undergraduate enrollments grew dramatically during the influx of the "baby boom" generation, from about twelve thousand in 1960 to twenty thousand in the early 1970s; today UCLA enrolls about twenty-five thousand full-time undergraduates. The University of California system as a whole gradually expanded to a ten-campus system. UCLA is now larger than UC Berkeley and UC Davis (both have about twenty-three thousand full-time undergraduates), and UC San Diego, UC Santa Barbara, and UC Irvine (all have about twenty thousand full-time undergraduates). UCLA is surrounded by some of the wealthiest neighborhoods in the United States.

The undergraduates at UCLA once came almost entirely from Los Angeles. Today, however, they come from a broader geographic area. In 2005, 34 percent of the freshmen came from Los Angeles County, 26 percent from elsewhere in southern California, and 35 percent from elsewhere in California. Only 5 percent came from outside California, including 1 percent from outside the United States. Colleges and universities in California, unlike many in the East, draw almost exclusively from the public school system: 81 percent came from California public schools, while only 5 percent came from private schools in Los Angeles County.

UCLA today is also among the most selective public undergraduate institutions in the nation. In the fall of 2005, more than fifty-five thousand students applied to be admitted to the undergraduate program, said to be the largest number of applications to any American university. Of them, 27 percent were admitted, and 39 percent of the admittees enrolled. The mean high school GPA of new freshmen was 4.13, and the mean SAT score was 1277. Today UCLA is considered the premier public university in the second-largest metropolitan area of the United States. It thus expects itself to be a key training ground for the future elites of white, African American, Asian, and Latino communities.

Cultural Diversity at UCLA

Diversity-related issues have long been salient at UCLA. Jackie Robinson began his storied athletic career at UCLA before World War II, lettering in four different sports; Ralph Bunche was a prominent alumnus; and Tom Bradley, the former mayor of Los Angeles, attended UCLA. The campus has named major facilities after all three. Sadly, numerous Japanese American students were removed from the campus in 1942 and interned far from Los Angeles, and two black student leaders were assassinated on the campus in the racial turmoil of the late 1960s.

The trends in ethnic enrollment at UCLA have changed considerably over time. As late as the 1960s, UCLA was almost all white. As shown in table 3.1, even at the end of the civil rights era, in 1973, UCLA was overwhelmingly white: 71 percent white, 10 percent Asian, 7 percent black, and 4 percent Latino. The white population then dropped precipitously over the next two decades, from 71 percent to 34 percent in 1995, but it has remained constant since then. As can be seen, the hoped-for increase in black enrollment never materialized; instead, it has declined substantially. Today black enrollment is at 3 percent, about half what it was three decades ago.

As a consequence of the rapidly increasing immigration to California from Asia beginning in the mid-1960s, the proportion of Asian students began to rise sharply, doubling to 21 percent by 1985 and nearly doubling again, to 39 percent, by 1995. Since then, it has remained steady, and in 2005 it stood at 38 percent. The Latino population also rose

Table 3.1   Ethnic Enrollment Among UCLA Undergraduates

Year	Whites	Asians	Latinos	Blacks	Others or Unknown
1973	71%	10%	4%	7%	8%
1980	63	16	6	4	11
1985	58	21	10	6	5
1990	46	28	16	7	3
1995	34	39	17	6	4
2000	35	38	14	4	9
2005	34	38	15	3	10

Source: Author-generated data from University of California, statistical summary of students.

sharply, with the new waves of immigration starting in the 1960s, doubling to 10 percent by 1985, and then almost doubling again, to 17 percent, by 1995. Only 51 percent of the student body at this time said that English was their first language, and another 29 percent said that they spoke both English and another language. A massive 20 percent said that some other language was their first language—despite a very small proportion of international students at the undergraduate level. Bear in mind that these students, in order to be admitted, had to have scored very high on the verbal SAT, in English.

In short, UCLA is even more culturally diverse than the state as a whole and more than other colleges and universities. For example, in postsecondary institutions across the state, whites, Latinos, blacks, and Asians/Pacific Islanders make up 49 percent, 21 percent, 8 percent, and 18 percent of the student population, respectively. At UCLA, the ethnic demography shows even more diversity, and no one group has a clear numerical majority: the comparable proportions are 34 percent, 15 percent, 3 percent, and 38 percent. Like the state of California, UCLA is in the eye of a diversity hurricane.

UCLA graduates a high percentage of the freshmen who initially enroll. As of 2005, 85 percent of entering freshmen graduate within five years, with 89 percent eventually graduating. However, graduation takes considerably longer for ethnic minorities. Of the entering class of 1995, 52 percent of whites, 43 percent of Asians, 31 percent of Latinos, and 27 percent of blacks graduated within four years. The six-year graduation rate shows smaller ethnic differences: of the students who entered as freshmen in 1993, 84 percent of the whites, 85 percent of the Asian

Americans, 68 percent of the Latinos, and 64 percent of the blacks had graduated by 1999.

Affirmative Action at UCLA

In the 1970s, it was widely thought throughout the higher education system that affirmative action was the solution to the underrepresentation of African Americans. Attention to diversity rose sharply at UCLA after the murders in 1969 of two members of the Black Panthers on campus. UCLA had opened an Afro-American Studies Center, along with three other ethnic studies centers, and was conducting a search for a director. The position became involved in the competition between two black political factions, the Black Panthers and US (an acronym for "United Slaves"). The black students on campus assembled to discuss the issue. In the middle of the meeting, members of the US faction entered the meeting room and shot and killed two members of the Black Panthers faction. Soon a shocked campus attempted to use affirmative action to increase the enrollments of ethnic and racial minorities and diversify the faculty.

Nationally, affirmative action soon came under sharp legal attack. In 1978, the *Regents of the University of California v. Bakke* case put a narrowly divided Supreme Court on record as supporting the critics of affirmative action in one sense by rejecting the use of racial quota systems in admissions in higher education. But the Court supported affirmative action in another sense by allowing the use of race as one element in admissions decisions. In 1995 opponents of affirmative action succeeded in getting the University of California Board of Regents to end affirmative action in admissions. This decision was reaffirmed by the statewide electorate the next year by the passage of Proposition 209, which eliminated all state and local affirmative action programs. Both went into effect the year after the students in our study had entered college. Since then, in 2003, two cases from the University of Michigan went to the Supreme Court. In one, the Court narrowly affirmed the use of race as one factor in law school admissions. In the other, the Court rejected the use of a numerical "point" system in undergraduate admissions that gave heavy weight to minority status by itself. Then, in 2006, the voters of Michigan overwhelmingly passed a ballot measure that eliminated official affirmative action programs. Affirmative action remains, to say the least, highly contested.

Much of the political opposition to affirmative action in California appeared to rest on the belief that unqualified blacks were being admitted to the University of California at the expense of qualified whites. However, as can be seen in table 3.1, ending affirmative action had a disastrous effect on black enrollment at UCLA but no effect on whites. The black proportion had hovered around 6 percent until the end of affirmative action in 1996 and then began to drop precipitously, to 3 percent in 2005. Throughout that period white enrollment did not budge. Since the end of affirmative action, the proportion of Latino students has changed very little. It has fallen from 17 percent in 1996 to about 15 percent as of 2005. In absolute numbers, there has been a catastrophic decline in the number of blacks entering UCLA since Proposition 209. The peak number was 389 in 1985; by 2005 the number had fallen to 125. This was regarded as such a crisis that the interim chancellor, Norman Abrams, decided to convert admissions decisions to a more "holistic," less quantitative process.[1]

Multiculturalism at UCLA

For several decades, UCLA has been committed to addressing diversity-related problems with "multicultural solutions." Like many of its counterparts across the nation, it has taken a variety of measures to address these problems (Association of American Colleges and Universities 2000) and has put an extensive web of diversity-related initiatives in place. UCLA established four ethnic studies centers on campus in the late 1960s—among the first in the nation to do so. Subsequently, the university introduced ethnic studies majors; implemented ethnic studies research and teaching initiatives; established affirmative action admissions policies relating to ethnicity; and sponsored minority-targeted orientations, events, and tutorial programs. Further, the university has established programs that are intended to ease diversity-related tensions and has put into practice harsh punishments for students, staff, and faculty who violate or disrespect multicultural norms. Therefore, it is of urgent practical interest to know whether this training ground—a model of the kind of multiculturalism making appearances at universities across the country—is an effective one.

These efforts at multiculturalism have often been fraught with conflict, such as when Chicano students and faculty proposed converting the Chicano Studies Center from an ethnic studies center into an aca-

43

demic department, with full internal control over faculty appointments and promotions. In the spring of 1993, three years before the students in our sample arrived on campus, Chicano activists set up a tent city outside the administration building at UCLA and began a hunger strike. Eventually a compromise was negotiated: a center for Chicana and Chicano studies, named after César E. Chávez, would be created with its own full-time faculty. Subsequently, standard academic departments were created for Chicana-Chicano studies and for Asian American studies. To date, neither African American studies nor Native American studies has an academic department, perhaps partly because there are so few undergraduate students from these ethnic groups at UCLA.

Conclusion

In the immediate aftermath of the civil rights movement, the primary vehicle of diversification was expected to be the integration of African American students into nearly all-white universities. In practice, higher education has indeed been diversified, but in quite a different way. African Americans have not been fully integrated; blacks remain seriously underrepresented in almost all universities that were predominantly white in the 1960s. Rather, higher education has been diversified mostly by the swelling ranks of new immigrants, the great majority from Latin America and Asia. UCLA is a premier case in point: its increased diversification is entirely due to the incorporation of students from these new-immigrant groups.

In response to this diversification, and despite the fact that it has taken place in a quite unanticipated way—the hoped-for integration of blacks having failed badly—the university put in place numerous multicultural programs. In the late 1990s, during the time of our data collection, minority groups were represented in relatively large numbers and multicultural efforts were in high gear. Just as college students are a prime population for the study of attitude formation and change, UCLA appears to be an optimal setting for examining whether and when multiculturalism succeeds. Is UCLA witness to inter ethnic harmony and a sense of common purpose, or is there evidence of eroding inter ethnic relations and ethnic balkanization? This is the core question guiding our research, and one that we have sought to examine from a variety of viewpoints.

In the following sections, we discuss our study design and sampling

Figure 3.1   The Participants in Each Wave of Data Collection

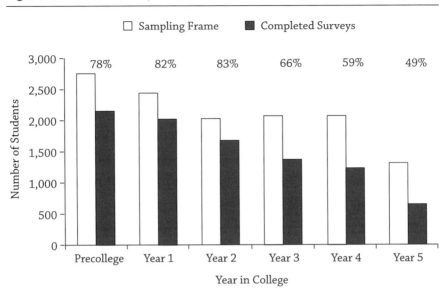

Source: Authors' compilation.

Note: The percentages above the bars in the figure are the response rates for each wave of data collection.

frames and the response rates for each wave of data collection. Then we present demographic information about our participants and provide an overview of the items that we used on the survey. In the final section, we report the results of the extensive attrition analyses we conducted in order to ascertain whether participants who completed our study differed in any way from those who dropped out at various points.

Study Design

Data for this longitudinal study were collected from students who were beginning their first year of college at UCLA in 1996. (Transfer students were not included in the study.) Data were collected during six time periods between 1996 and 2001: the summer before college entry (1996) and the end of the first through fifth years of college (1997 to 2001). Figure 3.1 shows the sampling frames and response rates for each wave of data collection.

Wave 1: Precollege

The first wave of data was collected through the mass administration of a written questionnaire at the beginning of the summer orientation program, which was a series of workshops spread throughout the summer before the students began their first year at UCLA (the summer of 1996). The incoming freshman class was composed of 3,877 students: 1,244 whites/Caucasians, 1,410 Asian Americans, 710 Latinos, 244 blacks/African Americans, and 269 students of other ethnicities (including Native Americans, Middle Easterners, and students from two or more ethnic-racial backgrounds) or unreported ethnicities. (Counts are based on enrolled students during the first week of the fall 1996 term.) Approximately 95 percent of the incoming freshmen (3,672 students) attended the 1996 summer orientation program. All students who attended orientation were eligible to participate in the first wave of data collection, except for the 923 summer orientation attendees who were under eighteen years of age and did not have written consent from their parents to participate. Therefore, the sampling frame for the baseline wave of data collection consisted of 2,749 students. Of these students, 2,156 returned their surveys, yielding a response rate of 78 percent. If we take the 2,156 completed surveys and divide by the 3,877 students in the freshman class, we find that 56 percent of the total freshman class participated in the precollege survey. The shortfall in this wave of data collection can be attributed about equally to the nonparticipation of students under eighteen years of age who did not have parental consent to participate in the study (24 percent of the total class) and nonparticipation for other reasons (20 percent of the total class). Nonparticipation was somewhat greater among black and Latino students than among other ethnic groups, so they were oversampled in the next wave.

At the end of students' first through fifth years in college (spring 1997 through spring 2001), data were collected through telephone interviews. These interviews averaged twenty-eight minutes in length and were conducted using the computer-assisted telephone interview (CATI) system run by the Institute for Social Science Research at UCLA.

Wave 2: End of First Year in College

Owing to the low number of Latino and African American participants in the first wave of data collection, contact information was obtained from the UCLA Office of the Registrar for all enrolled Latino and African American freshmen who did not complete the precollege survey. These students were added to the eligible population for the second wave of data collection, which took place at the end of students' first year in college. All black, Latino, and biracial students who returned the wave 1 precollege survey were also included in the wave 2 sampling frame. White and Asian respondents from wave 1 who had more than thirty missing values or missing contact information were excluded from the wave 2 sampling frame; all others were included. Therefore, our wave 2 sampling frame consisted of all the students who returned the wave 1 precollege survey, except for 179 white and Asian students with incomplete data or missing contact information. It also consisted of 471 additional Latino and black students who had not participated in the precollege wave and were added to our sampling frame at wave 2. Eighty-two percent of the 2,448 students in our sampling frame (2,016 students) completed the wave 2 telephone interview conducted at the end of students' first year in college.

Wave 3: End of Second Year in College

The sampling frame for wave 3 consisted of the 2,016 students who completed the wave 2 telephone interview at the end of their first year in college. Eighty-three percent of this eligible population (1,667 students) completed the wave 3 telephone interview conducted at the end of their second year in college.

Wave 4: End of Third Year in College

The sampling frame for wave 4 also consisted of the 2,016 students who responded at wave 2, in addition to two extra groups that were added to increase the number of African American students in our sample: forty-four black students who were in the sampling frame for wave 2 but did not participate in wave 2, and seven biracial students who were in the sampling frame for wave 2 but did not participate in wave 2 and indicated on the open-ended ethnicity question in wave 1 that one of the ethnic-racial groups they most closely identified with was African Americans. Five students were excluded because their contact information could not be obtained. The sampling frame for wave 4 therefore consisted of 2,062 students. Sixty-six percent of this eligible population

(1,360 students) completed the wave 4 telephone interview conducted at the end of their third year in college.

Wave 5: End of Fourth Year in College

The sampling frame for wave 5 was the same as for wave 4, except that one person was excluded owing to missing contact information. Fifty-nine percent of the eligible population of 2,061 students (1,215 students) completed the wave 5 telephone interview conducted at the end of their fourth year in college.

Wave 6: End of Fifth Year in College

The sampling frame for wave 6 consisted of the 2,061 students who were in the sampling frame for wave 5, except for those students who graduated from UCLA during or before data collection for wave 5 (that is, during or before the spring of 2000). Of the 2,061 students who were in the sampling frame for wave 5, 758 graduated during or before spring 2000 (18 in spring 1999, 8 in summer 1999, 14 in fall 1999, 57 in winter 2000, and 661 in spring 2000). Thirteen additional students were excluded because they indicated in their wave 5 interviews that they did not wish to remain in the sample. The sampling frame for wave 6 therefore consisted of 1,290 students. Forty-nine percent of this eligible population (627 students) completed the wave 6 telephone interview conducted at the end of their fifth year in college.

Participant Characteristics

Figure 3.2 shows the racial and ethnic demographics of the students in the precollege wave of our longitudinal sample compared to all the entering freshmen at UCLA in 1996, the population of Los Angeles County, and the population of the United States. The majority of UCLA freshmen attended high school in Los Angeles County. In Los Angeles County, there is now no clear majority ethnic group, although Latinos are the most numerous group. Blacks and Latinos were substantially underrepresented and Asian Americans were substantially overrepresented in the UCLA freshman class entering in 1996. The participants in our entering freshman (precollege) sample were approximately representative of the ethnic distribution of the entire freshman class of that year. However,

48

Figure 3.2   The Racial and Ethnic Composition of Entering
Freshman Sample, All UCLA Freshmen, and All Residents
of Los Angeles County and the United States

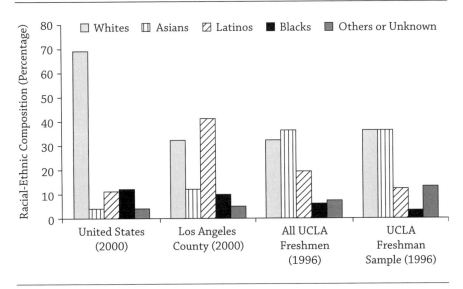

Source: Authors' compilation.

Note: Data on the number of all UCLA freshmen are based on enrolled students during the first week of the fall 1996 term. Data on the number of residents of Los Angeles County and the United States are taken from the U.S. Census Bureau (2000).

nonparticipation was somewhat greater among black and Latino students than among other ethnic groups, so they were oversampled in the next wave of data collection. The ethnic and gender compositions of the sample for each wave of data collection are shown in table 3.2, and the entire longitudinal sample is shown in figure 3.3. As was the case for the UCLA freshman class entering in 1996 as a whole, there are more women than men in the sample, especially among African Americans (69 percent of whom are women, compared to 56 percent of Latinos, 53 percent of Asians, and 54 percent of whites).

Overall, the entire longitudinal sample was composed of 17 percent Protestants, 33 percent Catholics, 6 percent Jews, 5 percent Buddhists, 23 percent students with no religious preference, and 16 percent students with some other religion. There are thus more Catholics than members of any other religious group in the sample as a whole, owing to

The Diversity Challenge

Table 3.2   The Ethnic and Gender Composition of the Sample for Each Year in College

	Precollege	Year 1	Year 2	Year 3	Year 4	Year 5
Ethnicity						
Whites	748	550	426	351	311	111
Asians	753	603	519	419	389	199
Latinos	255	430	356	295	252	167
Blacks	68	130	102	84	67	46
Others or unknown	332	303	264	211	196	104
Gender						
Males	937	901	758	633	525	309
Females	1,218	1,115	909	725	690	318
Others or unknown	1	0	0	2	0	0
Total	2,156	2,016	1,667	1,360	1,215	627

Source: Adapted from Levin, van Laar, and Sidanius 2003.

Figure 3.3   Gender Composition by Ethnicity in the Entire Longitudinal Sample

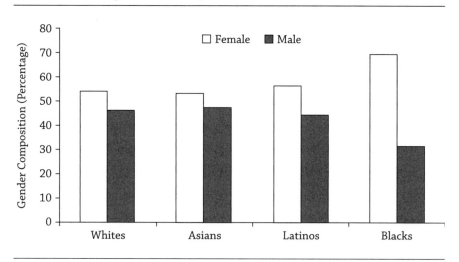

Source: Authors' compilation.

Figure 3.4   Parental Education by Ethnicity in the Entire
Longitudinal Sample

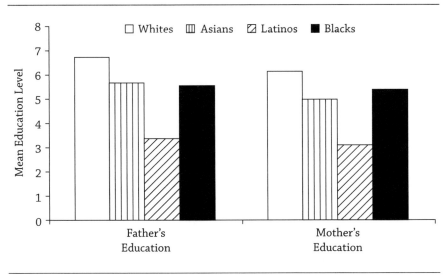

Source: Authors' compilation.

Note: 1 = elementary school; 2 = some high school; 3 = completed high school; 4 = trade school; 5 = some college; 6 = completed degree (BA or BS degree); 7 = some graduate or professional school; 8 = completed graduate or professional degree.

the large number of Latinos (77 percent) who indicated they were Catholic. Approximately 20 percent of the whites and Asians were Catholic (only 12 percent of the blacks were Catholic), and about 20 percent of the whites, Asians, and blacks were Protestant (only 6 percent of the Latinos were Protestant). An additional 15 percent of the whites were Jewish, and 14 percent of the Asians were Buddhist.

As shown in figure 3.4, whites had the highest mean levels of parental education and Latinos had the lowest. While the mean level of father's education among whites was at least completion of an undergraduate degree, for Asians and blacks it was at least some college, and for Latinos it was just above high school completion. Mean levels of mother's education were similar, but slightly lower for whites and Asians than mean levels of father's education. As shown in figure 3.5, these ethnic differences in parental education are also reflected in ethnic differences in family social class.

In this study, the students from the new-immigrant groups, Latinos

Figure 3.5   Family Social Class by Ethnicity in the Entire
Longitudinal Sample

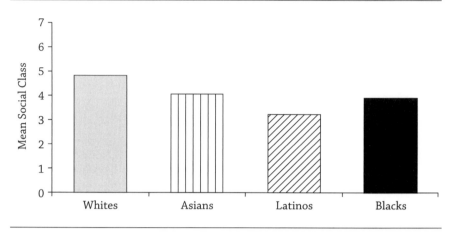

Source: Authors' compilation.

Note: 1 = poor; 2 = working class; 3 = lower-middle class; 4 = middle class; 5 = upper-middle class; 6 = lower-upper class; 7 = upper class.

and Asian Americans, were disproportionately immigrants themselves or the children of immigrants rather than descendants of earlier generations of hyphenated Americans. Table 3.3 shows the basic data on the birthplace of the students, their parents, and grandparents. Translated into generational terms, 49 percent of the Asian students were first-generation (self, parents, and grandparents all born elsewhere) and 41 percent were second-generation (all parents and grandparents born elsewhere); only 3 percent had at least three U.S.-born grandparents. Nearly half (43 percent) were of Chinese background, 18 percent were Korean, 12 percent were Filipino, 11 percent were Southeast Asian, and 7 percent each were Japanese and East Indian. The Latino students, on average, came from families who had been in the United States only slightly longer: two-thirds had neither a U.S.-born parent nor grandparent. Fewer Latinos (15 percent) than Asians were first-generation, 47 percent were second-generation, and only 9 percent had at least three U.S.-born grandparents. The great majority (76 percent) were of Mexican background, 11 percent were Central American, and 8 percent were South American.

By contrast, the great majority of black and white students were rather remote from any immigration experience. The overwhelming ma-

Table 3.3   The Immigration-Linked Status of UCLA Freshmen in the Sample, by Ethnicity

Immigration-Linked Status	Whites	Asians	Latinos	Blacks
Generation in the United States				
First-generation (self, parents, and grandparents all born outside the United States)	4%	49%	15%	9%
Second-generation (self born in the United States, all parents and grandparents born elsewhere)	3	41	47	10
Second-generation-mixed (self, one parent, and no more than two grandparents born in the United States)	9	3	13	4
Third-generation (self, both parents, and no more than two grandparents born in the United States)	13	3	8	9
Fourth-generation-plus (self, parents, and at least three grandparents born in the United States)	67	3	9	67
Unclassifiable	3	1	7	1
Language spoken at home				
English only	86	10	19	87
Primarily English	7	42	31	11
Primarily other languages	5	40	38	2
Only other languages	2	7	12	0

Source: Authors' compilation.

Note: Columns may not add to 100 percent owing to rounding.

jority of blacks (76 percent) and whites (80 percent) had been in the United States for three or more generations. In short, the Asian and Latino students were mostly the products of quite recent immigration rather than being descendants of ethnic minorities who had long resided in the United States. Almost all had either direct personal memories of, or at least close family connections with, other countries. By contrast, black and white students principally came from families that had long resided in the United States.

A closer look at their backgrounds underlines this vast experiential gap between the new-immigrant Asian and Latino students and the predominantly native-born blacks and whites. Theories of assimilation use language adoption as an indicator of the first stage of assimilation. The turn-of-the-century European immigrants came predominantly from non-English-speaking origins in Southern and Eastern Europe. Similarly, as table 3.3 shows, about half of the Asian and Latino students in our sample came from homes in which the predominant language was not English. Obviously, the students themselves had to be fluent in English or they would not have been able to survive the competitive process of admission to UCLA, which demands high scores in academic subjects such as English as well as verbal fluency in English on SAT tests. Nevertheless, at home at least half still used languages other than English to communicate with family members. Again, the contrast with blacks and whites is a sharp one. In over 85 percent of the homes of blacks and whites, only English was spoken. This reveals the persistence of foreign cultures in these recent immigrant families, even though the students themselves had passed what is usually considered the first stage of assimilation (Gordon 1964).

Overview of the Measures

We turn now to a discussion of the measures used in the study. Our survey items examined many aspects of students' academic, social, and psychological experiences during college, specifically focusing on attitudes toward and contact with members of four main ethnic groups: whites/Caucasians, Asians/Asian Americans, Latinos/Hispanics, and blacks/African Americans. The variables were classified into seven categories:

1. Demographics and background

2. Group identification

3. Sociopolitical attitudes, orientations, and behavioral intentions

4. Psychological and academic adjustment, commitment, and performance

5. Expectations and attributions

6. Perceptions and experiences on campus

7. College financing and postcollege preparation and planning

Demographic variables assessed basic information about the students, including their age, gender, and ethnicity-race, as well as information about their families, including parental ethnicity, parental education, and family socioeconomic status. Background variables assessed students' precollege academic performance and precollege contact with members of the four main ethnic groups. Group identification variables measured the students' identification with the different social groups to which they belonged, such as their ethnic identification and gender identification. A host of sociopolitical attitudes, orientations, and behavioral intentions were studied, many addressing ethnic issues in society at large. These included questions about sociopolitical and ethnic orientations, perceptions of the structure of the ethnic-status hierarchy, ethnic attitudes, social policy attitudes, political preferences, intentions, and behaviors. Variables measuring psychological and academic adjustment, commitment, and performance explored both actual and perceived academic performance as well as self-esteem and other psychological constructs. The expectations and attributions variables assessed the respondents' expectations about their future socioeconomic status and that of other members of their ethnic group, as well as the attributions they made for their future economic life outcomes. Variables assessing perceptions and experiences on campus included measures of campus climate, university involvement, classroom and residential experiences, inter-ethnic contact, and personal and work life. Finally, college financing and postcollege preparation and planning variables informed us of how the students paid for their education and what directions they planned to take after graduation.

The constructs measured in each category of variables are presented here. An alphabetical list of all constructs, including all survey questions and scales, can be found in appendix A. The scale reliabilities for each wave of data collection are located in appendix B.

1. Demographics and Background

In the first wave of their participation in the study (wave 1 for those who participated in the precollege wave and wave 2 for those who did not participate in wave 1), students were asked a series of demographic questions about themselves and their families. They were also asked a number of background questions about their prior academic performance and their exposure to members of the four main ethnic groups in their precollege neighborhoods, classrooms, and friendship circles. Some of these questions were asked in more than one wave of data collection, and some questions, rather than being asked in the first wave in which respondents participated, were asked in later waves (see appendix A for wave information).

Background
 Precollege academic performance (SAT scale and ACT test score)
 Precollege contact with the four main ethnic groups (as neighbors, friends, and classmates in high school)
Family demographics
 Father's ethnicity
 First in family to go to college
 Language spoken at home
 Mother's ethnicity
 Number of grandparents born in the United States
 Number of parents born in the United States
 Socioeconomic status scale/items (mother's and father's education, subjective family SES)
Personal demographics
 Age
 Ethnicity-race
 Gender
 Religion
 U.S.-born
 U.S. citizen
 Years lived in the United States

2. Group Identification

This category contains the measures of the participants' identification with larger societal groups, including ethnic and gender groups.

American identification
Ethnic identification scale

Ethnic private collective self-esteem scale
Ethnic versus American identification
Gender identification scale
Time spent learning about ethnic ingroup

3. Sociopolitical Attitudes, Orientations, and Behavioral Intentions

This category includes variables assessing the students' orientations, perceptions, attitudes, and behaviors regarding a number of social and political issues in society at large, with a particular emphasis on ethnic issues.

Ethnic attitudes
    Affect toward the four main ethnic groups
    Groups should maintain their distinctive cultures versus
        change and blend
    Opposition to miscegenation scale
    Self-perception as an individual American rather than as a
        group member
    Stereotypes of the four main ethnic groups (violent, intoler-
        ant, unintelligent, lazy)
Perceptions of the structure of American society
    Legitimacy of the ethnic-status hierarchy scale
    Permeability of the ethnic-status hierarchy scale
    Societal ethnic discrimination items
    Stability of the ethnic-status hierarchy scale
    Status perceptions of the four main ethnic
        groups
Social policy attitudes, political preferences, intentions, and
    behaviors
    Attitude toward bilingual education
    Attitude toward English as the official language of the United
        States
    Attitude toward government helping minority
        groups
    Attitude toward immigrants
    Attitude toward solving the crime problem
    Attitude toward welfare recipients

Feeling of "having a say" about what the government does
Frequency of political discussions
Intention to vote
Interest in politics
The more important duty of a good citizen is to obey laws versus vote
Opposition to affirmative action scale
Political candidate preference and voting behavior
Preference for smaller versus larger government
Registered to vote
Sociopolitical and ethnic orientations
Best way to get ahead in society is to improve personal status versus ethnic group status
Classical racism scale
Ethnic activism scale
Gender activism scale
Intergroup anxiety scale/items
No attempt to befriend people from other ethnic groups
Perceived zero-sum group conflict
Political conservatism scale/items
Pressure from one's own ethnic group not to interact with members of other groups
Religiosity
Social dominance orientation (SDO) scale
Symbolic racism scale

4. Psychological and Academic Adjustment, Commitment, and Performance

Many of the variables in this category measured students' psychological and academic adjustment to the university. We also measured several academic experiences.

Academic commitment and performance
Academic performance scale (self-reported cumulative GPA, perceived academic performance)
Academic term expects to earn UCLA degree
Average number of hours per week spent studying or doing homework

Consideration of dropping out of UCLA before earning a degree
Degree attained by the end of the seventh year after college
   entry
Importance of getting a high GPA
Last term registered
Length of time taken to earn a degree
Number of academic terms enrolled during data collection
   period
Number of incompletes taken this year
Perceived smartness compared to other UCLA students
Units passed during each academic term
Psychological and academic adjustment
   Discounting scale
   Disidentification scale
   Feeling of being admitted to UCLA because of affirmative action
   Personal identity stereotype threat
   Self-esteem scale
   Social identity stereotype threat

5. Expectations and Attributions

In this series of variables, students were asked to make predictions about themselves and members of their ethnic group at UCLA and in society at large.

Attributions for future outcomes of ethnic group in society at large
   scale
Attributions for future outcomes of same-ethnicity UCLA students
   scale
Attributions for future self economic life outcomes scale
Expectancies of future ethnic prejudice and discrimination scale
Expectancies of future socioeconomic status scale/items

6. Perceptions and Experiences on Campus

These variables measured students' UCLA experiences, once again focusing on the interaction between members of different ethnic groups. We inquired about perceptions of the campus climate and also looked at students' involvement in university activities, giving special attention to ones with a racial or ethnic focus. Finally, to determine their exposure to multicultural ideas and contact with members of the four main ethnic groups, we asked the students a number of questions about the ethnic focus of their classes and the ethnicity of their professors, friends, roommates, and dates.

Campus climate
    Atmosphere at UCLA allows versus prevents expression of true feelings about ethnic-racial issues
    Belonging
    Ethnic organizations promote separatism
    Perceived conflict between groups on campus
    Perceived ethnic discrimination on campus scale/items
    Perceived gender discrimination on campus items
    Perceived professor bias items
    Preference for ingroup professors
    Representation of the student body as one group, different groups, or individuals
    Support for increasing diversity on campus
    UCLA is not at all ethnically diverse versus very ethnically diverse
    UCLA promotion of diversity items
Classroom experiences
    College major
    Extent to which curriculum allowed learning about different cultures
    Extent to which learned about ethnic minority groups in classes
    Number of Asian American, African American, Latino, and female professors had each year at UCLA
    Number of ethnic studies courses taken each year
Interethnic contact
    Dating members of the four main ethnic groups
    Ethnicity of roommates
    Ethnicity of the person respondent is currently dating
    Friendships with members of the four main ethnic groups at UCLA
Personal and work life
    Employment and hours worked
    Involvement in a steady relationship, and its duration

Residential experiences
    Chose own roommate(s) or roommate(s) randomly chosen
    Feeling of exclusion versus belonging in the dormitory
    Feeling that dorm floor or suite is ethnically diverse
    Number of roommates
    Place of residence
University involvement
    Hours per week spent at most important organization
    Membership in fraternity or sorority
    Membership in student organizations
    Most important student organization of which one is a member
    Participation in the Academic Advancement Program
    Participation in the summer orientation program for minorities
    University identification

7. College Financing and Postcollege Preparation and Planning

Finally, we asked students how they shouldered the financial burden of college life (including tuition, fees, supplies, living expenses, and transportation) and what their immediate and long-term professional and academic goals were.

    Amount of education paid for by parents or other relatives, scholarships or fellowships, or own earnings or savings
    Future career or occupation
    Graduate or professional school test achievement (GRE, LSAT, GMAT, MCAT)
    Highest degree interested in getting (and field)
    Immediate plans after graduation
    Intention to attend graduate or professional school
    Money owed for undergraduate education

Sample Attrition

To examine whether the respondents who participated in each wave of the study differed in any way from those who dropped out of the study at various points, we conducted extensive attrition analyses. In these analyses, we defined and compared four groups of respondents. "Persisters" were those who participated in all waves of the study. They were compared to three attrition groups called "partway persisters," "voluntary early dropouts," and "involuntary early dropouts." Specifically, persisters were those who were present in waves 1 to 5 or 1 to 6, plus any black or Latino respondents who were added at wave 2 and participated in waves 2 to 5 or 2 to 6. Partway persisters were those who participated in only the first few waves, completing waves 1 and 2 only or waves 1 to 3 only. This group also included the black and Latino oversample added at wave 2 who participated in waves 2 and 3 only. The voluntary early dropouts dropped out early in the study after completing wave 1 only or wave 2 only if they were in the black and Latino oversample added at wave 2. The involuntary early dropouts consisted of the white or Asian students we decided not to recontact after wave 1 either because they had failed to complete a substantial portion of the wave 1 questionnaire (having at least thirty missing values) or because they had failed to provide contact information. These involuntary early dropouts consisted solely of whites and Asians.

Since most of our key variables were strongly correlated with ethnicity, we performed the attrition analyses within ethnicity in an effort to unconfound attrition from ethnicity. We compared these four attrition groups with respect to five different factors: demographic indicators, background variables (for example, ethnicity of high school and college friends), major sociopolitical attitudes, the consistency of these major attitudes at wave 1, and the stability of these major attitudes across the first two waves of data collection.

Our central concern was that attrition from the study might be selective rather than random. In particular, we were concerned that those students who dropped out of the study might have been more ethnocentric and more indifferent to issues of multiculturalism than those who remained in the study. We addressed this and several related questions in a set of attrition analyses described in detail in appendix C. The conclusion we drew from this series of analyses was that, while whites (especially white women) were more likely to drop out of the study than other groups, we found no evidence that this higher attrition rate was due to differential attitudes about race or ethnic diversity. Furthermore, since the differences between the four attrition groups appeared to be largely due to chance, the results of these extensive attrition analyses provided no evidence that the major conclusions reached in this study needed to be modified in any substantial fashion.

PART II

SOCIOPOLITICAL ATTITUDES AND GROUP IDENTITIES: THE ENTERING STUDENT AND PERSISTING DIFFERENCES

Chapter 4

Cultural Diversity and Sociopolitical Attitudes at College Entry

The next three chapters of this volume take a life-history perspective on the attitudes of the college students in our study, tracking their political and racial attitudes across the life course. This approach builds from the scholarly traditions of political socialization and life-span developmental psychology (Sears 1975; Sears and Levy 2003). It typically examines the pre-adult acquisition of attitudes, the college experience as a key intervention in what has been called "the impressionable years" of the life span, and the long-term persistence of such attitudes through adulthood. In these chapters, we deal with three central domains of political and social attitudes. We begin with two traditionally paradigmatic cases of early-acquired attitudes, partisan orientation and racial prejudice. In chapter 4, we examine whether or not our entering freshmen brought meaningful and stable attitudes to college in these domains. In chapter 5, we examine how those attitudes changed through college. Then, in chapter 6, we turn to a third domain, ethnic identity, as an indicator of ingroup attitudes.

Introduction

Are students essentially prepolitical at college entry? In other words, are they preoccupied with other life tasks and largely ignorant of the broader societal issues they will mainly confront later in college? Or in terms of consciousness about the broader society, are they already at approximately the level of the average adult? This chapter focuses on how developed the political socialization of students is at college entry. Here we examine political socialization broadly defined in terms of both incorporation into the electoral system, through which most Americans have their primary voice in decisions about the society, and views of America's racial and ethnic diversity.

Throughout most of its history, American society has been composed largely of two racial-ethnic groups: the descendants of European immigrants and the descendants of African slaves. The political socialization of both groups, broadly considered in terms of their incorporation into both the party and electoral system and the American system of ethnic and racial relationships, has been widely studied. However, traditional studies of political socialization have largely ignored young people's location in America's racial and ethnic system. Cultural diversity is central to our own story, but it is a new kind of diversity. Over the past several decades, the demography of the American electorate has changed in important ways. Like many other Western societies, the United States has become much more culturally diverse. Most notably, recent waves of immigration—comparable in magnitude to those of the early twentieth century—have led to rising numbers of Latinos and Asians within the United States (Alba and Nee 2003). We refer to these as the new-immigrant groups because they dominate immigration to the United States today. The political socialization of these immigrant groups, however, has not been closely examined.

We start by assessing whether the essential findings from traditional research on the acquisition of political and racial attitudes replicate with our white students. Then we turn to the question of whether such patterns also describe the socialization of the so-called new immigrants, whose political incorporation into their new nation, as either immigrants themselves or the descendants of very recent immigrants, is a crucial issue for their future. In what cases do these groups depart from the traditional patterns of whites and African Americans? It is particularly important to understand students at selective public universities, such as UCLA, for they promise to be the future leadership class for these growing ethnic groups.

The Completeness of Sociopolitical Socialization

This chapter is theoretically framed by symbolic politics theory (Sears 1983, 1993; Sears and Valentino 1997). As indicated in chapter 2, this theory takes a life-course approach to describing the process of attitude acquisition. Each attitude exhibits a learning curve over time as the attitude gradually becomes stronger. As with any learning curve, attaining an asymptote would reflect a mature, adult-like acquisition. Put another way, it would indicate that socialization is complete.

The speed with which any attitude approaches and reaches an asymptote in attitude strength depends on a variety of factors, particularly the intensity and homogeneity of the information flow to which the individual is exposed and the individual's opportunity to practice the attitude. For example, Philip Converse (1976) reports that Americans' political partisanship tends to strengthen gradually through the life course as they repeatedly enact it at the voting booth. Party systems that remain stable over years generate stronger partisanship than new or reformulated party systems. Exposure to an event that stimulates a strong information flow, such as an intense presidential campaign, sharply strengthens young people's partisanship (Sears and Valentino 1997). Exposure to intense political debate over many years on certain issues, such as abortion or civil rights, creates quite strong symbolic predispositions. In that sense, the life stage at which people acquire meaningful attitudes seems to depend partly on context.

One result is that adults' attitudes vary widely in strength across issues. The strongest are described as "symbolic predispositions," such as the strong racial prejudice in the old white South or the partisan cleavages in the very divided and stable party system of the present-day United States. Other issues remain obscure and generate "non-attitudes" in most members of the general public (Converse 1964; Converse and Markus 1979; Sears 1983).

To understand properly the actual and potential impact of the college experience on undergraduates, then, we need first to understand how completely they were socialized when they began college. Herbert Hyman (1959, 74) provided a traditional view of political partisanship when he stated, "A man is born into his political party just as he is born into his probable future membership in the church of his parents." That is, a meaningful party preference is acquired early in life, before the student leaves home for college, and it then remains quite stable through the rest of life. In chapter 2, we described this pattern of pre-adult acquisition and later persistence as the persistence model. An alternative, also cited earlier, is the impressionable years model, which proposes that people are more vulnerable to influence in late adolescence and early adulthood than they are later in life. As a result, significant political socialization can extend beyond adolescence and into young adulthood (Alwin, Cohen, and Newcomb 1991; Jennings and Niemi 1981; Sears 1975, 1990; Sears and Levy 2003). An early example, relevant to our study, was reported by Theodore Newcomb (1943) in his well-known study of the political orientations of undergraduate students before and after attending Bennington College. This study yielded evidence that young adulthood continues to be a time of political change for young adults (see also Alwin, Cohen, and Newcomb 1991).

What is the typical pattern for the most central symbolic predispositions of eighteen-year-olds setting off for college? Is their attitude strength already largely at adult levels? Remember that Newcomb's example was an unusual one. Most Bennington women entered college as conservatives, and in college they encountered a broadly and consensually progressive atmosphere. What about the presumably more common case of broadly pluralistic undergraduate experiences, such as would be the case at a large public university? Do these experiences build on and reinforce attitudes that are already fairly crystallized at college entry? Or do they help form and develop initially rather weak and diffuse attitudes? We begin this chapter, then, by asking how complete is the socialization of students' central political and racial attitudes is at college entry.

But what do we mean by "complete"? The traditional criterion is acquisition of the values and attitudes that are normative in one's social environment—that is, the most culturally or subculturally "correct" attitudes, such as socially approved religious beliefs, moral values, political preferences, and intergroup affections and prejudices. By analogy to the Bennington study, we would expect many students to enter college reflecting the conventional conservatism of their upbringing. A closely related but separable of the same criterion assesses whether the students already show the sociopolitical attitudes normatively appropriate for their subcultures, as reflected in the cleavages that most sharply divide today's adults. If so, political and racial liberalism should be more common at college entry among ethnic and racial minorities, women, the secular, and those with egalitarian values.

A second criterion for completeness of attitudes, often more implicit than explicit, is the acquisition of a coherent belief system en route to the successful attainment of a more general personal identity. Has the individual accomplished the basic tasks of acquiring that sociopolitical identity by college entry? By this criterion, socialization would be complete when the individual has moved beyond the tentative and sparse beliefs of late childhood and early adolescence to a fully crystallized belief system. In other words, socialization is complete when attitude crystallization reaches adult levels, irrespective of the specific content of the attitude. Such increasing attitude crystallization would be reflected in greater internal consistency and greater stability of attitudes over time.

Sociopolitical Socialization Across Racial and Ethnic Groups

Within this chapter, we compare the socialization of different ethnic groups in several ways. We begin with the status of key partisan and racial predispositions among white students at college entry. Have they attained adult levels—in terms of both preference and crystallization—or is that a task that remains for the college years and thereafter? Here our central focus is on the student's life stage. To what extent is the socialization of two central predispositions, political conservatism and symbolic racism, already complete at college entry? Or are these attitudes still somewhat unformed and susceptible to substantial later change?

Our second question focuses on the extent to which the new-immigrant groups have politically assimilated at this early life stage. Have new-immigrant groups already become incorporated into the American system of partisan and racial attitudes, as reflected in attitudes similar in content and crystallization to whites' attitudes? Past research has demonstrated substantial differences in political and racial attitudes and behaviors across racial and ethnic groups (to mention just a few, Bobo and Johnson 2001; Hochschild 1995; Kinder and Sanders 1996; Schuman et al. 1997; Sears et al. 1999; Sears and Savalei 2006; Sidanius and Pratto 1999). As a result, we might expect to find substantial racial-ethnic differences in our sample. The large Asian and Latino subsamples give us a special opportunity, however, to explore the political and racial incorporation of new-immigrant groups. Our assessment of the white students establishes a benchmark against which to compare Asians and Latinos, most of whom are the products of immigration within the past couple of generations. Do they show levels of precollegiate political and racial socialization at college entry—in both political positioning and attitude crystallization—comparable to that of whites?

Third, what about those students who are themselves immigrants? If Asian and Latino immigrants are in the process of attaining full political incorporation, we should see substantial differences not just between whites and the new-immigrant groups, but between the most recent immigrants and their counterparts with longer tenure in the United States.

Symbolic politics theory offers us some guidelines on what to expect. In general, strongly crystallized parental attitudes are a strong predictor of offspring attitudes (Jennings and Stoker 1999). It may be recalled from chapter 3 that about half the Asian sample was foreign-born and almost all of the remainder had foreign-born parents. (Incidentally, very few undergraduates were non-immigrant foreign students.) Most of the Latinos also were first- or second-generation Americans. Most of these students were likely to have been exposed to relatively weak flows of information in adolescence about American political and racial issues, at least from their newly immigrated, often noncitizen and nonvoting parents. Even the second-generation Asians and Latinos were likely to have parents with incompletely developed preferences about American social and political issues, themselves being foreign-born and often noncitizens. The same is likely to have been true of their peer groups in adolescence: the more recent immigrants were more likely to live in neighborhoods where they were surrounded by largely immigrant peers, weakening that source of potential socialization (Valentino and Sears 1998). In that sense, the new immigrants may resemble whites from relatively unpoliticized families.

This line of reasoning would lead us to many of the same expectations as a classical or canonical assimilation theory (Alba 1990; Alba and Nee 2003; Gordon 1964). That is, new immigrants are obviously initially different from people born in the United States, especially whites, who are historically by far the dominant majority. More telling, the longer immigrants and their families are in the United States, the more they should resemble the longer-tenured white majority. In other words, the symbolic politics hypothesis is that Asian Americans and Latinos assimilate to the mainstream American culture over time by adopting political and racial attitudes similar to those of whites, in terms of both their preferences and their attitude crystallization. One specific empirical implication is that Asian and Latino students whose families have longer tenure in the United States should already have assimilated to some extent, so that even at college entry they may already share the sociopolitical attitudes and level of crystallization shown by white students. A second implication is that those who are the products of more recent immigration will fall short of the level of socialization shown by either their native-born counterparts or white students.

The assimilation hypothesis has been challenged in recent decades, however, as indicated in chapter 2. A "people of color" hypothesis is a prime alternative, suggesting that the fate of immigrant Asians and Latinos in American society is wrapped up with their being "peoples of color" like African Americans (Chan 1991; see also Sears and Savalei 2006). This alternative hypothesis derives from social structural theories that posit a clear ethnic hierarchy in the United States, wherein whites are the dominant majority and the various peoples of color are—to a greater or lesser extent—subordinate groups (Bonilla-Silva 2003; Sidanius and Pratto 1999). Asian Americans and Latinos, like African Americans, have suffered various kinds of discrimination and disadvantage. According to the people of color hypothesis, this should heighten their sense of ethnic identity and group consciousness, as it has for blacks, and perhaps produce somewhat oppositional political and racial attitudes. Most important for our purposes, the longer such ethnics and their families have been in the United States, the more they should have experienced group-based discrimination. This experience may further broaden the gap between them and the dominant whites in their attitudes about race and ethnicity.

The symbolic politics view suggests, however, that these new-immigrant groups may not follow the black model so closely. Instead, it offers a "black exceptionalism" hypothesis (Sears et al. 1999; Sears and Savalei 2006; Sears and van Laar 1999). It suggests that in American society the color line restricts African Americans from full assimilation considerably more than it does other groups. Indeed, Asian Americans are sometimes described as the "model minority," suggesting that their trajectory is likely to propel them toward more complete assimilation than has been the case for blacks. If so, native-born Asians and Latinos, long-term residents of the United States, might increasingly resemble whites, rather than blacks, in their political and racial attitudes, especially compared to their immigrant counterparts.

This analysis does not distinguish between Asians and Latinos but rather treats both as alternative cases of the effects of the immigration experience. However, there may be important differences. The Asian students at UCLA enter college with considerably higher socioeconomic status (SES) on average, and with far greater parental education, than the Latino students (see chapter 3). They also carry that familiar positive stereotype of being a "model minority" group. To the extent that Asians are more accepted and assimilated, their precollege experiences could therefore be very different. Latinos might well resemble a classic ethnic group of the kind often seen in the immediate aftermath of the waves of European immigration in the last century, with stronger group consciousness and more political distinctiveness (Alba 1990; Alba and Nee 2003).

Sociopolitical Predispositions

As indicated in chapter 2, we focus here on two key attitudes. The first, political conservatism, combines ideology (or "political outlook," as we describe later) and party identification.[2] These are perhaps the most important sociopolitical attitudes in the United States today. They are the most powerful determinants of voting behavior among American adults. Indeed, party loyalty is now at an extraordinarily high level. Moreover, as mentioned earlier, party identification is the single most stable political attitude in the United States, and the benchmark by which the crystallization of other attitudes is judged (Converse 1964; Converse and Markus 1979; Green, Palmquist, and Schickler 2002; Jennings and Stoker 1999; Sears 1983; Sears and Valentino 1997). General political outlook is also quite stable over time, and relatively highly crystallized, even if often cognitively impoverished. Here we combine party identification and political outlook into a composite index of political conservatism, as has been done in other studies of persistence through the life span (Alwin, Cohen, and Newcomb 1991; Sears and Funk 1999).

Our second key dependent variable is symbolic racism, arguably the most powerful contemporary form of racial prejudice in the United States. The original theory of symbolic racism embodied three essential propositions (Kinder and Sears 1981; McConahay and Hough 1976; Sears and Kinder 1971; Sears and McConahay 1973; see also Sears and Henry 2005). First, it proposed that the nature of white racism has changed markedly over time. Even after World War II, the dominant

72

form of racial prejudice was the Jim Crow belief system, or "old-fashioned racism," which included belief in blacks' inherent biological inferiority and support for the physical segregation of blacks and formal discrimination against them. This form of racism has gradually disappeared, both in terms of much reduced white support for these essential beliefs and the now-marginalized political influence of these beliefs (Schuman et al. 1997; Sears et al. 1997). Instead, it has gradually been replaced by the more contemporary "symbolic racism," a coherent post–civil rights era belief system. This contemporary racism is manifested in beliefs that blacks no longer face much prejudice or discrimination, that their failure to progress results from their unwillingness to work hard enough, that they are demanding too much too fast, and that they have already gotten more than they deserve. Symbolic racism is now more common and politically influential than such traditional racial attitudes as old-fashioned racism, negative racial stereotypes, or anti-black affect (Kinder and Sanders 1996; Sears and Henry 2005).

Moreover, the origins of symbolic racism were hypothesized to lie in a blend of early-socialized, negative feelings about blacks and traditional, conservative moral values (Sears and Henry 2003). The word "racism" reflects these roots in racial antipathy. The word "symbolic" highlights not only the roots of this form of racism in abstract moral values rather than in concrete self-interest or personal experience, but also the focus of such beliefs on blacks as an abstract collectivity rather than on specific black individuals.

Finally, the concept of symbolic racism grew out of the broader theory of symbolic politics, especially the proposition that much adult political behavior is influenced by stable symbolic predispositions acquired before adulthood. Symbolic racism is also thought to be rooted partly in early-learned racial fears and stereotypes. Racial attitudes are generally more stable over time than most other sociopolitical attitudes (see, for example, Converse and Markus 1979; Jennings and Stoker 1999; Sears 1983). As a result, early-acquired racial attitudes are likely to have a strong and lasting impact on adults' attitudes and behavior. That is particularly true of symbolic racism, which, like party identification, proves to be quite stable through the life span (Henry and Sears 2002; Kinder and Sanders 1996). To date, there has not been much evidence addressing the life-stage hypothesis that symbolic racism is already a highly crystallized, stable predisposition in late adolescence. We hope this and the next chapter shed light on this aspect of the theory.

Empirical Questions

Our concrete research questions in this chapter focus on students at college entry. The chapter addresses five empirical questions:

1. *Liberalism at college entry*: The oft-cited stereotype is that today's university students are predominantly liberal, both politically and racially. That seems likely to be true of black students at college entry, but what about whites? Are they as conservative as the social structural theories would suggest? What about the new-immigrant groups? The first section compares the four major ethnic groups—whites, Asians, Latinos, and blacks—in terms of their political conservatism and symbolic racism at college entry.

2. *Sociopolitical cleavages at college entry*: Has socialization prior to college entry already generated the standard sociopolitical cleavages in American society, in forms similar to those present among adults? We look at five cleavages in particular: gender, race and ethnicity, religiosity, which increasingly is driving a wedge between the more liberal seculars and the more conservative faithful; and racial conservatism and egalitarian values, two important attitudinal contributors to the cleavage between liberal Democrats and conservative Republicans. What political resonance do these four areas of cleavage have among young people just entering college?

3. *Crystallization of political and racial attitudes at college entry*: How complete is student socialization at college entry in terms of the crystallization of political conservatism and symbolic racism? Is it already similar to adult levels? The persistence model suggests that the two attitudes are fairly well crystallized already. But it is also plausible that these entry-level attitudes are largely meaningless, quite malleable, and expressed by young people who are prepolitical and preoccupied with other issues in their lives.

4. *The new-immigrant groups*: We would take evidence of an initial dissimilarity of Asians and Latinos to whites in the completeness of their socialization as signs of incomplete incorporation into the American sociopolitical system. To test for this, we compared Asians and Latinos with whites in terms of their liberalism, showing subgroup cleavages like those among adults and attitude crystallization.

5. *Recent immigrants*: Finally, we consider the effects of immigration among Asians and Latinos. The assimilation hypothesis would

suggest that U.S.-born Asians and Latinos and those with English-language fluency resemble whites more than their foreign-born counterparts. In contrast, the people of color hypothesis suggests that native-born ethnics are more politically liberal than either whites or recent immigrants at college entry, owing to their longer and more extensive experience as disadvantaged minorities in the American ethnic hierarchy.

Liberalism at College Entry

How conservative or liberal are students' political and racial views at college entry? Is there evidence of sharp racial-ethnic differences at that early point? We begin with a description of students' political conservatism in the simplest possible terms, based on a cross-tabulation of the two scales measuring party identification and general political outlook.[3] We included all students who participated in the precollege wave of data collection and who identified themselves as whites, Asians, Latinos, or blacks. As shown in table 4.1, all four groups tilted toward both the Democratic and liberal side at college entry. Moreover, liberal Democrats outnumbered conservative Republicans within each broad ethnic and racial group. That said, Latinos and blacks tended to be somewhat more liberal than Asians and whites on both measures: 67 percent of the Latinos and 78 percent of the blacks were liberal Democrats, whereas just half of the whites and 39 percent of the Asians were. But even among whites and Asians, only one-third began college as conservative Republicans.

As mentioned, throughout this and the next chapter we analyze political conservatism in parallel with symbolic racism. As can be seen in table 4.2, mean levels of symbolic racism toward blacks varied substantially across ethnic groups at college entry. Specifically, Asians and whites were considerably more racially conservative than were Latinos or blacks.

We also measured several other predispositions in this study. An obvious comparison with political conservatism and symbolic racism is religiosity. Another is social dominance, which we subdivided into two subscales, inegalitarianism and dominance.[4] Mean levels of these predispositions within each ethnic group are also shown in table 4.2. As can be seen, blacks and Latinos tended to be more religious and more egalitarian and expressed stronger opposition to group dominance than whites and Asians.

We were also interested in students' attitudes toward certain issues of

The Diversity Challenge

Table 4.1   Party Identification and Political Outlook at College Entry

Party Identification	Political Outlook			
	Liberal	Moderate	Conservative	Total
Whites (N = 730)				
Democrat	50%	1%	0%	51%
Independent	3	9	2	14
Republican	0	1	34	35
Total	53	11	36	100
Asians (N = 721)				
Democrat	39	1	0	40
Independent	6	16	2	24
Republican	0	1	33	34
Total	45	18	35	98
Latinos (N = 245)				
Democrat	67	2	0	69
Independent	5	8	1	14
Republican	1	0	15	16
Total	73	10	16	99
Blacks (N = 65)				
Democrat	78	3	0	81
Independent	5	8	2	15
Republican	2	0	3	5
Total	85	11	5	101

Source: Authors' compilation.

Note: Independents and moderates are defined as falling at the absolute midpoint on the seven-point party identification and political outlook scales, respectively. All available participants are included. Percentages may not total 100 percent owing to rounding.

broad social policy: opposition to affirmative action; attitude toward immigrants (opposition to increasing the rate of legal immigration into the United States); attitude toward solving the crime problem (beliefs that more money should be invested in prisons versus schools as a crime remedy); and attitude toward welfare recipients (beliefs that most welfare recipients do not really need welfare). As shown in table 4.2, the same basic pattern emerged: Latinos and blacks were more liberal on these issues than whites and Asians.

Our first conclusion, regarding how liberal students' political and racial

Table 4.2   Mean Group Differences on Predispositions and Policy Attitudes at College Entry

Variable	Whites	Asians	Latinos	Blacks	F	p	η^2
Predispositions							
Party identification	3.72[a]	3.87[a]	3.13[b]	2.51[c]	30.33	<.001	.043
Political outlook	3.63[ab]	3.81[a]	3.33[bc]	3.10[c]	14.69	<.001	.021
Symbolic racism	3.87[a]	4.03[a]	3.54[b]	2.57[c]	58.08	<.001	.083
Religiosity	3.57[c]	3.76[bc]	4.01[ab]	4.44[a]	9.03	<.001	.013
Inegalitarianism	2.70[a]	2.72[a]	2.13[b]	1.57[c]	29.03	<.001	.044
Dominance	1.86[ab]	2.11[a]	1.67[b]	1.10[c]	25.68	<.001	.039
Policy attitudes							
Opposition to affirmative action	4.29[a]	4.27[a]	2.61[b]	2.05[c]	177.63	<.001	.222
Attitude toward immigration	4.64[a]	4.44[a]	4.42[a]	4.61[a]	4.70	.003	.008
Attitude toward welfare recipients	2.10[a]	2.16[a]	1.97[ab]	1.75[b]	3.25	.021	.005
Attitude toward solving the crime problem	4.44[ab]	4.53[a]	4.45[ab]	4.13[b]	1.75	.155	.003

Source: Authors' compilation.

Note: Entries under each ethnicity are mean scores for each ethnic group on seven-point scales. Scales have been coded so that high numbers indicate more identification with the Republican party, political conservatism, negative racial attitudes, religiosity, support of group inequality and dominance, opposition to affirmative action and increasing the rate of legal immigration, and stronger beliefs that more money should be invested in prisons versus schools as a crime remedy and that most welfare recipients do not really need welfare. The F values refer to one-way analysis of variances. Different superscript letters indicate significant Tukey t post-hoc mean differences across each row.

views were, is that UCLA freshmen were politically somewhat to the left of the broader American public as they entered college, regardless of race or ethnicity. Among the public as a whole in the mid-1990s, Democrats and Republicans were almost equally numerous, and conservatives considerably outnumbered liberals (Miller and Shanks 1996). However, this national division did not replicate among these entering freshmen. Among the white students, liberal Democrats outnumbered conservative Republicans by 16 percent. Latinos and blacks tilted even more heavily to the liberal side, with liberal Democrats outnumbering conservative Republicans by 52 percent and 75 percent, respectively. Even among the somewhat more conservative Asian students, liberal Democrats had a slight plurality.

Second, although we considered Newcomb's (1943) Bennington College study to be a precedent for assessing the effects of college experience on partisanship, the results of that study also stand in contrast to those we obtained at UCLA. In the Bennington study, of course, most of the students entered college as relative political conservatives, even in the depths of the Great Depression. In contrast, UCLA, like many large research universities, has the reputation today of having a liberal political climate of opinion. Given our results, that reputation seems largely justified, even in terms of incoming white students.

Sociopolitical Cleavages at College Entry

How fully socialized were these students' political and racial attitudes at college entry? Our first approach looks at their demographic and attitudinal correlates. We have three alternative hypotheses. A "prepolitical" hypothesis is that their key attitudes are quite incompletely socialized at that stage, and have few meaningful correlates. A "social background" hypothesis would pose the minimal criterion that the students' attitudes are at least beginning to sort themselves out according to such major demographic categories as race, gender, and parental education. A "pre-adult socialization" hypothesis suggests that the students have already acquired fairly mature levels of political and racial attitudes by college entry, reflected in cleavages in the attitudinal predispositions that divide today's adults, such as religiosity, racial prejudice, and egalitarian values (see, for example, Miller and Shanks 1996; Valentino and Sears 2005).

The familiar ethnic differences are clearly present at this early stage of political life, as already seen in tables 4.1 and 4.2. Blacks and Latinos were significantly more liberal than whites and Asians on almost every dimension. Also, at this stage Asians were the most politically conservative. The main exception was immigration: not surprisingly, the Asian and Latino students were the most liberal on this issue, but the differences among the four groups are not significant.

For the remaining analyses in this chapter, we developed a composite measure of political conservatism by averaging the party identification and political outlook items for each student.[5] They also required subdividing students within ethnic groups. The number of African Americans at college entry was too small to yield reliable estimates for subdivisions within that group. As a result, we restrict the remaining analyses in this chapter to whites, Asians, and Latinos.

White Students

We begin with white students, who have provided the model for the traditional sociopolitical socialization of young Americans. In the United States today, the divides between liberals and Democrats, on the one hand, and conservatives and Republicans, on the other, take numerous forms. Here we focus on four of the most important cleavages in mainstream American politics: gender, religiosity, racial conservatism, and inegalitarianism.

The social background hypothesis suggests that students adopt the "correct" partisanship for their social environments without necessarily being aware of or accepting all the values normally associated with it. To test this, we correlated the students' demographic characteristics with the composite political conservatism and symbolic racism scales, as shown in table 4.3. We used several demographic and background measures: gender, parental education, SAT scale, subjective family socioeconomic status, and precollege contact with the three main ethnic outgroups (number of neighbors, high school friends, and classmates of other ethnicities).[6] For example, under the social background hypothesis, we would expect political conservatism to be associated with higher SES. Gender, though a standard demographic variable, has a somewhat different theoretical interpretation to which we will return.

Social background, in its own right, appears to have very little bearing on the political conservatism of whites at college entry (see table 4.3). None of the correlations exceeded r = .11. The social background hypothesis, however, may be more plausible for white students' symbolic racism. Greater education is associated with more tolerance among adults; therefore, better-educated parents, who tend to have higher SES, may teach more tolerance to their pre-adult children. Academically more able students and those with family members who attended college may engage in a process of anticipatory socialization, showing increased tolerance before they even reach college. As shown in table 4.3, however, parental education, family socioeconomic status, and students' SAT scores failed to demonstrate significant relationships to white students' symbolic racism at college entry. Another possibility is that having highly racially and ethnically segregated experiences prior to college con-

Table 4.3 Associations of Political Conservatism and Symbolic Racism with Social Background and Predispositions at College Entry

	Whites		Asians		Latinos	
Variable	Political Conservatism	Symbolic Racism	Political Conservatism	Symbolic Racism	Political Conservatism	Symbolic Racism
Social background						
Gender	.11**	.14***	.09*	.09*	.17**	.10
Parental education	-.07*	-.02	.06	-.04	.09	.02
Family socioeconomic status	.09**	-.03	.10**	-.06	.15**	.05
Precollege contact with main ethnic outgroups	.04	.00	.16***	.12**	-.15**	-.05*
Mean SAT	-.01	.03	.09*	-.04	.11	-.03
Predispositions						
Religiosity	.32***	.12**	.22***	.05	.20***	-.10
Symbolic racism	.39***	—	.25***	—	.39***	—
Inegalitarianism	.34***	.44***	.24***	.31***	.27***	.35***
Antiblack affect	.09**	.14***	.14***	.27***	.02	.16**
Political conservatism	—	.39***	—	.25***	—	.39***
Dominance	.16***	.24***	.11**	.21***	.20***	.22***
Ethnic identification	.10**	.17***	.11**	.02	-.13*	-.23***

Source: Authors' compilation.
Note: Entries are Pearson correlations between the scales indicated in the first column and political conservatism (odd data columns) and symbolic racism (even data columns). Political conservatism is the combination of political outlook and party identification. Scales have been coded so that high numbers indicate male, more parental education, higher subjective family socioeconomic status, less precollege contact with the student's three main ethnic outgroups, higher SAT scores, more religiosity, more symbolic racism, more antiblack affect, more inegalitarianism, more conservatism, more support of group dominance, and stronger ethnic identification.

* p < .05; ** p < .01; *** p < .001

Table 4.4   The Gender Gap in Political Conservatism at College
Entry, by Ethnicity

Ethnicity	Female		Male		Gap
Whites	+21%	(n = 387)	+8%	(n = 343)	+13%
Asians	+13	(n = 390)	−1	(n = 329)	+14
Latinos	+60	(n = 147)	+40	(n = 98)	+20

Source: Authors' compilation.
Note: The entry is the percentage of liberal Democrats minus the percentage of conservative Republicans in each category of ethnicity and gender. Partisan categories are the same as those in table 4.1. Numbers are based on all available respondents at college entry.

tributes to whites' symbolic racism, as the "contact" hypothesis might predict. But the relationship between our scale of precollege contact with the three main ethnic outgroups and symbolic racism did not reach significance at college entry for white students.

The partisan gender gap has been a staple of American political life since the early 1980s. It is normally found to be based in greater support for a social safety net and greater opposition to violence among women than among men. As such, it fits better with the pre-adult socialization of standard attitudinal predispositions than with the less thoughtful and reflective the social background hypothesis. To test for the gender gap, we started by comparing males' and females' political conservatism, using the typology developed in table 4.1. By this criterion, the white students already show a substantial gender gap at college entry, as shown in table 4.4. Liberal Democrats outnumbered conservative Republicans by 21 percent among white females, but only by 8 percent among white males. Similar findings hold for Asians and Latinos. As shown in table 4.3, males also tended to be higher than females in political conservatism and symbolic racism. By the criterion of the gender gap, then, we again see that the students' partisan socialization is well on its way to adult levels at college entry.

What about the pre-adult socialization hypothesis? Strong associations of fundamental predispositions and values with political conservatism and symbolic racism at college entry would suggest that students arrive at college already divided along the lines of the attitudinal predispositions that undergird adults' political and racial divisions and give them substantive meaning. For predispositions, we used the "usual suspects": religiosity, symbolic racism, inegalitarianism, antiblack affect, dominance, and ethnic identification.[7] As shown in table 4.3, the pre-adult socialization hypothesis seems to fit the data for white students reasonably well. All six of these predispositions were significantly associated with political conservatism at college entry. The associations at college entry resembled those of white adults more generally: white liberal Democrats tended to be more secular, racially liberal, and egalitarian than conservative Republicans. These white UCLA students showed the same political divisions as white American adults do, even as early as their entry into college.

Did these incoming students already base their symbolic racism in their subjective predispositions, rather than simply reflecting their social backgrounds? Inspection of table 4.3 shows clearly that all of the same predispositions have significant and consistently larger correlations with symbolic racism than do the demographic variables. Of particular note is that the original theory of symbolic racism located its origins in a blending of negative feelings toward blacks with traditional, conservative American values. Subsequent research on white adults has generally supported that view (see, for example, Sears and Henry 2003). Among these students, too, antiblack affect and political conservatism were significantly correlated with whites' symbolic racism at college entry.

There is one further important political implication of the association between these two central political attitudes, political conservatism and symbolic racism. Previous research on white adults has shown that symbolic racism is an attitude that is very much at the heart of today's partisan divisions (Sears et al. 1997; Valentino and Sears 2005). This was true for the white students in this study as well. As can be seen in table 4.3, symbolic racism at college entry was strongly correlated with political conservatism. That correlation ($r = .39$) was almost identical to the correlation of symbolic racism with party identification ($r = .44$ and $.38$) and political outlook ($r = .39$ and $.43$) among adult whites in the broader Los Angeles community in the same era, as reflected by the 1995 and 1997 Los Angeles County Social Surveys (Sears et al. 1997; Tarman and Sears 2005).

Beyond that, as indicated in chapter 2, much theory in recent years has focused on a darker side of American intergroup relations, hypothesizing a powerful ethnic hierarchy in which whites are the dominant group to whom minorities of color are subordinated (Bobo and Tuan 2006; Sidanius and Pratto 1999). These theories use several key predictors of the divide between liberal and conservative whites in political and racial attitudes. For example, social dominance theory focuses on social dominance orientation as an index of support for perpetuating the ethnic hierarchy. Rejected theories focus on such unfavorable attitudes toward minorities as "laissez-faire" or "benevolent" racism (Jackman 1994).

Still other theories have emphasized a self-conscious awareness of white ingroup ethnic identification, attitudes about "whiteness," and perceptions of white privilege as perpetuating racial inequality (see, for example, Branscombe, Schmitt, and Harvey 1999). It should be noted that the original theory of symbolic racism assumed that attitudes about the white ingroup no longer played an important role in American politics, since white group consciousness was concentrated most powerfully in the old South. In that view, whites do not generally perceive much discrimination being targeted at them, nor do they think about their whiteness very much. As a result, they are not likely to have developed a strong sense of racial identity or racial common fate. In line with that view, white adults' perceptions and attitudes about "whiteness" generally have not been significantly empirically related to either their symbolic racism or their racial policy preferences (Sears and Henry 2005; Sears and Jessor 1996; Sears and Savalei 2006; Sears et al. 1997).

As indicated earlier, we treat inegalitarianism and dominance (the two subdimensions of SDO) separately because of indications elsewhere that they have divergent effects and often are not highly correlated. In this study, too, the inegalitarianism subdimension of SDO had a much stronger relationship to whites' political conservatism ($r = .34$) than did the dominance subdimension ($r = .16$), consistent with other research. In addition, white identity, perhaps mainly a legacy of the old South, was not strongly linked to whites' political conservatism ($r = .10$). Symbolic racism had a stronger relationship with inegalitarianism ($r = .44$) than with dominance ($r = .24$) or white ethnic identification ($r = .17$), though all were statistically significant. Among the white students, conservative Republicans, like their adult counterparts, had reservations about promoting greater equality among various groups in society. But they seemed to have little appetite for the old Jim Crow ideology of "keeping inferior groups in their place" in a rigidly categorized, ascriptive racial hierarchy. That ideological notion seems to be a historical relic, closer to the political debates of the old South than to today's partisan debates.[8]

In sum, most of the evidence suggests that, for whites, the pre-adult socialization hypothesis holds up well. Their political and racial attitudes were already grounded in their fundamental predispositions and values. The standard political cleavages along the lines of gender, religiosity, racial prejudice, and egalitarianism usually observed among American adults were already present among the white students at college entry.

The New-Immigrant Groups

How do the prepolitical, social background, and pre-adult socialization hypotheses fare among the new-immigrant groups? The prepolitical hypothesis might be especially fitting if these immigrants are markedly less politically incorporated into American political life than whites. A quick glance at table 4.3 indicates that was not so: political conservatism and symbolic racism correlated significantly with most of the demographic and predisposition variables.

In addition, the social background hypothesis did not fare markedly better among the new immigrants than among whites. The top panel of table 4.3 shows that a similar number of demographic correlations were significant for Asians and for whites. Again, there was a tendency for high family SES to be associated with political conservatism. The gender gap was clearly present among new immigrants. Asian females were 14 percent more likely to fall on the political left than were Asian males, as shown in table 4.4. The most interesting divergence is that growing up in an ethnically homogeneous precollegiate background was associated with conservatism for Asians. Presumably, this reflects a norm of greater political conservatism in traditional Asian communities. That foreshadows a possible dilemma to be faced in college by conservative Asian students, similar to that faced by Newcomb's Bennington students. The conservative norms of their family and other precollege environments may conflict with those of a predominantly liberal college climate of opinion. We address this in the next chapter.

Nevertheless, for the Asians as for the whites, the pre-adult socialization hypothesis again seems to be the best fit. The correlations of Asians' predispositions with their political conservatism and symbolic racism were significant, as shown in table 4.3. The same basic political cleavages had already arisen at college entry among the Asian students as among the white students, meeting the second criterion for political incorporation. Yet there is a discernible difference that suggests their somewhat incomplete initial socialization of partisanship. In almost all cases, religiosity, symbolic racism, and inegalitarianism were all more weakly linked to political conservatism among Asians than among whites, as shown in table 4.3. In particular, the Asian students at college entry seemed not to associate partisan divisions with the large issues of racial and other intergroup equality that have been so visible over the past several decades. However, they did show evidence of having learned about racism. If anything, Asians rooted their symbolic racism in anti-black affect even more strongly than did whites.

Latinos showed less disparity from whites. Again, higher subjective family socioeconomic status was associated with greater political conservatism. The gender gap was very similar in both groups: Latino females were 20 percent more likely than Latino males to fall on the political left, as shown in table 4.4. To be sure, religiosity and inegalitarianism produced smaller cleavages among Latinos than whites, as the delayed-incorporation view would expect. But their racial and ethnic attitudes seem to have been in place. The association of political conservatism with symbolic racism was just as strong in Latinos as it was in whites (r = .39). The more liberal norms of the Latino community seem evident. Growing up in an ethnically homogeneous environment was associated with greater liberalism (r = −.15), and stronger Latino ethnic identification was significantly associated with more liberal political and racial attitudes (r = −.13 and −.23, respectively). In contrast, white ethnic identification was associated with greater political conservatism and symbolic racism (r = .10 and .17, respectively).

In sum, Asian students, and to a lesser extent Latino students, looked less completely socialized at college entry than the white students. Although the same political cleavages seemed to be emerging, they were less firmly established. Still, even in these new-immigrant groups, the pre-adult socialization hypothesis seemed to fit the best.

The Crystallization of Political and Racial Attitudes at College Entry

The third criterion for complete socialization is holding fully crystallized attitudes. As indicated in chapter 2, crystallization has often been defined in previous research (for example, Sears and Valentino 1997) in terms of four indicators, based on the classic early work of Converse (1964): the internal consistency of attitudes; the stability of an attitude over time; constraint with other attitudes, like that holding in the broader electorate and among political elites; and power over attitudes toward psychologically relevant, new attitude objects, such as the effect of partisanship on candidate preferences. For space reasons, we focus here only on consistency and stability.

Whites' Crystallization at College Entry

The first index of the crystallization of political conservatism is consistency across its two components, party identification and political outlook. White students exhibited high levels of consistency at college entry. The correlation of party identification with political outlook, both measured on seven-point scales, was .78, as shown in table 4.5. Similarly, the correlation of political conservatism with support for President Clinton in the 1996 election also yielded a very high level of consistency $(r = .78)$.[9]

How developed at college entry was whites' symbolic racism toward attaining adult levels of internal consistency, as indexed by the Cronbach's alpha for the four symbolic racism items? At college entry, the alpha for the white students was .68, as shown in table 4.5. That was already close to adult levels of internal consistency, as evidenced by comparison to results from national surveys of general population samples. For example, also using four-item symbolic racism scales, four National Election Studies (NES) surveys from 1985 through 2000 yielded very similar alphas of .67, .67, .75, and .75, and in the 1994 General Social Survey (GSS), an alpha of .65 was attained (Sears and Henry 2003; Sears et al. 1997). Longer scales in the 1997 and 1998 Los Angeles County Social Survey yielded reliabilities of .77 (seven items) and .78 (eleven items). Similarly, longer scales in the 1986 NES (eight items) and 1992 NES (six items) yielded reliabilities of .78 and .76, respectively.[10] Differences between entering freshmen and these general population samples in educational level are minimal and, in any case, do not explain these similarities (Henry and Sears 2002).

A second indicator of crystallization is the stability of individual attitudes over time. The stability of entry-level attitudes is indicated by the test-retest correlations for political conservatism, symbolic racism, predispositions, and policy attitudes from college entry to sophomore year.[11] As shown in table 4.6, all test-retest correlations for white students were reasonably strong, and all were significant beyond the $p < .01$ level. Party identification showed the strongest test-retest correlation $(r = .80)$, thus

Table 4.5   The Internal Consistency of Key Sociopolitical
            Predispositions at College Entry

Predispositions	Whites	Asians	Latinos
Symbolic racism (α)	.68	.54	.58
Political conservatism (r)	.78	.61	.66

Source: Authors' compilation.
Note: Entries are Pearson correlations of political outlook and party identification for political conservatism and Cronbach's alpha for the four symbolic racism items. Significance tests are not available for Cronbach's alpha. All other entries are significant at p < .01.

resembling the coefficients for mature adults in earlier surveys (see Converse and Markus 1979; Sears 1983; Sears and Valentino 1997).

As may be recalled, Hyman's (1959) standard for the pre-adult acquisition of party identification was comparability with religion. Among the white students in this study, religiosity was a highly stable attitude at college entry (r = .80 from precollege to sophomore year). Inegalitarian values also yielded evidence of reasonably high levels of crystallization

Table 4.6   The Stability of Predispositions and Policy Attitudes at
            College Entry

Variable	Whites	Asians	Latinos
Predispositions			
Religiosity	.80	.71	.74
Political conservatism	.78	.63	.68
Party identification	.80	.64	.72
Political outlook	.58	.46	.52
Symbolic racism	.57	.46	.39
Ethnic identification	.54	.60	.61
Inegalitarianism	.44	.42	.44
Dominance	.35	.35	.27
Policy attitudes			
Opposition to affirmative action	.52	.36	.38
Attitude toward immigration	.46	.27	.39
Attitude toward welfare recipients	.51	.29	.38
Attitude toward solving the crime problem	.24	.23	.19

Source: Authors' compilation.
Note: Entries are test-retest correlations for each scale between college entry and sophomore year (wave 1 to wave 3). All entries are statistically significant at p < .01.

among entering white students (stability coefficient of r = .44). The stability of symbolic racism at college entry was r = .57, as shown in table 4.6. That fell somewhat short of the two-year stability levels for symbolic racism in samples of white adults. In both the 1990 to 1992 and 1992 to 1994 NES panel studies, the test-retest correlations were r = .68 for whites.

The stability of symbolic racism at college entry among white students compared favorably with that of other important political attitudes. As shown in table 4.6, its stability was not as high as those for religiosity or for party identification, by far the most stable political attitude that Americans hold (Converse and Markus 1979; Jennings and Stoker 1999; Sears 1983). But it was just as stable as political outlook and white ethnic identification, and considerably more stable than inegalitarian or dominance values. The stability correlations for the policy preference measures were somewhat weaker, ranging from .24 to .52, as would be expected from earlier research on adults.[12]

Using these indicators of consistency and stability, then, white students' political orientations were, in aggregate, close to a mature level of crystallization at college entry. As seen earlier (table 4.3), most white students arrived at college with a broad and normative understanding of what it means to be a liberal Democrat or conservative Republican. Symbolic racism, too, was strongly crystallized as an affective predisposition. Its internal consistency was already at adult levels, and its stability across time was not far behind adult levels. Overall, the pre-adult socialization hypothesis seems to be a good fit for white students' most important political and racial attitudes.

New Immigrants' Crystallization at College Entry

Presumably, white students form the standard for gauging the assimilation of new-immigrant groups. Again, we start with internal consistency as an indicator of crystallization. For Asian and Latino students, the correlations between party identification and political outlook at college entry were r = .61 and .66, respectively, as shown in table 4.5. These were lower than the relationship for whites (r = .78). The relationship of political conservatism with support for Bill Clinton was also weaker among both of the new-immigrant groups (for Asians, r = .57, and for Latinos, r = .61) than among whites (r = .78). The same pattern held for symbolic racism. The alpha coefficient for whites was .68, compared to .54 for Asians and .58 for Latinos. In terms of internal consistency, whites showed substantially more crystallized political orientations and racial attitudes.

The second criterion for crystallization, stability of these college-entry attitudes over time, showed the same pattern of relatively lower crystallization for the new-immigrant groups than for whites, as shown in table 4.6. Party identification was noticeably less stable for Asians and Latinos ($r = .64$ and $r = .72$, respectively) than it was for whites ($r = .80$) across the first two years of college. Whites also showed substantially more stable levels of symbolic racism ($r = .57$) than either Asians ($r = .46$) or Latinos ($r = .39$). Political outlook followed a similar pattern ($r = .46$ and $r = .52$ for Asians and Latinos, as compared to $r = .58$ for whites). On all policy issues, Asians and Latinos demonstrated markedly less stable attitudes at college entry than did whites, with average correlations of .29 for Asians, .33 for Latinos, and .43 for whites.

Recent Asian and Latino Immigrants

Our guiding hypothesis has been that new-immigrant groups of Asians and Latinos would initially show shortfalls in political socialization because of their relatively recent immigration. Not having grown up in families steeped in the American political culture, they had not been politically socialized as thoroughly as white students, almost all of whose families were longtime residents of the United States. We have found support for that hypothesis in two ways. The standard political cleavages among adult Americans were present, but somewhat muted, among Asian and Latino students at college entry, compared to whites. Second, the crystallization of Asians' and Latinos' political conservatism and symbolic racism fell well short of whites' at college entry in terms of consistency and stability.

The assimilation hypothesis would further suggest that the political incorporation of those ethnic minority groups was slowed owing to the many relatively recent immigrants among them. Next, we test this hypothesis directly. Are the most recent immigrants less incorporated into the American political system at college entry than their longer-tenured counterparts, and does that explain the relatively incomplete political incorporation of the Asian and Latino students, taken in aggregate?

We have two comparisons. First, we test for the progress of political incorporation and assimilation of this new wave of immigrants. It would seem to be well along if the U.S.-born, English-fluent Asians and Latinos resemble whites. Second, we would expect students who, with their families, have been in the United States for a longer period of time to be further along in political incorporation than the most recent Asian and Latino immigrants. Again, we defined the "old" Asians and Latinos as those born in the United States and primarily speaking English at home. However, as seen earlier in chapter 3, the term "old" should not be taken very literally, since few were more than second-generation Americans. The "new" Asians and Latinos were defined as those who were born outside the United States *or* who spoke a foreign language as the primary language in their parents' home. At college entry, 64 percent of the Asians and 49 percent of the Latinos were classified as "new," while only 7 percent of the whites and African Americans were classified as such.

Sociopolitical Liberalism

One sign of assimilation of the new-immigrant groups would be a similarity between the levels of political conservatism and symbolic racism among the old Asians and Latinos and the levels found among whites. Figure 4.1 shows a somewhat different trajectory for Asians and Latinos. In terms of political conservatism, the old Asians were actually somewhat more conservative than whites were at college entry. However, the difference is not significant; old Asians had, on average, almost exactly the same level of symbolic racism as whites (see figure 4.1). In contrast, the old Latinos showed a tendency toward the emergence of ethnic politics rather than pure assimilation. They were more liberal than whites in terms of political conservatism, though the difference was not significant. However, the old Latinos were significantly more liberal than the old Asians. In terms of symbolic racism, the old Latinos were more liberal than whites, and significantly so, consistent with the people of color hypothesis.

In sum, we do not see much difference between the old Asians and whites in levels of political conservatism and symbolic racism. The old Asians may be slightly more conservative, but the differences are small and nonsignificant. On the other hand, the old Latinos are markedly more liberal than whites, and significantly so in symbolic racism.

Do we see greater differences between the most recent immigrants and their native-born, English-fluent counterparts? The most recently immigrated "new" Asians were almost exactly as politically liberal as their longer-tenured "old" counterparts. However, the new Asians—

Figure 4.1   Mean Levels of Political Conservatism and Symbolic Racism Across Groups

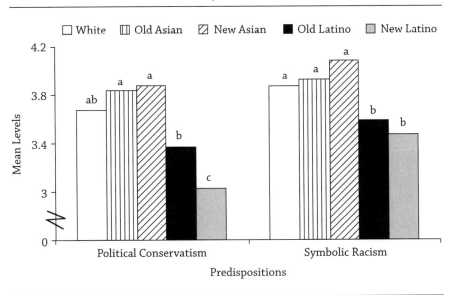

Source: Authors' compilation.

Note: Higher numbers indicate greater conservatism and more symbolic racism. Different letters indicate significantly different means for that variable across groups at p < .05.

those who were foreign-born or did not speak English at home—initially demonstrated even higher symbolic racism scores, thus demonstrating more racial conservatism, than did native-born Asians and whites. However, none of these differences was significant.

One might expect the new Latinos to be the least-assimilated students, both because of their lower socioeconomic position and because Latinos have generally integrated into the broader society more slowly than Asian Americans. We venture forward with an analysis of them somewhat hesitantly, because the relatively small sample size of new Latinos (n = 88) makes the estimates tend to be unstable. However, at college entry the new Latinos were significantly more liberal than the old Latinos in terms of political conservatism, and they were more liberal than whites and both groups of Asians. They were no different in symbolic racism than the old Latinos, and again, they showed significantly lower symbolic racism scores, thus demonstrating more racial liberalism, than whites and both groups of Asians at college entry.

Overall, then, the Asians, both old and new, did not differ much at college entry from whites in either political conservatism or symbolic racism. This suggests that the Asians were already well on their way to political assimilation, at least in terms of the direction and strength of their political preferences. The old Latinos tended to be more liberal than whites, suggesting a trajectory that would define them as a politically distinctive ethnic group. The new Latinos were substantially more liberal than either whites or Asians, and more liberal in terms of political conservatism than the old Latinos.

This suggests two conclusions. The Latinos, more than the Asians, seemed to be on their way to a distinctively liberal ethnic politics, as the people of color hypothesis would suggest. Second, the new Latinos in particular were distinctively liberal. As we will see later, this reflected a larger pattern of similarity between Latinos and blacks that, again, seems to be consistent with the people of color hypothesis. However, this similarity was present only when the Latinos were newly immigrated, as suggested by the black exceptionalism alternative.

Crystallization

The assimilation hypothesis would lead us to expect that the crystallization of native-born Asians' and Latinos' political and racial attitudes would resemble those of whites at college entry. That assimilation hypothesis seems to hold better for the old Latinos than for the old Asians in terms of the consistency of political conservatism, as shown in figure 4.2. The correlation of party identification with political outlook for the old Latinos was only slightly below that for whites at college entry. But among the old Asians, it fell substantially short. On the other hand, symbolic racism among the old Asians and old Latinos was nearly indistinguishable in its internal consistency from that among whites at college entry, as shown in figure 4.2. When we turn to the stability of these two attitudes over a two-year period, the assimilation hypothesis receives further support. Stability for the old Asians and old Latinos of both political conservatism and symbolic racism approached but fell somewhat short of that for whites, as shown in figure 4.3.

At college entry, then, the "old" Asian and Latino students showed slightly less crystallization of political conservatism and symbolic racism

Figure 4.2   Internal Consistency of Predispositions at College Entry

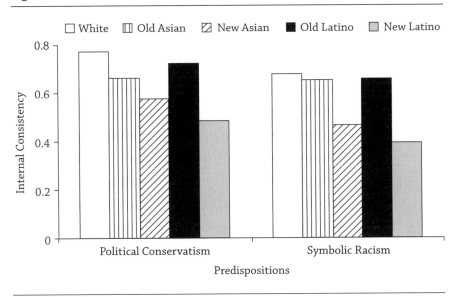

Source: Authors' compilation.
Note: Data points are correlations between party identification and political outlook for political conservatism and alpha coefficients for the symbolic racism scale.

than did white students. By the standard of attitude crystallization, then, those who were native-born and spoke English at home already seemed at college entry to be on the way to incorporation into the American political mainstream, though their attitudes were not yet as crystallized as white students' attitudes. In the next chapter, we assess whether or not the college experience fully closed that gap.

Most evidence suggests that recent immigration was a central factor preventing full attitude crystallization among the Asian students. Consistency in political conservatism at college entry was higher for the old than for the new Asians ($r = .66$ and $.58$, respectively), as shown in figure 4.2. The correlations of political conservatism with support for Bill Clinton in 1996 were also higher among old Asians ($r = .66$) than among new Asians ($r = .52$). This effect of recent immigration is replicated with symbolic racism. In terms of both the internal consistency and stability of symbolic racism, the new Asians showed far less crystallized attitudes than did the old Asians, as shown in figure 4.2.

Figure 4.3   Stability of Predispositions at College Entry

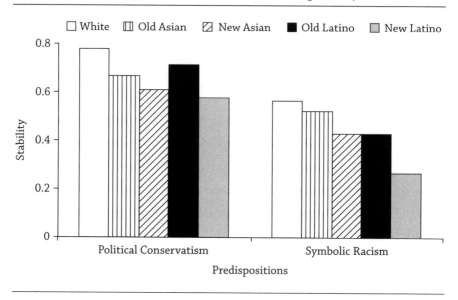

Source: Authors' compilation.
Note: Entries are test-retest correlations for each scale between college entry and sophomore year (wave 1 to wave 3). All entries are statistically significant at p < .02.

Recent immigration posed similar obstacles to attitude crystallization at college entry for the Latino students. Internal consistency of political conservatism for the old Latinos (r = .73) was considerably higher than for their newer-immigrant counterparts (r = .48), as shown in figure 4.2. The internal consistency of symbolic racism was far lower among the new Latinos than among the old Latinos. Stability of political conservatism over time also showed similar patterns, as shown in figure 4.3, with the old Latinos showing considerably higher stability (r = .71) compared to the new Latinos (r = .58). Similarly, the stability of symbolic racism was considerably higher among the old Latinos than among the new Latinos. The new Asians and Latinos were clearly not as assimilated at college entry as either their "old" counterparts or whites. By the criteria of both consistency and stability, they showed substantially less attitude crystallization than did either whites or the "old immigrants" at college entry.

In sum, the evidence on the crystallization of political conservatism and symbolic racism generally supports the assimilation hypothesis for these new-immigrant groups. By most indicators, Asians and Latinos who were the products of earlier waves of immigration showed just slightly less attitude crystallization at college entry than did whites. The "new" ethnics showed considerably less crystallization, however, than either whites or "old" ethnics.

Summary and Conclusions

In this chapter, the phenomenon we were concerned with was the completeness of college students' sociopolitical socialization at college entry, in terms of both basic political orientations and racial prejudice. One general issue is whether socialization is largely complete at college entry, when young people first become eligible to participate formally in the political system. We used Newcomb's (1943) classic study of Bennington College students as a benchmark. Newcomb's finding that many students changed their political orientations in college suggested that their political socialization was incomplete at college entry. Additional research (for example, Jennings and Niemi 1981) has supported Newcomb's results: basic political identifications generally are not fully crystallized until people reach their late twenties.

A second general issue was the incorporation of the new-immigrant groups into the American political and racial system. The great majority of these Latino and Asian students were immigrants themselves, or their parents were, or both were. Many of their homes were populated by noncitizens, who therefore could not participate in formal American political life. Parental communication of clear American political and social norms is a critical prerequisite for the development of attitudes about American politics among pre-adults (Jennings and Niemi 1974; Jennings and Stoker 1999). Many of these students could not have had that experience. Within this chapter, we were concerned with assessing whether, by college entry, new immigrants had acquired crystallized political and racial preferences, which they might have absorbed through exposure to a broader environment in which American racial minorities and minority politics are quite salient.

We offered two orthogonal criteria for determining whether socialization was complete: conformity to the conventional norms for political and racial attitudes of one's social groups and acquisition of coherent, crystallized attitudes. When maturing individuals reach a life stage at which their attitudes reach an asymptote by both criteria, neither increasing further with age, we can say that political socialization is complete. The two attitudes we focused most attention on were general political conservatism and symbolic racism.

The Completeness of Whites' Political Socialization at College Entry

Our first criterion for the completeness of political socialization was conformity to normative expectations. The college environment is generally thought to have predominantly liberal sociopolitical norms. For example, the Bennington students, on average, entered college as conservatives and exited as political progressives. In our study, by contrast, liberal Democrats outnumbered conservative Republicans in all ethnic groups at college entry. It is more difficult to set a clear dividing line between racial liberals and racial conservatives. However, whites and Latinos were lower than the absolute midpoint in symbolic racism, and thus more racially liberal, whereas Asians hovered close to it.

We also found evidence that the students' political conservatism and symbolic racism conformed to their cultural subgroups in the same fashion as they do among mainstream adults in terms of ethnicity, gender, and religiosity. Latinos and blacks were significantly more liberal than whites and Asians, as is generally true for adults. A sizable gender gap existed among students of all ethnicities at college entry, with women being more liberal and men more conservative. Divisions between the most religiously faithful and the more secular were also significantly associated with divisions in political conservatism at college entry among students of all ethnicities.

We also considered the predictors of political conservatism and symbolic racism among white students in terms of the other attitudes and values with which they were correlated. Strong associations like those among adults would suggest that the students' socialization had already been internalized. For example, our data demonstrate a consistently central role for symbolic racism in the students' political orientations at college entry. Similarly, important predictors of symbolic racism were antiblack affect, political conservatism, and inegalitarianism, as is true in adults' attitudes. By these standards, the students gave evidence of understanding the conventional substantive meaning of partisanship and symbolic racism quite well. Rather than merely parroting parental sociopolitical preferences, they had adopted those appropriate to their fundamental values.

Our third criterion for the completeness of socialization concerned the crystallization of conventional partisan and racial attitudes, as indexed in terms of internal consistency and attitude stability. White students at college entry demonstrated a rather high level of crystallization of the most central political attitudes, party identification and political outlook. Their partisan socialization seemed to be well along before they enrolled at college, and not far behind adults' levels of crystallization. This is not surprising, since the regular recurrence of partisan elections provides numerous opportunities for pre-adult socialization (Sears 1983; Sears and Valentino 1997). White students' symbolic racism was also quite crystallized already at college entry, almost at adult levels, according to each of our indicators of crystallization. At college entry, symbolic racism was not as stable as party identification, but it was more stable than attitudes such as white ethnic identification or inegalitarianism. This too parallels stability data among adults, as noted earlier.

The Completeness of the New-Immigrant Groups' Political Socialization at College Entry

We also assessed the completeness of the Asian and Latino students' sociopolitical socialization at college entry, partly by comparison to the white students. Both political conservatism and symbolic racism seemed markedly less crystallized among Asians and Latinos than among whites, in terms of both their internal consistency and their stability. This led us to conclude that, taken as a whole, the new-immigrant groups had not received as much political socialization to the American sociopolitical system as had white students prior to arrival at college.

To address the question of the role of recent immigration directly, we described the earlier immigrants (those who had been born and reared in the United States and spoke English at home) as "old Asians" and "old Latinos," and we compared them with the most recent immigrants (those who were immigrants or did not speak English at home), whom we described as "new Asians" and "new Latinos." The answer seems clear: the longer-tenured Asians and Latinos were more likely to have become politically incorporated. At college entry, the old Asians looked much like whites in terms of their levels of political conservatism and symbolic racism, their levels of crystallization, and the correlates of those key attitudes. The old Latinos also resembled both whites and old Asians at college entry in terms of crystallization, showing similar levels of consistency and stability of sociopolitical attitudes, as well as similar correlations of their political and racial attitudes with their fundamental predispositions. The old Latinos departed from whites and Asians, however, in being considerably lower in symbolic racism, and thus more racially liberal, and in linking that racial attitude to their own ethnic identities. This provided some support for the people of color hypothesis among the old Latinos, suggesting that they might have had a heightened sense of group consciousness. In contrast to the old Asians and Latinos, who by and large were already politically incorporated at college entry, the new Asians and Latinos were considerably lower in crystallization and thus much more likely to find college to be a socializing experience.

In aggregate, the Latinos seemed to have been more meaningfully politically incorporated into the American sociopolitical system at college entry than Asians were. We would suggest two explanations for this difference. First, significantly more Latino students were second-generation rather than first-generation Americans (only 15 percent were first-generation, against 49 percent for Asians; see chapter 3). That, by itself, should have provided greater precollege socialization among Latinos than among Asians. A second possible explanation is suggested by the role of external political events as crucial catalysts for socialization (see Sears and Valentino 1997). In general, the speed of political socialization should partly depend on context. The timing of our study was propitious for increased Latino socialization in certain respects. Two years before the study began, the California electorate passed the highly divisive Proposition 187, which explicitly denied illegal immigrants access to local and state public services, even enrollment in public schools. That created a firestorm of opposition among Latinos. In 1995, a year before our students enrolled at UCLA, the Regents of the University of California ended affirmative action in UC admissions, which directly affected UC students, especially Latinos. Finally, our study began in the summer of 1996, when the presidential campaign was well under way. All these events might have contributed to the crystallization of our students' sociopolitical attitudes.

In sum, these findings are consistent with the view that whites' political and racial attitudes at college entry bear coherent relationships to other fundamental political attitudes and have already crystallized rather strongly. This suggests that white students have acquired an adult-like political identity by the time they begin college. This finding is reminiscent of the early theories about political socialization that argue that much of this socialization has already been accomplished before college begins. On the other hand, the new-immigrant groups do not seem to be arriving at college as speedily and fully incorporated into the American political and racial systems as the white students; crystallization of political attitudes may occur during or after college for these students. This was most clear for the Asian students, about half of whom were immigrants themselves and by and large not strong partisans at college entry. The data are more mixed for the Latino students, who by some indications were further along in the process of sociopolitical incorporation into the United States, perhaps because they were far less likely to be immigrants themselves.

Although these findings assist in shedding light on the extent to which students' sociopolitical attitudes were crystallized at college entry, relatively little is known about the impact of the college process on students' attainment of adult-like attitudes. Chapter 5 further assesses the crystallization of students' attitudes through examination of their change, or lack thereof, through college.

Chapter 5

The Overall Effects of College on Students' Sociopolitical Attitudes

To what extent did the overall college experience influence the students' sociopolitical attitudes? Had they completed the basic life task of acquiring such attitudes by college exit? That is, how did their key sociopolitical predispositions stand at college exit relative to those of adults in the general population? This chapter, like the previous one, is framed by symbolic politics theory (Sears 1983, 1993; Sears and Valentino 1997). To reiterate briefly, that theory takes a life-course approach to describing the process of attitude acquisition and thus views the students as being at a particular stage in the political life cycle. Each attitude presumably exhibits a learning curve over time as the attitude gradually becomes stronger. Attaining an asymptote would reflect complete acquisition. Our question here is whether or not the socialization of major political and racial attitudes is complete upon the life stage of college graduation.

We again use two quite different criteria to assess the completeness of socialization. The traditional criterion is acquisition of the attitudes that are most normative in one's social environment—that is, the most culturally or subculturally "correct" attitudes. The second criterion for completeness of socialization is the acquisition of a coherent belief system. By this criterion, socialization should be considered complete when attitude crystallization reaches adult levels, irrespective of the specific content of the attitude. This too gives reason to expect substantial college effects. As in the previous chapter, we rely here primarily on political conservatism and symbolic racism as measures of sociopolitical attitudes.

This chapter, then, focuses on the effects of the college experience taken as a whole. We look first at how the college experience influences the trajectory of students' attitudes through the life cycle and thus at how complete their socialization is at college exit compared to its status at college entry. As indicated earlier, the persistence model assumes that much sociopolitical socialization has already occurred by late adolescence. That model would lead us to expect normatively appropriate and rather crystallized political and racial attitudes—at least the most central predispositions—prior to college entry. In the last chapter, we found that the persistence model fit at least the white students' core predispositions pretty well at college entry. However, the impressionable years model suggests that young adults remain substantially open to change, even in strong sociopolitical attitudes such as general political orientations and racial prejudice. If so, the college years may be a crucial period of attitude development in terms of both content and crystallization.

By tracing students through the college years, then, we examine them during the presumably critical "impressionable" years of early adulthood. This was what made Newcomb's (1943) study of Bennington College undergraduate students so interesting: it showed that the normal transmission of attitudes from the family to offspring, apparently quite effectively executed prior to college, could be reversed by the college experience.

Our second focus in this chapter is on differences among racial and ethnic groups. During the civil rights era, the movement to extend equal opportunity began to promote greater diversification within institutions of higher education. The principal goal was to incorporate and integrate African Americans more fully into predominantly white institutions. A by-product of racial integration was expected to be reduced prejudice among whites, in line with the contact theories of prejudice reduction that were in vogue at the time (Allport 1954). In practice, higher education has indeed been substantially diversified, but in a way quite different from the hoped-for mass integration of African American students into nearly all-white institutions. The doors of America's colleges and universities have not been fully opened to African Americans: blacks remain seriously underrepresented in almost all institutions of higher education that were predominantly white in the 1960s. Nor have those black students who did manage to get inside been fully integrated into the mainstream.

Rather, higher education has been diversified mainly by the swelling numbers of new immigrants over the past few decades, the largest share of whom come from Asia and Latin America. The UCLA student body is a good case in point. It has become increasingly diverse, primarily owing to the incorporation of students from the new-immigrant groups. As indicated in chapter 3, in 1973, 71 percent of the undergraduates at UCLA were self-classified as white, 16 percent as either Asian or Latino, and 7 percent as black. By 2000, when some of our respondents began their fifth year in college, only 35 percent were white, almost 50 percent were either Asian or Latino, and the black proportion had actually declined substantially, to 4 percent (University of California, Los Angeles, statistical summary of students and staff).

The core phenomena addressed by this book are the consequences of increased ethnic diversification of our colleges and universities, and immigration is central to that story. Have the new-immigrant groups achieved parity with white students at college exit? Beyond that, we are particularly interested in learning whether or not college is more important for the socialization of the most recent immigrants than it is for earlier arrivals from Asia and Latin America. At college entry, the relatively recent immigrants were less incorporated into the American political system than either whites or U.S.-born Asians and Latinos. Subsequently, the college experience might have been especially important in helping these newest immigrants to attain the level of sociopolitical incorporation that their U.S.-born counterparts had at college entry.

Liberalization

Throughout this chapter, we first consider the white students and then determine whether Asian and Latino students follow the patterns of whites. Most research has shown that having had a college education is associated with greater liberalism among Americans, especially on racial issues. The most common explanation posits that college has significant effects and that college students are influenced by liberal norms in the college environment. Does today's highly diverse public university produce the traditional liberalization of attitudes? Or does it produce a

backlash against liberalism in the form of greater conservatism, prejudice, intolerance, conflict, and separation or segregation?

There are two reasons why symbolic politics theory would lead us to
expect the traditional liberalization of white students' political and
racial attitudes during their college years. First, the norms of their college environments are generally liberal in a variety of ways. The dominant institutional norms at large universities seem to be predominantly
liberal. Peer norms clearly leaned to the liberal side at UCLA at college
entry, as seen in the previous chapter. Those liberal norms, whose specific effects we examine in later chapters, are communicated in several
ways: through institutional practices, the attitudes of faculty and teaching assistants, the formal curriculum, many student organizations, and
direct peer contact.

Second, symbolic politics theory suggests that the speed with which
any attitude approaches asymptote depends on a variety of factors, but
two of the most notable are the intensity of the information flow to
which the individual is exposed and opportunity to practice the attitude. The considerable cultural diversity of the UCLA campus and the
surrounding metropolitan area would suggest that sociopolitical issues
are the subject of a relatively strong information flow. Confronted
with a strong and predominantly liberal information flow, white students should become more liberal as they proceed through college.
However, as we saw in the last chapter, they were already fairly liberal
at college entry, which may prevent much further change through the
college years. Another alternative, drawn from a parallel with Newcomb's (1943) Bennington study, is that the students most immersed
in the campus and the college experience undergo the most liberalization.

In addition to liberal norms on the college campus, a second set of
norms is represented by the major cleavages that generally divide American adults along left-right political lines: race and ethnicity, the gender
gap, religiosity, racial conservatism, and egalitarian values. Symbolic
politics theory would expect that this presumed intense information
flow leads these normative cleavages to expand further as white students move through college. On the other hand, these cleavages were already quite marked among the white students in our study at college entry, so a ceiling effect might have prevented them from expanding very
much. An alternative explanation is that college actually reduces those

cleavages, swamping students in a more general movement toward the liberal norms of the college.

Symbolic politics theory would also expect the new-immigrant groups initially to hold different sociopolitical attitudes than the white students because of cultural differences in prior socialization, as we found in the previous chapter. The further trajectory of new-immigrant students should depend heavily on whether or not they are substantially integrated into the mainstream. In general, the longer immigrants and their families are in their country of destination, the more they should resemble historically mainstream groups. Exposure to concentrated assimilation experiences, such as a university education, might well play a role that is functionally equivalent to longer tenure in the host country. Symbolic politics theory would suggest that, among Asians, Latinos, and whites, the college experience results in both greater liberalization and expanded sociopolitical cleavages along the usual lines. Both U.S.-born and recently immigrated Asians and Latinos should show substantial movement through college. Recently immigrated Asians, however, should start out more similar to whites and perhaps continue to be more similar to them through college.

But alternative predictions are plausible. As indicated in chapter 2, a people of color hypothesis suggests that the fate of Asians and Latinos in American society is similar to that of African Americans. Social structural theories posit a clear ethnic hierarchy in the United States, wherein whites are the dominant majority and peoples of color are—to a greater or lesser extent—subordinate groups (Bobo 1999; Bonilla-Silva and Glover 2004; Chan 1991; Sidanius and Pratto 1999). They suggest that Asian Americans and Latinos, like African Americans, have suffered various kinds of discrimination and disadvantage in the United States; therefore, they should have more liberal sociopolitical attitudes than whites. The college experience, especially at an institution as culturally diverse as UCLA, might raise their consciousness still further about the ethnic hierarchy and their group's place in it, thereby expanding these differences between whites and minorities. Similarly, those who have resided in the United States for longer periods or who are of a later post-immigration generation may have experienced more group-based discrimination, everything else being equal, and so they may adopt attitudes more consonant with their position in the ethnic hierarchy. In short, the people of color hypothesis suggests that college moves students of color more to the left, on average, than white students.

The most important difference between symbolic politics theory and the people of color hypothesis can be found in the notion of "black exceptionalism." This notion argues that the color line restricts African Americans from full assimilation considerably more than it does other peoples of color in American society (Sears et al. 1999; Sears and Savelei 2006; Sears and van Laar 1999). The "model minority" stereotype, for example, suggests that Asian Americans are on a trajectory closer to full assimilation than is the case for blacks. If so, the new-immigrant groups might increasingly assimilate to the mainstream with longer tenure in the United States, and this increased assimilation would be seen in politics as well as in other domains of life. Therefore, we should see more political assimilation among those who are native-born, long-term residents of the United States than among their more recent immigrant counterparts, although the college experience might even facilitate such incorporation among recent immigrants.[1]

In this form, neither symbolic politics theory nor the people of color hypothesis distinguishes between Asians and Latinos. Social dominance theory, however, provides a more finely grained portrait of the American ethnic hierarchy. This theory proposes that whites are the dominant group, with Asians close behind, Latinos trailing, and blacks as the most subordinated group (see, for example, Sidanius and Pratto 1999; see also Bonilla-Silva and Glover 2004). Indeed, as seen in chapter 3, the Asian students entered UCLA with far greater parental education and considerably higher SES than the Latinos students, on average. They might therefore have become more accepted and assimilated in college than Latinos and may have followed a trajectory more like that of whites. In contrast, a people of color hypothesis might better fit the Latino case because Latinos have been considerably more politicized than Asians on the UCLA campus in recent decades. From that perspective, college might lead Latinos to move more to the left than both Asians and whites.

Crystallization

Is the college experience likely to increase the crystallization of basic sociopolitical attitudes, perhaps to typical adult levels, by college exit? A college education is intended to help students learn to think for themselves and would presumably thereby help them develop more coherent values and attitudes. If so, this should be reflected in increased crystallization of students' political and social attitudes through college. However, the trajectory of attitude crystallization through college may vary across different sociopolitical attitudes and ethnic groups. As seen in the previous chapter, the crystallization of whites' political conservatism and symbolic racism was already approximately at typical adult levels at college entry. As a result, the college experience might not increase their crystallization much more. However, the crystallization of other sociopolitical attitudes was not at such a high level initially. The crystallization of those other attitudes might increase with exposure to increasing amounts of information through college.

At college entry, the crystallization of Asian and Latino students' predispositions was, for the most part, below that of white students' and below typical adult levels. The most recently immigrated or non-English-fluent Asian and Latino students had especially uncrystallized attitudes. The simplest expectations would be that the flow of sociopolitical information in college would be about the same for Asians and Latinos as it is for whites, and that this information flow would be relatively heavy compared to precollege levels. If so, symbolic politics theory would suggest that attitude crystallization increases through college for Asians and Latinos.

What about the immigrants themselves? If the college experience truly is a major socializing experience for native-born Asians and Latinos, it might well eliminate the differences between them and whites, since whites are already close to asymptote at college entry. Similarly, because the newest immigrants start college with the least crystallized attitudes, college could be a prime vehicle by which they begin to close the crystallization gap, even if they do not fully eliminate it.[2]

Empirical Questions

We address four empirical questions in this chapter:

1. *Liberalization or conservative backlash against diversity*: We start by assessing whether the students follow the familiar pattern documented in the research literature: becoming increasingly liberal on political and racial issues during their college years. Beyond that, we examine whether or not immersion in the UCLA campus and the college experience produce particularly strong liberalization, as in the Bennington study.

2. *Widening or blurring conventional cleavages*: We examine possible changes through college in the standard group and value cleavages that are usually found among adults in the general population and that we found at college entry. They might diminish through college in response to the homogenizing pressures of a liberal college environment. Alternatively, any liberalizing changes might be across-the-board and might simply preserve those cleavages found at college entry. Yet another possibility is that the college experience enlarges those cleavages as students find friends and curricula that reinforce their initial attitudes.

3. *Increased attitude crystallization*: We test whether or not the crystallization of political conservatism and symbolic racism increases over the college years. We found in the last chapter that white students were already close to typical adult levels of crystallization at college entry. Do their political attitudes crystallize any further, or have they already reached asymptote? Students from the new-immigrant groups seem to have less crystallized attitudes than whites at college entry. Is that difference erased by the end of college?

4. *College effects among recent immigrants*: Finally, we examine the role of immigration in these processes. Does the college experience play an especially important socializing and incorporating role for the most recent immigrants? At college entry, the foreign-born or non-English-fluent immigrants depart more sharply from whites than do their native-born ethnic counterparts. The college experience might advance the sociopolitical socialization of the more recent immigrants in particular, helping them to raise their initially lower levels of attitude crystallization. Alternatively, it might freeze that initial gap, with all groups showing similar trajectories across the college years.

The Effects of Diversity: Liberalization or Conservative Backlash?

College effect studies have typically found that college has a net effect of creating more liberal students in terms of both political orientation and racial prejudice (see chapter 2). This liberalization has been found in panel studies like our own that show change through the college years, and it has been inferred from the attitudinal correlates of educational attainment among adults in cross-sectional studies. But it is possible that the rapidly increasing ethnic diversity within colleges in recent years has interrupted such traditional effects. Today diversity may instead produce increasing ethnic conflict, and with it, more interethnic hostility. Therefore, college may now be producing both a conservative backlash and greater prejudice.

Aggregate Change

To assess whether college is liberalizing students or producing a conservative backlash, we begin at the aggregate level. First, we use the simple taxonomy of political conservatism introduced in the previous chapter to determine whether political attitudes became more liberal during college.[3] As shown in table 5.1, liberal Democrats outnumbered conservative Republicans at college entry within each broad ethnic and racial group. That said, Latinos tended to be somewhat more liberal than Asians and whites: 73 percent of the Latinos were liberal Democrats, whereas about half of the whites and 41 percent of the Asians identified themselves as such. But even among whites and Asians, only one-third began college as a conservative Republican.[4]

Four years after enrolling in college, students in each of the ethnic groups had moved even more strongly to the left. Table 5.1 shows that liberal Democrats added 12 percent among whites, 19 percent among Asians, and 12 percent among Latinos, while the number of conservative Republicans shrunk in each group. As in the previous chapter, we turn to the composite measure of political conservatism to help simplify the data presentation, averaging the party identification and political outlook items for each student. The data are shown in table 5.2 and make the same point. Whites had moved significantly to the left by their sophomore years, and then again by their senior years ($p < .01$; $p < .05$). So did the Asian ($p < .001$ in both cases) and Latino ($p < .001$, not significant) students. In other words, the students in all groups surged toward the political left during college, including those in the initially most conservative ethnic group, Asian Americans. It might be noted that the change is greater in party identification than in political outlook. This difference may be due to the greater salience of political partisanship than outlook in a period with two presidential campaigns and the impeachment of a president.

Did this shift to the left occur mainly among students who were ini-

Table 5.1   Change Through College in Political Conservatism, by Ethnicity

	Precollege	Sophomore	Senior	Total Change
Whites (N = 229)				
Liberal Democrats	49%	56%	61%	+12%
Conservative Republicans	36	34	31	−5
Moderate independents	10	4	2	−8
Other	5	6	6	+1
Asians (N = 294)				
Liberal Democrats	41	55	60	+19
Conservative Republicans	34	30	26	−8
Moderate independents	14	3	4	−10
Other	11	12	10	−1
Latinos (N = 116)				
Liberal Democrats	73	82	85	+12
Conservative Republicans	14	10	8	−6
Moderate independents	7	0	1	−6
Other	6	8	6	0

Source: Authors' compilation.

Note: Includes only those who participated in all three waves.

tially apolitical and still in the acquisition phase of their learning? Or did it reflect the resocialization of those who were previously conservative, as in the case of the Bennington students? At the aggregate level, both occurred. As shown in table 5.1, the most substantial change is the reduction in "moderate independents." About 11 percent of the students entered college wholly nonpartisan: they chose the neutral point on both seven-point party identification and ideology scales. By the end of college, this uncommitted "moderate independent" group had almost completely disappeared, constituting only slightly over 2 percent in their senior year. The vast majority had staked out a position on one side or the other of the political divide in the United States. At the same time, in each ethnic group there was some reduction in the number of conservative Republicans, which dropped 6 percent in the sample as a whole.

Another important norm on a multicultural campus is the abandonment of any racial prejudices over the course of one's college education.

Table 5.2 Liberalization Through College on Predispositions and Policy Issues

Variable	Whites				Asians				Latinos			
	Pre-college	Sopho-more	Senior	F	Pre-college	Sopho-more	Senior	F	Pre-college	Sopho-more	Senior	F
Predispositions												
Political conservatism	3.6	3.5	3.3	13.5***	3.9	3.7	3.5	24.1***	3.2	3.0	2.9	7.2**
Party identification	3.7	3.4	3.2	21.0***	3.8	3.4	3.2	27.9***	3.1	2.5	2.4	20.7***
Political outlook	3.6	3.5	3.4	3.4*	3.9	4.0	3.7	9.4***	3.4	3.4	3.3	0.6ns
Symbolic racism	3.9	3.7	3.4	42.0***	4.1	4.0	3.8	22.1***	3.6	3.4	3.1	12.3***
Religiosity	3.6	3.9	3.6	8.3***	3.9	4.1	4.0	8.2***	4.2	4.5	4.3	6.3**
Inegalitarianism	2.7	2.4	2.3	15.6***	2.8	2.7	2.5	5.8**	2.1	2.0	1.8	3.6*
Dominance	1.7	1.7	1.6	1.2ns	2.1	2.0	1.9	4.0*	1.6	1.5	1.5	<.1ns
Social policy attitudes												
Opposition to affirmative action	4.3	3.8	3.6	45.2***	4.3	3.8	3.5	64.5***	2.7	2.6	2.5	2.3ns
Attitude toward immigrants	4.5	4.2	3.9	39.7***	4.4	4.1	3.9	35.9***	4.5	4.0	3.6	28.0***
Attitude toward solving crime problem	2.1	1.9	1.9	3.0*	2.2	2.0	1.9	6.8**	1.9	1.8	1.6	2.8ns
Attitude toward welfare recipients	4.3	4.1	3.7	25.6***	4.6	4.2	3.8	36.0***	4.5	4.0	3.7	16.2***

Source: Authors' compilation.

Note: Entries are mean scores for each ethnic group at each time point, on seven-point scales. Scales have been coded so that high numbers indicate more political conservatism, more symbolic racism, more religiosity, more inegalitarianism, more dominance, and more conservative social policy attitudes. These analyses were limited to participants who responded to the precollege, sophomore year, and senior year waves. The F value refers to an analysis of variance across the three waves.

* $p < .05$; ** $p < .01$; *** $p < .001$; ns = not significant

In our study, this should be reflected in consistently lower levels of symbolic racism as the students moved through college. Indeed, all groups showed substantially lower symbolic racism scores over time (that is, they became more racially liberal), as shown in table 5.2. Contrary to the people of color hypothesis, these data show no dramatic differences between whites and the minority groups in the extent of liberalizing change. Rather, there is a substantial general liberalizing change. For example, among whites, the change from college entry to the end of the senior year was 7 percent (about 0.5 on the seven-point scale). The story of racial prejudice among today's college students seems to be the same as the story of yesterday's students: racial liberalization is a general consequence of exposure to higher education. Moreover, we see this not only among the "people of color" from the new-immigrant groups, but among the presumably advantaged white students as well.

The liberalizing shift through college was not simply stronger identification with the Democratic Party, a more liberal political outlook, and reduced racial prejudice. We also tested the effects of college on other key predispositions, namely inegalitarianism, dominance, and religiosity.[5] As shown in table 5.2, the students in all ethnic groups consistently and significantly became more egalitarian. However, no significant changes occurred in opposition to group dominance. This contrast should come as no great surprise, for two reasons. Inegalitarian values are closely connected to both political conservatism and racial prejudice, while support for group dominance is not closely associated with either, as we saw in the previous chapter. Also, the fact that students were nearly consensual in rejecting dominance at college entry placed a ceiling on how much more liberalizing change was possible.

The exception in the shift toward liberalization is subjective religiosity. No net movement occurred from college entry to college exit. Rather, students in all ethnic groups became more religious in their first two years, but had reverted to their initial positions by college exit. This departure from the pattern shown on our other measures is difficult to explain. It is possible that religiosity is the product of even earlier and more profound socialization than any of these other attitudes.

Liberalization occurred on each of the four policy issues we addressed, across all three ethnic groups. A statistically significant trend toward liberalization was found in ten of the twelve comparisons. Interestingly, perhaps the most dramatic change to the left occurred on attitudes toward affirmative action among white and Asian students, who moved from opposition at college entry to net support. In 1995, the University of California Board of Regents had eliminated affirmative action from university admissions. In November 1996, shortly after these students began attending their first classes, the state's voters passed Proposition 209, outlawing affirmative action in all state and local programs. Throughout that period, the issue was hotly debated on campus. Although neither whites nor Asians had been eligible for affirmative action, the consensus in both groups of students shifted strongly to the pro–affirmative action side.

What was the trajectory of this liberalizing change through college? Did it occur almost immediately as students entered college? Or did it happen mostly during the last two years when most students were immersed in such popular liberal arts majors as psychology, political science, English, and history, which are often taught by disproportionately liberal faculty and graduate students? Looking at the political conservatism taxonomy (table 5.1), we see that change seems to have occurred most dramatically in the first two years. The advantage of liberal Democrats over conservative Republicans in all three groups of students surged from college entry to the end of their second year, then increased more modestly over the final two years. But on the other measures, liberalization occurred more steadily through college. On average, the liberal norm seems to have resulted in steady and uniform liberalization across all years, groups, and measures. The presidential campaign that was under way just as the students entered college may have had an unusually strong effect on basic partisan orientations at that stage, as would be expected from earlier studies of the effects of a presidential campaign on young people (Sears and Valentino 1997).

Individual-Level Change

This pattern of liberalization at the aggregate level might reflect either of two quite different underlying patterns of change at the individual level. The changes could be across the board, with all students showing some shift. Since these attitudes had been quite highly crystallized at college entry, particularly among white students, continuity with many small changes might be more common than large changes among a few students. Alternatively, the overall liberalizing change may have resulted from the initial acquisition of liberal attitudes by the few students who were largely prepolitical at college entry.

To test these two alternatives, we cross-tabulated precollege positions on the political conservatism taxonomy by the students' senior positions (see table 5.1). Only 3 percent, 5 percent, and 3 percent (for whites, Asians, and Latinos, respectively) of the senior liberal Democrats came from the ranks of the apolitical "moderate independents" at college entry, whereas 8 percent, 16 percent, and 10 percent came from the ranks of "other"—those with initially more mixed preferences. In other words, liberalization mainly came from changes among students who had some initial preferences, even if mixed, rather than from acquisition of liberal preferences among those who were initially apolitical.

We repeated the same exercise with symbolic racism by dividing the students at college entry and exit into three groups: those above, at, or below the absolute midpoint on the symbolic racism scale. In this case, we see substantial shifts into the low symbolic racism category, even among those who had initially been above the midpoint. The shift from high to low symbolic racism was made by 18 percent, 17 percent, and 14 percent of the white, Asian, and Latino subsamples, respectively. This is a critical finding, given the objectives of our study. It indicates that experiencing college in the midst of extreme cultural diversity encouraged numerous racial conservatives to liberalize.

In conclusion, the sociopolitical attitudes of these students became more liberal through college, in all ethnic groups and across a wide variety of attitude dimensions, including political conservatism, symbolic racism, sociopolitical predispositions, and social policy attitudes. In the case of both political conservatism and symbolic racism, the aggregate-level shift appears to have come predominantly from widespread individual-level attitude changes among students who already had fairly firm attitudes at college entry, rather than from the initial acquisition of liberal attitudes among students who were largely prepolitical at college entry. This is an important finding of our study, and most of the later chapters analyze how it happened.

Immersion in Campus Life

Sociopolitical liberalism seems to have been the prevailing norm among undergraduates in all ethnic groups. The model of the Bennington College experience would lead us to expect that such increased conformity to campus norms would be greatest among the students most strongly involved, both physically and psychologically, with the institution. That is, the students most immersed in the UCLA community should have shifted the most to the left. Alternatively, a blanket and undifferentiated leftward shift might have affected even students more tentatively attached to the campus.

To test these two alternatives, we used five items to measure students' immersion in campus life. Three were relatively subjective: measures of university identification, belonging, and consideration of dropping out of UCLA before earning a degree (reverse-coded). These items were fairly strongly associated with one another, so we combined them into a composite index of subjective immersion. The remaining two items were more objective: membership in student organizations and place of residence (living on campus versus off campus). These two items were significantly correlated with neither the subjective items nor with one another, so we left them as stand-alone items.[6]

How well does immersion in the campus explain movement to less political conservatism and less symbolic racism at college exit? To make a long story short, subjective immersion does little or nothing to explain students' liberalization. As the most sensitive test, we estimated regression equations for both political conservatism and symbolic racism with only the immersion variables included as predictors of senior attitudes and no controls. To conserve space, we do not present these results in detail. Overall, subjective immersion had a very weak effect, accounting for anywhere from 0.8 percent to 2.2 percent of the variance. Of the eighteen immersion coefficients, only three were statistically significant. Membership in student organizations contributed to greater conservatism among whites. That may have been due to the effects of their membership in predominantly white fraternities or sororities, as we will see in chapter 10. Surprisingly enough, greater university identification also contributed to greater political conservatism among Asians and Latinos.

Of course, the logic of the immersion hypothesis is that it should contribute to change through college above and beyond students' attitudes at college entry. In a second stage of this analysis, we therefore controlled for the students' precollege sociopolitical attitude (political conservatism or symbolic racism). The relatively weak conservatizing effects of membership in student organizations among whites, and of university identification among Asians, persist. However, the effects among Latinos are no longer significant. The variance explained by immersion above and beyond that of precollege sociopolitical attitudes is small, however, ranging from 0 to 1.9 percent. We followed up these analyses by controlling for key demographic variables, but that had little material effect on the results, leaving the two significant findings already cited—that whites' organizational memberships and Asians' university identification contributed to increasing levels of political conservatism.

This weak conservatizing impact of immersion in campus life contrasts with its much stronger liberalizing role in the Bennington case. The analogy with the far smaller Bennington campus, however, may not be useful. UCLA is the equivalent of a small city, said to average a population of seventy thousand on any given weekday. It has many different groups, no doubt each with its own norms. As we see in chapter 10, the fraternity and sorority world is to some extent its own enclave, as are ethnically based organizations, the athletic teams, honors organizations within the larger majors, religious groups, and many others. Even though UCLA has a well-deserved reputation for political liberalism, that is not a universal norm, since more conservative political views prevail in some departments and schools, such as business and engineering, and in the fraternities and sororities.

That political liberalism is not the universal norm at UCLA suggests that the general liberalization among the students in the study occurred because of liberal teachings in particular academic areas, such as the social sciences, humanities, and the arts, as often charged by conservative critics of academia. To assess this possibility, we classified all college majors into two groups: "liberal majors" and "conservative majors."[7] We assigned students according to their declared major in their senior year (wave 5), which we assumed would best capture the predominant unique subject material of their college course work. We used the categories given in table 5.1 to assess their sociopolitical attitudes, indexing the liberalism of any given group in terms of the excess of liberal Democrats over conservative Republicans. By that standard, the liberal majors did indeed contain substantially more liberal students than did the conservative majors at college exit. The liberalism index was +40 percent in the liberal majors and +20 percent in the conservative majors in the senior year wave.

Although the difference might have reflected the differential effects of the majors themselves, it is more likely that it reflected the self-selection of students into politically congenial majors from the beginning. In the precollege wave, the liberalism index was +26 percent among the students who would ultimately indicate a liberal major in the senior year interview, but only +4 percent among the students who would ultimately indicate a conservative major. That 22 percent difference between the two sets of majors before college enrollment is very similar to the 20 percent difference between them at the end of the senior year. Although there are some differences across ethnic groups, the bottom line is that all groups became more liberal through college, with no evident pattern to the differences. Indeed, the largest pro-liberal shift (+19 percent) was among white students in conservative majors, and the smallest (+8 percent), among white students in liberal majors. The shifts among Asians and Latinos ranged from +19 percent (Asians in liberal majors) to +10 percent (Latinos in conservative majors). At the aggregate level, the liberalization of the students through college seems to have been more a product of a general campus liberal norm than of shifts among the most involved students or those in particularly liberal academic bastions.

Widening or Blurring Conventional Cleavages

As we saw in the previous chapter, a number of standard sociopolitical cleavages were firmly in place at college entry. Most notable were ethnic and racial divisions, the gender gap, and cleavages in terms of values and attitudinal predispositions, such as religiosity, racial conservatism, and inegalitarianism. How did the general political and racial liberalization of the students through college affect these cleavages?

One possibility is that the campus norm of liberalization might have been so pervasive that it blurred those initial differences. Alternatively, college might have reinforced, strengthened, and expanded the cleavages already present at college entry. That is, the college experience might have produced continued normative socialization. The students may have increasingly aligned themselves with these "correct" adult political divisions over time, which would have produced even stronger congruity with demographic and attitudinal characteristics by college exit. After all, more information does tend to polarize people around their predispositions (Zaller 1992). This tendency might also result in increased adherence by the new-immigrant groups to the norms of mainstream politics, as manifested in the rooting of their sociopolitical attitudes in the attributes common among adult whites. Expansion of the cleavages that are standard among adult whites to new-immigrant students as well would suggest that college contributed to further political incorporation and assimilation.

Ethnicity and Gender

The first of these standard cleavages is based in ethnicity. There were, in fact, almost no changes in ethnic divisions through college, as seen in table 5.1. In terms of political orientation, the proportion of liberal Democrats increased and the proportion of conservative Republicans decreased in all three ethnic groups almost equally. The net change toward liberalism was +7 percent for whites, +11 percent for Asians, and +6 percent for Latinos.[8] As a result, the students were no more divided by race and ethnicity at the end of college than they had been at college entry. The increases in liberal racial attitudes, egalitarian values, and policy-issue liberalism were also almost exactly the same in all ethnic groups, as shown in table 5.2. College had few overall polarizing effects on the sociopolitical divisions among racial and ethnic groups, consistent with the multicultural goals (and hopes) of the campus.

The gender gap has also been a salient feature of American political divisions over the past twenty-five years. Men have typically been considerably more likely to be conservative Republicans than women have been. In figure 5.1, we present the gender gap at college entry and exit for each group in terms of the proportion of liberal Democrats minus the proportion of conservative Republicans in each ethnic group. If whites were already substantially socialized at college entry, as we concluded in the previous chapter, the gender gap might not have changed much through college. However, among whites it almost doubled. By the end of the senior year, liberal Democrats dominated conservative Republicans by 42 percent among white women, against only 18 percent among white men. The norm of a political gender gap among whites had already been well established by college entry, but it widened substantially over the course of the college years.

Why did the gender gap increase through college for the white students? Earlier we found that liberal college majors were not directly responsible for producing liberalizing attitude changes through college. Still, it is possible that female students chose more liberal majors than did male students and for that reason shifted more to the political left

The Diversity Challenge

Figure 5.1 The Gender Gap in Political Liberalism at Precollege and Senior Year, by Ethnicity

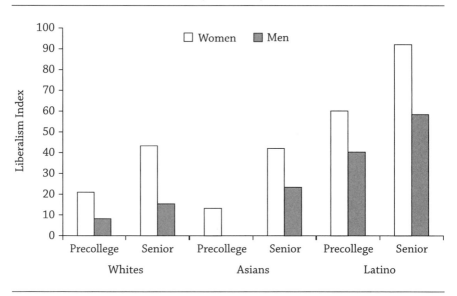

Source: Authors' compilation.

Note: Data reflect the percentage of liberal Democrats minus the percentage of conservative Republicans.

through college than did men. To test this, we again used the liberalism index presented in figure 5.1, which describes the excess of liberal Democrats over conservative Republicans in any given group.

Indeed, there was a large gender difference in the political complexion of the majors ultimately chosen by the students. That gender difference was present even before college entry. For example, among white students at college entry, 61 percent of those who ultimately selected a liberal major in their senior year were women, while only 40 percent of those ultimately selecting a conservative major were women. But at college entry, the political gender gap was quite similar in both groups. The gender gap in the liberalism index was +11 percent among students who would ultimately select a liberal major and +13 percent among those ultimately selecting a conservative major. We saw earlier that students self-selected into politically congenial majors. That self-selection process, however, did not seem to generate differential political gender gaps at college entry across ultimate majors.

Moreover, the gender gap in the liberalism index actually increased through college a little less among students in the liberal majors (+9 percent) than among those in conservative majors (+15 percent). The tendency for women to select more liberal majors than men was not responsible for the increased gender gap among white students through college. Put another way, the gender gap among white students increased even after the political leanings of the college major were controlled. The biggest liberalizing shift, in fact, was among women in conservative majors (+28 percent), and the smallest liberalizing shift occured among men in liberal majors (+2 percent). The other two groups were intermediate. Therefore, it looks as if choice of major was not relevant to the increased gender gap. It flowed from a more general gendered norm that produced continuing socialization through college.

There also was a substantial gender gap among Asians and Latinos at college entry. However, it failed to expand through college in either group. Most noteworthy, the general shift of Latinos to the liberal Democratic side through college was actually sharper among men than among women, so the gender gap shrank from 33 percent at college entry to 20 percent at college exit. Still, the gender gap remained evident in both groups. Indeed, by the end of college, 63 percent of the Latina women described themselves as liberal Democrats, with only one saying she was a conservative Republican![9]

In short, both females and males became much more liberal through college in all ethnic and racial groups. But among whites, women liberalized more than the men did, enlarging the gender gap. In this respect, we see evidence of continuing political socialization among white students through college as they increasingly conformed to adult norms.[10]

Predispositions and Values

Next, we turn to cleavages based in standard predispositions and values. In the last chapter, we found that political conservatism was fairly closely associated with symbolic racism, religiosity, and inegalitarianism at college entry, just as it is among adults in the broader electorate. Similarly, symbolic racism was closely associated with antiblack affect and political ideology, as it is among typical adults. Did these cleavages enlarge through college, resulting in even stronger associations of these key sociopolitical attitudes with other predispositions, thereby reflect-

Table 5.3   Associations of Political Conservatism and Symbolic Racism with Predispositions

	Political Conservatism		Symbolic Racism	
	Precollege	Senior Year	Precollege	Senior Year
Whites				
Antiblack affect	—	—	.12*	.30***
Political conservatism	—	—	.39***	.47***
Symbolic racism	.40***	.46***	—	—
Religiosity	.35***	.40***	.24***	.25***
Inegalitarianism	.42***	.46***	.45***	.51***
Dominance	.10	.26***	.22***	.32***
Asians				
Antiblack affect	—	—	.30***	.27***
Political conservatism	—	—	.22***	.24***
Symbolic racism	.22***	.29***	—	—
Religiosity	.24***	.25***	.00	.00
Inegalitarianism	.23***	.21***	.29***	.41***
Dominance	.16**	.11*	.22***	.28***
Latinos				
Antiblack affect	—	—	.21**	.21**
Political conservatism	—	—	.41***	.31***
Symbolic racism	.44***	.34***	—	—
Religiosity	.33***	.26***	−.03	.06
Inegalitarianism	.30***	.25**	.40***	.48***
Dominance	.25**	.13	.23**	.37***

Source: Authors' compilation.

Note: Entries are Pearson correlations between the scales indicated in the first column and political conservatism (columns 2 and 3) and symbolic racism (columns 4 and 5). Scales have been coded so that high numbers indicate more antiblack affect, more symbolic racism, more political conservatism, more religiosity, more inegalitarianism, and more dominance. Entries include only those who participated in both the precollege and senior year waves.
* p < .05; ** p < .01; *** p < .001

ing continuing socialization? Or were such associations weakened by the general shift to the left? Table 5.3 presents the bivariate correlations of both political conservatism and symbolic racism with these other attitudes and predispositions at college exit (senior year) compared to such correlations at college entry (precollege).[11]

All the correlates of whites' political conservatism increased, though not dramatically. The average correlation rose from $r = .32$ to $r = .40$. For symbolic racism, all the correlations also rose, from an average of $r = .28$ to $r = .37$. Table 5.3 shows that two of the greatest increases were in the associations of symbolic racism with its presumptive foundational elements, antiblack affect and political conservatism. A third noteworthy advance was in the association of dominance with both political conservatism and symbolic racism, which rose from an average correlation of $r = .16$ at college entry to $r = .29$ at college exit. This suggests that dominance is relatively weakly socialized in pre-adulthood, and since its content is rare in contemporary political discourse, that is not too surprising. The college experience did strengthen attitudes about group dominence, however. On the other hand, inegalitarianism, the other and more contemporary component of social dominance orientation (SDO), had already achieved some crystallization at college entry.

These cleavages were generally lower among the Asian students (average $r = .21$) than among the white students (average $r = .30$) at college entry, and they did not advance much among the Asian students—only to an average of $r = .23$ at college exit. The liberalization of Asians' sociopolitical attitudes through college was not accompanied by increased correlations with standard predispositions among the Asian students, unlike whites. As seen earlier, Latinos tended through the course of the college experience to be swept fairly uniformly into the liberal Democratic camp. They began to resemble a fairly solidly partisan group on the political left, like African Americans, rather than being internally split along the standard cleavage lines found in the broader electorate. This general liberal movement seems to have diminished the associations of political conservatism with other predispositions: all four correlations were reduced. The correlations of symbolic racism with other predispositions rose, but not consistently, with three of the five correlations increasing. Except for the gender gap, then, Latinos' general liberal movement somewhat reduced the internal cleavages present at college entry.

In sum, the conventional cleavages in political conservatism and symbolic racism, breaking along the lines of gender and key attitudinal predispositions, were substantially in place among white students at college entry. The college experience seems to have enhanced all of these cleavages somewhat, but the only dramatic increase was in the gender gap. Whites' sociopolitical socialization continued through the college years, then, albeit at a slower pace. The gender gap was visible at college entry for both Asian and Latino students but did not increase through college, since both women and men became equally more liberal. More broadly, the college experience seems not to have strengthened the conventional political divisions among Asians or Latinos. Latinos moved so uniformly to the political left that the conventional political divisions did not expand, and indeed they remained smaller than among whites. In short, the clearest evidence for a college effect in expanding standard sociopolitical divisions is the increased gender gap among whites. The other standard cleavages increased more modestly among whites, but none did so among Asians and Latinos.

Increased Attitude Crystallization?

Another criterion for complete socialization is holding fully crystallized attitudes. The impressionable years model would suggest that the students' attitudes were not fully socialized at college entry and thus that the crystallization of their political and racial attitudes might increase over the college years as they became more educated and coherent in their social and political thinking. In contrast, the persistence model would suggest that many entered college with fairly mature attitudes already and that college simply reinforces and strengthens preexisting preferences. Again, we focus primarily on political conservatism and symbolic racism, using internal consistency and stability over time as indicators of attitude crystallization.

Whites' Attitudes

In the last chapter, we found that the essentials of whites' socialization were already largely in place at college entry, at least on their most central sociopolitical attitudes. As might be expected, then, the college experience did not make their attitudes systematically more consistent. Figure 5.2 shows that the internal consistency of whites' political conservatism scarcely changed at all during the college years, and on balance it actually dropped off somewhat from precollege to the sophomore year before rising a bit in the senior year. On the other hand, the consistency of whites' symbolic racism steadily and substantially increased through the college years, as shown in figure 5.3.[12]

If the college experience was crucial in politically socializing students to conventional partisan politics, we might expect increased sta-

Figure 5.2   The Internal Consistency of Political Conservatism over
Time in College

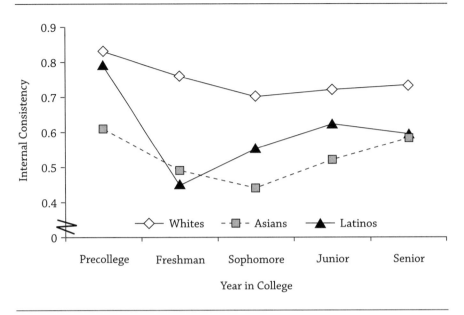

Source: Authors' compilation.
Note: Data points are correlations between party identification and political outlook.

bility of their attitudes as well. To test this we compared the stability of entry-level attitudes across students' first year of college with the stability of their attitudes across their last year of college, as shown in table 5.4. Political conservatism (as well as party identification and political outlook, treated separately) and symbolic racism all had only modestly more stability in the later years than they had in the early years. These increases in crystallization were clear and consistent but generally not large—hardly surprising given the high level of stability in these attitudes at college entry. By the end of college, white students' political conservatism was almost completely stable, as shown in table 5.4. Both party identification and political outlook had attained typical adult levels (compare with Converse and Markus 1979). By college exit, white students' acquisition of crystallized attitudes toward the symbolic racism belief system also seems to have been sub-

Figure 5.3　The Internal Consistency of Symbolic Racism over Time in College

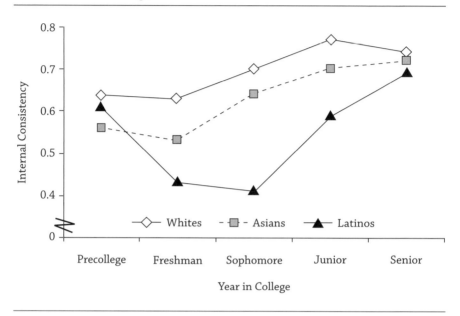

Source: Authors' compilation.
Note: Data points are alpha coefficients for the symbolic racism scale.

stantially complete, by the standard of having reached typical adult levels.[13]

In sum, the crystallization of whites' political conservatism did not dramatically change through college, in terms of either consistency or stability. The decline in consistency may itself be a bit anomalous, since both the precollege and senior year waves were conducted amid presidential campaigns. According to other studies (Sears and Valentino 1997; Valentino and Sears 1998), those campaigns alone should have stimulated greater crystallization. In any case, there is no sharp increase through college. The crystallization of white students' symbolic racism did increase substantially through college, by both indicators. The greater improvement for symbolic racism is instructive, since political conservatism was, by all indications, considerably more crystallized at college entry (see chapter 4) and remained so at college exit.

124

Table 5.4   Year-to-Year Stability of Attitudes Through College

	Whites		Asians		Latinos	
Variable	Precollege to Freshman	Junior to Senior	Precollege to Freshman	Junior to Senior	Precollege to Freshman	Junior to Senior
Predispositions						
Political conservatism	.83	.87	.73	.67	.80	.71
Party identification	.88	.92	.81	.80	.81	.84
Political outlook	.62	.70	.52	.45	.56	.50
Symbolic racism	.63	.72	.59	.71	.56	.55
Religiosity	.79	.87	.81	.84	.80	.85
Inegalitarianism	.44	.69	.45	.45	.37	.47
Dominance	.41	.54	.32	.34	.23	.46
Social policy attitudes						
Average correlation	.57	.62	.36	.40	.44	.50

Source: Authors' compilation.

Note: Entries are test-retest Pearson correlations across the precollege and freshman waves, and the junior and senior waves, respectively. The bottom entry is the average test-retest correlation across opposition to affirmative action, attitude toward immigrants, attitude toward solving the crime problem, and attitude toward welfare recipients.

The New-Immigrant Groups

In chapter 4, we saw that whites had considerably more crystallized attitudes at college entry than did Asians and Latinos, even those who were U.S.-born. Does the college experience allow students from the new-immigrant groups to erase that earlier gap? Or does it simply strengthen, and possibly enlarge, those initial ethnic differences? The crystallization of Asians' political conservatism seemed to change little through college. Both the consistency and stability of political conservatism were slightly lower by the end of the senior year than at college entry, as shown in figure 5.2 and table 5.4. In addition, there was no increase in the stability of the constituent parts of political conservatism, party identification and political outlook. Asians had arrived at college with considerably less crystallized political conservatism than did whites, and that remained true at college exit. Symbolic racism, again, was a markedly different story. Asians showed substantial increases in both internal consistency and stability, as shown in figure 5.3 and table 5.4, and in fact the difference between whites and Asians was eliminated altogether. In other words, we find little change in the crystallization of Asians' political conservatism through college, but there was substantial development of their racial attitudes. In the next section, we examine the role of the many recent Asian immigrants in producing these differences between our two key sociopolitical attitudes.

As noted earlier, Latinos represent a somewhat different phenomenon. The consistency and stability of their political conservatism fell off quite sharply through the college years, as shown in figure 5.2 and table 5.4. As a result, the difference between whites and Latinos in crystallization actually increased. Although the consistency of Latinos' symbolic racism increased, its stability did not change. Overall, then, Latinos failed to show systematic increases in crystallization. Again, their wholesale, nearly consensual, movement toward the left may have smoothed over the individual differences that would be required to register high levels of crystallization on our indicators.

In sum, a key indicator of the completeness of sociopolitical socialization is crystallization. In the last chapter, we concluded that the new-immigrant groups showed substantially less crystallization prior to college than did whites, who were already close to typical adult levels. The college experience appears to have pushed the white students further toward complete acquisition, but it does not seem to have produced more crystallization of political conservatism among either Asian or Latino students. Both groups' attitudes remained less crystallized than whites' attitudes. This lack of a college effect on their political conservatism is somewhat surprising in view of our expectation that Asians are politically acculturating to American society and that higher education is an important instrument in that process. The crystallization of the new-immigrant groups' symbolic racism did increase substantially, however, largely erasing the initial differences from whites. The college experience does appear to have been broadly effective in promoting sophistication about race relations. One noteworthy effect of the contemporary college multicultural experience is growing elaboration and coherence of students' attitudes about other racial groups.

Comparisons Across Attitude Objects

Our final question about crystallization concerns differences across attitude objects. In the previous chapter, we saw considerable variation at college entry in crystallization over different attitudes. Party identification and symbolic racism were relatively highly crystallized, while social dominance orientation and social policy attitudes were less so. Those variations paralleled the differences usually found in adults, among whom objects recurrently in the public arena draw considerably more crystallized attitudes than do objects that are transient or only episodically salient (Sears 1983). Presumably, the reason is that strong information flows promote crystallization. On the other hand, the college experience might affect previously less-crystallized attitudes, which have room to grow, but it might not affect attitudes that are highly crystallized and already close to typical adult levels at college entry. Does the college experience allow attitudes toward less salient attitude objects to catch up to the presumably more salient and earlier-acquired attitudes? Comparisons across attitude objects are better tested with stability than consistency, because estimates of consistency are more influenced by the number of items used to measure each attitude dimension. As in the last chapter, we compare symbolic predispositions with a broader set of predispositions and attitudes. The data are shown in table 5.4.

Among the white students, the major symbolic predispositions drew the most stable attitudes at college entry. The two attitudes advertised in the last chapter as "the gold standard," party identification and religiosity, were extraordinarily stable. Symbolic racism and general political outlook were not far behind. Symbolic racism still was not as crystallized as party identification, but it was just as crystallized as other important political attitudes.[14] The four social policy attitudes lagged substantially behind, and the two subcomponents of SDO, inegalitarianism and dominance, were the least stable.

White students' college experiences increased the stability of all these categories of attitudes. The stability of the symbolic predispositions rose from an average correlation of $r = .73$ to an average of $r = .80$. The average stability for social policy attitudes rose from an average of $r = .57$ to $r = .62$.[15] The initially least crystallized predispositions, the subcomponents of SDO, showed especially large increases in stability, from an average of $r = .42$ to $r = .62$. The variation across attitude objects did not disappear, then, as would be expected, since adults' attitudes show such variation quite clearly. But the college experience did narrow the variation somewhat.

As was the case for whites, differences across attitude objects were very similar at college entry for Asians and Latinos, with the symbolic predispositions showing considerably more stability than did either the social policy attitudes or the subcomponents of SDO. There was little change through college in the stability of the new-immigrant groups' symbolic predispositions: an average test-retest correlation of $r = .69$ from the precollege to the freshman waves rose only to $r = .70$ from the junior to the senior waves. Moreover, social policy attitudes and the subcomponents of SDO showed little increase in stability. Averaging across Asians and Latinos, the stability of social policy attitudes rose from $r = .40$ to $r = .45$, and for the subcomponents of SDO from $r = .34$ to $r = .43$. Put another way, the same rank order held for these attitude objects at college exit as at college entry. Since it parallels the rank order that we see in the broader electorate, this may serve as another indication of the completeness of much socialization at college entry, especially among whites, along with the maintenance of ethnic gaps through college.

College Effects Among Recent Immigrants

Our assimilation hypothesis would suggest that the political incorporation of ethnic minority groups is slowed by relatively recent immigration. Not having grown up in families steeped in the American political culture, Asians and Latinos should not have been as thoroughly politically socialized as white students, almost all of whose families are long-time natives of the United States. Nor should the most recent immigrants be as thoroughly incorporated as fellow ethnics who, with their families, have been in the United States for longer periods of time. But in introducing them both to partisan politics and to the dynamics of racial diversity in the United States, the college experience might play a special compensatory role for those students who are the products of recent immigration.

We again treat as longtime residents the "old Asians" and "old Latinos" who were born in the United States and for whom English is the primary language at home. We classify as "new Asians" and "new Latinos" those who were born outside of the United States *or* for whom English is not the primary language at home.[16] The assimilation hypothesis suggests three empirical comparisons: Did "old" immigrants or "new" immigrants show greater political incorporation at college exit than they had at college entry? Had the longer-resident old Asians and old Latinos

Figure 5.4   Mean Levels of Political Conservatism and Symbolic Racism Through College, by Ethnicity and Immigration Status

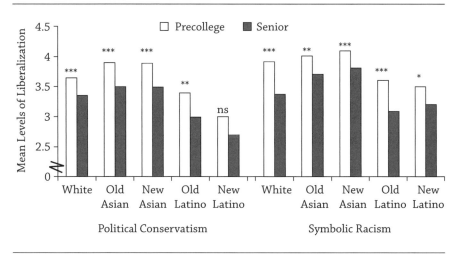

Source: Authors' compilation.

Note: Higher scores reflect higher levels of political conservatism and symbolic racism. Statistical significance of changes through college are indicated by the asterisks above each pair of bars.

p < .05; ** p < .01; *** p < .001; ns = not significant

attained the same levels of political incorporation as whites by college exit? And had more recent immigrants, new Asians and new Latinos, attained the same levels of incorporation as their longer-tenured counterparts?

Liberalization

To test for differential liberalization through college, we compared changes in mean levels of political conservatism and symbolic racism from college entry to exit across these groups, as shown in figure 5.4. First, all four groups of Asians and Latinos had become more liberal by college exit than they had been at college entry, on both attitude dimensions, with all but one of the changes reaching statistical significance.[17] Second, old Asians had been a little more conservative than whites at college entry, and the old Latinos somewhat more liberal, in both political conservatism and symbolic racism. By the end of college, the old Asians and old Latinos had become significantly more liberal on both dimensions. But the differences between them and white students remained more or less unchanged.

Third, the new Asians had been almost identical to the old Asians at college entry. The old Latinos were slightly more conservative than their new counterparts, as might be expected from traditional assimilation theories. All four groups of Asians and Latinos seem to have adapted equally to the general norm of becoming more liberal through college, without any discernible differences among them in the magnitude or pace of change. The end point, however, was different. At the conclusion of college, both groups of Asians remained somewhat more conservative than whites, while both sets of Latinos remained more liberal than white students.

Taking recency of immigration into account does not change the liberalization story line very much. By the end of college, Asians as a whole had nearly assimilated to the political norms set by whites, while Latinos had become a distinctive political bloc on the left, more like blacks. Either way, immigration status played a minor role. The college experience had a broadly liberalizing effect on all groups of students.

Crystallization

Finally, we return to crystallization. Figures 5.5 and 5.6 present the data for consistency and stability, respectively, of both political conservatism and symbolic racism. This yields three possible criteria for assessing change through college for each ethnic group. The first is a comparison of old and new immigrants. In fact, both tended to show somewhat greater crystallization at college exit than at college entry, especially for symbolic racism. That is, the college experience seems to have been especially important in the new-immigrant groups' learning about America's most central racial cleavage. The crystallization of political conservatism also increased in most cases, though less consistently. College had the least impact on the old Latinos, who came from families with longer residence in the United States and presumably had less to learn on average.

A second criterion assesses sociopolitical incorporation of the new-immigrant groups by comparing their change through college with whites. How did they compare at college exit? Even old Asians and old Latinos

Figure 5.5   Internal Consistency of Political Conservatism and
              Symbolic Racism over College, by Ethnicity and
              Immigration Status

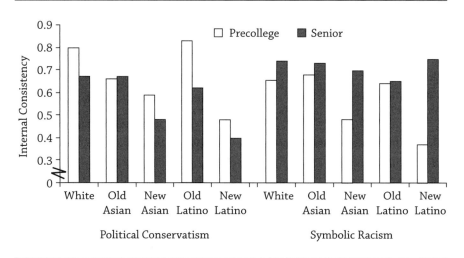

Source: Authors' compilation.
Note: Data points for political conservatism are correlations between party identification and political outlook, and alpha coefficients for the symbolic racism scale.

had shown substantially less attitude crystallization than had whites at college entry, as we saw in the previous chapter. The old Asians did eliminate that crystallization gap by all four tests: the consistency and stability of both political conservatism and symbolic racism. In that sense, the college experience seems to have succeeded in assimilating them to the mainstream of the broader culture. It was not successful, however, in producing that level of incorporation among the old Latinos, whose attitudes remained substantially less crystallized than whites' attitudes, as indicated by all four tests.

Third, the more recent new immigrants had markedly less crystallized attitudes than their longer-resident counterparts at college entry. Was that still true at the end of college? The answer is no. The new immigrants did show consistently increased crystallization, but generally not by enough to reach the old immigrants' levels (falling short in six of the eight comparisons). Among the most recent immigrants, however, there was one important impact of the college experience. The new Latinos

Figure 5.6   Stability of Political Conservatism and Symbolic Racism
over College, by Ethnicity and Immigration Status

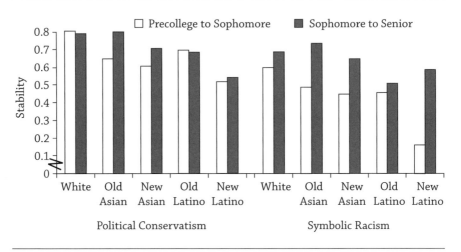

Source: Authors' compilation.
Note: Data points are test-retest correlations.

showed both greater consistency and stability of symbolic racism by college exit than did the old Latinos. As we have seen at several junctures in
this chapter, the college experience apparently was most successful in
bringing students up to speed about racial norms in the United States,
and here we see that it was especially successful with the newest immigrants.

We draw three main conclusions about recent immigration. The college experience generally enhanced the new-immigrant students' attitude crystallization, except for the consistency of political conservatism,
no matter how recent their immigration. College did promote their sociopolitical incorporation into the United States. But even the boost
given by college was insufficient to overcome the reality that the incorporation process is generally more intergenerational than intragenera-
tional. College allowed the more recently immigrated to advance, not to
catch up. Third, at college entry political conservatism was more crystallized in all ethnic groups than was symbolic racism. However, the impact
of college on the crystallization of political conservatism among the
newest immigrants was quite mixed. Indeed, the consistency of party
identification and political outlook actually fell for the new immigrants,

unlike our other indicators of crystallization. Our suspicion is that this is a consequence of the greater liberalization of party identification than of political outlook seen earlier in table 5.2. "Conservatism" can reflect more than just a tendency exercised in the voting booth; it may also reflect other lifestyle issues, such as religiosity, moral values, attachment to family, and so on. By all indicators, however, the crystallization of symbolic racism rose, as would be expected. In this sense, symbolic racism seems to be a clear example of the impressionable years hypothesis, with the college experience as the driving influence, while political conservatism seems more clearly an example of the persistence hypothesis involving pre-adult acquisition.

Summary and Conclusions

In this chapter, we addressed several questions regarding the overall effects of college on students' sociopolitical attitudes. Our first and perhaps most basic question was whether the college experience liberalized the students' political and racial attitudes, or whether the new cultural diversity created a conservative backlash among them. The symbolic politics hypothesis was that the college experience was likely to have liberalized the students, because of the liberal norms present at both the institutional and peer levels when the students entered college. In fact, in terms of both political conservatism and symbolic racism, students in all ethnic groups did move to the left, in the aggregate, and did so rather steadily throughout college. A broader set of predispositions and social policy attitudes showed the same liberalization. At the individual level, the students with somewhat inconsistent initial attitudes were the ones who most often changed to more liberal political orientations. With respect to race, liberalization more clearly reflected a conversion of some racial conservatives—those showing higher levels of symbolic racism— to greater racial liberalism. Although this quite pervasive trend toward liberalism parallels the findings of Newcomb's (1943) famous Bennington study, we failed to find any evidence that it was most prominent among the students who were most identified with and involved in the campus and its activities. The dynamics of sociopolitical change seem quite different on a large, diverse, urban campus such as today's UCLA from those in a small, rural, homogeneous liberal arts college such as the Bennington College of the 1930's. Later chapters address the dynamics of this change in more detail.

The Diversity Challenge

Our second question was whether the sociopolitical cleavages characteristic of adults in the American electorate, and present already among the students at college entry, persisted through college. Alternatively, they might have been blurred by the general trend toward sociopolitical liberalism, or they might have even expanded through college, as part of students' continuing political socialization. The ethnic divisions in political conservatism and symbolic racism present at college entry—with Latinos more liberal and Asians slightly more conservative than whites—did not expand through college. In that sense, the multicultural ideals of the campus were not met with a backlash driven by ethnic conflict. The gender gap did increase throughout college among white students, yielding a convincing sign that college had some continuing socialization effects. But it was not simply due to the concentration of female students in more liberal curricular majors; the gender gap increased just as much among students in conservative majors such as the sciences and engineering as it did among those in the social sciences and humanities. Partisan cleavages due to racial attitudes, gender, religiosity, and egalitarian values continued to expand through college among whites but not among Asians or Latinos, a somewhat puzzling halt to their continuing acculturation.

In the previous chapter, we found considerable crystallization of basic sociopolitical attitudes already at college entry, as if pre-adult political socialization had been highly effective. Our third question was whether or not the college experience promoted still greater crystallization, as an impressionable years model might suggest. A symbolic politics theory would expect continuing advances, especially in attitude domains that had shown only modest crystallization initially. In fact, there were only modest increases in the crystallization of political conservatism, which had already been close to typical adult levels at college entry, especially among white students. More telling advances occurred in symbolic racism, even though it too had initially approached typical adult levels. There was much evidence in this chapter that the college experience played a more important role in facilitating students' understanding of race relations in the United States than in helping them achieve a clear political identity, much of which had already been accomplished by college entry.

Fourth, we repeatedly compared whites with the Asian and Latino new-immigrant groups throughout the chapter and, in the last section, specifically with the most recently immigrated of them. At college entry,

134

whites had shown the most evidence of closing in on complete political socialization, followed by the Asian and Latino students from families who had lived longest in the United States; the most recent immigrants showed the least complete political socialization. All groups showed some increase in crystallization through college. For the most part, however, the initial differences between whites and new-immigrant groups persisted at college exit. The exception was the group of old Asians who had lived longer in the United States. By the end of college, they did not differ from whites. Our conclusion is that full sociopolitical acculturation generally is not accomplished within one generation, even with the advantage of a college education. It remains an intergenerational task.

Finally, did the college experience facilitate the development of a people of color perspective among Asians and Latinos or the sense of being in an inferior position in a racial hierarchy, either of which might promote more progressive sociopolitical attitudes relative to whites? At college entry, Asian students did not fit either model very closely since they held more conservative attitudes than whites. The college experience did not alter that pattern. On the other hand, Latinos, who held more progressive attitudes than did whites at both junctures, did fit these models better at both college entry and exit. But perhaps the most important finding is that the college experience did not increase differences of sociopolitical opinion between whites and these new-immigrant groups. Rather, all moved, on average, in a more liberal direction. Therefore, it appears that college does not convert Asians and Latinos into balkanized minorities, as the harshest critics of multicultural education fear.

These findings provide a simple, broad-canvas sketch of the effects of the college experience. The remaining chapters examine the specific details of how college affected the students. We simply close here with the caveat that what we have described as the "effects" of college are confounded irretrievably with two other factors: more experience in responding to these survey questions, and the effects of maturing over four years of what were still rather short lifetimes. The analytic focus of later chapters on specific determinants of change through college provides the volume as a whole with protection against the uncertainties introduced by these inevitable confounds.

Chapter 6

The Origins and Persistence of Ethnic Identity Among the New-Immigrant Groups

The previous two chapters charted the introduction of our students to the American political and racial systems. The fact that most of them are members of minority groups, however, raises other questions that focus more directly on their specifically racial and ethnic experiences on a multicultural campus. UCLA, like the broader American society and many other Western nations, has become increasingly culturally diverse since the 1960s. The social and political effects of cultural diversification have been much debated. One particular concern is that it might produce ethnic balkanization, stimulating communal conflict and, in extreme cases, violence and the disintegration of nation-states. Samuel Huntington (2004), for example, argues that heavy waves of immigration from Mexico and the rest of Latin America could diminish national unity in many ways and perhaps even lead to a loss of American control over significant regions of the present United States. Huntington believes that the only way to maintain a unified America is through a common creed and culture.

Presumably, ethnic balkanization is intimately connected to the social identities of members of ethnic minority groups—the psychological markers of their relationships to their own groups and the broader society. A student body at a large university that includes a relatively high proportion of ethnic minorities and no single numerically dominant group could provide a "critical mass" that encourages the enhanced salience of ethnic identity and the formation of ethnic enclaves. At UCLA, the issue of possible balkanization hinges most on the trajectory of Asian and Latino students because of the relatively small numbers of African Americans on the campus. Accordingly, our primary empirical focus in this chapter is on the social identities of students from what we earlier called the new-immigrant groups, Asians and Latinos.

Two American Prototypes

Two popular prototypes exist for thinking about ethnic minority groups in the United States and their social identities. We describe the first as the European assimilation prototype. It focuses on the European immigrants who arrived in the United States in the nineteenth and early twentieth centuries and their descendants. The term "melting pot" is often used to symbolize their general assimilation into the broader society. This assimilation is reflected in much-reduced geographical concentration, fluency in original languages, ethnically based social organization, and intraethnic friendship preferences, as well as increased interethnic intermarriage and socioeconomic convergence with Anglo-American whites. It is also reflected in a lessened burden of stereotypes and prejudice against them and in their own gradual transition from ethnic to American social identities. Of course, this process usually is not depicted as trouble-free or free of discrimination. Moreover, full assimilation has normally occurred across rather than within generations, an important point to which we will return. Still, the assimilation prototype has become a dominant symbolic model of intergroup relations in the United States, and it is often described as part of the "dominant ideology" of American life (see, for example, Alba 1990; Alba and Nee 2003; Gordon 1964; Huber and Form 1973; Perlmann and Waldinger 1996).

A second prototype is the black discrimination prototype, deriving from America's history of legalized discrimination against blacks. African Americans were subjected first to slavery and later to the Jim Crow system before finally being given equal formal status in the 1960s. In the aggregate, blacks have not followed the same assimilatory trajectory as the European immigrants, either in terms of socioeconomic convergence or social integration. They persistently fall at the bottom of most indicators of well-being, such as income, wealth, longevity, infant mortality, health, education, employment, and housing. These racial gaps have not generally decreased very much in recent decades. Moreover, blacks remain the most residentially segregated, show the least intermarriage with other groups, and are the targets of the strongest prejudice from whites (see, for example, Farley 1996; Sears et al. 2000; Stoll 2005). In turn, the continuing separateness and disadvantage of African Americans promotes the continuation of their strong sense of perceived societal discrimination, racial identity, and common fate (Dawson 1994; Hochschild 1995; Sears and Savalei 2006).

Which of these prototypes best fits the waves of new immigrants who have entered the United States in the past few decades? A people of color hypothesis, which generalizes the black discrimination prototype to Asians and Latinos, is plausible, given the parallels between these groups and blacks. The new immigrants too are regarded as "peoples of color" and as groups that have experienced a history of prejudice and discrimination in the United States. Sucheng Chan (1991, 42) has noted that "racial discrimination is what separates the historical experience of Asian immigrants from that of Europeans, on the one hand, and makes it resemble that of enslaved Africans and dispossessed Native Americans and Mexican Americans, on the other hand" (see also Takaki 1993).

The European assimilation prototype, however, is a plausible alternative for thinking about the future trajectory of Asians and Latinos, given the many parallels between them and the turn-of-the-century European immigrants. Almost all Asians and Latinos have immigrated to the United States voluntarily, pulled by economic opportunity or pushed by political expulsion. The great majority arrived in a post–civil rights era in which formal discrimination has been banned. Moreover, they differ in salient ways from African Americans. Because of the recency of their immigration, most lack the long history of discrimination and exclusion in American society that blacks and their ancestors have experienced. As Nathan Glazer (1997, 120–21) writes, "The difference that separates blacks from whites, and even from other groups 'of color' that have undergone a history of discrimination and prejudice in this country, is not to be denied." Elsewhere, we have termed this view the black exceptionalism hypothesis (Sears et al. 1999; Sears and Savalei 2006). Its core idea is that obstacles to assimilation are considerably more intractable for blacks than for other minority groups, given the nearly impermeable color line that blacks have historically confronted.[1]

Ethnic Identity

Several social-psychological theories are relevant to the inquiry into ethnic identity, as indicated in chapter 2. In particular, cognitive categorization theories suggest that people automatically and even unconsciously categorize individuals (themselves as well as others) into social groups. Social identity theory further suggests a basic need for a specifically *social* identity as a key to self-esteem and, with it, universal tendencies to form solidarity groups and to allocate resources selectively in favor of the ingroup, even in the absence of any especially self-interested reason to do so. Social-structural theories of group competition, such as realistic group conflict theory or sense of group position theory, also assume the ubiquity of group formation based on a need for social identity. But they go further, variously assuming the inevitability of intergroup competition and pressures toward stable hierarchies of status and power.[2]

In most of these theories, the exact group divisions that display the sharpest conflicts are thought to depend on the particular historical and social context.[3] But in the contemporary United States, the most important applications of these theories have been to ethnic and racial cleavages.[4] These theories would generally lead us to expect that greater diversity strengthens ethnic group boundaries, provoking the dominant whites to protect their own privileges and leading the subordinate ethnic minority groups to demand more resources to satisfy their own group's interests. In this view, the most likely effect of greater diversity is to generate ethnic polarization over resource allocations.

A key political-psychological prerequisite in these processes is a strong sense of ethnic identity. Among a dominant white majority, ethnic identity can protect group privileges. Among ethnic and racial minorities, it can motivate actions to seek greater resources for one's own group. Most relevant for our purposes is *politicized* ethnic identity, which goes beyond placing oneself in a particular social category: those with a politicized ethnic identity have adopted a political group consciousness and perhaps are even impelled toward collective action to further the goals of their group. Such a politicized collective identity is engaged when people perceive themselves as self-conscious group members in a power struggle on behalf of their group. This identity can motivate *group*-interested action even when *self*-interest is not at stake. For example, ingroup favoritism may be linked to "collective," but not "personal," self-esteem (Crocker and Luhtanen 1990). Symbolic political

139

manipulation can make ethnic identity more salient and stronger in the service of mobilizing group-based political action by disadvantaged groups (Rhea 1997; Simon and Klandermans 2001). Sometimes such a strategy can help to rectify inequalities. But it can also lead demagogues to use their followers' ethnic identities to arouse either support for the ingroup or hostility toward their enemies, as has happened in recent years in nations as diverse as Bosnia, Rwanda, and Iraq. In such cases, more strongly politicized senses of ethnic identity can be vehicles for moving democratic societies closer to ethnic balkanization and societal disintegration (Eriksen 2001).

Most applications of such thinking to American ethnic and racial groups have focused on African Americans. The people of color hypothesis suggests that these applications may extend to Asians and Latinos as well, such that strongly politicized ethnic identities may also be common and desirable for the new-immigrant groups. But such applications are not necessarily a clean fit for today's Asians and Latinos. Most blacks are descendants of Africans brought to the United States two or more centuries ago, not within the past few decades. Many more generations of blacks have lived in the United States than is the case for the new-immigrant groups. Still, most blacks' integration into the broader society is frustratingly incomplete. Blacks' long history of privation and disadvantage is likely to have contributed to their relatively politicized racial identities. Adult blacks have been shown to have a stronger sense of racial identity and common fate with fellow group members than do adults from other ethnic and racial groups. Moreover, blacks' strong racial identities and sense of common fate strongly affect their political attitudes (Bobo and Johnson 2001; Citrin and Sears 2007; Dawson 1994; Sears and Savalei 2006).

As a result, the turn-of-the-century European immigrants might also be plausible benchmarks for understanding the new immigrants' social identities. To be sure, on average, ethnic identity remains more important among their adult descendants than among those still earlier European immigrants. But the erosion of objective ethnic differences and of behavioral manifestations of ethnic identity and the extensive intermarriage that has occurred across ethnic groups have led to a decline in the subjective importance of ethnic identity across generations. Ethnic identity may now primarily represent a "symbolic ethnicity" among most of the turn-of-the-century immigrants' descendants (Alba 1990; Alba and Nee 2003; Gans 1979).

Emprical Questions

In this chapter, we begin with the ethnic identities of Asians and Latinos at college entry. Our first empirical question is whether their ethnic identities mainly operate like those of any other new immigrants to the United States, as suggested by the black exceptionalism hypothesis. Alternatively, as suggested by the people of color hypothesis, the ethnic identities of Asians and Latinos may operate more like those of African Americans in terms of their content, strength, and origins. Concretely, we seek to determine whether Asians' and Latinos' social identities derive more from the transitional phase of recent immigration or from long-standing discriminatory experiences in the American racial and ethnic system.

This leads us to our second empirical question: what is the effect of the college experience on the ethnic identities of the new-immigrant groups? In addition to considering the ethnic identities of these new-immigrant groups at college entry, we also consider the influence of the college experience on students' thoughts regarding their ethnicity, thereby further assessing the process of identification with a certain ethnicity. This experience may contribute either to ethnic balkanization or to the gradual assimilation of recent immigrants. Our focus here is on people who have "made it" in the sense of having gained admission to a highly selective institution of higher education. They are thus likely to join the ranks of the most educated and advantaged members of their cohorts. Many from the new-immigrant groups are destined to be the core of future Asian American and Latino elites. How will these future elites think about their own ethnicity? And what role will their college experience play in that thinking?

The two prototypes described here suggest several possibilities. A college education could lead them to adopt more strongly politicized ethnic identities, accompanied by a rhetoric of self-conscious identification with fellow members of an oppressed minority group, as the people of color hypothesis suggests. Alternatively, like the earlier European ethnics, they may follow a trajectory of assimilation, perhaps transitioning through the traditional model of conventional ethnic bloc politics, as the black exceptionalism hypothesis suggests. The political debate about these possibilities as usual often puts it in even more extreme terms: are college campuses spawning "activist radicals" who, through identity politics, will take the lead in promoting the advancement of their groups, balkanizing the society as they go? Or are campuses preparing future "solid citizens" who will engage in the more traditional quests for personal mobility and leadership positions in the community?[5]

On the campus itself, the people of color hypothesis might predict a pattern of "reactive ethnicity"—that is, the strengthening and politicizing of ethnic identity through the college years because of the salience of ethnic diversity, the ubiquity of ethnic categorization, and intergroup competition. Indeed, ethnic studies programs and ethnically based activities directly aim at promoting cultural awareness for minority students and seek to recover and recognize the contribution of groups that may have been neglected by the mainstream of American society. There is some evidence that, at least in the past, higher education increased blacks' group consciousness. David Sears and John McConahay (1973) found, in the 1960s, that more-educated blacks had stronger black identities (but not more antiwhite hostility). In the 1980s, Patricia Gurin, Shirley Hatchett, and James Jackson (1989) found that more education was associated with a number of attitudes supportive of mobilization on behalf of blacks' distinctive political interests. Similarly, Jennifer Hochschild (1995) found that middle-class blacks were more pessimistic about blacks' opportunities than were poor blacks.

On the other hand, with gradual assimilation might come the supplanting (or at least supplementing) of ethnic identity with other forms of identity and the weakening of ethnic identity per se. As we saw in chapter 3, most Asian and Latino students today are the products of recent immigration and do not come from families with long histories in the American racial system. Moreover, shared campus experiences may override their diverse pasts, working against separate ethnic identities and encouraging a more inclusive American identity. As noted earlier, the ethnic identity of descendants of the turn-of-the-century European immigrants now tends to be less grounded in a sense of disadvantage or deprivation and is more of a "symbolic ethnicity" (Alba 1990; Gans 1979).

For our third empirical question, we ask: what do the new-immigrant groups' ethnic identities look like at college exit? Have they changed, or do they remain substantially the same at the conclusion of the college experience? During the college experience these groups may become increasingly politicized, and at college exit there may be polarization between or within ethnic groups. Their ethnic identities may become increasingly rooted in perceived discrimination against the ingroup. Alternatively, they may show continuity with their ethnic identities at college entry.

At the broadest level, then, we seek to assess how the American color line is playing out in the social identities of the growing numbers of college-educated people in the new-immigrant groups, Asians and Latinos. To put it in extreme terms, we are seeking to determine whether a pattern of increasingly politicized ethnic identity, and thus ethnic balkanization, arises as Asians and Latinos become defined as "people of color," in the mode of African Americans. Alternatively, a pattern of assimilation over time, in the mode of the turn-of-the-century European immigrants, may arise. These possibilities raise our fourth and final empirical question: Is it appropriate to treat Asians and Latinos alike, as fellow new-immigrant groups? Or are there such significant differences between these two groups that they should be treated separately?

Ethnic Identity at College Entry

First, at a descriptive level, what can we say about the content of the students' ethnic identities? In particular, how widely accepted are the politicized pan-ethnic identities commonly used to describe American ethnic groups, such as the labels of "white," "black," "Asian," and "Latino"? Such category labels are ubiquitous in Americans' lives, and especially in their interactions with bureaucracies like those on any campus. But such pan-ethnic labels may force many individuals of quite disparate cultural roots and ethnic consciousness into a few artificially created superordinate categories that do not reflect their own thinking about their ethnicity.

The Content of Ethnic Identity

We wanted to assess the spontaneous content of the students' ethnic identities as free of any expectations or context as possible. As described in chapter 3, the college entry questionnaire was administered on the first day of summer orientation, which for most students was the first day spent on campus after accepting admission to UCLA. At college entry, an open-ended question, "Which ethnic-racial group do you most closely identify with?" was posed early in the questionnaire, preceded only by four relatively neutral questions (on age, gender, college major, and SAT scores).[6] This procedure seems to have freed many students from feeling obligated to use the conventional pan-ethnic labels, since they gave a very large number of different responses: 138 coding categories were necessary at college entry (n = 2,080), and in the senior year 87 categories were needed (n = 1,192).

Table 6.1 displays the data, grouped into pan-ethnic and specific nationality categories.[7] The latter includes any response mentioning a specific country. Most of the students from the new-immigrant groups began college identifying with their national origins rather than with the pan-ethnic political labels that are socially constructed in the United States. This was particularly true of the Asian students, who, on average, were newer to this country: 63 percent described themselves in terms of national origins at college entry. The Latinos split evenly, with 50 percent describing themselves in terms of national origins.[8] In contrast, almost all of the whites and blacks, predominantly from families with long histories in the United States (see chapter 3) used the standard pan-ethnic labels. At college entry, 98 percent of the black students used "black," "African American," or "Afro-American," and 93 percent of the whites used "white," "Caucasian," or "Anglo-Saxon." That is, the social identities of many of the students from the new-immigrant groups hearkened back to their nations of origin rather than invoking American ethnic group labels, whereas blacks and whites almost all described their identities in terms of standard American pan-ethnic labels. This is the first of several ways in which the new-immigrant groups differed from blacks in particular, consistent with the black exceptionalism hypothesis.

The Strength of Ethnic Identification

An ethnic identification scale was generated in each wave.[9] The mean strength of ethnic identification for each ethnic group is shown in table 6.2. Most important for our purposes here, at college entry Asians' and Latinos' strength of ethnic identification was just as strong as that of blacks. This finding, in contrast to the last one, is consistent with the people of color hypothesis. All three ethnic minority groups had a stronger sense of ethnic identification than did whites. Whites much less frequently thought about their ethnicity, which most thought of in terms of being white, Caucasian, or Anglo-Saxon rather than in terms of national origins.

Table 6.1   "Which Ethnic-Racial Group Do You Most Closely
             Identify With?"

Ethnic-Racial Group	At Entry	Sophomore	Senior
Whites			
Pan-ethnic categories	93%	94%	94%
White, Caucasian, Anglo-Saxon	93	94	93
European American	0	0	1
Specific nationalities	6	6	5
British, Irish, Italian, et cetera	6	5	5
Irish American, et cetera	0	1	0
Number of respondents	816	496	362
Asians			
Pan-ethnic categories	37%	39%	32%
Asian or Southeast Asian	25	28	20
Asian American	11	10	10
Pacific Islander	1	1	2
Specific nationalities	63	61	69
Chinese, Asian Chinese, et cetera	58	50	55
Chinese American, et cetera	5	11	14
Number of respondents	760	554	414
Latinos			
Pan-ethnic categories	50%	62%	55%
Hispanic	23	28	18
Latino or Latina	14	22	25
Chicano or Chicana	11	10	10
Hispanic American, et cetera	2	2	2
Specific nationalities	50	38	45
Mexican, Spanish, et cetera	22	12	14
Mexican American, et cetera	28	26	31
Number of respondents	305	386	255
Blacks			
Pan-ethnic categories	98%	98%	100%
African or Afro-American	78	78	74
Black	20	20	26
Specific nationalities	2	2	0
Number of respondents	95	125	86

Source: Authors' compilation.

Note: Respondents include those who responded to any of the three waves. Percentages may not add up to 100 percent owing to rounding.

Table 6.2   Mean Strength of Ethnic Identification Across Time

Time	Whites	Asians	Latinos	Blacks
At college entry	3.6[b]	5.3[a]	5.3	5.3[b]
At end of sophomore year	3.8[a]	5.0[b]	5.1	5.8[a]
At end of senior year	3.6[ab]	4.9[b]	5.2	5.6[ab]

Source: Authors' compilation.

Note: Data are from respondents who participated in all three waves. Entries are means on seven-point scales averaging three items. Entries within a column with different superscript are significantly different at $p < .05$.

Origins of Strong Ethnic Identification

Within the new-immigrant groups, which of the entering students had the strongest ethnic identities? Was it the descendants of the Asian and Latino families long resident in the United States, who had much experience with American-style ethnic and racial subordination, as the people of color hypothesis would suggest? Or was it students from recently immigrated families who were entering college with a sense of separateness and difference, and transitioning from homes dominated by foreign customs and non-English languages to an American-style, English-speaking college environment? If so, later generations might show weaker ethnic identification, consistent with the black exceptionalism hypothesis. To test this contrast, we compare the explanatory power of the background factors related to immigration with that of perceptions of societal ethnic discrimination against the student's own group. The bivariate correlations and multivariate regression coefficients are shown in table 6.3.[10]

Among the Asian students, the best predictors of ethnic identification at college entry were characteristics of traditional Asian homes rather than of Westernized and secularized Asian American homes. These predictors included speaking a foreign language at home, religiosity, and having high school friends primarily of one's own ethnicity. Foreign language use was particularly telling, since retaining a native language is one crucial index of the preservation of cultural roots after immigration (Alba 1990; Alba and Nee 2003; Phinney 1990). In contrast, societal ethnic discrimination has little impact; it is not significant in the regression analysis. For the Asian students, then, ethnic identification seemed to be more closely associated with the transitional stage of recent immigration, as the black exceptionalism hypothesis would have it, than with a

146

Table 6.3   Antecedents of Strong Ethnic Identification at
             College Entry

	Asians		Latinos	
Variable	r	beta	r	beta
Distal background				
Generation in the United States	−.13***	.05	−.21***	−.05
Father's education	−.04	−.06	−.29***	−.10
Mother's education	−.08*	.06	−.24***	.10
Religiosity	.15***	.12*	.09	.05
Proximal background				
Language spoken at home	.23***	.19***	.33***	.18*
Closest friends in high school				
Own ethnicity	.34***	.26***	.42***	.34***
Other ethnicities	−.21***	−.08*	−.23***	.00
Societal ethnic discrimination	.08*	.05	.20*	.09
Adjusted R^2		.156		.222

Source: Authors' compilation.

Note: All variables measured in wave 1. Maximum Asian n = 743, maximum Latino n = 249.

* p < .05; *** p < .001

long history of discrimination, as the people of color hypothesis would have it.

Among Latinos, the bivariate correlations show the same picture. A strong sense of ethnic identification was based most strongly in recent immigration, speaking Spanish in the home, having high school friends drawn predominantly from fellow Latinos, and having less-educated parents. Again, these seem to be attributes associated with recent immigration that might make a student feel ethnically distinctive in a large public research university. The regression model shows that coming from a household in which Spanish is the dominant language and having ingroup friends in high school seem to mediate the effects of that immigrant history. For Latinos, as for Asians, societal ethnic discrimination was not significantly associated with ethnic identification.

In short, the black exceptionalism hypothesis, tying strong ethnic identification to recent immigration, seems to fit the data better than the people of color hypothesis, for both Asians and Latinos. The effects of recent immigration seem to be mediated in particular by not speaking English at home and by having precollege friendships dominated by same-ethnicity peers. The links among these immigration-related variables were strong. In other analyses not shown here, generation in the United States was found to be strongly associated with speaking English at home and with having fewer ingroup and more outgroup close friends in high school, among both Asians and Latinos (p < .001, by analysis of variance).

Have we modeled the people of color hypothesis too simply? Perhaps more complex versions would bear more fruit. One possibility is that the discriminatory impact of America's racial system may be felt more strongly in generations further removed from immigration, as families increasingly experience the brunt of it. However, societal ethnic discrimination fails to increase with generation in the United States for both Asians and Latinos (at the bivariate level, F < 1 for both groups).[11] Another possibility is that societal ethnic discrimination affects ethnic identification more powerfully in later generations as its victims learn the appropriate ethnically politicized response to it. The interaction of generation and discrimination, however, when added as a separate term to the models of ethnic identification in table 6.3, is nonsignificant for both Asians and Latinos (with betas of .04 and .07, respectively).[12]

Therefore, the strength of ethnic identification among the new-immigrant groups seems to be most closely linked to recent immigration and falls away in later generations, perhaps as they gradually assimilate to American society. A "reactive ethnicity" driven by perceived discrimination in the American racial and ethnic hierarchy, expected from parallels with the African American experience in the people of color hypothesis, seem to only weakly promote their ethnic identification.

Ethnic or American Identity?

Strong ethnic identification would be indicated if it were preferred to an American national identity. At college entry, the students were asked about ethnic versus American identification, with lower scores representing greater identification with other members of their ethnic group and higher scores representing greater identification with Americans in general. The mean scores for each ethnic group on this item at college entry are similar to those shown in table 6.2 for ethnic identification by itself: for whites, 4.6; for Asians, 3.6; for Latinos, 3.9; and for blacks, 3.6 (F = 60.56; p < .001). When scores on this item were reverse-coded (so that high scores indicate greater preference for ethnic rather than Amer-

Table 6.4 Antecedents of Preference for Ethnic Rather than American Identification Prior to College Entry

	Asians		Latinos	
Variable	r	beta	r	beta
Distal background				
Generation in the United States	−.17***	−.01	−.22***	−.05
Father's education	−.05	−.01	−.15*	.14
Mother's education	−.06	.04	−.23***	.01
Religiosity	.12*	.05	.03	.02
Proximal background				
Language spoken at home	.25***	.18***	.34***	.26*
Closest friends in high school				
Own ethnicity	.30***	.19***	.37***	.20*
Other ethnicities	−.32***	−.21***	−.28***	−.13
Societal ethnic discrimination	.12***	.09*	.30***	.24***
Adjusted R^2	.180		.229	

Source: Authors' compilation.

Note: Maximum Asian N = 696, maximum Latino N = 217. A high score on the item trading off ethnic and American identification indicates greater preference for ethnic than American identity.

* $p < .05$; *** $p < .001$

ican identity), they correlated positively with scores on the ethnic identification scale at similar levels for the ethnic minorities—for Asians, $r = .50$; for Latinos, $r = .49$; for blacks, $r = .57$—and more strongly than for whites ($r = .30$).

But we wanted to know if ethnic and American identity were truly reciprocal or had somewhat different origins. As can be seen in table 6.4, the determinants of responses to this item trading off two identities are partly like those explaining strength of ethnic identification by itself. Again, more recent immigrants tend to prefer ethnic identification, as indicated by the effects of not speaking English at home and having had primarily own-ethnicity friends in high school. But there are also some interesting differences between this trade-off item and ethnic identification measured by itself. Among both Latinos and Asians, societal ethnic discrimination significantly contributed to weaker American identity, whereas it had no effect on ethnic identification considered by itself (see table 6.3). Evidently, perceiving one's own group to be the victim of societal discrimination distanced the new-immigrant groups from identifying with the United States, but it did not draw them closer to their own ethnic group, contrary to fears about its role in stimulating ethnic balkanization.

At college entry, then, we find more evidence for the black exceptionalism hypothesis than for the people of color hypothesis. To be sure, the new-immigrant groups initially show ethnic identities similar in strength to blacks' identities. But Asians and Latinos prefer their original national identities over Americanized pan-ethnic labels much more than do blacks or whites. In addition, their ethnic identities are more rooted in experiences related to recent immigration, such as using foreign languages or having fellow co-ethnics as friends, than in the societal ethnic discrimination that is more central to the people of color hypothesis.

Change and Stability Through the College Years

Next we turn to the trajectory of ethnic identity through the college years. Does college increase ethnic balkanization in terms of ethnic identities?

The Content of Ethnic Identity

The people of color hypothesis might predict that the content of the new-immigrant groups' ethnic identities would increasingly incorporate conventional pan-ethnic labels as the students move through college and become more sensitized to color-based inequalities within the American ethnic system. At college entry, Asians and Latinos showed far greater preference for national-origin identities than did the largely native-born whites and blacks. That difference did not change much over the college years. If anything, Asian students were *more* likely to use national origins by their senior year, as shown in table 6.1. On the other hand, the Latino students did show a slight shift toward standard American pan-ethnic identities. Perhaps the two groups were different because the Latino students were on average one generation more removed from immigration than the Asian students were. In any case, almost all blacks and whites continued to use the broad pan-ethnic self-labels rather than refer to national origins.[13]

The preference for national identities among students who had initially selected one also showed substantial, though far from perfect, continuity at the individual level. Of the Asian students who selected national identities at college entry, 79 percent did so again at college exit; of the Latinos, 60 percent did so again. Similar continuity held among Latinos who had initially selected pan-ethnic identities: 68 percent also selected a pan-ethnic identity at college exit. However, Asians' initial pan-ethnic identities were less stable: only 48 percent of those selecting pan-ethnic identities at entry did so again at college exit. Perhaps "Asian American" did not have much resonance as an identity for the Asian students, most of whom were the products of rather recent immigration from quite separate (and sometimes hostile) nations. However, labels like "Latino" and "Hispanic" seem to have had more resonance for Latino students, most of whom were longer removed from immigration than were the Asian students and the vast majority of whom shared the same Mexican national origin.

The new-immigrant groups' greater preferences for national-origin identities, their continuing ambivalence about American pan-ethnic labels, and the stability of these identity choices at both the aggregate and individual levels are findings that are all more consistent with the black exceptionalism hypothesis than with the people of color hypothesis.

The Aggregate Strength of Ethnic Identity

What was the effect of college on ethnic identification? The black exceptionalism hypothesis suggests that black students' ethnic identities would strengthen. But for the new-immigrant groups, would exposure to a culturally diverse educational experience similarly strengthen their ethnic identities? The people of color hypothesis would expect parallels to the black case, with college strengthening ethnic identity through exposure to large numbers of fellow ethnics and various ethnically oriented programs. The black exceptionalism hypothesis would expect instead that their college experiences in a mainstream university might have a less politicizing effect on Asians and Latinos, as the products of relatively recent immigration who might be drawn into a common cultural mainstream through college. Therefore, we might instead see a progressive weakening of ethnic identification through college.

Consistent with the black exceptionalism hypothesis, the college experience appears to have strengthened blacks' racial identity as early as the end of the sophomore year, as shown in table 6.2. On the other hand, the mean strength of Asians' ethnic identification significantly declined over time. Asians, unlike blacks, showed signs of gradual assimilation into the broader society through college, reflected in weakened ethnic identification, among other things. Latinos' ethnic identification did not change significantly over time. Put another way, blacks' ethnic identities were no stronger than the new immigrants' ethnic identities at college entry. But at the end of the sophomore and senior years, blacks' racial identities were significantly stronger than those of either Asians or Latinos (t(457) = 5.46, p < .001, and t(315) = 2.07, p < .04, respectively). Consistent with the black exceptionalism idea, then, blacks' group consciousness was strengthened by college, whereas the new-immigrant groups showed no such change.[14]

The Stability of Individuals' Ethnic Identities

Third, the people of color hypothesis might expect that a college experience on a highly diverse campus would produce fluctuations in ethnic identities for a variety of reasons, such as experiencing discrimination, engaging in peer interaction, or being exposed to coursework that might influence ethnic group consciousness. But if the immigrant experience normally yields a steady intergenerational process of assimilation, as the literature on European immigrants suggests, ethnic identification might actually be quite stable within generations, and so stable across the college years.

The conventional tests of the individual-level stability of youthful attitudes through college use simple test-retest correlations, as seen in the previous chapter.[15] Ethnic identification was indeed quite stable over the first two years of college, with test-retest correlations over r = .50 in all groups, as shown in table 6.5. Over the final two years, from the end of the sophomore year to the end of the senior year, they were more stable still, with all correlations over r = .60. These are high levels of stability over time relative to most other political attitudes (see chapter 5; see also Sears 1983; Sears and Levy 2003).

Politicized Ethnic Identity

Did the ethnic identities of the new-immigrant groups become more politicized as a result of the college experience, contributing to more ethnic balkanization? If so, they should have been more closely associ-

Table 6.5   The Stability of Strong Ethnic Identification, Correlations Across Time

Time	Whites	Asians	Latinos	Blacks
Over two years				
At entry through sophomore year	.51	.59	.51	.55
Sophomore through senior year	.67	.69	.65	.69
Over four years				
At entry through senior year	.43	.47	.54	.35

Source: Authors' compilation.

Note: Respondents included are those participating in all three waves (at college entry, sophomore year, and senior year). Entries are Pearson correlations.

ated with other ethnically relevant social and political attitudes at college exit than at college entry. Table 6.6 presents such correlations for both the college entry and senior year waves.[16] Ethnic identification became increasingly correlated with these other ethnically relevant attitudes among both Asians and Latinos through college. The average correlation of ethnic identification with the ethnic orientations and social policy attitudes shown in table 6.6 was $r = .10$ for Asians at college entry, and $r = .23$ at college exit. For Latinos, the average correlation rose from $r = .28$ to $r = .36$.[17]

Polarization Within Ethnic Groups

To switch gears slightly, increased ethnic balkanization through college might also be reflected in polarization around ethnicity *within* the new-immigrant groups. Some students' ethnicities might have become more politicized, while other students may have become more integrated into the broader campus community and broader society and thus would have shown weakened ethnic identities. To test for this within-group polarization, we tested for changes in variance and kurtosis through college in strength of ethnic identification and the other items shown in table 6.6. To make a long story short, we found no evidence of systematically increased polarization in any group. In most cases, variance decreased and kurtosis became more positive, reflecting more peaked distributions.[18]

In sum, we offer several findings indicating that the new-immigrant

Table 6.6   The Correlates of Strong Ethnic Identification at College Entry and at the End of Senior Year in College

Variable	Whites		Asians		Latinos	
	At Entry	Seniors	At Entry	Seniors	At Entry	Seniors
Ethnic orientations						
Ethnic activism	.37*	.51*	.31*	.47*	.44*	.59*
Prejudice against group imposes barriers	.07*	.33*	.16*	.21*	.31*	.42*
Minorities get unfair treatment	-.01	-.11*	.16*	.17*	.24*	.30*
Social policy attitudes						
Support for increasing diversity on campus	.04	-.06	.03	.18	.20	.28*
Attitude toward immigrants	-.16*	-.18*	.01	.14	.19	.21*
Attitude toward English as official language of the United States	n.a.	-.24*	n.a.	.04	n.a.	.35*
Attitude toward government helping minority groups	n.a.	-.07	n.a.	.10	n.a.	.06
Maximum number of respondents	355	364	407	412	177	181

Source: Authors' compilation.

Note: Entries are Pearson correlations of ethnic identification with other variables, measured at college entry (wave 1) and at the end of senior year (wave 5). Respondents are all those responding to both waves. All variables are coded such that ethnic consciousness is high.

* $p < .05$

groups' early ethnic identities tended to persist through college rather than changing in ways that would have fostered ethnic balkanization. Most Asian students continued to prefer labels describing their national origins over the politicized American pan-ethnic labels, and nearly half of the Latino students showed a similar preference.[19] Their ethnic identities did not strengthen through college; indeed, in the aggregate, Asians' ethnic identities became weaker. Only blacks showed any evidence of strengthened racial identity. In all groups, ethnic identification was quite stable over time at the individual level. Continuity and stability, rather than systematic change or volatility, marked the trajectory of ethnic identity through the college years for the new-immigrant groups. Strength of ethnic identification showed modest increases in correlations with other ethnic attitudes through college, implying some increased politicization of ethnic identification. Finally, we did not find evidence of increased polarization around ethnicity within ethnic groups.

Most of these findings are inconsistent with the people of color hypothesis. The college experience did not induce the new-immigrant groups to identify increasingly with subordinate pan-ethnic groups in an American racial hierarchy, nor did they show significant strengthening of ethnic identities. Blacks, on the other hand, almost all accepted pan-ethnic identities and showed strengthened ethnic identification through college, consistent with the black exceptionalism hypothesis. The college experience may have promoted ethnic balkanization, but only the balkanization of African Americans, not of Asians or Latinos.

Ethnic Identity at the End of College

If the college experience promotes systematic politicization of ethnic identity, several observable outcomes should be detectable by college exit. For example, ethnic identification should be closely related to other ethnically relevant sociopolitical attitudes about one's own and other groups. Strong ethnic identities could be grounded in widespread perceptions of societal ethnic discrimination, and ethnic identities might be strongest in social contexts that most resemble ethnic enclaves dominated by other fellow ingroup members.

Were the ethnic identities of the new-immigrant groups strongly politicized at college exit? As shown in table 6.6, ethnic identification was significantly correlated with most other ethnically relevant attitudes among both Asians and Latinos at college exit, one sign of ethnic

Table 6.7 Predictors of Ethnic Identification at the End of Senior Year

Variable	Asians		Latinos	
	r	beta	r	beta
Background (at college entry)				
Generation in the United States	−.02	.07	−.16	−.08
Language spoken at home	.14**	.08	.17	−.12
Ethnic identification	.47***	.41***	.54***	.46***
College experience (end of sopho-more year)				
Friendships with members of the four main ethnic groups at UCLA				
Own ethnicity	.25***	.12*	.37***	.24*
Other ethnicities	−.12*	−.04	−.20*	−.08
Societal ethnic discrimination	.20***	.13**	.22*	.05
Adjusted R^2	.258		.314	

Source: Authors' compilation.

Note. Respondents include all those with data at the college entry, sophomore year, and senior year waves. Maximum Asian n = 352, maximum Latino n = 124.

* p < .05; ** p < .01; *** p < .001

balkanization. The correlations for Asians were generally smaller than those for Latinos (although most were still significant), suggesting that Asians' ethnicity was somewhat less politicized.

Were stronger ethnic identities based in societal ethnic discrimination and socializing in homogeneous ethnic enclaves? The predictors of ethnic identification at the end of college are shown in table 6.7. Recall that the strength of ethnic identification was highly stable through college; therefore, it is not surprising that its strength at college exit is best explained by its strength four years earlier, at college entry. One important story, then, picks up on a major theme of the last chapter: key sociopolitical attitudes, like political conservatism, symbolic racism, and ethnic identification, tend to be quite stable through college, despite all the pressures to change that they presumably involve.

In addition to these persisting effects of early experience, however, the immigration-related factors that had been important at college entry, such as generation in the United States and speaking a language other than English at home, no longer had a significant impact at college exit. Even the bivariate correlations are small and nonsignificant. By college exit, ethnic identification seems to have become somewhat autonomous of the effects of recent immigration.

Finally, there is other evidence that not much ethnic balkanization was occurring among Asians and Latinos. Most important, ethnic identification was considerably *less* closely associated with the exclusion of outgroups from the students' circles of friends than it had been at college entry, as seen through comparison of tables 6.7 and 6.3. In addition, having ingroup college friends at the end of the sophomore year had no more impact on ethnic identification at college exit than having ingroup friends in high school had at college entry.[20] A substantial amount of variance in senior year ethnic identity is explained by these models—25.8 percent for Asians and 31.4 percent for Latinos. This is noteworthy considering that almost all the predictor variables had been measured either two or four years earlier and the models are extremely simple, with only six predictors.

In sum, we find evidence of meaningful patterns of association between ethnic identification and other ethnicity-related political and social attitudes among the new-immigrant groups at the conclusion of college. The strength of attachment to one's ethnic group has some political and social resonance at college exit. However, the dominant predictor of ethnic identification at college exit is its strength before the student even began college. The indicators of heightened group consciousness suggested by the people of color hypothesis have no greater impact at college exit than they had at college entry. Continuity, rather than ethnic balkanization or more politicized ethnic identities, seems to mark the new-immigrant groups by the end of college.

Summary and Conclusions

At the most general level, the central question of this volume is how a society comes to grips with cultural diversity, with particular focus on higher education. America's recent diversification has been especially stimulated by a heavy flow of new-immigrant groups from Asia and Latin America, and its social impact has been exacerbated by the incomplete assimilation of the large African American minority. Many observers have expressed fears that rapid cultural diversification could lead to ethnic balkanization, for both psychological and political reasons.

Our focus in this chapter was on politicized ethnic identities as possible psychological vehicles for such effects, particularly among the more educated and youthful cadres of the new-immigrant groups.

We began with two common prototypes for understanding ethnic minority status in the United States. The black discrimination prototype refers to the unique historical experience of African Americans, centering on the centuries-long struggles they have waged against caste-based inequality that have led many to a powerful sense of common racial identity and common fate. Parallels between their experiences and the past oppression of Asian Americans and Latinos, such as the interned Japanese Americans of the 1940s or the Mexican farm laborers of the 1920s and 1930s, generated what we have called the people of color hypothesis.[21] It essentially expands the color line to include Asians and Latinos as fellow "peoples of color." In this view, the college experience is likely to heighten ethnic group consciousness, and with it ethnic balkanization. Alternatively, application of a European assimilation prototype to Asians and Latinos suggests that these new-immigrant groups may be less like African Americans, corralled behind an impermeable color line, and more like turn-of-the-century European immigrants, most of whose descendants have now assimilated into the broader American society. That is, this prototype would shift the spotlight on the new-immigrant groups to their recent immigration and away from continuity with their oppressed predecessors of a half-century or more ago. From this second prototype we derived the black exceptionalism hypothesis, positing that the American color line most powerfully distinguishes people with some African ancestry from all others. According to this hypothesis, a college experience is more likely to promote the gradual assimilation of the new-immigrant groups than their ethnic balkanization.

Our first set of empirical analyses focused on the content, strength, and origins of the ethnic identities of Asian and Latino students at college entry. These data gave only modest support to the people of color hypothesis. To be sure, at college entry the strength of the new-immigrant groups' ethnic identities did not differ from the strength of African Americans' ethnic identities. More generally, ethnic identity was linked to immigration, not to position in the American racial hierarchy. Asians especially, and Latinos to a large extent, tended to describe themselves in terms of their national origins rather than using the standard American pan-ethnic labels. The strongest ethnic identities were held by the students who were closest to immigration, coming from families that were not fluent in English and being surrounded by the ethnically homogeneous peer ingroups common in immigrant neighborhoods. Societal ethnic discrimination against one's own ethnic group was not a significant factor, either by itself or in interaction with other factors. Ethnic identification at college entry among Asians and Latinos, then, seemed to be associated more closely with their recent immigration than with historical connectedness to oppressed minorities of the past, thus lending support to the black exceptionalism hypothesis.

The centrality of recent immigration to strong ethnic identities among Asians and Latinos is not limited to college students. Surveys of adult Latinos consistently find that the foreign-born have stronger ethnic identities and weaker American identities than do the U.S.-born, and their ethnic identities are more likely to refer to their national origins. Studies of children find that identification with national origins is more common among the foreign-born, while "American" or hyphenated American identities are much more common among the U.S.-born. The psychological effects of recent immigration tend to be mediated by living in more ethnic neighborhoods, having more ingroup friends, and speaking foreign languages at home (Citrin and Sears 2007; Ethier and Deaux 1994; Pew Hispanic Center/Henry J. Kaiser Family Foundation 2002; Sears and Savalei 2006; see also Phinney 1990; Rumbaut and Portes 2001).

Our second empirical question was whether the new-immigrant groups' ethnic identities changed through college in ways that would contribute to ethnic balkanization. In fact, both the content and strength of ethnic identification were quite stable over time, both in the aggregate and within individuals. Asian Americans' preferences for national rather than pan-ethnic identities actually increased. The average strength of both Asians' and Latinos' ethnic identities did not increase. The fact that the strength of individuals' ethnic identities was highly stable through college lends further support to the black exceptionalism hypothesis.

The bottom line seems to be that the college experience did not promote much ethnic balkanization. This is especially noteworthy given the presence of several conditions conducive to ethnic enclaves, including high levels of diversity both on campus and in the broader community, a strong institutional emphasis on cultural diversity, and the fact that UCLA is a large public university embedded in an urban megalopolis rather than a small private college in a predominantly white college town. The stability of ethnic identity through college despite substantial pressure to change once again suggests that social identities may not be as context-dependent in real life as they often seem to be in the laboratory (Huddy 2001; see also Oakes 2002).

Our third empirical question concerned the level of politicized ethnicity and ethnic balkanization at college exit. We found that the new immigrants' ethnic identities were somewhat more meaningfully linked to other ethnically related political attitudes at college exit than at college entry. However, strong ethnic identities at college exit were rooted more in strong ethnic identities at college entry than in any increased impact of the ethnically conscious variables emphasized by the people of color hypothesis, such as societal ethnic discrimination against one's own ethnic group or having predominantly own-ethnicity friends. Especially noteworthy was the *decline* in the association between strong ethnic identities and an absence of outgroup friends, perhaps the most direct indicator of a lack of ethnic balkanization. These findings do not yield much evidence of highly politicized ethnicities at college exit. Continuity with attitudes at college entry is more apparent than balkanizing changes.

Rather than being readily subject to change, the new-immigrant groups' ethnic identities may be relatively static through college. That may be one piece of a broader pattern of stability within the life of any given generation. However, each generation seems to be moving another step away from the immigration experience—in terms of language usage, residential segregation, education, and so on. At a broader level, too, the fears of Huntington (2004) and others that American society will be compromised by taking in too many unassimilable minorities may be misplaced.

This stability, despite the potential for change inherent in the pressures of the college experience, has several important implications. First, ethnic balkanization may not be as prominent a feature of American higher education as some conservative critics maintain. At the other extreme, a college education may not promote the full assimilation of recent immigrants as much as its supporters advertise. After all, many of the college graduates from the new-immigrant groups still go home with their bilingual friends to visit parents who speak minimal English and attend churches filled with fellow ethnics. That same stability would also seem to cast a dark shadow over universities' hopes that all students, regardless of ethnicity, will join in identification with common institutional goals rather than isolating themselves in ethnic enclaves. We take up that question in the next chapter.

In all these analyses, we have treated Asian and Latino students as if they were similar new-immigrant groups functioning in parallel. Our fourth empirical question asked whether we should have drawn sharper distinctions between them. There were several reasons to expect that Latinos would fit the people of color hypothesis better than would Asian students and so would be more likely to show ethnic balkanization. Latinos were less likely to be immigrants themselves (see chapter 3). The primarily Mexican and Spanish-speaking Latinos, coming from a narrower range of national and linguistic backgrounds, were more ethnically homogeneous. There had also been a stronger tradition of political activism at UCLA among Latinos, especially among Chicano students. And finally, Latinos came on average from considerably less-educated parents (see chapter 3) and so presumably from poorer, more segregated, underclass backgrounds. That might have led to a more "reactive ethnicity" (Portes and Rumbaut 2001) and perhaps stronger ethnic identities as a result.

Nevertheless, most of our conclusions hold for Asians and Latinos alike. To be sure, Latinos were somewhat more likely to use pan-ethnic identities (see table 6.1) and had slightly more politicized ethnic identities at college exit (see table 6.6). But their ethnic identities were no stronger than Asians' at either college entry or exit (see table 6.2). Also, Latinos' identities were not significantly associated with societal ethnic discrimination at either college entry or exit, while Asians' identities were, at least at college exit (see tables 6.3 and 6.7). Nor was there any difference in ethnicity-based polarization within the two groups.

These similarities between Asians and Latinos add credibility to the black exceptionalism hypothesis. It is perhaps not surprising that Asians, the "model minorities," seem to be following the paths of earlier waves of immigrants rather than that of blacks, even setting aside their slightly greater initial racial prejudice (see chapter 4). Latinos, on the other hand, should look similar to blacks, by many accounts. Both are often described as being in similarly subordinate positions in the American racial hierarchy (see, for example, Sidanius and Pratto 1999). In our study, Latinos stood in contrast to blacks in most respects. Unlike Latinos, blacks almost universally used pan-ethnic labels. The college experience strengthened blacks', but not Latinos', ethnic identities. Since ethnic identity is strongest among recent immigrants, the apparent similarity of Latinos and blacks in ethnic identification at college entry may simply reflect the predominance of recent immigration among Latinos. Consistent with this view, we find elsewhere that black adults generally have stronger ethnic identity than do native-born Latinos (Citrin and Sears 2007; Sears and Savalei 2006).

Our study considers relatively advantaged college students, of course. Less-advantaged Latinos and Asians might well be expected to respond differently. Indeed, Alejandro Portes and Rubén Rumbaut's (2001) notion of "segmented assimilation" suggests that, rather than experiencing upward mobility and assimilation to the broader society, some Latinos and Asians drift downward over time, toward the largely African American urban underclass with its "adversarial culture," participating in gang-related activities and declining educational aspirations. Still, the black exceptionalism hypothesis might argue for a somewhat more nuanced approach to such possible downward drifts. Portes and Rumbaut find it to be particularly common among children with some African ancestry. Douglas Massey and Nancy Denton (1993) also note that the residential segregation levels for black Puerto Ricans are at high levels, like those of African Americans, while those for white Puerto Ricans are at the more moderate levels of Latinos more generally. A black exceptionalism view would interpret these findings as reflecting the continuing importance of the narrowly Afrocentric color line in the United States.[22]

We close this chapter by underlining the disjuncture between American social scientists' and bureaucrats' treatments of ethnic identity, on the one hand, and those of our students, on the other. The former almost universally classify people into a handful of large pan-ethnic categories. But the students did not. Despite living in a social world in which they are described by others and are asked to self-classify themselves in terms of the major pan-ethnic categories on a daily basis, the students spontaneously described themselves in rich and diverse terms, using a broad multiplicity of ethnic identities in response to our open-ended self-categorization items. Moreover, the students nearly unanimously rejected the labels of "European American"—much in vogue in some liberal academic circles as a synonym for "white" (only three white students in the senior wave used that self-label)—and "Asian Pacific Islander," the official campus identity for Asians (only eight spontaneously used that label after four years of exposure to it). There is considerable merit, we believe, in assessing ethnic identity in the respondents' own words if we want to know how they think about race and ethnicity.

Chapter 7

In Search of a Common Ingroup Identity: National and University Identities

In chapter 6, we argued that, in some contexts, the ethnic identities of Asian American and Latino students vary more as a function of how close they are to the immigrant experience than as a function of how much discrimination they have experienced as members of minority ethnic groups in the United States. This pattern is consistent with a black exceptionalism hypothesis of race and ethnicity, which proposes that, at least in the United States, a color line divides those of African ancestry from everyone else. According to this model, African Americans are unique in that their high levels of ethnic identification are driven by strong and persistent beliefs that they and other members of their ethnic group are discriminated against in American society. As such, the previous chapter emphasized similarities in the content, origins, and effects of the college experience on the ethnic identities of Asian Americans and Latinos and the uniqueness of blacks along these dimensions. By contrast, this chapter highlights ways in which the ethnic identities of people in the dominant ethnic group in the United States, whites, differ from the ethnic identities of people in ethnic minority groups—Asian Americans, Latinos, *and* blacks. This chapter also differentiates the experience, on the one hand, of Latinos and African Americans—minority ethnic groups with relatively low socioeconomic status—from the experience, on the other hand, of Asian Americans—a minority ethnic group with intermediate socioeconomic status.

The main distinction between this chapter and the previous one is in how the ethnic groups are categorized. In the previous chapter, ethnic groups were categorized according to immigrant status. On average, Asian Americans and Latinos in the United States are much closer to the immigrant experience than whites and blacks. For this reason, they tend to describe themselves in terms of their national origins more than whites and blacks do, and those with stronger ethnic identities tend to be those who have immigrated to the United States more recently. In another important way, however, the ethnic identities of Asian Americans and Latinos are more similar to the ethnic identity of African Americans, with whom they share subordinate ethnic status in the United States, than to that of whites. For example, some recent research suggests that for the three ethnic minority groups, ethnic identity tends to bolster feelings that minorities get unfair treatment in the United States. For whites, on the other hand, ethnic identity appears to be associated with a *denial* that minorities get unfair treatment (see, for example, Levin et al. 1998; Peña and Sidanius 2002; Sidanius et al. 1997). Findings such as these suggest that ethnic identity reflects not only the unique immigrant experience of Asian Americans and Latinos but also the experience of subordination shared by all ethnic minority groups in the United States.

Using both social dominance theory and the common ingroup identity model as interpretive frameworks, this chapter examines the intersection between students' subgroup identities as members of specific ethnic groups and superordinate identities as members of larger groups such as Americans or UCLA students. The social dominance model argues that the experience of ethnic subordination within a society creates similarities in the meaning of ethnic identity for all subordinated groups and that this subordinate ethnic identity is distinct in many ways from the ethnic identity of the dominant group. In the United States, for example, ethnic identity among whites should imply a "group dominance" orientation that favors group-based inequality, because ties to the high-status white ingroup afford greater access to the economic and political resources used in maintaining social hierarchy. In contrast, for members of minority groups, ethnic identity should imply a counterdominance orientation or a rejection of the system that relegates one's ethnic group to a subordinate position in the social hierarchy. In the United States, then, ethnic identities may be imbued with either support for or opposition to group-based hierarchy, depending on the status of one's ethnic group.[1]

Given these contrasting group identities, many fear that tensions will rise as members of different ethnic groups come together on the college campus. One way to reduce such intergroup tension, as suggested by Samuel Gaertner and John Dovidio in the common ingroup identity model, is to get people to accept higher-order, superordinate identities that emphasize what members of all groups have in common (see chapter 2; Gaertner et al. 1993, 1994; see also Gaertner and Dovidio 2000). The core idea is that when members of different groups come to think of themselves as members of a single, superordinate group, they will extend to former outgroup members the favorable evaluation previously bestowed only upon members of the original, limited ingroup. For example, from this perspective, encouraging members of different ethnic groups on the UCLA campus to embrace a common identity as a UCLA student should reduce inter-ethnic conflict by extending the ingroup favoritism formerly lavished solely on fellow UCLA ethnic ingroup members to all fellow UCLA students. This process of recategorization (extending the boundaries of the ingroup to include former outgroup members) elevates the evaluation of previous outgroup members to the level of ingroup members, thus reducing intergroup bias and discrimination.

According to social dominance theory, however, not all superordinate identities offer fertile ground for the development of such positive outcomes. Rather, the degree to which members of diverse ethnic groups are likely to find common ground in different superordinate group memberships—such as being an American or a student at UCLA—is contingent on the degree to which the superordinate social system is, on balance, relatively more hierarchy-enhancing (promoting group inequality) or hierarchy-attenuating (promoting group equality). In this chapter, we examine two specific social systems—the United States, a relatively more hierarchy-enhancing social system, and the university, a relatively more hierarchy-attenuating social system. According to social dominance theory, common ingroup identities that promote intergroup harmony are more likely to be found in the latter setting than the former. We explore this possibility by first discussing superordinate group membership within the relatively hierarchy-enhancing environment of American society as a whole.

Superordinate Group Identification

Although the United States is characterized by a tension between hierarchy-enhancing and hierarchy-attenuating tendencies, we argue that the former tendency predominates in the nation as a whole. For example, there is substantial evidence that African Americans and Latinos experience discrimination across several different domains of American life, including the criminal justice system, the labor market, the educational system, the health care system, and the retail sales market (Sidanius and Pratto 1999). In addition, public opinion data indicate that the relative status ranking of different American ethnic groups has remained fairly stable over the last several decades, with white Americans consistently ranked at the top of this status hierarchy, followed by Asian Americans, and Latino and African Americans consistently ranked at the bottom (Smith 1991). Finally, although white Americans overwhelmingly claim to endorse racial equality and integration in principle, national surveys consistently show that they are much less supportive of concrete social policies designed to instantiate these egalitarian principles in practice (Schuman et al. 1997). Therefore, despite the presence of both egalitarian and inegalitarian forces within American society, we argue that hierarchy-enhancing forces predominate in practice.

Superordinate Group Membership in a Hierarchy-Enhancing Social System

In hierarchical social systems like the United States, social dominance theory argues that high-status ethnic groups often dominate the value system and collective identity of the society (Sidanius and Pratto 1999; see also Brewer 2000). For example, because whites are the dominant ethnic group in American society, the image of what it means to be an American is strongly associated with being white (see, for example, Devos and Banaji 2005). This overlap between white ethnic identity and American identity should make the development of an American identity easier for whites than for members of subordinate ethnic groups such as Latinos and African Americans. In other words, native-born white Americans should have higher levels of American identification than native-born Latinos and African Americans (hypothesis 1). This logic also suggests that there should be asymmetry in the interface between ethnic identification and American identification. Specifically, ethnic identification should be more positively related to American identification among native-born whites than among native-born Latinos and African Americans (hypothesis 2). Among whites, positively embracing one's ethnic identity should imply a positive orientation toward the American social system—a system in which whites are advantaged. In contrast, members of subordinate groups who have a strong ethnic identity should not be as positively disposed toward the system that relegates their group to a position of relative disadvantage.

Consistent with these expectations, Jim Sidanius and his colleagues (1997) have found that white Americans have higher levels of patriotism than Latino and African Americans. They also found that the more white Americans identify as "white," the more patriotic they feel toward the United States. In contrast, the more Latino and African Americans identify with their respective ethnic groups, the *less* patriotic they feel toward the United States (see also Sidanius and Petrocik 2001; Tropp 2006). As suggested by social dominance theory, this type of asymmetry in the interface between ethnic group identification and superordinate group identification (in this case, American identification) should be found in all environments in which members of one group dominate the sociopolitical landscape at the expense of members of other groups.[2]

The predictions of social dominance theory are most relevant to comparisons between high-status and low-status ethnic groups. But what might the theory suggest regarding Asian Americans, an ethnic group of intermediate status? Given their intermediate status, it is likely that native-born Asian Americans would be less inclined than white Americans to adopt an inegalitarian superordinate American identity and that they would be less inclined to perceive ethnic identification as compatible with American identification.

As mentioned earlier, the patterns of superordinate group identification that emerge among the members of various ethnic groups should deviate between social systems that treat group-based distributions of status and resources differently. Specifically, clear differences should emerge in the patterns seen among ethnic groups in a hierarchy-enhancing social system—which generates and sustains group-based inequality—and a hierarchy-attenuating social system—which promotes social equality among groups. Our next hypotheses address patterns of group identification among ethnic groups within a relatively hierarchy-attenuating social system.

Superordinate Group Membership in a
Hierarchy-Attenuating Social System

In contrast to the inequality that characterizes American society as a whole, specific settings within American society may be relatively more egalitarian and inclusive. As a result, they may allow superordinate identities to be equally embraced by members of different ethnic groups. For example, a large and consistent body of research suggests that American universities are relatively tolerant and inclusive environments (see, for example, Bobo and Licari 1989; Lipset 1982; McClintock and Turner 1962). Universities are run and populated by individuals with relatively high levels of commitment to egalitarian praxis as compared to the general public (Feldman and Newcomb 1969; Lipset 1982). Furthermore, cross-sectional and longitudinal research shows that increasing exposure to this environment is positively associated with greater levels of egalitarianism (see, for example, Bobo and Licari 1989; Lipset 1983; McClintock and Turner 1962; Sidanius et al. 1991; but see also Jackman 1978; Jackman and Muha 1984; Weil 1985). For example, in chapter 5 we saw that levels of symbolic racism among the students in our sample significantly declined from precollege to the senior year. Therefore, despite the likely presence of some competing inegalitarian forces on college campuses, we argue that the net effect of the university environment is predominantly hierarchy-attenuating and relatively more egalitarian than American society at large.

In addition to this difference in the relatively hierarchy-enhancing versus hierarchy-attenuating norms that predominate in the two settings, the university environment and American society at large differ in another important respect. In the Unites States as a whole, whites are dominant not only in terms of their higher group status but also, as the clear numerical majority, in size. By contrast, the superordinate student body at UCLA has no clear dominant group in terms of either group status or group size. In such a multiethnic context, where identification with a common ingroup does not imply a desire to dominate or be dominated within a hierarchical system, it may be easier for all subgroup members to feel equal "ownership" and endorsement of the superordinate identity. As such, students of all ethnicities at UCLA should have similar levels of identification with the larger university student body (hypothesis 3). In addition, ethnic identification should be similarly related to university identification among members of all ethnic groups (hypothesis 4). That is, the interface between ethnic and university identification should be symmetrical among members of all ethnic groups. It may be either uniformly neutral, indicating that ethnic identification does not have much of an impact on university identification one way or the other, or uniformly positive, indicating that the two identities are complementary among members of all ethnic groups. In sum, we argue in this chapter that it is precisely the type of relatively hierarchy-attenuating setting in which students find themselves at UCLA that should lend itself to the development of a common ingroup identity that is compatible with the ethnic identities of both white and minority students.

Changes in Superordinate Group Identification over Time

In addition to providing the opportunity for replication over the four-year span of the study, the longitudinal design employed here also allows for an initial examination of the impact of exposure to the relatively hierarchy-attenuating university environment on levels of American identification. One possibility is that greater exposure to this relatively egalitarian university environment may cause a reduction in American identification among all ethnic groups over time. Members of both high-status and low-status ethnic groups may come to perceive the relatively hierarchy-enhancing superordinate American identity as incommensurate with their values. This heightened egalitarianism may also lead to a decrease in the perceived compatibility between ethnic identification and American identification among all ethnic groups. That is, increasing socialization within a hierarchy-attenuating environment may stimulate awareness among members of high-status groups that inequalities in outcomes and opportunities exist for members of different ethnic groups in the United States. This increased awareness of the inequities that characterize American society may, in turn, lead these high-status group members to become less identified as Americans and change their understanding of their ethnic identification such that they begin to separate it from their American identification. Exposure to a hierarchy-attenuating campus environment might also improve the ability of members of low-status groups to discern the injustice they face and thus also reduce their American identification and decrease the perceived compatibility between their ethnic and American identities.

In sum, this chapter examines the nature of the interface between ethnic identification, on the one hand, and American identification and university identification, on the other hand.[3] The longitudinal nature of the research design allows us to examine these relationships over the four-year college experience. For this reason, data collected at the end of students' freshman through senior years of college are analyzed, and because we are interested in relationships with American identities, we include in our analyses only those white, Asian American, Latino, and African American students who were born in the United States.

Hypothesis 1: Asymmetry in Mean Levels of American Identification

First, we assessed American identification among the different ethnic groups. Given the notion that American society is a relatively hierarchy-enhancing environment, native-born white Americans should have higher levels of American identification than native-born Latinos and African Americans. Further, given that Asian Americans are of intermediate status, we speculated that native-born white Americans would have higher levels of American identification than native-born Asian Americans as well.[4] Mean levels of American identification by ethnic group and year in college can be found in table 7.1. As shown in the table, the four ethnic groups differed significantly in their levels of American identification across all four years in college.[5] Pairwise comparisons of ethnic groups within each year using Scheffé tests revealed that whites tended to have higher levels of American identification than African Americans and Latinos, but similar levels to Asian Americans (see table 7.1 for the significance tests of all pairwise comparisons).

These results suggest that the ethnic group with the highest status in a society that awards status and resources according to group membership shows the greatest identification with that society as a whole when compared to subordinate ethnic groups. In other words, the dominant group within the hierarchical system shows more support for that system than groups with less status. This provides support for the existence of an asymmetrical pattern in superordinate group identification among ethnic groups in a relatively hierarchy-enhancing society.

170

Table 7.1   Mean Levels of American Identification for Native-Born Respondents, by Ethnic Group and Year in College

Ethnicity	Freshman	Sophomore	Junior	Senior
Whites	6.07[a]	5.79[a]	5.71[a]	5.74[a]
Asians	5.64[b]	5.68[ab]	5.67[a]	5.64[ab]
Latinos	5.53[bc]	5.43[bc]	5.49[ab]	5.19[c]
Blacks	5.19[c]	5.05[c]	5.04[b]	5.18[bc]
p-value for ethnicity effect (within-year)	< .001	< .001	= .001	< .001

Source: Authors' compilation.

Note. Within each column (year in college), superscripted letters that are the same for two or more ethnic groups indicate that the groups do not significantly differ in American identification, p > .10.

Changes over Time in American Identification

We also speculated that increasing exposure to a relatively hierarchy-attenuating college environment might cause a reduction in American identification among members of all ethnic groups over time. To assess the change in levels of American identification across time for each of the four ethnic groups, we conducted hierarchical linear modeling (HLM).[6] Analyses using the HLM technique revealed that American identification significantly declined among whites across the college years (b = −.12, p < .001). The slopes for Latinos and blacks did not significantly differ from the slope for whites, indicating that, consistent with our expectations, whites, Latinos, and blacks all declined in American identification across the college years (and to a similar extent). However, contrary to expectations, the slope for Asians showed that American identification did not decline as much as it did for whites; in fact, Asian Americans' levels of American identification appear to have remained fairly constant across the college years.[7]

Hypothesis 2: Asymmetry in the Relationship Between Ethnic and American Identification

Consistent with the notion that American society is a relatively hierarchy-enhancing environment, we expected ethnic identification to be more positively related to American identification among native-born whites than among native-born Latinos and African Americans. Again, given the intermediate status of Asian Americans, we speculated that ethnic identification would also be more positively related to American identification for native-born whites than for native-born Asian Americans.[8]

To allow comparisons across ethnic groups, table 7.2 reveals the unstandardized regression coefficients for the effect of ethnic identification on American identification. As expected, these analyses demonstrated that ethnic identification and American identification were more positively associated among native-born whites, members of the highest-status group in the United States, than among native-born Asian Americans, Latinos, and blacks, members of lower-status groups. Whereas white students who identified more with their ethnic group also identified more as Americans, among students of the other ethnic groups, higher levels of ethnic identification were either associated with lower levels of American identification or were not associated with American identification at all.[9] Thus, there appears to be asymmetry among ethnic groups in the relationship between ethnic identification and American identification. Members of the dominant ethnic group who identified more with their group showed more identification with the social system that perpetuated their dominance. However, members of subordinate groups who identified more with their ethnic group either did not identify systematically with or identified less with the hierarchical social system that perpetuated their subordination.

Changes over Time in the Relationship Between Ethnic and American Identification

We also speculated that there might be a decrease in the perceived compatibility between ethnic identification and American identification for members of all ethnic groups over the four years in college. However, use of the LISREL chi-square difference test showed that these relationships did not vary significantly over time for any ethnic group.[10] It thus appears that the relatively hierarchy-attenuating nature of the university environment did not lead students to perceive their ethnic and American identification as less (or more) compatible over time.

In addition to assessing identification with a relatively hierarchy-en-

Table 7.2 Unstandardized Regression Coefficients for the Effect of Ethnic Identification on American Identification for Native-Born Respondents

Ethnicity	Freshman	Sophomore	Junior	Senior
Whites	.19**	.31**	.32**	.23**
Asians	−.09+	−.08	−.02	−.12+
Latinos	−.33**	−.18**	−.22**	−.34**
Blacks	.00	.10	.00	.03
p-value for ethnicity effect (within-year)	<.001	<.001	<.001	<.001

Source: Authors' compilation.
+ p < .10; ** p < .01

hancing environment, we also examined how superordinate group identification might compare across ethnic groups in a social system that predominantly attenuates hierarchy. We now shift from analyses focused on the relatively hierarchy-enhancing social system of the United States to an examination of identification with the relatively hierarchy-attenuating social system of the university.

Hypothesis 3: Symmetry in Mean Levels of University Identification

Given the notion that the university campus is a relatively hierarchy-attenuating environment, members of all ethnic groups should have similar levels of university identification. Mean levels of university identification by ethnic group and year in college can be found in table 7.3. Contrary to what was expected, there were significant ethnic group differences in students' levels of university identification for three of the four college years.[11] Further pairwise comparisons of ethnic groups within year, however, using Scheffé tests, revealed that the overall effect of ethnicity was entirely due to higher levels of university identification among Asian Americans compared to whites during the freshman, junior, and senior years.[12] Whites, Latinos, and blacks all demonstrated similar levels of university identification, which generally supports the hypothesis of symmetry among ethnic groups in identification with a relatively hierarchy-attenuating environment.

173

Table 7.3   Mean Levels of University Identification for Native-Born Respondents, by Ethnic Group and Year in College

Ethnicity	Freshman	Sophomore	Junior	Senior
Whites	5.66[b]	5.60[a]	5.55[b]	5.41[b]
Asians	5.92[a]	5.74[a]	5.96[a]	5.83[a]
Latinos	5.70[ab]	5.75[a]	5.78[ab]	5.62[ab]
Blacks	5.75[ab]	5.57[a]	5.64[ab]	5.56[ab]
p-value for ethnicity effect (within-year)	<.05	>.10	<.01	=.01

Source: Authors' compilation.

Note: Within each column (year in college), superscripted letters that are the same for two or more ethnic groups indicate that the groups do not significantly differ in university identification, p > .10.

Hypothesis 4: Symmetry in the Relationship Between Ethnic and University Identification

Consistent with the notion that the university campus is a relatively hierarchy-attenuating environment, ethnic identification was expected to be similarly related to university identification among members of all ethnic groups. The analyses for university identification are exactly the same as those for American identification. Table 7.4 reveals the unstandardized regression coefficients for the effect of ethnic identification on university identification.[13] As expected, these analyses demonstrated that ethnic identification and university identification tended to be similarly associated across ethnic groups within each year in college.[14] All students tended to identify more as a UCLA student the more they identified with their ethnic group.[15] Thus, the relationship between subgroup and superordinate group identification was symmetrical across ethnic groups within this relatively hierarchy-attenuating environment. This supports the notion that when a larger social system is relatively egalitarian, ethnic and superordinate identities can be compatible, and compatible to the same extent, across different ethnic groups.

Summary and Conclusions

The purpose of this chapter was to integrate the common ingroup identity model with social dominance theory. The common ingroup identity

Table 7.4   Unstandardized Regression Coefficients for the Effect of Ethnic Identification on University Identification for Native-Born Respondents

Ethnicity	Freshman	Sophomore	Junior	Senior
Whites	.11**	.18**	.27**	.27**
Asians	.10*	.22**	.27**	.22**
Latinos	.10*	.12**	.15**	.15*
Blacks	.34**	−.05	.09	.37**
p-value for ethnicity effect (within-year)	>.10	>.10	>.10	>.10

Source: Authors' compilation.

* $p \leq .05$; ** $p \leq .01$

model advocates the creation of a superordinate group identity in order to reduce intergroup conflict. Building on this model, social dominance theory specifies the conditions that facilitate the development of a superordinate group identity that is endorsed to approximately the same extent by members of all ethnic subgroups and complements rather than contradicts ethnic subgroup identification. According to social dominance theory, the development of such a common ingroup identity depends on the relative hierarchy-enhancing or hierarchy-attenuating nature of the superordinate social system or context within which the subgroups interact.

Hierarchy-Enhancing Environments

Relatively hierarchy-enhancing environments, like American society as a whole, tend to promote the dominance of high-status groups and the subordination of low-status groups. Within hierarchy-enhancing environments, social dominance theory argues that groups that have access to more economic and political resources often dominate the value system and collective identity of the superordinate group. When this happens, two asymmetries should result. Compared to members of low-status groups, members of high-status groups should exhibit higher levels of superordinate identification, and high-status groups should also demonstrate a more positive relationship between subgroup and superordinate identification.

175

The results reported in this chapter generally confirmed these predictions. The four ethnic groups differed significantly in their levels of American identification across all four years in college, and generally in order of their social status within American society. Specifically, native-born members of the dominant ethnic group (whites) tended to have the highest levels of American identification, native-born members of the lowest-status ethnic groups (African Americans and Latinos) tended to have the lowest levels of American identification, and the intermediate-status group (native-born Asian Americans) tended to have an intermediate level of American identification. The predicted asymmetrical pattern was also found in the relationship between ethnic and American identification across all four years of college: ethnic identification was more positively related to American identification among native-born whites than among native-born members of the three other ethnic groups.

As pointed out by Jim Sidanius and his colleagues (1997), the fact that native-born whites display greater patriotic attachment to the United States than other native-born ethnic groups (especially blacks) cannot be easily attributed to the idea that white Americans have deeper roots in American history or culture than other groups. Although blacks consistently show the lowest levels of American identification, they also have the longest average tenure in the United States compared to their white, Asian American, and Latino counterparts.[16] In addition, recent evidence using national probability samples suggests that this asymmetrical pattern is not just restricted to university samples in the United States but can be found among more representative samples across several other nations as well. For example, using data from nine countries and more than eleven thousand respondents, Christian Staerklé and his colleagues (2005) have found that ethnic majorities have higher levels of national attachment than do ethnic minorities and that the relationship between ethnic subgroup identification and national attachment is more positive for majorities than for minorities.

Viewed from a social dominance perspective, this asymmetry stems directly from differences in the *meaning* of superordinate and subgroup membership for members of dominant and subordinate subgroups within hierarchical social systems. For members of dominant subgroups, both identification with the common ingroup and identification with the subgroup imply a dominance orientation and so should be positively related to one another. For members of subordinate groups, by contrast, identification with the common ingroup implies acquiescence in the hierarchical social system, while identification with the subgroup implies a counterdominance orientation, or a rejection of the system that relegates one's group to a subordinate position in the social hierarchy. Because these two identifications have dominance implications that operate in different directions, they should not be as positively associated with one another.

These predictions are also consistent with a system justification perspective. From this perspective, John Jost and his colleagues have argued that two distinct but related motives underlie intergroup behavior: a "system-justification" motive, or a desire to maintain the existing system of hierarchical relations, regardless of the consequences for one's own group; and a "group-justification" motive, or a desire to promote the interests, status, and power of one's own group. Within a hierarchical social system, superordinate identification should reflect a system-justification motive, and subgroup identification should reflect a group-justification motive. Relevant to our discussion here, John Jost and Erik Thompson (2000) emphasize that for members of high-status groups, system justification and group justification are congruent motives. That is, support for a system of hierarchy that privileges one's own group is consistent with the promotion of that group's interests and status. System justification theory would therefore also expect a positive association between subgroup and superordinate identification among members of high-status groups. For members of low-status groups, by contrast, these two motives are incongruent: system justification implies a rejection of the ingroup's interests in favor of support for existing hierarchical arrangements, whereas group justification implies a rejection of the system in favor of the interests of the ingroup. System justification theory would therefore expect a negative association between subgroup and superordinate identification among members of low-status groups in hierarchy-enhancing environments.

Interestingly, the relationships between ethnic identification and American identification did not become less positive for native-born whites or more negative for native-born Asians, Latinos, or blacks with longer tenure in the hierarchy-attenuating college environment, as we had speculated they might. Consistent with our earlier speculation, however, we did find that levels of American identification decreased to a similar degree among native-born whites, Latinos, and blacks over the college years. As students from these ethnic groups gained more exposure to the hierarchy-attenuating college environment, their increased awareness of the inequities that characterize American society may have led them to identify less with the superordinate American group. We did not find, however, that Asian Americans declined in American identification to the same extent that whites did. Rather, Asian Americans had similar levels of American identification during all four years of college.

In general, we also found that the relationships between ethnic identification and American identification exhibited by native-born Asian Americans tended to be less positive than the relationships exhibited by native-born white Americans, but not as negative as those exhibited by native-born Latinos and African Americans. These findings are consistent with Tom Smith's (1991) notion that Asian Americans occupy an intermediate-status position in American society. According to social dominance theory, asymmetry in mean levels of superordinate identification and in the relationship between subgroup and superordinate identification should be greater between high-status and low-status groups than between high-status and intermediate-status groups.

Hierarchy-Attenuating Environments

Social dominance theory also makes specific predictions about the nature of the relationship between subgroup and superordinate identification within relatively hierarchy-attenuating environments. Within these environments, social dominance theory suggests that all subgroup members feel equally entitled to "ownership" of the superordinate identity and that, as a result, there should be symmetry in the mean levels of superordinate identification across the different subgroups, as well as symmetry in the interface between subgroup and superordinate identification. Specifically, mean levels of superordinate identification should be essentially the same among members of all groups, and the two types of identification should be similarly related among all group members.

As predicted, the results reported in this chapter were generally consistent with the expectation that the university environment would yield symmetry with regard to superordinate group identification. If anything, native-born whites had *lower* levels of university identification than native-born Asian Americans (contrary to the pattern for American identification). Other than this one group difference, all other comparisons (within each year of college) between different ethnic groups in their mean levels of university identification were not significant. Furthermore, ethnic identification and university identification tended to be positively associated across all ethnic groups, and there were no significant ethnic-group differences in the nature of this relationship within any of the four college years.

Clearly then, the context and the hierarchical flavor of superordinate identity make a difference. The type of superordinate context one is dealing with appears to be related to whether or not the superordinate and subgroup identities of members of dominant and subordinate groups will be compatible. While identification with the American nation as a whole seems substantially easier and less problematic for members of dominant groups than for members of subordinate groups, multicultural university environments appear to be ones in which students from all ethnicities can experience positive associations between their ethnic and institutional identities.

Caveats

We must add three important caveats to these general findings. First, the number of black participants in the sample was considerably lower than the number of whites, Asian Americans, and Latinos. Therefore, the analyses for blacks had less statistical power than the analyses for the other three groups.

Second, although American identification was asymmetrically endorsed by different native-born ethnic groups, and there were asymmetrical relationships between American and ethnic identification among these groups, other researchers have shown some benefits to endorsement of this superordinate identification through a reduction in prejudice and discrimination against members of other ethnic groups. For example, Samuel Gaertner and his colleagues (1994) found that intergroup bias was lower among ethnic minority students attending a multicultural high school when they thought of themselves simultaneously as "Americans" and as members of their ethnic subgroup than when they thought of themselves just as members of their ethnic subgroup. Linda Tropp (2006) also found that stronger identification with the superordinate group of Americans is associated with more positive orientations toward members of other ethnic groups. Yuen Huo and her colleagues (1996) drew similar conclusions in their research on the group-value model of justice. Therefore, a strong American identity can have beneficial effects for intergroup relations, even though it may be relatively more difficult to sustain among members of low-status ethnic groups in the face of substantial power asymmetries.

There is a third important caveat to note. Social dominance theory expects—and much evidence has confirmed (Sidanius et al. 1997; Staerklé et al. 2005)—that asymmetry in the interface between subgroup and superordinate identity will be found in all environments in which members of one group dominate the sociopolitical landscape at the expense of members of other groups. There appear to be some circumstances, however, in which this generalization may not hold. For example, Jim Sidanius, Yesilernis Peña, and Mark Sawyer (2001) found evidence that the Dominican Republic is organized as a group-based social hierarchy in which group status distinctions are consensually agreed upon, based largely on skin color (a system also known as a "pigmentocracy"). However, they found no evidence of an asymmetric relationship between national and racial identity across the social status hierarchy. Altogether, the accumulated data now appear to suggest that while group-based social hierarchy might be a necessary condition for the emergence of an asymmetrical interface between national and ethnic identity, it is not a sufficient condition for the emergence of this asymmetry. Future cross-cultural research needs to identify more fully the specific moderating conditions that enable a symmetrical interface between national and racial identities, despite the existence of race-based social hierarchy.

Conclusions

As a whole, these results are noteworthy in that they appear to paint a slightly different picture of the dynamics of ethnic identification than that presented in chapter 6. As discussed earlier in the volume, the black exceptionalism model emphasizes the uniqueness of African Americans as opposed to other minority ethnic groups in the United States. Within the social dominance framing used in this chapter, African Americans appear to have more in common with the recent Asian American and Latino immigrant groups than was implied in previous chapters. We would like to suggest, however, that this contradiction is more apparent than real. Whether the black exceptionalism or social dominance narrative is the best framing for understanding the dynamics of ethnic identity depends on exactly what question we are asking. If we focus on the contents and origins of ethnic identity, then it is clear that the children of recent immigrants frame their identities in terms of their countries and cultures of origin rather than in terms of the pan-ethnic identities, such as "Asian American" or "Latino," that are so widespread in American culture. Furthermore, there is reason to believe that, unlike African American identities, these particular ethnic identities become less salient and politicized over time and are replaced by an increasingly important identification as simply "American." However, if we are instead focused on the degree to which ethnic subgroup identities intersect with larger superordinate group identities, then it appears that the social dominance framing may be the more appropriate one. Within relatively hierarchy-enhancing environments, the intersection between these two identities should be asymmetrical for dominant and subordinate groups. By contrast, within relatively hierarchy-attenuating environments, the intersection between these two identities should be more symmetrical across the different groups.

In closing, this chapter focused on the university setting as an example of a relatively hierarchy-attenuating environment. The next several chapters more closely examine particular elements of the university experience and the degree to which these elements influence intergroup relations. Using contact theory, chapters 8 and 9 assess how intergroup contact in university friendships, dating, and roommate relationships affects intergroup attitudes, thereby shifting our focus from how students' exposure to the university environment affects their own group identities to how their experiences within this setting affect their responses to members of other groups.

PART III

THE IMPACT OF SPECIFIC UNIVERSITY EXPERIENCES ON SOCIOPOLITICAL ATTITUDES AND ACADEMIC ADJUSTMENT

Chapter 8

The Effects of Close Intergroup Contact:
Interethnic Friendship and Dating in College

In part III of the book, we examine the effects of specific elements of the college experience on students' intergroup attitudes and social and academic adjustment. In this chapter, using contact theory as our theoretical framework, we examine the effects of interethnic friendships and dating relationships on ethnic attitudes, feelings of belonging in college, and academic commitment, motivation, and performance. Prior work on contact theory has emphasized the importance of favorable conditions of contact for creating positive change in intergroup attitudes. Despite good-faith efforts at promoting positive campus racial climates, many colleges and universities are still struggling to establish and maintain institutional norms of intergroup acceptance, and UCLA is no different. Furthermore, although efforts to diversify college campuses have led to the increased representation of minorities in the student body, students from all ethnic groups remain largely segregated by ethnicity. Such ethnic segregation—the tendency for ethnic groups to be socially distanced from one another on campus—is a growing concern on many college campuses (McDermott 2002).

Some fear that ethnic segregation leads to increased ethnocentrism and racial intolerance on campus and that it can foster negative attitudes toward the university (D'Souza 1991). Others share these concerns but adopt a contact theory perspective, arguing that segregation is a barrier to racial integration because it undermines efforts to establish firm institutional norms of intergroup acceptance (Pettigrew 1998b).[1] Contrary to contact theory, others argue that segregation is beneficial and should not be discouraged, especially among students of color on predominantly white campuses. Those adopting this perspective argue that segregation may actually have positive effects on minority students' social and academic adjustment in college because, for these students, same-race peer groups provide the social and academic resources necessary to overcome barriers erected by a hostile campus racial climate (Hurtado et al. 1998, 1999; Loo and Rolison 1986).

In this chapter, we explore the validity of these claims by first testing the basic contact theory notion that more positive ethnic attitudes should develop at the end of college as a result of the interethnic friendships and dating relationships that students form during college. We also examine whether students who have more positive ethnic attitudes at the beginning of college are more likely to have friends and dating partners of different ethnicities during college. In addition to examining the reciprocal relationships between interethnic contact and ethnic attitudes, we go on to test four specific hypotheses regarding the reciprocal relationships between students' perceptions of ethnic discrimination on campus and their interethnic friendship choices and the subsequent effects of these perceptions of discrimination and friendship patterns on students' feelings of belonging and academic adjustment in college.

The first of these four hypotheses, the peer support hypothesis, examines whether people have more friends of their own ethnicity when they perceive more ethnic discrimination on campus. If spending time with members of one's own ethnic group provides critical social support for those who find themselves in culturally unsupportive environments, then students may develop ingroup friendships as a coping strategy to deal with perceptions of ethnic discrimination on campus. However, this relationship may operate in the opposite direction as well: ingroup friendships may promote the development of perceptions of ethnic discrimination, a second prediction we call the peer socialization hypothesis. We speculate that one mechanism responsible for the development of negative perceptions of the campus climate may be the socialization process that students are exposed to when they have more friends of their own ethnic group. Peer socialization studies indicate that students are likely to modify their attitudes and behaviors to be consistent with those of the groups to which they belong (Feldman and Newcomb 1969). Groups that are more homogeneous in terms of racial-ethnic background (or age, sex, social class, or religious beliefs) exert a particularly strong influence because people with similar backgrounds and experiences are more likely to share similar attitudes and ideas. When people who share similar attitudes and ideas are isolated from other groups with different views and attitudes, this isolation may serve to strengthen the belief that the group's views are "right," thus leading to greater perceptions of ethnic discrimination if these perceptions are viewed as normative within the group (see chapter 10).

Our last two hypotheses examine the effects of ingroup friendships and perceptions of discrimination during college on social and academic adjustment at the end of college. If minority students gain academic and social support within same-ethnicity friendship groups, these friendships may serve to enhance their academic commitment, motivation, and performance, although these friendships may also reduce their sense of belonging to the larger campus community. We refer to this third prediction as the ethnic segregation hypothesis. Finally, beyond the effects of ingroup friendships on social and academic adjustment, we also explore whether perceptions of discrimination on campus harm students' subsequent social and academic outcomes—a fourth prediction we call the hostile climate hypothesis.

In the first section of the chapter, we discuss how students' ethnic attitudes at the beginning of college affect their friendship choices during college and how their interethnic friendship patterns during college affect their ethnic attitudes at the end of college. In the next section, we examine similar longitudinal relationships between ethnic attitudes and dating patterns to see if they resemble those for friendship patterns. We then go on to examine the reciprocal relationships between students' perceptions of the campus racial climate and their friendship choices. In the next section, we examine the subsequent effects of these campus climate perceptions and friendship patterns on students' social and academic adjustment in college. We end the chapter with an overall summary and set of final conclusions.

Relationships Between Ethnic Attitudes and Interethnic Friendships

In one of the most extensive tests to date of the relationship between intergroup friendship and prejudice, Thomas Pettigrew (1997) analyzed data from seven national probability samples of majority group members in four Western European countries (see also Hamberger and Hewstone 1997). He found that having more friends of another nationality, race, religion, culture, or social class is associated with less prejudice toward minority group members, even after controlling for political conservatism, group relative deprivation, political interest, national pride, urbanism, education, and age. In a study of friendship groups at UCLA, Anthony Antonio (2001) also found that friendship group diversity is positively associated with interracial interaction outside the friendship group, commitment to racial understanding, and gains in cultural awareness. These positive effects of intergroup friendships on intergroup outcomes are exactly what contact theory would expect to find. We might also expect that the opposite direction of causality operates as well—that is, people who are less prejudiced may also be more likely to seek out intergroup contact in the first place. Using correlational data in a nonrecursive structural equation model, Pettigrew (1997) did find that less prejudice leads to more intergroup friendships, but, consistent with contact theory, the reverse causal path—from more intergroup friendships to lower levels of prejudice—was larger (see also Herek and Capitanio 1996). Daniel Powers and Christopher Ellison (1995) also found that close interracial friendships lead to more positive racial attitudes among African Americans, even when accounting for possible selection bias.

Although advanced statistical procedures certainly go a long way toward helping us compare the reciprocal paths between contact-reducing prejudice and prejudice-reducing contact, our longitudinal design affords us a much better way to isolate causal effects. Specifically, we can first examine the effects of students' ethnic attitudes at the beginning of their college careers on their friendship choices during college in order to see the extent to which their prior ethnic attitudes affect subsequent interethnic friendship patterns. Then we can control for the effects of these prior ethnic attitudes when we look at the effects of friendship choices on later ethnic attitudes. This allows us to ascertain the size of the effect that close interethnic contact during college has on changes in students' ethnic attitudes from the beginning to the end of college.

In addition to examining the effects of having more friends of other ethnicities (outgroup friends) on ethnic attitudes, we also examine the effects of having more friends of one's own ethnicity (ingroup friends). It is possible that the positive effects of outgroup contact on prejudice reduction found in previous research are due to less ingroup contact rather than to more outgroup contact per se. There are few previous studies that have examined the effects of ingroup contact in addition to outgroup contact (see, for example, Wilder and Thompson 1980). In this chapter, we examine the separate effects of both ingroup and outgroup contact to see if outgroup contact leads to more positive ethnic attitudes at the same time that ingroup contact leads to more negative ethnic attitudes.

The ethnic attitudes that we assess are ingroup bias (more positive feelings in favor of one's own group compared to one's feelings toward the ethnic outgroups) and intergroup anxiety (feelings of incompetence and unease interacting with people from different ethnic groups).[2] In their meta-analysis, Thomas Pettigrew and Linda Tropp (2006) found strong effects of intergroup contact on affective measures of prejudice. Walter Stephan and Cookie White Stephan (1992, 2000) found that intergroup contact has similar effects on intergroup anxiety (see also Islam and Hewstone 1993). In our study, we examine whether students who have more ingroup bias and more intergroup anxiety at the end of their freshman year have fewer outgroup friends and more ingroup friends during their sophomore and junior years of college. We also control for these effects of prior ethnic attitudes and orientations in order to examine whether those with more outgroup contact and less ingroup contact during their sophomore and junior years of college show less ingroup bias and less anxiety interacting with members of different ethnic groups at the end of college. In line with previous findings that the relationship between contact and prejudice is significantly weaker among low-status minority groups than high-status majority groups (Pettigrew and Tropp 2006; Tropp 2006), we also examine whether these relationships vary by ethnic group.

In presenting the results of these analyses, we first examine whether students tend to have more friends of their own ethnic group rather than from other ethnic groups during college. We then examine the effects of students' ethnic attitudes at the beginning of their college career on their friendship choices during college in order to see the extent to which students choose their friends in college on the basis of prior ethnic attitudes. In our final set of analyses, we control for these effects of prior ethnic attitudes when we look at the effects of friendship choices during college on ethnic attitudes at the end of college (for a more detailed description of these analyses, see Levin, van Laar, and Sidanius 2003).

Friendship Patterns

At the end of both their sophomore and junior years, students were asked about their friendships with members of the four main ethnic groups at UCLA.[3] As can be seen in figure 8.1, the highest proportions of students' closest friends came from their own ethnic group. In addition to these findings for ingroup friends, blacks were least likely to have white and Asian friends on campus, and Asians were least likely to have Latino and black friends on campus.

The Effects of Prior Ethnic Attitudes on Ingroup and Outgroup Friendships

Figure 8.2 shows the overall model that we test in a series of hierarchical regression equations, first using outgroup friendships as our college friendship variable and then using ingroup friendships.[4] Results indicate that students who were more biased in favor of their ethnic group and higher in intergroup anxiety at the end of their freshman year in college had a smaller proportion of outgroup friends and a greater proportion of ingroup friends during their sophomore and junior years in college, even when controlling for the background variables.[5] These relationships did not vary across ethnic groups.

The Effects of Ingroup and Outgroup Friendships on Subsequent Ethnic Attitudes

We turn now to measure the subsequent effects of these friendship choices on ingroup bias and intergroup anxiety at the end of the senior year of college. Here we seek to answer the question of whether students become less biased and less anxious interacting with members of different ethnic groups at the end of college when they have relatively more outgroup friendships and fewer ingroup friendships during college, even when we take into account preexisting differences between people in

Figure 8.1   Ethnicity of Friends During the Sophomore and Junior Years Combined, by Ethnic Group

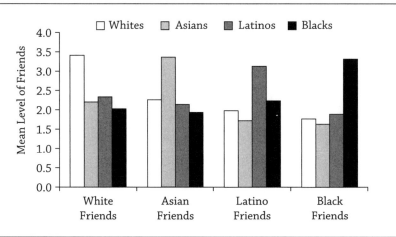

Source: Authors' compilation.

Note: Means range from 1 to 5 (1 = none, 2 = few, 3 = many, 4 = most, 5 = all).

Figure 8.2   Predicted Model of the Relationships Between Ethnic Attitudes and Interethnic Friendships in College

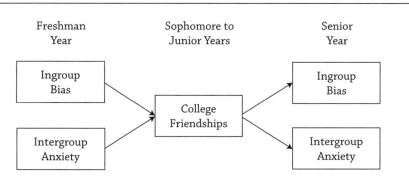

Source: Authors' compilation.

Note: Effects on all outcome variables control for several background variables: precollege friendships, gender, religion, foreign cultural closeness, socioeconomic status, and political conservatism. Effects on senior year ingroup bias and intergroup anxiety also control for both ethnic attitudes measured in freshman year.

these ethnic attitudes and in background variables related to these attitudes.[6]

In our assessment of outgroup friendships, the results indicate that students who had a greater proportion of outgroup friends during their sophomore and junior years in college showed less bias in favor of their ethnic group and felt less anxious being around people of different ethnic groups at the end of their senior year in college, even when controlling for their ethnic attitudes at the end of their freshman year and the background variables.[7] These relationships were the same for all ethnic groups.

Turning to our assessment of ingroup friendships, results show the predicted opposite effects: students who had a greater proportion of ingroup friends during their sophomore and junior years in college showed more bias in favor of their ethnic ingroup and felt more anxious being around people of different ethnic groups at the end of their senior year in college, even when controlling for the previous ethnic attitudes and background variables.[8] Again, these effects did not vary across ethnic groups.

Summary

Overall, these results indicate that white, Asian, Latino, and black students selected outgroup and ingroup friends during their sophomore and junior years of college partially on the basis of the ethnic attitudes they held at the end of their freshman year. Specifically, students from these four ethnic groups had a smaller proportion of outgroup friends and a greater proportion of ingroup friends during college when they were more biased in favor of their ingroup and when they felt more uneasy and less competent interacting with members of different ethnic groups at the beginning of college. These results also demonstrate the positive effects of outgroup contact and the negative effects of ingroup contact over the college years on ethnic attitudes. Specifically, students who had a greater proportion of friends from different ethnic groups and students who had a smaller proportion of friends from their own ethnic group during their sophomore and junior years of college were less biased in favor of their ethnic ingroup and felt less anxious interacting with members of different ethnic groups at the end of their senior year in college. These results hold even when controlling for previous ethnic attitudes and a number of background variables.

Relationships Between Ethnic Attitudes and Interethnic Dating

Now we examine the relationships between ethnic attitudes and in-terethnic dating to see if we find the same pattern of results for interethnic dating that we found for interethnic friendships. Previous studies on interethnic dating have focused extensively on demographic correlates of relationship patterns, particularly with respect to ethnicity, gender, previous ethnic contact, socioeconomic status, and closeness to a foreign culture. In a previous analysis of the data in our sample (Levin, Taylor, and Caudle 2007), we found that white, Latino, and African American men were generally more likely to date outside their ethnic group than their female counterparts (whereas Asian women were more likely to do so than Asian men). There were also some consistent patterns across ethnic groups. Specifically, those who had more close friends of their own ethnic group in high school were more likely to date members of their own group and less likely to date members of other ethnic groups during college. Beyond these effects of gender and precollege ingroup friendships, socioeconomic status and foreign cultural closeness did not greatly contribute to explaining interethnic dating patterns in college. The few consistent patterns that did emerge indicated that whites and Latinos of higher socioeconomic status were more likely to date whites. In addition, Asians of higher socioeconomic status were less likely to date other Asians, and Asians whose families had been in the United States relatively longer were more likely to date whites. Latinos whose families had been in the United States relatively longer were less likely to date other Latinos.

Although most of the previous research on this topic has focused on the demographic correlates of interethnic dating, Belinda Tucker and Claudia Mitchell-Kernan (1995) suggest that psychological factors must be considered along with demographic variables to get a more complete picture of the correlates of interethnic dating. As stated earlier, we examine the independent effects of students' ingroup bias and intergroup anxiety before college entry on their interethnic dating patterns during their first three years of college, controlling for the demographic variables of gender, precollege friendships, socioeconomic status, and closeness to a foreign culture. This allows us to see if precollege ethnic attitudes affect interethnic dating in college even when we take into account other demographic variables that might explain why people date mem-

193

Figure 8.3   Ethnicity of Dating Partners During the Freshman Through Junior Years, by Ethnic Group

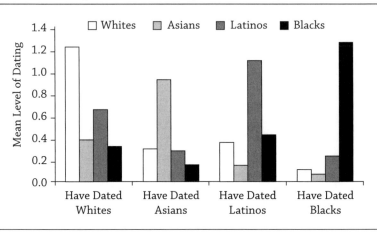

Source: Authors' compilation.

Note. Means range from 0 to 2 (0 = have not dated at all, 1 = have dated either by end of sophomore year or during junior year, 2 = have dated both by end of sophomore and during junior year).

bers of other ethnic groups in college. We then examine whether interethnic dating during the first three years in college has subsequent effects on ingroup bias and intergroup anxiety at the end of the fourth year of college, even when controlling for the precollege ethnic attitudes and demographic variables. These two sets of analyses require data from the precollege wave of data collection, but few blacks who participated in the precollege wave also participated in the final wave (n = 23). Therefore, we were only able to examine whites, Asians, and Latinos in the longitudinal analyses of the relationships between ethnic attitudes and interethnic dating in college (for a more detailed description of these analyses, see Levin, Taylor, and Caudle 2007).[9]

Patterns of Dating

As can be seen in figure 8.3, students were more likely to have dated members of their own ethnic group during their first three years of college than they were to have dated members of other ethnic groups.[10] However, to varying degrees, students did also date members of other

Figure 8.4   Predicted Model of the Relationships Between Ethnic
Attitudes and Interethnic Dating in College

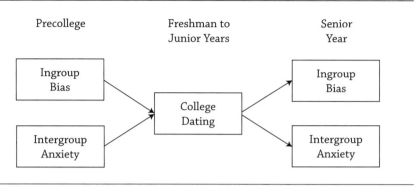

Source: Authors' compilation.

Note: Effects on all outcome variables control for several demographic variables: gender, foreign cultural closeness, socioeconomic status, and precollege friendships. Effects on senior year ingroup bias and intergroup anxiety also control for the same ethnic attitude measured before college entry.

ethnic groups. Latinos dating outside of their ethnic group were more likely than Asians and blacks to choose whites as their partners, and they were more likely than whites and Asians to choose blacks as their partners. Asians were the groups least likely to have dated Latinos.

The Effects of Prior Ethnic Attitudes on Interethnic Dating

Figure 8.4 shows the overall model we test in a series of hierarchical regression equations, this time examining the relationships between ethnic attitudes and interethnic dating in college.[11] Overall, results indicate that the ethnic attitudes held by white, Asian, and Latino students prior to college entry affected the degree to which they dated members of other ethnic groups during their first three years of college. Specifically, students from these three ethnic groups were more likely to date outside their ethnic group during their first three years of college when they were less biased in favor of their ingroup and felt less anxious interacting with members of different ethnic groups before college, even when controlling for the demographic variables.[12] The results did not vary across the three ethnic groups.

The Effects of Interethnic Dating on Subsequent Ethnic Attitudes

Overall, results also demonstrate the positive effects of interethnic dating over the college years for whites, Asians, and Latinos.[13] Specifically, the more these students dated members of other ethnic groups during their first three years of college, the less biased they were in favor of their ingroup and the less anxious they felt interacting with members of different ethnic groups at the end of college.[14] This was especially true regarding the intergroup anxiety of Asians and Latinos.[15]

Summary

The purpose of the first two sections of this chapter was to examine the reciprocal relationships between interethnic contact and ethnic attitudes. We were interested in two primary sets of relationships: the net effects of early ethnic attitudes on the interethnic friendships and dating relationships that students form in college, and the net effects of interethnic friendships and dating during college on students' ethnic attitudes at the end of college. We measured intergroup attitudes and behaviors across several years and controlled for many other potentially contaminating influences—including the individual's prior ethnic attitudes and various other factors such as precollege friendships, gender, socioeconomic status, and foreign cultural closeness. Therefore, we believe that we have been able to isolate some of the causes and effects of interethnic friendships and dating in college.

As expected, we found that students who exhibited more ingroup bias and more anxiety interacting with people from different ethnic groups at the beginning of college had fewer interethnic friends and dates during college, controlling for precollege friendships and other background variables. Once formed, then, ethnic attitudes may become causal factors affecting interethnic friendships and dating in college. Our results also support earlier contact research suggesting the importance of intergroup contact for improving ethnic attitudes (Allport 1954; Hamberger and Hewstone 1997; Pettigrew 1997, 1998a; Pettigrew and Tropp 2000; Powers and Ellison 1995; Stephan and Stephan 1992, 2000). Specifically, we found that students who had more interethnic friends and dates in college were less biased in favor of their ingroup and less anxious interacting with members of different ethnic groups at the end of college. These effects hold even when controlling for other factors that make people more likely to have positive ethnic attitudes at the end of college (such as having positive ethnic attitudes at the beginning of college and having more interethnic contact prior to college entry).

Relationships Between Campus Climate Perceptions and Ingroup Friendships

The previous analyses show that outgroup contact tends to facilitate positive ethnic attitudes and ingroup contact tends to facilitate negative ethnic attitudes in college. From a strict contact theory perspective, these findings suggest that if college administrators are interested in promoting positive intergroup attitudes, they should promote ethnic integration and discourage ethnic segregation on campus. However, lest we draw this conclusion too hastily, we should examine some of the reasons why students tend to form segregated friendship groups in the first place. If, in line with contact theory, the development of outgroup friendships is facilitated by positive conditions of contact, then the development of ingroup friendships may be facilitated by negative conditions of contact, such as perceptions of ethnic discrimination on campus. Furthermore, if ethnically similar peers provide critical social and academic support for students of color who find themselves in culturally unsupportive environments, then these ingroup friendships may go on to enhance students' academic commitment, motivation, and performance in college—a positive outcome despite the negative intergroup attitudes that may also result from ingroup friendships. To facilitate the positive effects of intergroup contact, then, we need to understand *why* people tend to have more ingroup friends in the first place, as well as the beneficial role these ingroup friendships may serve. This may allow us to encourage interethnic friendships to fulfill a similar role and at the same time foster positive interethnic attitudes.

Figure 8.5 shows the overall model of the relationships between ingroup friendships, perceptions of discrimination, and social and academic adjustment that we test in a series of hierarchical regression equations (for a more detailed description of the model and the following analyses, see Levin, van Laar, and Foote 2006).[16]

Figure 8.5   Predicted Model of the Antecedents and Consequences of Ingroup Friendships in College

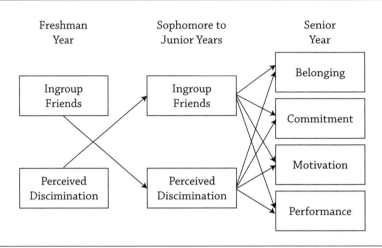

Freshman Year

Sophomore to Junior Years

Senior Year

Source: Authors' compilation.

Note: Effects on all outcome variables control for previous measures of the same variables.

The Peer Support Hypothesis

In the first set of analyses, we examine whether negative perceptions of the campus climate facilitate the formation of ingroup friendships, as we would expect if students seek friends of their own ethnic group in order to gain refuge from a hostile campus racial climate. To test this peer support hypothesis, we examine the extent to which students form more ingroup friendships during college when they report at the beginning of college that they and other members of their ethnic group have experienced more discrimination on campus.[17]

Results indicate that students who perceived more ethnic discrimination on campus at the end of their freshman year of college had a greater proportion of ingroup friends during their sophomore and junior years of college, controlling for precollege friendships.[18] This was especially true for black students.[19] As such, these results provide support for the peer support hypothesis. Students appear to seek out same-ethnicity friends in response to perceptions that they and other members of their ethnic group experience discrimination on campus.

198

The Peer Socialization Hypothesis

We also examine the reciprocal relationship between ingroup friendships and perceptions of discrimination in the peer socialization hypothesis. According to this hypothesis, the more friends that students have of their own ethnicity at the beginning of college, the more they will perceive ethnic discrimination against themselves and other members of their ethnic group during college.[20]

Consistent with the peer socialization hypothesis, results indicate that students who had a greater proportion of friends of their own ethnicity at the end of their freshman year in college perceived more ethnic discrimination on campus during their sophomore and junior years, even when controlling for precollege expectations of perceived ethnic discrimination on campus.[21] Again, this was especially true for black students.[22]

Summary

Taken together, these tests of the peer support and peer socialization hypotheses indicate that perceptions of discrimination and ingroup friendships mutually influence one another. Consistent with the peer support hypothesis, negative perceptions of the campus climate at the end of their freshman year lead members of different ethnic groups, especially blacks, to have a greater proportion of ingroup friends during their sophomore and junior years. In addition, consistent with the peer socialization hypothesis, having a greater proportion of ingroup friends at the end of their freshman year leads students, especially black students, to perceive more ethnic discrimination on campus during their sophomore and junior years.

The Effects of Campus Climate Perceptions and Ingroup Friendships on Social and Academic Adjustment

We next examine the subsequent effects of ingroup friendships and perceptions of ethnic discrimination on campus during students' sophomore and junior years on their social and academic adjustment at the end of their senior year in tests of the ethnic segregation and hostile climate hypotheses.

The Ethnic Segregation Hypothesis

In our test of the ethnic segregation hypothesis, we seek to answer the question of whether students become more alienated from the university but more academically committed, motivated, and successful at the end of college when they have more ingroup friendships during college, even when we take into account preexisting differences between students in their social and academic adjustment at the beginning of college. In these analyses, depicted in figure 8.5, we use belonging, academic commitment, motivation, and performance measured at the end of senior year as our dependent variables (one in each analysis).[23]

Regarding belonging, results indicate that Latino students who had a greater proportion of ingroup friends during their sophomore and junior years of college were the only ones to feel a reduced sense of belonging to the larger university at the end of their senior year.[24] Results for academic performance also reveal negative effects of ingroup friendships for Latinos. Latino students who had a greater proportion of ingroup friends during their sophomore and junior years of college exhibited significantly lower academic performance at the end of their senior year.[25]

Consistent with the ethnic segregation hypothesis, however, results for academic commitment indicate that black and Asian students who had a greater proportion of friends of their own ethnicity during their sophomore and junior years in college were more committed to staying in school at the end of their senior year.[26] Similar results were found for black students' academic motivation. Black students who had a greater proportion of friends of their own ethnicity during their sophomore and junior years in college were more motivated to get a high GPA at the end of their senior year.[27]

Overall, these results indicate that Latinos exhibited both reduced feelings of belonging to the larger university and reduced academic performance at the end of college when they had more friends of their own ethnicity during college. However, black students showed positive effects of having more ingroup friends on academic commitment and motivation. The more friends they had of their own ethnicity during their sophomore and junior years in college, the more committed they were to staying in school (a marginally significant relationship) and the more motivated they were to get a high GPA at the end of their senior year in college (a statistically significant relationship).

The Hostile Climate Hypothesis

In testing the final prediction, the hostile climate hypothesis, we control for these effects of ingroup friendships in order to see if we find independent negative effects of perceptions of discrimination during college on feelings of belonging and academic commitment, motivation, and performance at the end of college. Here we seek to answer the question of whether students become more alienated and less academically committed, less motivated to get a high GPA, and less successful at the end of college when they perceive more discrimination against themselves and other members of their ethnic group during college, even when we take into account already existing differences between students in their ingroup friendships and social and academic adjustment.[28]

Consistent with the hostile climate hypothesis, results for belonging indicate that Latino and white students who perceived more ethnic discrimination on campus during their sophomore and junior years in college exhibited significantly reduced feelings of belonging on campus at the end of their senior year.[29] Coupled with the results from the ethnic segregation hypothesis, these findings reveal that both ingroup friends and perceived ethnic discrimination on campus had negative effects on belonging among Latinos.

Weaker support for the hostile climate hypothesis was found for academic commitment and academic performance. Overall, students who perceived more ethnic discrimination on campus during their sophomore and junior years in college were less committed to staying in school at the end of their senior year. However, this effect was only marginally significant, and none of the separate regression analyses reached statistical significance.[30] Furthermore, perceived discrimination during sophomore and junior years was unrelated to academic performance at the end of senior year, and none of the separate regression analyses showed significant relationships.[31]

Interestingly, results for academic motivation contradicted the hostile climate hypothesis. The separate regression analyses for each ethnic group indicate that black students who perceived more ethnic discrimination on campus during their sophomore and junior years actually exhibited *stronger* motivation to get a high GPA at the end of their senior year.[32] The appropriate interpretation of these results may be that it is not so much perceiving discrimination that is beneficial for motivation but that making *attributions* to discrimination is. That is, African American students who attribute some of their negative experiences to discrimination rather than to the self may evidence stronger motivation to get a high GPA (see also van Laar 1999, 2000). Such external attributions tend to be good protectors of the self as they draw negative inferences away from the self (Weiner 1986). At the same time, attributions to discrimination may play an important role in helping members of disadvantaged groups understand their social world and make contact with members of their ethnic groups. Such attributes may thereby positively affect motivation both directly and indirectly by increasing contact with ingroup friends, which increases motivation. Coupled with the results from the ethnic segregation hypothesis, these findings reveal that both ingroup friends and attributions to discrimination had positive effects on academic motivation among African Americans.

Summary

Taken together, these results demonstrate the protective effects of having more ingroup friends and perceiving more ethnic discrimination (or making more attributions to discrimination) for African American students, and the negative effects of these variables for Latino students, on academic and social adjustment in college. Specifically, Latino students who had more Latino friends during their sophomore and junior years of college exhibited reduced feelings of belonging on campus and poorer academic performance at the end of their senior year in college, even when controlling for previous levels of social and academic adjustment. Furthermore, perceiving more ethnic discrimination on campus during college reduced Latino students' sense of belonging on campus at the end of college, beyond the negative effects of having more ingroup friends. For African American students, on the other hand, having more friends of their own ethnicity during their sophomore and junior years of college enhanced academic commitment and motivation at the end of their senior year in college, even when controlling for previous levels of commitment and motivation. Moreover, perceiving more discrimination during college or making more attributions to discrimination enhanced black students' academic motivation at the end of college. These results highlight important differences between Latino and African American students in how they respond to having ingroup friends and perceiving ethnic discrimination on campus.

Summary and Conclusions

This chapter examined the reciprocal relationships between interethnic contact and ethnic attitudes and the relationships between students' perceptions of ethnic discrimination on campus, their ingroup friendship choices, and their sense of belonging in college and general academic adjustment. Not surprisingly, results indicated that prior ethnic attitudes influenced choices regarding future interethnic relationships. Specifically, students who were initially less biased in favor of their ingroup and less anxious interacting with members of other ethnic groups were more likely to have friends and dating partners outside their ethnic group later in college.

The results painted a mixed picture of both the beneficial and harmful effects of interethnic and ingroup contact on campus. First, supporting the predictions of contact theory, interethnic friendships and dating relationships during college appeared to have positive effects on ethnic attitudes at the end of college. Specifically, students who had more friends and dates of other ethnicities developed more positive feelings toward other ethnic groups relative to their own group and felt less anxious interacting with members of other ethnic groups. These effects occurred even when we took into account other reasons why positive ethnic attitudes may have developed. Such results suggest that further actions taken by the university to encourage interethnic contact should have positive effects on students' intergroup attitudes. These conclusions are bolstered by other findings, reported in the next chapter of this book, showing that contact with randomly assigned roommates of other ethnic groups also has positive effects on subsequent interethnic attitudes, friendships, and dating patterns.

Second, and more disturbingly, the results reported in this chapter indicated that having more ingroup friends had negative effects in terms of increasing ingroup bias and intergroup anxiety. In addition, as the peer socialization hypothesis would suggest, our results demonstrated that having a greater proportion of same-ethnicity friends at the end of a student's first year in college was associated with greater perceptions of ethnic discrimination on campus in later years. Notably, there appeared to be a reciprocal relationship between perceiving more discrimination and having more ingroup friends. Specifically, students who perceived more discrimination on campus early in their college experience appeared to seek out comfort through a greater proportion of ingroup friends later in college, as would be suggested by the predictions of the peer support hypothesis.

These and other results were especially evident for African American students. Having more ingroup friends had an especially strong effect on increasing black students' perceptions of ethnic discrimination on campus. Further, greater perceptions of ethnic discrimination on campus appeared to lead black students in particular to have more ingroup friends. These findings are consistent with previous research suggesting that black students who face a negative racial climate may seek out ingroup others for support and that this may protect their psychological well being. Consistent with the ethnic segregation hypothesis, we also found that ingroup contact increased the importance that black students placed on getting a high GPA and lowered the likelihood that they would consider dropping out of college before earning a degree. Furthermore, contrary to the predictions of the hostile climate hypothesis, making more attributions to discrimination was also associated with stronger motivation to attain good grades among black students. Therefore, the tendencies to form ingroup friendships, although potentially harmful for feelings of ingroup bias, intergroup anxiety, and perceived discrimination, may be particularly adaptive for protecting the psychological well-being and academic motivation and commitment of African American students. These effects may have been heightened among the African American students in our sample because of their low representation on campus (6 percent of the entering freshman class) compared to Asian students (36 percent), white students (32 percent), and Latino students (18 percent).

Unlike the findings for African Americans, our results showed that Latino students who perceived more ethnic discrimination on campus felt a greater sense of alienation from the general campus life. Latino students who had more ingroup friendships also felt a lower sense of belonging to the campus and did not perform as well academically. These results are consistent with previous work by Melvin Oliver, Consuelo Rodriguez, and Roslyn Mickelson (1985), who found that alienation from general campus life is a significant predictor of poor academic performance among Latino students but not among black students. The researchers speculated that Latino students' ties to the university structure may provide them with a sense of comfort and security that enables the positive expression of their academic abilities. The researchers suggested that because they are more similar to whites in speech, dress, and physical appearance than African Americans and therefore do not necessarily signal their nonwhite status to the extent that black students do, Latino students are able to integrate more smoothly into predominantly white campuses. According to this view, the more Latino students integrate into general campus life, the better they perform academically.

By contrast, Robbie Steward, Marshall Jackson, and James Jackson (1990) found that for African American students, interaction with other blacks does not correlate significantly with alienation from the campus. These results support the thesis of Chalsa Loo and Garry Rolison (1986) that relationships with other blacks do not influence black students' feelings of alienation from the campus in general in a way that harms their academic outcomes. Rather, through same-ethnicity friendships, African American students may feel well integrated into their own ethnic subculture, which can then provide the social integration necessary for academic success.

Overall, the findings reported in this chapter emphasize the need to consider the causes and consequences of ingroup contact separately for members of different ethnic groups. While outgroup contact positively influences ethnic attitudes among all ethnic groups and ingroup contact negatively influences these attitudes, the effects of ingroup contact are not uniformly negative. Ingroup contact may fulfill important psychological needs for social support among ethnic minority students who perceive a negative racial climate on campus and may also improve the academic adjustment of students from the most underrepresented groups on campus.

Chapter 9

The Effects of Contact with Ethnically Diverse Roommates

Like chapter 8, this chapter examines predictions derived from contact theory. While the previous chapter focused on contact with ethnically diverse friends and dating partners, this chapter examines the effects of living with white, Asian, Latino, and African American roommates on affective, cognitive, and behavioral indicators of prejudice. Specifically, we use data from precollege through students' senior year to examine the effects of roommate contact in two different ways. First, through a field experimental test, we examine prejudice as a function of living with randomly assigned roommates during students' freshman year; and second, net of preexisting attitudes, we examine the effects of voluntary roommate contact during students' sophomore and junior years on prejudice levels during their senior year. Because most of the students in our sample were randomly assigned to their living situation during their freshman year, the field test we conducted meets the rigorous standards of an experimental test of the prejudice-reducing effects of roommate contact. Because of the longitudinal nature of the research design in subsequent years, we are able to gain additional insights into the causal direction of the relationship between roommate contact and prejudice by controlling for preexisting attitudes when we examine the effects of voluntary roommate contact during students' sophomore and junior years on their senior year prejudice levels.

The Effects of Contact with Ethnically Diverse Roommates

Like contact with ethnically diverse friends and dating partners, contact with ethnically diverse roommates meets many of the conditions thought to facilitate prejudice reduction. First, although differences in ethnic-group status are evident in society at large (Smith 1991), within a given living situation on the university campus members of different ethnic groups are likely to have equal status. Furthermore, even though the college classroom environment can be a competitive one, roommates must work together cooperatively to achieve the common goal of maintaining a home environment that is mutually satisfactory. Roommate situations are also characterized by high acquaintance potential. The familiarity afforded by living together is likely to facilitate the development of positive affective ties between roommates (Festinger, Schachter, and Back 1950). Also, the wide range of activities that roommates may share (such as studying, socializing, and dining together) provides them with the opportunity to learn about one another and reduce the degree to which they view one another through the prism of group stereotypes. Finally, a wealth of research has shown that universities are egalitarian socializing environments (see, for example, Bobo and Licari 1989; Lipset 1983; McClintock and Turner 1962; but see also Jackman 1978; Jackman and Muha 1984). For this reason, it is highly likely that students in this environment will perceive that the relevant authorities are supportive of interethnic contact, and thus all the conditions for optimal intergroup contact are likely to be present among ethnically diverse roommates.

Unlike the design of previous studies, the design of our study allows us to examine whether contact with ethnically diverse roommates causes reductions in prejudice, in two ways. First, because most students at UCLA were randomly assigned to their roommate situation in their freshman year, we are able to control for many confounding influences when we examine students' ethnic attitudes at the end of their freshman year as a function of their roommate situation during that year. This random assignment and control over confounding variables means that we are essentially able to conduct a field experimental test of contact theory. To our knowledge, there were only three previous experimental examinations of residential contact, and these were limited in that they either examined the effects of residence hall contact in general, as opposed to close, extended contact between roommates, or examined only interactions between white and African American roommates, as opposed to interactions among multiple groups (Nesdale and Todd 1998, 2000; Towles-Schwen 2003; Towles-Schwen and Fazio 2002). Second,

207

we utilize a longitudinal design to examine the effects of choosing to live with an outgroup roommate during the sophomore and junior years on changes in students' intergroup attitudes from their freshman to their senior year. Both of these methodological strategies offer substantial advantages over cross-sectional, non-experimental research in overcoming the causal sequence problem.

In essence, the experimental and longitudinal design of our study allows us to test two main hypotheses and three additional research questions derived from contact theory. First, individuals randomly assigned to live with an outgroup roommate during their freshman year in college should show improved intergroup attitudes at the end of freshman year as a function of this contact. Second, individuals who choose to live with an outgroup roommate during their sophomore and junior years should show improved intergroup attitudes at the end of their senior year as a function of this contact. The ethnically heterogeneous nature of our sample also enables exploration of the following three research questions. First, do roommates' ethnic group memberships moderate the relationship between contact and prejudice? Second, do the positive effects of contact with one ethnic outgroup also create more positive attitudes toward other ethnic outgroups? Third, does contact with one's own ethnic group actually increase prejudice?

To gain a thorough understanding of the effects of roommate contact, we examine three different dimensions of prejudice: affective, cognitive, and behavioral. The affective indicators of prejudice that we use are affect toward the four main ethnic groups, intergroup comfort, and intergroup competence.[1] The cognitive indicators of prejudice are symbolic racism, social dominance orientation (SDO), and opposition to miscegenation (that is, opposition to interethnic dating and marriage). Finally, the behavioral indicators of prejudice are the ethnic heterogeneity of one's friends and dating partners.[2] These behavioral indicators of prejudice are of particular interest because they allow us to determine whether contact with ethnically diverse roommates begets contact with ethnically diverse friends and dating partners, thus creating a ripple effect of prejudice reduction.[3]

Within this chapter, we examine descriptive data regarding roommate assignment to gain a basic understanding of the nature of roommate contact within our sample. After doing so, we examine the effects of freshman year contact with randomly assigned roommates on our indicators of prejudice. Then we assess the influence of longitudinal contact with roommates on these indicators. Finally, we discuss both the theoretical and practical implications of our findings (for a more detailed discussion of these analyses, see van Laar et al. 2005).

The Nature of Roommate Contact and Assignment

Before examining our hypotheses, we need to determine the nature of roommate contact among students, and we must establish whether roommate assignment satisfies the requirements of random assignment.

The Nature of Roommate Contact

First, we examine some basic facts regarding roommate contact. Specifically, we determine where students lived, how many people they lived with, and whether they chose their own roommates or had roommates who were randomly chosen.[4] The students were asked a number of questions about their roommates. If they lived in a dormitory, they were instructed to consider persons in the dormitory with whom they shared their room as their roommates. If they lived off-campus in a house or apartment, they were instructed to consider persons with whom they shared their residence as their roommates. The range of the number of roommates indicated by respondents was zero to more than three. Most of the students in our sample spent their freshman year in a dormitory (85 percent). Another 11 percent lived at home, and 4 percent lived in off-campus housing. In the dormitories during freshman year, students tended to share their room with one (58 percent) or two (32 percent) other freshman students, and occasionally three (4 percent) or more (5 percent).

During students' freshman year at UCLA, university policy dictates that same-sex roommates are randomly assigned to students (after certain lifestyle preferences are taken into account, such as smoking, drinking, sleeping, studying, and cleaning habits). Although it is not the norm, students can be assigned a specific roommate if they specify that they want to share a room with a particular person. As such, most of the students in our sample who lived in the dorms their freshman year had a randomly assigned roommate (78 percent, n = 1,130), while 20 percent (n = 292) lived with a roommate they chose themselves. In their sophomore year, many students chose to remain in a dormitory (52 percent), although a substantial number (31 percent) chose to live in off-campus housing. Another 14 percent lived at home. In off-campus housing, students tended to have one (28 percent), two (21 percent), or three roommates (32 percent), and occasionally zero (6 percent), four (7 percent), or more than four (6 percent) roommates.

The Nature of Roommate Assignment

We also needed to ensure that students who lived in the dormitory during their freshman year were indeed randomly assigned to their roommate situation. Recall that 85 percent of the students in our sample reported living in the dorms during their freshman year and that, of these students, 292 (20 percent) reported having a self-selected roommate and 1,130 (78 percent) reported having a randomly assigned roommate. If roommate assignment was indeed random, we should find two main results. First, the precollege ethnic attitudes of students who reported having randomly assigned roommates during their freshman year should be unrelated to the ethnic heterogeneity of their roommates that year. On the other hand, it is likely that the precollege ethnic attitudes of students who reported selecting their own roommates would be related to the ethnic heterogeneity of their roommates. For example, students who felt less comfortable interacting with people from different ethnic groups before college entry should be less likely to choose members of other ethnic groups as roommates during their freshman year. Second, at the end of freshman year, it is reasonable to suppose that students with randomly assigned roommates should have more ethnic heterogeneity among their roommates than students with self-selected roommates. Moreover, given that students were more likely to select their own roommates in their sophomore year and beyond, students with randomly assigned roommates in their freshman year should show a sharper decline in the ethnic heterogeneity of their roommates between their freshman and sophomore years than students with self-selected roommates.

To examine the ethnic heterogeneity of students' roommates, we created a roommate heterogeneity variable, which we define as the proportion of roommates who were members of ethnic outgroups. In each year, the students were asked to identify the ethnicities of all the people with whom they were living. Specifically, respondents indicated the number of roommates they had who were white, Asian, Latino, or black. The an-

Table 9.1 Relationships Between Precollege Ethnic Attitudes and Behaviors and Roommate Heterogeneity During Freshman Year, Among Those with Self-Selected or Randomly Assigned Roommates

Ethnic Attitudes and Behaviors Prior to University Entry	Roommate Heterogeneity Among Freshman Students with Self-Selected Roommates (N = 292)	Roommate Heterogeneity Among Freshman Students with Randomly Assigned Roommates (N = 1,130)	T-Value of Slope Difference Between Those with Self-Selected Versus Randomly Assigned Roommates
Intergroup competence	.04**	.00	2.22*
Intergroup comfort	.06**	.01	−1.96+
Symbolic racism	.02	−.08	n.s.
Social dominance orientation (SDO)	.02	−.02	n.s.
Opposition to miscegenation	−.01	−.02	n.s.
Friendship heterogeneity	.01*	.00	2.23*

Source: van Laar, Levin, Sinclair, and Sidanius 2005, reprinted with permission from Elsevier.

Note: All entries are unstandardized regression coefficients, except for those in the rightmost column.

+ p < .10; * p < .05; ** p < .01; n.s. = not significant

swers were recoded such that roommates belonging to the same ethnic group as the student were considered ingroup roommates and all other roommates were considered outgroup roommates. Roommate heterogeneity in a given year was calculated as: 1 − [number of ingroup roommates/total number of roommates].[5]

To examine whether precollege ethnic attitudes and freshman year roommate heterogeneity were unrelated among students with randomly assigned roommates but significantly related among those with self-selected roommates, we regressed degree of freshman year roommate heterogeneity on the precollege measures of intergroup competence, intergroup comfort, symbolic racism, SDO, opposition to miscegenation, and friendship heterogeneity.[6] These regressions were conducted separately for dormitory residents with self-selected roommates and those with randomly assigned roommates.[7] As shown in table 9.1, consistent with our

The Diversity Challenge

Figure 9.1   Roommate Heterogeneity over the College Years for
Those with Randomly Assigned or Self-Selected
Roommates During Freshman Year

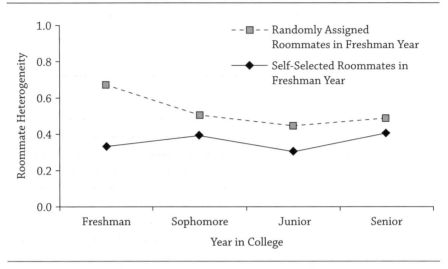

Source: van Laar, Levin, Sinclair, and Sidanius 2005, reprinted with permission from Elsevier.
Note: All entries are unstandardized regression coefficients, except for those in the rightmost column.
+ p < .10; * p < .05; ** p < .01; n.s. = not significant

expectations, dormitory residents with randomly assigned roommates did not show any significant relationships between their freshman year roommate heterogeneity and precollege ethnic attitudes and behaviors. In contrast, those with self-selected roommates had more ethnically heterogeneous roommates as they showed more intergroup comfort, more intergroup competence, and more ethnic heterogeneity among their precollege friends.[8] We also see in table 9.1 that neither students with self-selected roommates nor those with randomly assigned roommates showed any relationships between freshman year roommate heterogeneity and precollege levels of symbolic racism, SDO, or opposition to miscegenation.

The results of our second preliminary analysis were also consistent with the notion that freshman year roommate assignment was truly random.[9] Figure 9.1 shows that at the end of freshman year, roommate heterogeneity was significantly higher among students with randomly assigned roommates than among students with self-selected roommates.[10] Also consistent with our expectations, we found a sharper de-

212

cline in the degree of roommate heterogeneity between freshman year and sophomore year for students with randomly assigned roommates than for students with self-selected roommates.[11] Students therefore had more ethnically heterogeneous living situations when the university randomly assigned roommates in the dormitories during their freshman year. However, when they selected their roommates in their sophomore year, they chose roommates with significantly less ethnic heterogeneity. Thus, by their senior year, there was only a marginally significant difference in roommate heterogeneity between those students who originally chose their own roommates and those who were randomly assigned roommates in the dormitories during their freshman year.[12]

We can conclude from these analyses that among those students who were randomly assigned roommates in the dormitories by the university during their freshman year, the ethnic heterogeneity of these roommates reflected actual variation in exposure to ethnic diversity that was independent of precollege ethnic attitudes and behaviors.

The Effect of Randomly Assigned Roommate Contact on Prejudice: An Experimental Test

In our assessment of the nature of roommate contact, we have thus far established that freshman year roommate assignment in the dormitory showed all the signs of being truly random. We now examine whether exposure to roommates of different ethnic outgroups changes the intergroup attitudes and behaviors of students. Since students who were randomly assigned to freshman year roommates showed no indication that they self-selected into these roommate situations on the basis of their prior intergroup attitudes and behaviors, restricting the analyses to this subsample represents an experimental test of contact theory. We may now assess our first hypothesis that randomly assigned contact with ethnically heterogeneous roommates during students' freshman year improves their ethnic attitudes and behaviors by the end of that year.

Freshman Year Contact with Ethnically Heterogeneous Roommates

To test this hypothesis, we conducted eleven hierarchical regression analyses using only those respondents who were randomly assigned

Table 9.2   Ethnic Attitudes and Behaviors at the End of Freshman Year as Functions of Roommate Heterogeneity and the Number of Roommates from Specific Ethnic Groups, Among Students with Randomly Assigned Roommates During Freshman Year

Intergroup Attitudes and Behaviors	Roommate Heterogeneity	Number of Roommates of Each Ethnicity				R^2
		Whites	Asians	Latinos	Blacks	
Affect toward whites	.06$^+$	.01	.00	.02	.00	.00
Affect toward Asians	.08*	.00	.07*	.01	.03	.01*
Affect toward Latinos	.12***	.01	.02	.05	.06$^+$	.02***
Affect toward blacks	.09**	.01	.00	.07*	.08**	.02***
Intergroup competence	.07*	.02	.01	.01	.01	.01
Intergroup comfort	.03	−.01	−.03	.04	.01	.00
Symbolic racism	−.06$^+$	.01	.04	−.04	−.06$^+$	.01*
Social dominance orientation (SDO)	−.04	−.04	.01	.00	−.04	.01
Opposition to miscegenation	−.08**	.00	−.03	.00	.02	.01
Friendship heterogeneity	.03	−.02	−.01	.01	.07*	.01
Interethnic dating	.02	−.06	.00	−.02	.01	.01

Source: van Laar, Levin, Sinclair, and Sidanius 2005, reprinted with permission from Elsevier.

Note: All entries are unstandardized regression coefficients, except for those in the rightmost column.

$^+$ p < .10; * p < .05; ** p < .01, *** p < .001

roommates at the beginning of their freshman year. In these analyses, degree of roommate heterogeneity and number of roommates from each of the four major ethnic groups (whites, Asians, Latinos, and blacks) were the independent variables, and each of the eleven ethnic attitudes and behaviors were the dependent variables. We conducted these analyses first for all the ethnic groups combined, and then separately for whites, Asians, Latinos, and African Americans.

As shown in table 9.2, the results for all ethnic groups combined showed a significant relationship between the ethnic attitude or behavior and either roommate heterogeneity or the number of roommates from a particular ethnic group for six of the eleven ethnic attitudes and behaviors. Another two of these relationships were consistent with the direction of the hypothesis but did not quite reach statistical significance. Consistent with other studies on the effects of intergroup contact, the effect sizes tended to be small (for the most extensive meta-analysis of the effects of contact, see Pettigrew and Tropp 2006), indicating that random roommate assignments explain a small portion of the variance in students' intergroup attitudes and behaviors (Cohen 1988). Of the five independent variables, roommate heterogeneity had the strongest and most consistent effects on the ethnic attitudes and behaviors. Five of the eleven ethnic attitudes and behaviors yielded statistically significant results. In addition, two yielded results that were consistent with the direction of the hypothesis but were not statistically significant at conventional levels. Specifically, as shown in table 9.2, the greater the ethnic heterogeneity of students' randomly assigned roommates during freshman year, the more positive their affect toward whites, Asians, Latinos, and blacks, and the greater their sense of competence in dealing with people from different ethnic groups. Further, roommate heterogeneity was also associated with lower symbolic racism and less opposition toward miscegenation (although the relationships with affect toward whites and symbolic racism did not reach conventional levels of statistical significance).

The Effect of Exposure to Members of Specific Ethnic Outgroups

Next, we examine the effect of contact with roommates of specific ethnicities. Our results show that, beyond the effects of roommate heterogeneity, exposure to roommates from specific ethnic groups also reduced various indicators of prejudice. As shown in table 9.2, the more students were exposed to Asian and African American roommates, the more positive affect they felt toward those two groups. For the two most stigmatized ethnic groups on campus (blacks and Latinos), results also indicated that exposure to one stigmatized group resulted in more positive affect toward the other stigmatized group. In other words, having randomly assigned Latino roommates caused more positive affect toward blacks, and having randomly assigned black roommates tended to result in more positive affect toward Latinos. Beyond these effects, exposure to randomly assigned black roommates increased levels of friendship heterogeneity and also tended to decrease levels of symbolic racism. It is noteworthy that, with the exception of the relationships between exposure to black roommates and symbolic racism and friendship heterogeneity just mentioned, the effects of exposure to randomly assigned roommates from specific ethnic groups were essentially restricted to affective reactions. These effects did not generally extend to the cognitive or behavioral indicators of prejudice—that is, to intergroup competence, intergroup comfort, SDO, opposition to miscegenation, or interethnic dating (see table 9.2).

The Effect of Exposure to Members of Specific Ethnic Outgroups Within Each Ethnic Group

When we analyzed the results within each ethnic group separately, we found that some of the effects of roommate contact depended on the combination of both respondent ethnicity and roommate ethnicity (not shown in table). Like the effects described earlier, these effects tended to be small, except that black respondents tended to show medium-sized effects of random roommate contact. The impact of exposure to Asian roommates was especially pronounced for white respondents and to some extent for black respondents. Contrary to contact theory, exposure to Asian roommates generally *increased* prejudice. Among white respondents, exposure to randomly assigned Asian roommates decreased comfort with being around students of other ethnicities, increased symbolic racism, increased SDO, and tended to increase opposition to miscegenation.[13] Exposure to Asian roommates also increased symbolic racism among black respondents and even tended to decrease the positive affect blacks felt toward other blacks.[14]

While exposure to Asian roommates had the largest number of anti-egalitarian effects, this was not the only group to produce such effects. Exposure to white roommates also increased symbolic racism among black respondents and tended to decrease black and Latino respondents' sense of intergroup comfort.[15] Exposure to white roommates also tended to decrease Latino students' sense of intergroup competence, tended to increase their opposition to miscegenation, and significantly decreased the heterogeneity of their friends.[16] Among Asian students, exposure to white roommates increased positive affect toward other Asian students (their ingroup members).[17] Exposure to white roommates also had some positive intergroup effects, however, in that it decreased SDO among black students, tended to decrease opposition to miscegenation among black students, and tended to increase positive affect toward Latinos among Asian students.[18]

216

Although having Asian and white roommates showed some negative effects on ethnic attitudes, Asian and white students both showed positive effects of being randomly assigned to Latino and black roommates or heterogeneous roommates more generally. Among Asian students, exposure to heterogeneous roommates increased interethnic dating.[19] Among white students, exposure to heterogeneous roommates also tended to increase interethnic dating, significantly decreased opposition to miscegenation, increased intergroup competence, and tended to increase feelings of intergroup comfort.[20] Similarly, Asian and white students showed more ethnic heterogeneity among their closest friends at UCLA after being exposed to randomly assigned African American roommates.[21] Among Asian students exposure to Latino roommates also tended to increase positive affect toward Latinos and to increase feelings of comfort being around students of different ethnicities.[22] However, white students who were exposed to randomly assigned Latino roommates showed significantly less interethnic dating.[23]

Exposure to Latino roommates also showed some negative effects for black students, as did exposure to heterogeneous roommates more generally for black and Latino students. Specifically, black students who were exposed to randomly assigned Latino roommates showed less intergroup competence.[24] Also, exposure to heterogeneous roommates tended to increase black students' opposition to miscegenation and significantly decreased interethnic dating among Latino students.[25]

The Effect of Exposure to Ethnic Ingroup Roommates

In our final set of group-by-group analyses, we explored the degree to which exposure to *ingroup* members actually *increased* prejudice. In these analyses for each ethnic group, we had eleven dependent variables and one independent variable—the number of roommates of one's own ethnic group. Inspection of all forty-four relevant analyses revealed that ingroup exposure had only one potential prejudice-inducing effect: among black students, exposure to randomly assigned black roommates increased opposition to miscegenation.[26] The three other significant ingroup exposure effects we found all tended to suggest decreased, rather than increased, prejudice as a result of ingroup exposure. Among blacks, exposure to black roommates decreased symbolic racism. Among whites, exposure to white roommates tended to increase intergroup comfort, and among Asians, exposure to Asian roommates increased interethnic dating.[27]

Summary of Experimental Effects

Overall, students who were randomly assigned to live with outgroup roommates in the dormitories at the beginning of their freshman year showed improved intergroup attitudes and behaviors by the end of this year, consistent with contact theory. The results were most consistent for the effects of roommate heterogeneity as a whole on the affective and cognitive indicators of prejudice. However, the effects of intergroup contact also depended on the particular ethnicity of students' roommates. Exposure to African American roommates had a particularly positive effect on respondents' intergroup attitudes, increasing positive affect toward blacks, increasing the ethnic heterogeneity of respondents' friendship circles, and tending to lower symbolic racism. Furthermore, the beneficial effects of exposure to African American roommates generalized beyond affect toward this group, tending to increase positive affect toward Latinos as well. Similarly, exposure to Latino roommates increased positive affect toward African Americans. Finally, consistent with contact theory, exposure to Asian roommates increased positive affect toward Asians. However, contrary to contact theory, the separate group analyses indicated that exposure to Asian roommates increased some of the prejudice indicators among white and black respondents. Similar effects were occasionally seen as a result of exposure to white roommates. However, Asian and white students themselves were positively influenced by exposure to black and Latino roommates, and heterogeneous roommates more generally. Exposure to roommates from one's own ethnic group had few negative effects.

The Effect of Voluntary Roommate Contact on Prejudice: A Longitudinal Test

We now assess our second hypothesis—that students who choose to live with an outgroup roommate during their sophomore and junior years show more positive intergroup attitudes by the end of their senior year. We turn to a longitudinal test of the effect of voluntary roommate contact on the affective, cognitive, and behavioral indicators of prejudice to assess this hypothesis. Because students were more likely to choose their own roommates after their freshman year, we must control for their earlier intergroup attitudes and behaviors when we assess the impact of roommate experiences during their sophomore and junior years on their intergroup attitudes and behaviors at the end of their senior year. We used hierarchical regression analysis to control for these previous attitudes and behaviors.[28]

Sophomore and Junior Year Contact with Ethnically Heterogeneous Roommates

As shown in table 9.3, the results of these analyses were generally consistent with the experimental results, and again, the effect sizes tended to be small (see Cohen 1988). Although overall roommate heterogeneity did not significantly influence affect toward whites, Asians, Latinos, or blacks—as it did in the first-year experimental analyses—it was associated with increased intergroup competence, increased intergroup comfort, decreased symbolic racism, decreased SDO, and increased degree of interethnic dating, even after controlling for baseline levels of the dependent variables.

The Effect of Longitudinal Exposure to Members of Specific Ethnic Outgroups

Exposure to roommates from specific ethnic groups had even more widespread effects. With one notable exception, these effects were generally consistent with contact theory and the first-year experimental results. Greater exposure to white, Latino, and black roommates during sophomore and junior years was associated with more positive affect toward those groups measured in the senior year. (For example, voluntary exposure to black roommates was related to more positive affect toward blacks, as in the experimental analyses.) There was also evidence of the same generalization effect for Latino and black roommates found in the experimental analyses. Greater exposure to black roommates was associated with more positive affect toward Latinos, and greater exposure to Latino roommates was associated with more positive affect toward blacks. In addition, increased exposure to Latino and black roommates was associated with decreased levels of symbolic racism and SDO. Increased exposure to white roommates was also associated with increased levels of friendship heterogeneity and tended to be associated with de-

Table 9.3 Ethnic Attitudes and Behaviors at the End of Students' Senior Year as Functions of Roommate Heterogeneity and the Number of Roommates from Specific Ethnic Groups During Sophomore and Junior Years, Controlling for Freshman-Year Ethnic Attitudes and Behaviors

Intergroup Attitudes and Behaviors During Senior Year	Effect of Freshman Year Attitude or Behavior	Roommate Heterogeneity	Number of Roommates of Each Ethnicity				R^2 Change
			Whites	Asians	Latinos	Blacks	
Affect toward whites	.46***	-.01	.10**	-.02	.01	-.02	.01*
Affect toward Asians	.41***	.05	.04	-.03	.04	-.01	.01
Affect toward Latinos	.45***	.01	.06+	-.10**	.08*	.06*	.03***
Affect toward blacks	.45***	.02	.05	-.09*	.08*	.07*	.03***
Intergroup competence	.27***	.08*	.03	-.05	-.09*	.05	.02**
Intergroup comfort	.21***	.08*	.00	-.11**	-.04	.05	.02**
Symbolic racism	.53***	-.07*	-.06+	.05+	-.09**	-.08**	.03***
Social dominance orientation (SDO)	.48***	-.08**	-.03	.06+	-.09**	-.06+	.03***
Opposition to miscegenation	.43***	-.02	.02	.06	-.06+	.02	.01
Friendship heterogeneity	.44***	-.05	.10**	-.07*	-.04	-.02	.02***
Interethnic dating	.44***	.10*	.00	-.05	-.05	.04	.02

Source: van Laar, Levin, Sinclair, and Sidanius 2005, reprinted with permission from Elsevier.

Note: All entries are unstandardized regression coefficients, except for those in the rightmost column.

+ p < .10; * p < .05; ** p < .01; *** p < .001

creased levels of symbolic racism. Surprisingly, exposure to Latino roommates was associated with a lower sense of intergroup competence.

However, while most of these findings support contact theory, there is one consistent set of contradictory findings. Specifically, as in the separate group analyses of the experimental data, the voluntary contact data show that exposure to Asian roommates was clearly and consistently associated with increased forms of prejudice, especially prejudice toward Latinos and blacks. As shown in table 9.3, increased exposure to Asian roommates was associated with the following forms of prejudice: increased negative affect toward Latinos and blacks; decreased intergroup comfort; and decreased friendship heterogeneity. Such exposure to Asian roommates also tended to be associated with increased levels of symbolic racism and SDO. Thus, the prejudice-inducing effects of exposure to Asian roommates found in the separate group analyses of the experimental data were found more consistently in these analyses of the longitudinal data.

The Effect of Longitudinal Exposure to Members of Specific Ethnic Outgroups Within Each Ethnic Group

When we analyzed the longitudinal data within each ethnic group separately, we found that the relationships between roommate heterogeneity and exposure to roommates of a specific group, on the one hand, and ethnic attitudes and behaviors, on the other hand, were essentially the same regardless of the ethnicity of the respondent. As was the case in the overall analyses, we found that roommate heterogeneity had positive effects on students. Among Latino students, increased roommate heterogeneity was associated with lower SDO and increased positive affect toward Latinos, African Americans, and Asians.[29] Among black students increased roommate heterogeneity was associated with increased interethnic dating, and among Asian students, it tended to be associated with stronger feelings of intergroup competence.[30]

Again, we found that exposure to white, Latino, and black roommates tended to be associated with positive intergroup attitudes, as was the case for the overall analyses. Among Asian students, increased exposure to white roommates was associated with decreased symbolic racism, and increased exposure to black roommates was associated with increased interethnic dating and increased positive affect toward

African Americans, Latinos, and Asians.[31] Asian students who were exposed to black roommates also tended to show increased positive affect toward whites, and those who were exposed to Latino roommates tended to show increased heterogeneity of friends.[32] For white students, increased exposure to black roommates was associated with increased interethnic dating, and increased exposure to Latino roommates tended to be associated with less opposition to miscegenation.[33] Although these results were generally consistent with contact theory, there were two notable exceptions. First, among Asian students, increased exposure to Latino roommates was associated with decreased feelings of intergroup comfort. Second, among Latino students, increased exposure to black roommates was associated with less positive affect toward whites.[34]

In these separate group analyses of the longitudinal data, we again found evidence for the negative effects of exposure to Asian roommates, but this evidence was not as strong as the evidence provided by the experimental results. For white students, increased exposure to Asian roommates tended to be associated with less positive affect toward Latinos.[35]

The Effect of Longitudinal Exposure to Ethnic Ingroup Roommates

We also examined whether exposure to roommates of one's own ethnic group increased prejudice in these separate group analyses. Once again, there was little support for this notion. Ingroup contact effects, to the extent that we found them at all, were almost exclusively associated with decreased rather than increased prejudice, especially among members of the two low-status ethnic groups (blacks and Latinos). Among Latinos, increased exposure to Latino roommates was associated with decreased levels of SDO and increased positive affect toward Latinos, Asians, and blacks.[36] Similarly, among blacks, increased exposure to black roommates tended to be associated with increased positive affect toward Latinos.[37] There were only two exceptions to this generally positive trend. Among whites, increased exposure to white roommates was associated with increased opposition to miscegenation, and among blacks, increased exposure to black roommates was associated with decreased interethnic dating.[38]

Why Does Contact with Asians Increase Prejudice?

In the last set of analyses in this chapter, we try to understand why both random and voluntary contact with Asian roommates increased prejudice levels. One possibility is that these findings are due to peer socialization. Peer socialization studies indicate that students are likely to modify their attitudes and behaviors to be consistent with those of their peers (Feldman and Newcomb 1969). If Asian students have significantly higher levels of prejudice than other students, then the increased prejudice associated with greater contact with them could be the result of an attitude shift in the direction of their higher levels of prejudice.

To explore the plausibility of this explanation we calculated the average prejudice levels of white, Asian, Latino, and black students across all five waves of data collection, from precollege to the end of senior year. We then computed the mean differences between the prejudice scores of Asian students and the prejudice scores of white, Latino, and black students (see table 9.4). These mean differences were calculated with respect to seven cognitive and affective indicators of prejudice: intergroup competence, intergroup comfort, symbolic racism, SDO, opposition to miscegenation, affect toward blacks, and affect toward Latinos. Results indicated that in twenty of the twenty-one contrasts, Asian students had significantly higher prejudice scores than white, Latino, and black students. These higher levels of prejudice are also consistent with the lower levels of interethnic contact (such as friendships and dating) found among Asians (see chapter 8). Therefore, one plausible explanation for why students become more prejudiced when they have more Asian roommates is that they may modify their attitudes and behaviors to be consistent with those of their roommates.

Summary and Conclusions

In this chapter, we explored the effects of living with ethnically diverse roommates on affective, cognitive, and behavioral indicators of prejudice. The design of our study conferred two major advantages in testing contact theory. First, as in the previous chapter on contact with ethnically diverse friends and dating partners, the longitudinal nature of the design allowed us to control for self-selection effects when we examined

Table 9.4   Contrasts Between Mean Intergroup Attitudes
            Measured from Precollege to Senior Year for Asians
            Versus Whites, Latinos, and Blacks

Intergroup Attitudes	Asians Versus Whites	Asians Versus Latinos	Asians Versus Blacks
Intergroup competence	−.47***	−.33***	−.48***
Intergroup comfort	−.48***	−.29***	−.38***
Symbolic racism	.24***	.55***	1.28***
Social dominance orientation (SDO)	.21***	.53***	.85***
Opposition to miscegenation	.28***	.39***	.15
Affect toward blacks	−.58***	−.71***	−1.03***
Affect toward Latinos	−.58***	−1.03***	−.70***

Source: van Laar, Levin, Sinclair, and Sidanius 2005, reprinted with permission from Elsevier.

Note: Entries are mean differences between groups (the means for Asians minus the means for whites, Latinos, or blacks).

*** $p < .001$

the effects of voluntary contact with outgroup roommates during sophomore and junior years on intergroup attitudes and behaviors during
senior year. Second, the random roommate assignment that occurred for
most students during their freshman year in the dormitories allowed us
to test experimentally the effects of randomly assigned contact with
outgroup roommates during freshman year on intergroup attitudes and
behaviors at the end of this year. Given that interactions between roommates were characterized by the conditions thought to facilitate prejudice reduction through intergroup contact (Allport 1954), we predicted
that living with outgroup roommates would reduce prejudice. Overall,
the findings tended to support this prediction. However, we also found
that the effect of interethnic contact on prejudice reduction depended to
some extent on the specific ethnic groups in the contact situation.

In our experimental test of the causal relationship between roommate ethnicity and intergroup attitudes within students' freshman year,
we found that interethnic roommate contact did indeed cause reductions in ethnic prejudice. Overall, the greater the ethnic heterogeneity of
students' roommates in their freshman year, the more positive affect

224

they exhibited toward all other ethnic groups, the more intergroup competence they felt, the less opposition they exhibited toward miscegenation, and the lower their symbolic racism tended to be at the end of their freshman year. Beyond these effects, exposure to roommates from specific ethnic groups made independent contributions to prejudice reduction, especially in terms of generating more positive affect toward the ethnic group of a student's roommate. Specifically, students assigned to live with more Asian roommates in the dormitories at the beginning of their freshman year had more positive affect toward Asians at the end of their freshman year, and students assigned to live with more African American roommates had more positive affect toward African Americans. Interestingly, students with more African American roommates also tended to have more positive affect toward Latinos, and students with more Latino roommates had more positive affect toward African Americans.

In our longitudinal test of the effect of voluntary interethnic roommate contact during students' sophomore and junior years on intergroup attitudes at the end of their senior year, we also found general support for contact theory. Findings from these longitudinal analyses indicated that the ethnic heterogeneity of students' roommates was associated with increased intergroup competence, increased intergroup comfort, decreased symbolic racism, decreased SDO, and increased interethnic dating. Beyond these effects, contact with roommates of specific ethnic groups again made independent contributions to intergroup attitudes. With the exception of Asian roommates, these analyses showed that interethnic roommate contact was consistently associated with more positive affect directed toward the ethnic group of a student's roommate. Choosing to live with more black or Latino roommates was also associated with lower levels of symbolic racism and SDO.

Of particular note were findings of crossover effects between exposure to black and Latino roommates and affect toward the other group, replicating findings from the experimental test. That is, in both the experimental and longitudinal analyses, contact with Latino roommates tended to improve affect toward African Americans, and contact with African American roommates tended to improve attitudes toward Latinos. Such crossover effects may have been found for these two groups because they have similarly low-status positions in the American ethnic hierarchy (Smith 1991). Insights and observations stimulated by contact with one low-status group may have influenced affect toward the other low-status group. Friendship patterns among Latinos and African Americans may also explain this effect. Relative to white and Asian students, African American students were more likely to have Latino friends, and Latino students were more likely to have African American friends (see chapter 8 on contact with ethnically diverse friends). Therefore, students with African American roommates may have had more positive affect toward Latinos because they had more contact with them by virtue of their association with their African American roommates. Students with Latino roommates may have had more positive affect toward African Americans for the same reason. Furthermore, according to research on the "extended contact effect," simply knowing that a close other has a friend of a particular ethnicity may improve one's attitudes toward that ethnic group (Wright et al. 1997). As such, knowing that one's Latino roommate has close friends who are African American may be enough to stimulate improved attitudes toward African Americans as a group, and vice versa.

In sum, both the field experimental and longitudinal tests provide converging evidence for the validity of contact theory. The experimental test is unique in that we were able to take advantage of the random roommate assignment that naturally occurs during students' freshman year in the dormitories to test the causal direction of the contact-prejudice relationship. The longitudinal test also provides an important contribution to the literature because we were able to observe the prejudice-reducing effects of contact despite the substantial stability of intergroup attitudes across students' freshman through senior years. (The eleven intergroup attitudes and behaviors measured in students' freshman year were strongly related to the same measures assessed in students' senior year.) We were also able to observe these effects even though roommate contact was a subtle prediction variable examined over a period of several years during which students were exposed to many other influences on their intergroup attitudes and behaviors. We therefore believe that the effects of both randomly assigned and voluntary contact with ethnically diverse roommates are very meaningful indeed.

However, although the findings reported in this chapter suggest that there is a clear tendency for interethnic roommate contact to decrease various kinds of ethnic prejudice, contact with Asian roommates was found to be an exception to this general trend. The longitudinal analyses showed that exposure to Asian roommates was associated with more negative affect toward both Latinos and blacks, reduced intergroup comfort, increased levels of symbolic racism and SDO, and decreased ethnic heterogeneity of students' friendships. Similar prejudice-inducing effects of living with Asian roommates were found in the separate experimental tests among members of different ethnic groups, especially among white and black students. Peer socialization may explain why exposure to Asian roommates increases prejudice. As we showed, Asian students have significantly higher levels of prejudice than white, Latino, and black students. As these white, Latino, and black students socialize with their Asian roommates, they may accommodate themselves to their roommates' attitudes and values, thereby increasing their own levels of prejudice during this socialization process (Feldman and Newcomb 1969; Hardin and Conley 2001; Hardin and Higgins 1996; Higgins and Rholes 1978; Lowery, Hardin, and Sinclair 2001; McCann and Hancock 1983).

A final question is whether contact with ingroup members increases prejudice. Contrary to this notion, findings from the experimental test tended to indicate that increased exposure to roommates of one's own ethnicity actually decreased rather than increased prejudice. The longitudinal analyses also provided little support for the notion that contact with ingroup roommates increases prejudice. We have, however, found negative effects of ingroup contact elsewhere in this study, most notably in terms of the consequences of ingroup friendships (see chapter 8) and the effects of ethnically segregated fraternities and sororities (see chapter 10). This suggests that the negative effects of ingroup contact may be more likely to occur when ingroup contact is oriented toward social activities, emphasizes self-disclosure, or consumes a great deal of individuals' discretionary time.

In conclusion, the results of these analyses suggest that although close interethnic contact is generally an effective means of reducing prejudice, it is not a panacea. Although living with an outgroup member on a university campus often meets the optimal conditions of contact specified by Gordon Allport (1954) and is rife with acquaintance potential, the effects of this situation on intergroup attitudes and behaviors clearly depend on which ethnic groups come into contact with one another.

Chapter 10

Ethnic Organizations and Ethnic Attitudes
on Campus

I n this chapter, we focus on an issue that has been a central focus of
the multiculturalism debate for some time, namely, whether ethnically oriented student organizations, such as the African Student
Union, the Vietnamese Student Union, and the Latin American Student
Association, increase or decrease the level of ethnic tension and conflict
on campus. As we recall from chapter 2, scholars weighing in on this debate fall into two camps. On the one hand, there are those who argue
that such ethnically oriented student organizations are detrimental to
the creation and maintenance of a common student identity and tend to
exacerbate ethnic tensions by further isolating students of different
racial and ethnic backgrounds into mutually suspicious and hostile ethnic enclaves (see, for example, D'Souza 1991). On the other hand, the
defenders of such student organizations argue that, rather than increasing the level of ethnic strife on campus, they contribute to student life
by providing minority students with a safe and welcoming environment
and a greater sense of belonging to the university community. This increased sense of belonging to the wider university community, they argue, leads to wider and more intimate contact with other ethnic groups
(see, for example, Ethier and Deaux 1994; Hurtado, Dey, and Treviño
1994; Hurtado et al. 1999; Moran, Algier, and Yengo 1994; Reyes 1998;
Rooney 1985; Treviño 1992). We refer to this as the "multicultural" or

"pluralist" argument. Despite the, at times, sharply argued debate concerning this issue, there has been surprisingly little research devoted to it.

The little work that has been done suggests that students join minority racial-ethnic organizations for the purpose of identity enhancement and that this increased comfort with their identity leads to greater interest in cross-cultural contacts, a richer sense of belonging to the university community, and greater integration into broader campus life. For example, Michelle Gilliard (1996) found that, for African American students, participation in ethnically oriented activities is correlated with enhanced social involvement, increased social interactions with faculty, and greater use of support services at predominantly white institutions. Overall, this line of research appears to support a multicultural perspective. Participation in ethnic organizations enables minority students to experience less threat to their social identities and to feel a greater sense of inclusion in campus life, and thus contributes to an improved intergroup atmosphere on campus.

While much of this earlier work has focused on the effects that minority ethnic organizations have on academic achievement (Gilliard 1996), attrition rates (Guiffrida 2003; Reyes 1998; Tinto 1993), and the integration of minority students into campus life (Treviño 1992), relatively little research has specifically focused on the broad effects of these student organizations on intergroup attitudes and behaviors. Furthermore, many of these earlier studies used cross-sectional research designs or panel studies over relatively short time intervals. In an extension of this earlier work, our longitudinal study explores both the possible effects of ethnically oriented student organizations that primarily serve minority students and the effects, both positive and negative, of student organizations that primarily serve white students. Primary among such predominantly white student organizations are the fraternities and sororities belonging to the "Greek system."

The history of American fraternities and sororities makes it clear that Greek organizations have served as exclusive enclaves of ethnic and economic privilege for most of American history. The first college social fraternity with a Greek-letter name, Phi Beta Kappa, included a secret initiation ritual and was established at William and Mary College in 1776. The first nonsecret social fraternity began in 1825 at Union College in Schenectady, New York. In the 1870s, men's fraternities were joined by women's fraternities, which were called "sororities." Although these fraternities and sororities were exclusionist in both racial and socioeconomic terms, explicitly discriminatory entrance requirements did not become widespread until the beginning of the twentieth century. By 1928, more than half of the national fraternities and sororities had written rules and constitutions explicitly excluding applicants on the basis of religious affiliation and "race." Furthermore, on a large number of American campuses interfraternity councils admitted only white Christian fraternities and sororities to their membership (Lee 1955a, 1955b). These explicitly discriminatory practices were not seriously challenged until the end of World War II. By the end of the 1970s, explicitly discriminatory entrance requirements had all but disappeared from American universities.

Despite the demise of these exclusionary practices, simple organizational inertia could lead one to expect that implicit norms of ethnocentrism, authoritarianism, and generalized prejudice remain associated with Greek organizations. These expectations are largely supported by empirical evidence. For example, a longitudinal study following 3,331 incoming students at eighteen colleges and universities (Pascarella et al. 1996) found that fraternity or sorority membership has a significant negative impact on openness to diversity among white students. Likewise, in a study of 1,242 male freshmen at the University of Pennsylvania, L. D. Miller (1973) found that fraternity members, as compared with nonmembers, were not only more politically conservative but also significantly less interested in issues concerning social justice. Similarly, and using a relatively small sample of students from a four-year liberal arts college, Bernard Segal (1965) found that fraternity members were significantly more anti-Semitic than nonmembers.

Thus, when exploring the effects of ethnically oriented student organizations, it was clear to us that we should not restrict our attention to minority student ethnic organizations, but that we should also extend our focus to include predominantly white student organizations within the Greek system. Therefore, unique to research in this area, in this chapter we examine the effects of both minority ethnic organizations among minorities and Greek organizations among whites across a broad array of intergroup attitudes. The longitudinal design of the study allows us to control for preexisting differences in attitudes and perceptions between students and allows us to examine the net effect of membership in ethnic organizations on students' attitudes and perceptions in later years.

Campus Organizations

There were 154 student organizations on the UCLA campus at the time of this study. We examined two particular types of student organizations: minority ethnic organizations and Greek organizations (sororities and fraternities). Minority ethnic organizations were identified as those groups whose names referred to a specific ethnic or racial minority group (for example, United Cambodian Students, Sikh Students Association, Iranian Students Group, African Student Union) or whose membership consisted of 80 percent or more of a specific ethnic or racial group. Of those students belonging to one of the four major ethnic groups, 548 students, roughly 26 percent of the sample, were members of at least one such ethnic organization at some point in their college careers, while 1,584 students were never members of such an organization.

Roughly 15 percent of the sample (324 students) were members of Greek organizations at some point in their college careers, while 1,808 students were never members of a Greek organization.

Membership in Ethnically Oriented Student Organizations

We begin our exploration by examining membership in minority ethnic organizations (excluding fraternities and sororities) at any point between students' freshman and senior years as a function of ethnicity (see table 10.1). Not surprisingly, while very few whites were members of traditional (minority) ethnic organizations (approximately 1.2 percent), very substantial proportions of Latinos (28.8 percent), Asians (42.0 percent), and especially African Americans (60.4 percent) were members of ethnic organizations.[1]

Turning our focus to the Greek organizations, we also found that membership in fraternities and sororities at any point during college was unevenly distributed across the four ethnic groups (see table 10.2). The results of this table show that white students were significantly underrepresented among nonmembers of sororities and fraternities and significantly and substantially overrepresented among the members of these Greek organizations. The exact opposite pattern was found for all three of the major minority groups (Asians, Latinos, and blacks). All three minority groups had a slight tendency to be overrepresented in the

Table 10.1 Distribution of Membership in Minority Ethnic
Organizations Across Ethnicity

Ethnic Category	Nonmember		Member		Total N
	N	Res	N	Res	
Whites	755	7.9	9	−13.4	764
	(98.8)		(1.2)		(100)
Asians	440	−5.2	318	8.8	758
	(58.0)		(42.0)		(100)
Latinos	332	−0.8	134	1.3	466
	(71.2)		(28.8)		(100)
Blacks	57	−4.8	87	8.2	144
	(39.6)		(60.4)		(100)
Total number of respondents	1,584		548		2,132

Source: Sidanius, van Laar, Levin, and Sinclair 2004, reprinted with permission from the American Psychological Association.

Note: The percentage of each ethnicity in each category of ethnic organization membership is in parentheses. Chi-square = 438.58, phi = .45, p < .01, res = standardized residual.

nonmember category, and all three groups were significantly underrepresented in the member category.

The Determinants and Effects of Membership in Greek and Ethnic Organizations

Before turning to our more substantive analyses, we examine the correlations among the various attitude and organizational membership variables of interest for all freshman students in order to gain an overall sense of the patterns of relationships. Our substantive analyses make use of twelve measures assessing intergroup attitudes, which we classify into four broad conceptual categories: social policy attitudes (opposition to affirmative action and opposition to increasing diversity on campus); social identity attitudes (ethnic identification, ethnic activism, common ingroup identity, and university attachment); ethnic prejudice (ingroup

Table 10.2 Distribution of Fraternity and Sorority Membership Across Ethnicity

| | Membership in a Greek organization | | | | |
| | Non-Greek | | Greek Member | | |
Ethnic Category	N	Res	N	Res	Total N
Whites	568	−3.1	196	7.4	764
	(74.3)		(25.7)		(100)
Asians	688	1.8	70	−4.2	758
	(90.8)		(9.2)		(100)
Latinos	418	1.1	48	−2.7	466
	(89.7)		(10.3)		(100)
Blacks	134	1.1	10	−2.5	144
	(93.1)		(6.9)		(100)
Total number of respondents	1,808		324		2,132

Source: Sidanius, van Laar, Levin, and Sinclair 2004, reprinted with permission from the American Psychological Association.

Note: The percentage of each ethnicity in each category of Greek organization membership is in parentheses. Chi-square = 101.04, phi = .22, p < .01, res = standardized residual.

bias, opposition to miscegenation, and symbolic racism); and perceptions of intergroup conflict (perceived ethnic discrimination, the perceived degree to which ethnic organizations promote separatism, and perceived zero-sum group conflict).[2]

We computed intercorrelations among all variables, for white and minority students, assessed during the freshman wave (see table 10.3). Importantly, as shown by the intercorrelations, this university context is one in which ethnic identification is related to various intergroup attitudes among both whites and minorities. For example, the greater students' ethnic identification, the greater the degree of bias in favor of their ingroup (see table 10.3). Similarly, the greater the students' degree of ethnic identification, the more opposed they were to interethnic marriage and dating, the more they felt discriminated against, and the greater their conviction that ethnic groups were locked into zero-sum conflict with each other.

Table 10.3 Correlations Among Student Organization Membership (Greek Groups for Whites, Ethnic Organizations for Minorities) and Ethnic Attitudes and Behaviors Among White and Minority Freshman Students

	1	2	3	4	5	6	7	8	9	10	11	12
1. Student organization membership	—	.03	.20**	.16**	.12**	.25**	.18**	.09*	.15**	.11**	.14**	.09*
2. Opposition to increasing diversity on campus	-.08**	—	.37**	.09*	.10*	-.11**	.22**	.16**	.47**	.09*	.32**	.17**
3. Opposition to affirmative action	.23**	-.28**	—	.22**	.18**	.10**	.25**	.18**	.48**	.26**	.42**	.40**
4. Ethnic identification	.32**	.30**	-.11**	—	.49**	.09*	.18**	.21**	.18**	.25**	.09*	.11**
5. Ethnic activism	.23**	-.28**	-.27**	.54**	—	.09*	.24**	.26**	.16**	.28**	.04	.14**
6. University attachment	.11**	-.06*	-.01	.13**	.04	—	.17**	.00	.07	-.08	-.07	.02
7. Ingroup bias	.11**	.04	.04	.23**	.17**	-.05	—	.21**	.19**	.05	.14**	.19**
8. Opposition to miscegenation	.09**	.20**	.21**	.10**	-.02	-.03	.19**	—	.19**	.14**	.12**	.20**
9. Symbolic racism	-.08**	.33**	.41**	-.16**	-.29**	.09**	-.01	.09**	—	.16**	.38**	.22**
10. Perceived ethnic discrimination	.21**	-.17**	-.09**	.23**	.34**	-.10**	.19**	.10**	-.22**	—	.27**	.25**
11. Ethnic organizations promote separatism	-.13**	.13**	.25**	-.20**	-.15**	-.07*	-.08**	.05	.23**	.07*	—	.23**
12. Perceived zero-sum group conflict	.07*	.07*	.18**	.15**	.09**	-.00	.11**	.20**	.06*	.22**	.05	—

Source: Sidanius, van Laar, Levin, and Sinclair 2004, reprinted with permission from the American Psychological Association.
Note: Entries above the main diagonal are for white students; entries below the main diagonal are for minority students. For student organization membership, 1 = member of a Greek organization for whites and member of an ethnic organization for minorities, 0 = ncnmember; for all other variables, higher numbers indicate greater levels of the construct.
* p < .05; ** p < .01

The Determinants of Membership in Greek and Ethnic Organizations

Past research has shown that, for minorities, the strength of one's ethnic attitudes is strongly related to joining a minority ethnic organization in college (Hurtado et al. 1999; Padilla et al. 1997). We therefore expected that, among whites, joining a sorority or fraternity would also be driven by attitudes about ethnic-racial issues. First, we examine the link between precollege ethnic attitudes and minority ethnic organization membership among minority students, and then we examine the link between these attitudes and Greek organization membership among white students.

The Determinants of Ethnic Organization Membership for Minority Students   We explored the decision to join minority ethnic organizations at any point in college as a function of the eleven scales that made up the four clusters of intergroup attitudes (social policy attitudes, social identity attitudes, ethnic prejudice, and perceptions of intergroup conflict) that were assessed just prior to the beginning of students' freshman year.[3] In the first set of analyses, we used a series of bivariate logistic regression analyses to predict membership in a minority ethnic organization based on the eleven precollege intergroup attitudes measured. Additionally, one overall multivariate logistic regression analysis was performed in which all of the eleven precollege attitudes were simultaneously included in the regression analysis, in addition to controls for minority ethnicity, gender, and social class.[4] The results of these analyses are presented in table 10.4.

Based on the bivariate analyses presented in table 10.4, four of the eleven variables examined were significantly related to minority student membership in minority ethnic organizations. As anticipated, using the odds-ratio as our measure of relationship, the strongest of these variables was ethnic identification.[5] The statistics shown in table 10.4 provide odds-ratio information; in the case of ethnic identification, this statistic indicates that a minority student's odds of joining a minority ethnic student organization are 1.40 times higher for every one-unit increase in precollege ethnic identification (p < .01). The bivariate analyses also indicate that a minority student's odds of joining a minority ethnic organization grew with increasing precollege ethnic activism and with increasing precollege ingroup bias.

Table 10.4   Membership in Minority Ethnic Organizations at Any Point in College Among Minority Students as a Function of Precollege Attitudes

Independent Variable in Precollege Year	Mean Levels by Membership in a Minority Ethnic Organization		Odds-Ratios of Logistic Regressions	
	Member	Nonmember	Bivariate	Multivariate
Social policy				
Opposition to increasing diversity on campus	2.74	2.91	.92	.92
Opposition to affirmative action	3.78	3.74	.96	1.00
Social identity				
Ethnic identification	5.64	5.04	1.40**	1.42**
Ethnic activism	3.74	3.44	1.15**	1.00
University attachment	4.97	4.82	1.12*	1.02
Ethnic prejudice				
Ingroup bias	.80	.61	1.13*	1.00
Opposition to miscegenation	1.81	1.83	.98	.95
Symbolic racism	3.84	3.82	1.01	1.05
Perceived group conflict				
Perceived ethnic discrimination	3.85	3.81	1.00	1.00
Ethnic organizations promote separatism	2.86	3.05	.92	.95
Perceived zero-sum group conflict	3.16	3.11	1.02	1.02

Source: Sidanius, van Laar, Levin, and Sinclair 2004, reprinted with permission from the American Psychological Association.

Note: Bivariate and multivariate analyses include controls for sex, social class, and minority ethnicity.

$^* p < .05; ^{**} p < .01$

At the same time, it should also be noted that there is some evidence here in support of the general ethnic pluralist argument. Specifically, the bivariate analyses reveal that, for minorities, ethnic organization membership was related not only to ethnic identification, ethnic activism, and ingroup bias but also to attachment to the larger, superordinate institution of the university. Thus, the more minority students thought of themselves as UCLA students and felt a strong sense of belonging at UCLA, the more likely they were to join an ethnically oriented minority student organization at some point during college.

The multivariate analyses presented in table 10.4 also reveal that, when all of the predictor variables were entered into the logistic regression equation simultaneously, only ethnic identification was found to have a significant effect on the likelihood that minority students would join a minority ethnic organization—above and beyond the effects of the other variables and the demographic controls. In short, and consistent with previous research, there was evidence that ethnic identification was a strong predictor of minority ethnic organization membership among minority students.

The Determinants of Greek Organization Membership for White Students   While it was not surprising to find that ethnic identification was the most important factor relating to minority ethnic organization membership among minorities, the role of ethnic identification and intergroup attitudes in white students' decisions to join sororities or fraternities is much less obvious. For reasons explored at the beginning of this chapter, we expect that racial-ethnic identification is associated with white students' decisions to join Greek organizations.

To explore this question, we repeated the types of analyses performed for the minority students. That is, looking only at white students' responses, we performed a series of bivariate logistic regression analyses and one multivariate logistic regression analysis in which Greek organization membership at any point in college was predicted as a function of precollege ethnic and racial attitudes.

As shown in table 10.5, these bivariate analyses indicate that, for whites, four of the eleven precollege attitudes examined were significantly related to Greek organization membership. First, paralleling the findings for the minority students, we found that, for the white students, there was a positive association between the likelihood of Greek organization membership and attachment to the university. Second,

The Diversity Challenge

Table 10.5   Membership in Greek Organizations at Any Point in College Among White Students as a Function of Precollege Attitudes

Independent Variable in Precollege Year	Mean Levels by Membership in a Greek Organization		Odds-Ratios of Logistic Regressions	
	Member	Nonmember	Bivariate	Multivariate
Social policy				
Opposition to increasing diversity on campus	3.22	3.22	1.04	.98
Opposition to affirmative action	4.66	4.29	1.19**	1.11
Social identity				
Ethnic identification	3.98	3.58	1.22**	1.19*
Ethnic activism	2.17	2.03	1.07	.96
University attachment	5.13	4.88	1.20**	1.14
Ethnic prejudice				
Ingroup bias	.60	.28	1.39**	1.23*
Opposition to miscegenation	1.83	1.65	1.10	1.00
Symbolic racism	3.97	3.82	1.15	1.00
Perceived group conflict				
Perceived ethnic discrimination	2.82	2.82	1.00	1.04
Ethnic organizations promote separatism	3.74	3.63	1.03	.99
Perceived zero-sum group conflict	3.21	2.99	1.08	1.00

Source: Sidanius, van Laar, Levin, and Sinclair 2004, reprinted with permission from the American Psychological Association.

Note: Bivariate and multivariate analyses include controls for sex and social class.

* $p < .05$; ** $p < .01$

consistent with our expectations, results also reveal that whites' ethnic identification was indeed positively associated with Greek organization membership. Specifically, for every unit increase in whites' ethnic identification, the odds of sorority or fraternity membership also increased by a factor of 1.22 ($p < .01$). Third, results show that the decision to join a

Greek organization was positively associated with one's degree of in-group bias. These first three findings, then, mirror those for minority students and minority ethnic organizations.

In contrast to the findings for the minority students, however, among white students, the decision to join a Greek organization was not related to ethnic activism but rather was related to one of the racial policy attitudes. Specifically, whites' decision to "go Greek" in college was positively associated with precollege opposition to affirmative action. This finding indicates that, among whites, for every unit increase in precollege opposition to affirmative action, the odds of joining a sorority or fraternity increased by a factor of 1.19 ($p < .01$).

Turning to the multivariate analyses, we see here that only two of the eleven precollege variables made net contributions in predicting whites' Greek organization membership. Namely, there were significant effects for precollege ethnic identification and for precollege ingroup bias. Thus, unlike the multivariate analysis for minority students and minority ethnic organizations, where ethnic identification turned out to be the only significant predictor variable, the analysis here for whites suggests that Greek organization membership was related not only to identification with the ingroup but to ingroup bias as well.

The Effects of Membership in Student Organizations on Intergroup Attitudes

The data thus far seem to suggest that ethnic identification is an important factor for minorities in deciding to join a minority ethnic organization and that both ethnic identification and ingroup bias are implicated for whites in the decision to join a Greek organization. It is not clear, however, whether or how membership in these student organizations affects students' ethnic and racial attitudes across their college years. We turn next to an examination of this issue.

In addressing this issue, we employed multiple regression analyses in which we examined students' ethnic attitudes at the end of their senior year as a function of their membership in (minority or Greek) ethnic organizations between their freshman and junior years. These analyses controlled for sex, social class, ethnicity (for minority students only), and the same (predicted) attitudes at "baseline" (precollege). For example, to examine the effect of membership in a minority ethnic organization on minority students' opposition to affirmative action, we regressed minority students' affirmative action opposition at the end of their senior year on their baseline (precollege) affirmative action opposition; demographic factors (sex, social class, and minority ethnicity); and whether the students belonged to a minority ethnic student organization at any point between their freshman and junior years. In brief, the purpose of these analyses was to ascertain if membership in student organizations had any effect on students' attitudes, net of their precollege baseline attitudes. Again, we first examine the effects of membership in minority ethnic organizations for minority students, and then we examine the effects of membership in Greek organizations for white students.

The Effects of Ethnic Organization Membership for Minority Students

Table 10.6 shows the effects for college senior year attitude (dependent) variables as a function of precollege baseline attitudes (shown in the first data column), and ethnic organization membership between the college freshman and junior years (shown in the second data column; 1 = membership, 0 = nonmembership). The effects of all of the variables together are shown in the last column.

For minority students, membership in minority ethnic organizations had significant effects on five of the twelve dependent variables examined. In order of strength of magnitude, these significant effects were: an increase in perceived ethnic discrimination, an increase in ethnic identification, an increase in ethnic activism, a *decrease* in the belief that ethnic organizations promote separatism on campus, and an increase in the perception of zero-sum conflict between ethnic groups.

Thus, while neither feelings of being victims of ethnic discrimination nor perceptions of zero-sum group conflict appear to be among minorities' motives for *joining* minority ethnic organizations (see table 10.4), these variables do appear to be among the *results* of joining. It is also important to note that the basic pattern of these effects did not dramatically change when we examined each minority group separately (Asians, Latinos, and blacks). Finally, these results are noteworthy for what they do *not* show. Namely, despite the fact that membership in minority ethnic organizations clearly increased the degree to which their ethnic identities were *politicized* (as witnessed by the increased sense of ethnic discrimination, perceived group conflict, and ethnic activism), this

Table 10.6   Ethnic Attitudes in Senior Year as a Function of Prior
Levels and Membership in Minority Ethnic
Organizations Among Minority Students

Dependent Variable in Senior Year	β for Same Attitude (Precollege)	β for Ethnic Organization Membership[a] (Freshman Through Junior Years)	Model R^2
Social policy			
Opposition to increasing diversity on campus	.25**	−.04	.17**
Opposition to affirmative action	.31**	-.06	.26**
Social identity			
Ethnic identification	.47**	.13**	.29**
Ethnic activism	.35**	.10**	.28**
Common ingroup identity[b]	.38**	−.05	.14**
University attachment	.18**	.03	.05**
Ethnic prejudice			
Ingroup bias	.34**	.03	.13**
Opposition to miscegenation	.35**	.03	.16**
Symbolic racism	.36**	−.05	.23**
Perceived group conflict			
Perceived ethnic discrimination	.30**	.13**	.18**
Ethnic organizations promote separatism	.21**	−.10*	.09**
Perceived zero-sum group conflict	.25**	.09*	.08**

Source: Sidanius, van Laar, Levin, and Sinclair 2004, reprinted with permission from the American Psychological Association.

Note: These analyses include controls for sex, social class, and minority ethnicity.

[a] For ethnic organization membership, 1 = member, 0 = nonmember.

[b] Common ingroup identity was first measured during freshman year; therefore the freshman year variable is used as the control variable, and membership in ethnic organizations between sophomore and junior years is used as the independent variable.

* p < .05; ** p < .01

membership did not seem to increase the minority students' ingroup bias.

The Effects of Greek Organization Membership for White Students We next examined the effects of Greek membership on white students' attitudes using the same regression strategy and controlling for the same variables as with the minority students (except ethnicity).

As can be seen in table 10.7, just as membership in minority ethnic organizations was associated with an array of senior year attitudes among minority students, membership in Greek organizations was associated with several senior year attitudes for whites. Net of precollege attitudes and demographic variables, and in order of effect sizes, membership in Greek organizations increased whites' sense that ethnic organizations promote separatism; increased their feelings of ethnic discrimination; increased their levels of symbolic racism; created more opposition to miscegenation; led to greater opposition to increasing diversity on campus; increased their attachment to the university as an institution; and marginally increased their levels of ingroup bias. In sum, while membership in Greek organizations seemed to increase various forms of ethnic prejudice and social distance to ethnic "others" among whites, it also, simultaneously, increased their attachment to the university as an institution.

Thus, among white students, membership in Greek organizations appears both to be affected by and to affect social identity, ethnic prejudice, and perceived group conflict. Although the perception of ethnic discrimination, opposition to miscegenation, and symbolic racism do not appear to be among the motives that white students have for joining Greek organizations (see table 10.5), they do appear to be among the consequences of joining these organizations. These effects of Greek organization membership among whites are quite consistent with social identity theory. Specifically, membership in Greek organizations increased whites' politicized identities, as shown in the effects on various indices of perceived group conflict and ethnic prejudice. However, for social identity theory to be more strongly confirmed, we must also show that ethnic identification *mediates* organizational membership—that is, we must show that it is the mechanism by which organizational membership expresses itself in various form of intergroup attitudes. It is to this last question, regarding both minority and white students, that we now shift our focus.

Table 10.7 Ethnic Attitudes in Senior Year as a Function of Prior Levels and Membership in Greek Organizations Among White Students

Dependent Variable in Senior Year	β for Same Attitude (Precollege)	β for Greek Membership[a] (Freshman Through Junior Years)	Model R^2
Social policy			
Opposition to increasing diversity on campus	.39**	.14*	.25**
Opposition to affirmative action	.47**	.08	.25**
Social identity			
Ethnic identification	.40**	.04	.19**
Ethnic activism	.47**	.08	.23**
Common ingroup identity[b]	.30**	−.10	.11**
University attachment	.14**	.13*	.06**
Ethnic prejudice			
Ingroup bias	.24**	.09+	.08**
Opposition to miscegenation	.23**	.15**	.09**
Symbolic racism	.43**	.17**	.28**
Perceived group conflict			
Perceived ethnic discrimination	.27**	.18**	.11**
Ethnic organizations promote separatism	.22**	.19**	.10**
Perceived zero-sum group conflict	.30**	.06	.10**

Source: Sidanius, van Laar, Levin, and Sinclair 2004, reprinted with permission from the American Psychological Association.

Note: These analyses include controls for sex and social class.

[a] For Greek membership, 1 = member, 0 = nonmember.

[b] Common ingroup identity was first measured during freshman year, and therefore the freshman year variable is used as the control variable, and membership in Greek organizations between sophomore and junior years is used as the independent variable.

+ p < .06; * p < .05; ** p < .01

The Mediational Effects of Ethnic Identification

Following the logic of social identity theory, we explored whether there is any evidence that ethnic identification during students' junior year mediated the effects of (minority or Greek) student organization membership during their freshman and sophomore years on intergroup attitudes during their senior year. We began these mediational analyses by examining opposition to increasing diversity on campus as a dependent variable. In this case, we were interested in whether organization membership during students' freshman and sophomore years increased ethnic identification during their junior year, which in turn might have led to increased opposition to increasing diversity on campus during their senior year. We repeated these analyses for all of the intergroup attitudes examined in the prior analyses. In all cases, the statistical significance of the mediation was assessed.[6] The mediational analyses made use of all five waves of the panel data and included baseline measures of precollege ethnic identification and precollege intergroup attitude (such as diversity opposition) as controls. The primary independent variable of interest here was membership in a minority or Greek student organization during the freshman and sophomore years; ethnic identification at the end of junior year functioned as the mediator; and intergroup attitudes (such as opposition to increasing diversity on campus) at the end of senior year served as the ultimate outcome variables.

The Mediational Effects of Ethnic Identification for Minority Students

We began by performing these mediational analyses among minority students for each of the dependent variables of interest (see table 10.8). First, the results of these analyses showed that the effect of minority ethnic organization membership (during freshman and sophomore years) on ethnic activism (at the end of senior year) was significantly mediated by ethnic identification (assessed at the end of junior year).

In terms of the other intergroup attitudes, for minority students, ethnic identification had a small yet statistically reliable mediational role for three of the remaining variables. Specifically, ethnic identification was shown to mediate the relationships between membership in an eth-

Table 10.8   The Indirect Effects of Student Organization Membership
             During Freshman and Sophomore Years on Intergroup
             Attitudes During Senior Year Through Ethnic Identification
             During Junior Year for Minority and White Students

Dependent Variable in Senior Year	Minorities		Whites	
	Size of Indirect Effect	t-Value for Indirect Effect	Size of Indirect Effect	t-Value for Indirect Effect
Social policy				
Opposition to increasing diversity on campus	−.01	−1.77	.03	1.49
Opposition to affirmative action	−.00	<1	.04	1.93*
Social identity				
Ethnic activism	.03	2.46**	.08	3.16**
Common ingroup identity[a]	.00	<1	.00	<1
University attachment	.02	2.08*	.02	1.29
Ethnic prejudice				
Ingroup bias	.02	2.21*	.02	1.50
Opposition to miscegenation	.01	1.64	.07	2.67**
Symbolic racism	.00	<1	.05	2.49**
Perceived group conflict				
Perceived ethnic discrimination	.02	1.64	.05	2.16*
Ethnic organizations promote separatism	−.01	−1.54	.03	1.83*
Perceived zero-sum group conflict	.02	2.10*	.03	1.22

Source: Sidanius, van Laar, Levin, and Sinclair 2004, reprinted with permission from the American Psychological Association.

[a] Common ingroup identity was first measured during freshman year, and therefore the freshman year variable is used as the control variable, and membership in student organizations during sophomore year is used as the independent variable.

* p < .05; ** p < .01 (for one-tailed test)

nic organization and university attachment, ingroup bias, and perceived zero-sum group conflict.

The Mediational Effects of Ethnic Identification for White Students

We used the same analytic strategy as employed for the minority students to examine the mediational effects of ethnic identification for white students. In this case, we uncovered small but significant mediated relationships for six of the eleven dependent variables examined (see table 10.8). Specifically, ethnic identification was shown to mediate the relationships between membership in a Greek organization and opposition to affirmative action, ethnic activism, opposition to miscegenation, symbolic racism, perceived ethnic discrimination, and the sense that ethnic organizations promote ethnic separatism.

Given the foregoing patterns of our results, and consistent with social identity theory, it appears that for both the minority students and the white students the effects of membership in ethnically oriented student organizations on intergroup attitudes were, at least partially, mediated by ethnic identification.

Summary and Conclusions

In this chapter, we have explored the intergroup antecedents and consequences of membership in ethnically oriented minority and Greek college student organizations among minority students and white students, respectively. Researchers using a multicultural framework have long argued that involvement in such student organizations, rather than increasing ethnic tensions on college campuses, is driven by a desire, at least among minority students, to engage in the broader university life and serves as a bridge to involvement in the broader university environment. In contrast, the logic of the social identity theory perspective would suggest that membership in an ethnically oriented organization, to the extent that it stimulates a politicized ethnic identification among minority students, is more likely to heighten ethnic segregation and exacerbate ethnocentric bias and tension. In speaking to these two discourses, and in contrast to the emphasis on minority organizations in the multicultural discourse, we argue that to the extent that membership in minority ethnic organizations affects minority students, membership in fraternities and sororities is likely to affect white students in a somewhat similar fashion.

Among minority students, our findings were more consistent with the expectations of social identity theory than with those of the multicultural perspective. However, in agreement with multicultural arguments and with previous empirical findings, our results did show that, among minority students, joining ethnically oriented student organizations was associated with high levels of ethnic identification and ethnic activism. Also in line with previous research within the multicultural tradition, we found that membership in such organizations among minority students led to an increased level of politicized identity (ethnic identification and ethnic activism).

On the other hand, and in direct contrast to previous research within the multicultural tradition, there was no indication that minorities' experiences in these ethnically oriented student organizations had the effect of increasing their sense of common identity with other ethnic groups or their sense of attachment to the wider university community. Furthermore, and in line with critics of multiculturalism, the evidence suggested that minority students' membership in ethnically oriented student organizations *increased* their perceptions that ethnic groups are locked into zero-sum competition and increased their feelings of being victims of ethnic discrimination. Also in line with the general expectations of social identity theory was the finding concerning the mediated effect of ethnic identification for minority students. All else being equal, membership in ethnic organizations among minorities increased their sense of ethnic identification, which in turn increased their perception of zero-sum competition among ethnic groups.

We have also reasoned that the conflict-inducing effects of membership in ethnically oriented student organizations should not be restricted to minority students but should be found among white students as well. Given the exclusionary history of fraternities and sororities on the American campus, we suspected that these organizations would tend to function as "ethnic clubs" for white students. Indeed, the data provided consistent evidence of the ethnic nature of Greek groups. First, white students were found to be significantly overrepresented in these organizations, while minority students were significantly underrepresented. Second, when we restricted analysis to white students only, we found that the probability of joining a Greek organization in college was significantly related to precollege levels of white ethnic identification.

Moreover, and in contrast to the findings among minorities, among white students, the decision to join a Greek organization showed a net association with outgroup prejudice. Thus, everything else being equal, the more ingroup bias white students displayed, the greater their likelihood of joining a Greek organization.

Membership in Greek organizations also appeared to have some effects on the ethnic and racial attitudes of white students. While such membership increased white students' attachment to the university as an institution, it also increased their opposition to an ethnically diverse campus, their belief that ethnic organizations promote separatism, their opposition to miscegenation, their levels of symbolic racism, and their sense of ethnic victimization (that is, their perceptions of ethnic discrimination). In other words, among whites membership in fraternities and sororities appeared to produce even more ethnocentric, conflict-inducing, and exclusionary effects than membership in ethnic student organizations produced among minority students. Furthermore, as with minority students, at least a portion of these conflict-inducing effects among white students were mediated by ethnic identification. In other words, membership in Greek organizations increased whites' ethnic-racial identity, which in turn affected a host of intergroup attitudes.

One of the more disturbing findings here was that membership in ethnically oriented student organizations appeared to increase the sense of ethnic victimization (the perception of being the target of ethnic discrimination) among both whites and minorities. The sense of group victimization has not been widely studied among contemporary social psychologists. There is strong ethnographic evidence, however, to suggest that this is a particularly central variable in driving intense intergroup conflicts around the world, as evidenced by events in Bosnia, Sri Lanka, Kosovo, Crimea, the Middle East, Northern Ireland, Rwanda, Sudan, and Kenya. Indeed, the sense of group victimization has shown itself to be easily "mobilizable," often with devastating effect.[7]

Of course, other research we have conducted using data from these students (reported in chapter 11) shows that such perceptions of victimization also appear to have important *benefits*. Specifically, controlling for earlier differences in actual abilities or skills among students, when black students make more attributions to discrimination in college they also perform better academically. Therefore, while possibly increasing ethnic tension on campus, the laying of blame more externally through perceptions of greater ethnic victimization may have important positive payoffs for minority achievement in college.

While some of the results reported here can be interpreted as being at odds with the limited research on the effects of ethnic organizations among minority students, our results, generally speaking, are clearly in line with the body of literature concerning the effects of Greek organizations among white students. With a few exceptions, the available literature suggests that sororities and fraternities foster somewhat xenophobic, authoritarian, and prejudiced attitudes and values among white students.[8] Moreover, while there has been a tendency to associate ethnically oriented student organizations with ethnic minorities, our results suggest that some of the most powerful ethnic environments among white students come in the form of sororities and fraternities, which function, in part, as "ethnic organizations" for these white students. Thus, even on campuses as ethnically heterogeneous as UCLA in the late 1990s, and even with the nondiscriminatory flavor of their membership clauses, Greek organizations still seem to have some of the same exclusionary overtones that characterized them during all of the nineteenth century and most of the twentieth century. Even more interesting, at least at this major California university, our results suggest that Greek student organizations also appear to be nurseries for the sense of white victimization.

We must qualify our conclusions somewhat by recognizing the fact that it is possible that the discriminatory effects of the Greek system on the UCLA campus were so strong because of this school's relatively high degree of ethnic heterogeneity. Indeed, universities at which these trends have not been found appear to be substantially more ethnically homogeneous (see, for example, Lottes and Kuriloff 1994). Thus, one of the questions remaining to be answered is whether the effects of Greek and other ethnic student organizations vary as a function of factors such as ethnic heterogeneity. For example, a recent multicampus study by Stanley Rothman, Seymour Martin Lipset, and Neil Nevitte (2003) suggests that the sense of ethnic victimization among the white student body increases with increasing levels of black enrollment at the university. In other words, instead of decreasing ethnic tension, multiethnic university environments appear to have the exact opposite effects for white students.

To conclude, the effects of both minority and white ethnically oriented student organizations appear to be somewhat more antagonistic and less benign than has been suggested in prior research.

Chapter 11

Minority Ethnic Groups and the University Experience

In the last few decades, social science researchers have obtained a much better understanding of the social and psychological factors impinging on the achievements of ethnic minority students. Students from some ethnic minority groups are still underrepresented in higher education and show lower academic achievement than their white counterparts. Much of the literature on minority achievement has addressed why these gaps in achievement between white and minority students remain. In this chapter, we take a more focused look at the social-psychological experiences of members of traditionally underrepresented ethnic groups on the university campus, and we examine how these experiences may affect their academic performance.

The literature on the college experiences and outcomes of underrepresented minority students is substantial (see, for example, Allen, Epps, and Haniff 1991; American Council on Education 2002; Bowen and Bok 1998; Massey et al. 2002; Nettles 1988). Much of the literature focuses on the experiences of the most prototypical underrepresented minority groups, African American and Latino students. Research has examined the barriers at college entry for minority students, the extra challenges faced by minority students during college, and the higher attrition rates of minority students in college. A large proportion of this literature is devoted to a discussion of the campus climate for underrepresented minority students (see Hurtado et al. 1999). In general, this research indicates that, in addition to the academic, social, and economic stresses faced by all students, students from underrepresented minority groups face an extra category of stressors known as minority status stressors, which include achievement stresses, social stresses, within-group stresses, and interracial stresses (Smedley, Myers, and Harrell 1993). Minority students may face negative expectations from other students and staff, lower feelings of belonging and exclusion on campus, and experiences with prejudice and discrimination. These stresses exert their influences on well-being and academic outcomes directly as well as indirectly by exacerbating the effects of the academic, social, and economic stresses faced by students in general (Sedlacek 1989; Tracey and Sedlacek 1984, 1985).

Differences in educational outcomes between white and minority individuals are most apparent in college education. While the gap in the rates at which blacks and whites completed at least high school began to close from 1971 to 2000, the gap between white and black high school graduates with at least some college remained similar, and the gap between blacks and whites who completed college widened (National Center for Education Statistics 2001). Similarly, while among Latinos there were increases in completion rates across all levels of education between 1971 and 2000, the differences in educational attainment between Latinos and whites remained about the same at every educational level.

However, Asian Americans are an exception. In 1995 Asian Americans and Pacific Islanders constituted the largest proportion of minority students at top research universities, accounting for 11 percent of the undergraduate enrollment (as compared to 2 percent of national undergraduate enrollment). On many campuses, Asian American students are considered a model minority—an immigrant group who came from a relatively disadvantaged background to achieve high levels of college participation and achievement. However, Asian students do not form a monolithic group. Within the Asian American superordinate group there are smaller subgroups, such as Filipino and Southeast Asian students (most of whom are Vietnamese in our sample), whose college experiences and precollege disadvantaged backgrounds are more similar to those of black and Latino students.

The purpose of this chapter, then, is to highlight the experiences of the minority groups in the sample who came from relatively disadvantaged backgrounds: African American, Latino, Southeast Asian, and Filipino students. Using white students as a comparison group, we conduct four main sets of analyses.[1] First, we examine differences in the academic backgrounds and academic preparation of the white and minority students. Second, we examine changes in academic performance and related variables among these ethnic subgroups over the college years. Third, we examine the degree to which noncognitive factors predict the academic performance of students within these ethnic groups. Fourth and finally, we explore the degree to which minority students' academic achievement is related to their belief that they were admitted to UCLA under affirmative action.

Students' Academic Backgrounds and Academic Preparation

There are likely to be important differences between the white and minority students in the anticipatory socialization for college that they received. Parental education is one important aspect of this socialization. High school graduates whose parents did not attend college tend to be less prepared academically, to receive less support from their families in planning and preparing for college, and to report lower educational expectations than peers whose parents did attend college (National Center for Education Statistics 2001; see also Billson and Terry 1982; Terenzini et al. 1994). We therefore examined the educational level of the parents of the students in the subsample and noted whether they were the first in their family to attend college.[2]

The results from these analyses indicate that the fathers of white students had the highest education level, followed by the fathers of Filipino, African American, and Southeast Asian students, respectively, and that the fathers of Latino students had the lowest average level of education. The mothers of white and Filipino students had the highest average education level, followed by the mothers of black students and Southeast Asian students, and the mothers of Latino students had the lowest education on average. Latino students were also significantly more likely than other students in the sample to be the first in their family to attend college. White and Filipino students were significantly less likely than other students to be the first in their family to go to college, with African American and Southeast Asian students falling in between.[3]

We also examined whether students in the different groups participated in the summer orientation program for new students. Student orientation programs are often the first orientation of nontraditional students to the norms of the institution and the expectations about their performance as college students (Terenzini et al. 1994). Controlling for incoming differences between students, studies have shown that students attending an orientation program develop higher levels of social integration during college and higher subsequent commitment to the institution than students who do not attend such an orientation. In turn, this higher level of social integration and commitment to the institution positively affects persistence (Pascarella, Terenzini, and Wolfe 1986). In 1996 UCLA had a generic orientation for all students, as well as a separate session that gave priority to students involved in a program for underrepresented minorities. Whereas 97 percent of white and all Filipino and Southeast Asian students participated in the generic orientation for all students, only 47 percent of African American students and 55 percent of Latino students attended this generic orientation. An additional 19 percent of black students and 15 percent of Latino students participated in the separate minority-oriented session only.

In stark contrast to white, Filipino, and Southeast Asian students, relatively large numbers of black (37 percent) and Latino (31 percent) students attended no orientation at all. When combined with the parental education results, these findings suggest that black students and, especially, Latino students may have received lower anticipatory socialization for college than white, Filipino, and Southeast Asian students.

There is much discussion in the literature regarding the "underpreparation" of students of color for college academics. This research, most of which has been conducted on African American students, has found evidence that black students are on average less academically prepared than their white peers (Cabrera et al. 1999; Nora et al. 1996). The results from our own study show that students in all of the ethnic groups at UCLA had mean verbal and math SAT scores that were substantially above the 1995 national average for college-bound seniors: 428 for verbal and 482 for mathematics. This indicates that these students at this select university entered with very strong academic credentials. However, there were significant differences in SAT scores between the ethnic groups (see figure 11.1). White students had significantly higher SAT verbal scores than the other groups in the subsample. Scores for blacks and Latinos, groups with similar mean scores, were lower than those of the other groups, and Filipino and Southeast Asian students fell in the middle. On mean SAT math scores, white and Southeast Asian students scored the

Figure 11.1   Mean SAT Verbal and Math Scores for the Ethnic
Groups in the Subsample

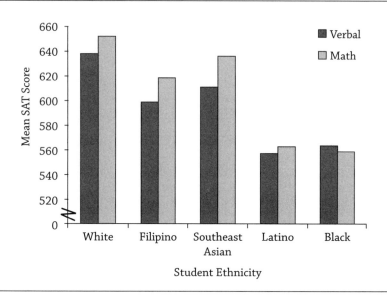

Source: Authors' compilation.

highest, followed by Filipinos (who did not differ significantly from the Southeast Asian students). Black and Latino students again scored the lowest on mean SAT math scores, and the two groups did not differ from each other.

In summary, the data reveal some similarities between black and Latino students. Relative to their white, Filipino, and Southeast Asian peers, black and especially Latino students received lower anticipatory socialization for college, and both groups were on average less academically prepared for college in terms of SAT scores.[4]

Changes over the College Years

To examine the orientation of students in the subsample toward academics through the college years, we explored a number of factors that have been examined in previous research. One of the specific concerns in the literature on minority achievement is that of the underperformance of students of ethnic minority groups, and of black students in particular, relative to white college students (National Center for Education Statistics 2001). In addition to examining students' academic performance, motivation, and commitment over the college years, we also examined the degree to which they discounted performance feedback as valid, "disidentified" from academics, and changed their self-evaluation over time.[5]

Academic Performance, Motivation, and Commitment

We measured both students' perceptions of their academic performance compared to other students at UCLA and their self-reported cumulative GPA in each of the years in college.[6] Examining perceptions of academic performance compared to other students, figure 11.2 indicates that white students perceive themselves as performing significantly better across the years than do other students in the subsample.[7] Also, while African American and Filipino students came into college expecting to do as well as white students did, their perceptions of their academic performance compared to other students dropped significantly in the first year of college and remained lower than whites across the remaining three years.[8] Latino and Southeast Asian students both began and ended college with lower perceptions of their academic performance relative to white students. As shown in figure 11.3, across freshman to senior years, white students also had an average GPA that was significantly higher than those of the minority ethnic groups.[9]

The importance of getting a high GPA declined significantly for all ethnic groups in the subsample, with no reliable differences across ethnic groups (not shown in figures). Whereas prior to college entry all students in the subsample considered getting a high GPA very important, by the end of the senior year of college, students in the subsample considered getting a high GPA significantly less important.[10] These results even hold for those who planned to continue with their education after the bachelor's degree, although for these students the importance of getting a high GPA declined to a lesser degree.

Regarding academic commitment, existing research shows that retention rates among African American students at predominantly white institutions are well below those of white students, and below those of African American students attending historically black institutions

Figure 11.2   Mean Perceived Academic Performance Compared
to Other Students at UCLA for Each of the Ethnic
Groups in the Subsample over Time

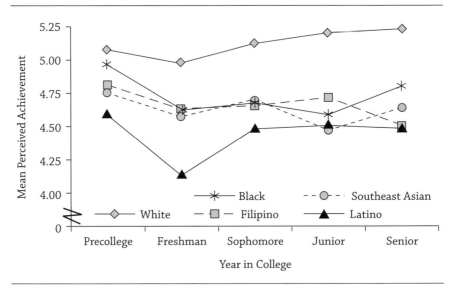

Source: Authors' compilation.

Note: Means are computed by wave for blacks, Filipinos, and Southeast Asians and with listwise deletion across
waves for whites and Latinos.

(Astin 1993). As figure 11.4 shows, for students of all ethnic groups in
this subsample, the tendency to think about dropping out of UCLA before earning a degree peaked at the end of freshman year and then declined. There are no significant differences in the patterns over time for
the different ethnic groups and no reliable differences between the ethnic groups in mean dropout considerations.[11]

By the summer of 2003, the end of the seventh year after college entry, 85 percent of the students in the subsample had obtained a bachelor
of arts or bachelor of science degree. Analyses of differences between the
ethnic groups, however, show that Latino and African American students were overrepresented in the group who did not obtain a degree by
this time, and white students were underrepresented in this group.
Southeast Asians and Filipinos did not differ from the percentages for
the subsample as a whole.[12] Of those students in the subsample who did
obtain a degree, the results also show that African American students

Figure 11.3   Mean GPA in College for the Ethnic Groups in the
                Subsample over Time

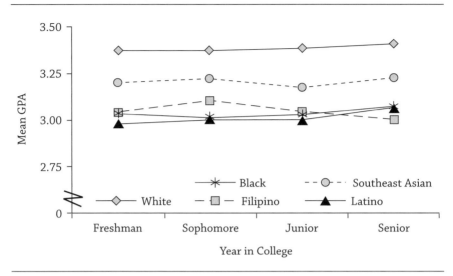

Source: Authors' compilation.

Note: Means are computed by wave for blacks, Filipinos and Southeast Asians and with listwise deletion across waves for whites and Latinos.

Figure 11.4   Mean Considerations of Dropping Out from College
                for the Ethnic Groups in the Subsample over Time

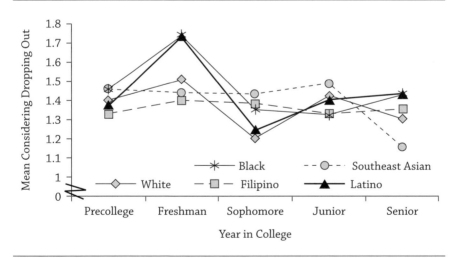

Source: Authors' compilation.

Note: Means are computed by wave for blacks, Filipinos, and Southeast Asians and with listwise deletion across waves for whites and Latinos.

and Latino students took significantly longer to get their degrees than did white students. While white students took an average of 4.38 years, African American and Latino students took 4.82 and 4.83 years, respectively, to obtain their degrees. Again, Southeast Asians and Filipinos did not differ significantly from the other groups, taking 4.68 and 4.61 years, respectively, to obtain their degree.

Discounting and Disidentification from Academics

One of the interpretations of the lower academic achievement of ethnic minority students emphasizes the role of discounting performance feedback as valid and disidentifying from academics (Crocker, Major, and Steele 1998; Fordham and Ogbu 1986).[13] Social-psychological research has shown that the suspicion that one has been discriminated against makes the cause of any feedback—both positive and negative—subject to uncertainty. To manage the attributional uncertainty regarding bias in performance evaluations by others, members of stigmatized groups may discount performance feedback as a valid indicator of skill and ability (Britt and Crandall 2000; Crocker et al. 1991; Crocker, Cornwell, and Major 1993; Major, Feinstein, and Crocker 1994; Schmader, Major, and Gramzow 2001). As shown in figure 11.5, and consistent with this reasoning, African American and Filipino students discounted academic feedback as valid more than all other ethnic groups across the college years, and Latino students discounted more than white students. Also, discounting increased significantly over time for all students, but especially for African American students.

The literature has also examined academic disidentification among minority students (Crocker, Major, and Steele 1998; Fordham and Ogbu 1986). Students are disidentified from academic performance to the degree that they consider their academic outcomes a less important part of their self-concept and to the degree that their feelings about the self are less responsive to feedback about academic performance. Jason Osborne (1995) directly examined the evidence for a dissociation between academic performance and self-esteem using the National Education Longitudinal Study (NELS), a national study of American high school students. He found that, during high school, the self-esteem of African American students became less related to academic performance, suggesting that black students devalue the academic domain as a source of

Figure 11.5   Mean Levels of Discounting Academic Feedback as Valid for the Ethnic Groups in the Subsample over Time

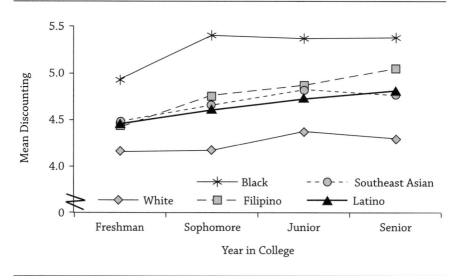

Source: Authors' compilation.

Note: Means are computed by wave for blacks, Filipinos, and Southeast Asians and with listwise deletion across waves for whites and Latinos.

their self-worth. The effects were strongest among black males but occurred to a lesser degree, and somewhat later, among black females as well. Meanwhile, the correlation between achievement and global self-esteem remained stable for white males and females. A further study showed no evidence of academic disidentification among Latino students (Osborne 1997).

Evidence for academic disidentification in college has been provided in an experimental study by Brenda Major, Steven Spencer, and colleagues (1998). They found that whereas white students showed the expected response of high self-esteem following success and low self-esteem following failure, black students' self-esteem was not responsive to either positive or negative feedback. Further results showed that black students were chronically more disengaged from the intellectual domain than white students and that racial priming led to a short-term situational disengagement. Furthermore, Major (1995) found that African American college students who were disidentified and disengaged had lower grade point averages, even when controlling for differences in SATs. In addition, African American students who were not doing well in college had higher self-esteem as they were less invested in school, whereas African American students doing well in college showed higher self-esteem following high investment in school. Ronald Taylor and his colleagues (1994) also showed that academic disidentification might be affected by perceptions of discrimination and prejudice. They found that the more discrimination African American high school students perceived, the less important they considered academic achievement and the less engaged they were in their schoolwork.

We measured disidentification from academics starting in the first year of college. As shown in figure 11.6, disidentification tended to increase for the subsample as a whole, especially in later years (between the end of sophomore and the end of senior year). Consistent with the literature, however, African American students at UCLA were significantly more disidentified from academics than the other ethnic groups in the subsample. Latino students were more disidentified than Filipinos, and Southeast Asian students tended to be the least disidentified from academics.

Self-Esteem

Theorists interested in motivation have long studied self-esteem because of associations between beliefs about the self and achievement behaviors. Self-esteem can derive from one's self-evaluation in multiple domains, such as academic competence, social acceptance, physical appearance, and athletic competence (Harter 1986). Individuals may, however, disidentify from one or more of these domains and base their self-esteem on other sources. Their self-esteem can then remain equally high or even increase, but it is no longer dependent on the old domains. In general, high self-esteem is seen to be a positive predictor of academic motivation and performance. Individuals who have high self-regard and strong feelings of self-worth are likely to be more motivated to engage in efforts to obtain higher outcomes (Astin 1993; Covington 1984a, 1984b; Rosenberg et al. 1995; Weiner 1985). Recent discussions in the literature, however, have also focused on the dangers of high (and especially unresponsive) self-esteem (see, for example, Baumeister, Heatherton, and Tice 1993; McFarlin, Baumeister, and Blascovich 1984). In his four-year longitudinal study of college students, Alexander Astin (1993)

Figure 11.6   Mean Levels of Disidentification from Academics for
Each Ethnic Group in the Subsample over Time

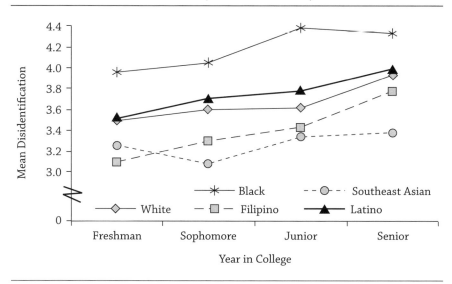

Source: Authors' compilation.

Note: Means are computed by wave for blacks, Filipinos, and Southeast Asians and with listwise deletion across waves for whites and Latinos.

found that college students who have high self-esteem have higher GPAs and are more likely to graduate with honors than students with equal ability levels but lower self-esteem, controlling for other differences. Positive self-esteem has also been shown to be particularly important in predicting the academic success of minority students on historically white campuses (Sedlacek and Brooks 1976; Tracey and Sedlacek 1984, 1985).

As shown in figure 11.7, and consistent with existing literature (for reviews, see Crocker and Major 1989), African American students in the sample evidence significantly higher mean self-esteem than all other ethnic groups.[14] Also, the mean self-esteem of African American students showed a marginally significant increase from precollege to the end of the first year in college and then remained stable. All other ethnic groups, however, showed rising mean levels of self-esteem during the college years, approaching that of black students. Combining these results with those for academic disidentification and academic perfor-

261

Figure 11.7   Mean Self-Esteem for Each Ethnic Group in the
Subsample over Time

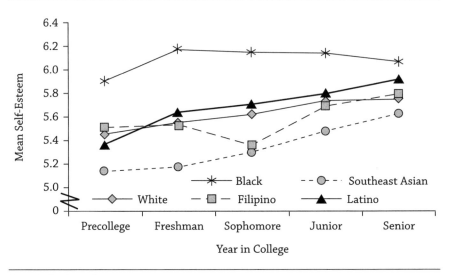

Source: Authors' compilation.

Note: Means are computed by wave for blacks, Filipinos, and Southeast Asians and with listwise deletion across waves for whites and Latinos.

mance suggests that black students were basing their self-esteem on domains other than academics and that the academic disidentification and discounting evidenced by them allowed them to maintain high self-esteem in the face of lower performance.

Summary of Changes over the College Years

In summary, white students' perceptions of their relative academic performance and their mean GPA across the college years were higher than those of the other students in the subsample. The end of freshman year, however, appears to be a particularly vulnerable time for all students. Perceptions of academic performance compared to other students at UCLA tended to decline, and considerations of dropping out of college before earning a degree, tended to peak at this time. The importance of getting a high GPA declined over the college years for all ethnic groups, and both discounting academic feedback as valid and disidentification from academics increased significantly over time for all students, but especially for African American students. Overall, mean levels of discounting and disidentification were also the highest for black students, as were mean levels of self-esteem across the college years. This suggests that black students were basing their self-worth on factors other than the academic domain. Like their Latino peers, black students were less likely than white students to have obtained a bachelor's degree by the end of their seventh year after college entry, and of those who did obtain one, their time to degree completion was significantly longer than that of white students.

Cognitive and Noncognitive Predictors of Academic Performance

These results show that traditionally underrepresented minority students differ from white students on a number of variables. Black and Latino students in particular show more doubts about their academic performance and display higher levels of discounting and disidentification from academics than white students. The literature on achievement among minority groups indicates that such noncognitive predictors of performance play an important role in explaining differences in academic achievement between white and ethnic minority students (Massey et al. 2002; Pascarella and Terenzini 1991; Sedlacek 1989; Sedlacek and Brooks 1976; Tracey and Sedlacek 1984, 1985; see also Oliver, Rodriguez, and Mickelson 1985). In this chapter, we examine seven noncognitive predictors of academic performance: disidentification from academics, self-esteem, feelings of belonging, several variables related to curriculum, participation in student organizations, the ethnicity of friends, roommates, and dates, and a number of ethnic outlook variables. Our main interest is in determining whether these noncognitive variables affect subsequent academic performance when differences between students in cognitive variables are taken into account. The cognitive variables that we control for are SAT verbal and math scores, GPA at the end of freshman year, and students' average GPA in their major. We use SAT scores and GPA at the end of freshman year as measures of cognitive potential, and we use the average GPA of students in their major to control for mean differences in GPA between majors.

We first examine how the ethnic groups in the subsample differ in terms of means on these noncognitive experiences and perceptions. We then consider whether these variables add anything in explaining the academic performance of the ethnic groups in the subsample beyond what can be accounted for by the cognitive factors. In each case, we take students' average on the noncognitive variable across the freshman, sophomore, and junior years and then use this as a predictor of subsequent academic performance.[15] We examine three indicators of academic performance: senior year GPA, whether the student had received a degree by the end of the seventh year after college entry, and how long it took the student to obtain a degree.[16]

In the first stage of these analyses, we examine the impact of the cognitive variables on the three indicators of academic performance. When the four cognitive variables (SAT verbal scores, SAT math scores, freshman GPA, and average major GPA) are entered into separate regression analyses for the five ethnic groups in the subsample, we find that they explain 65 percent of the variance in senior year GPA for white students, 45 percent for Filipinos, 61 percent for Southeast Asians, 43 percent for Latinos, and 58 percent for black students. Regarding degree attainment seven years after college entry, the cognitive variables explain 9 percent of the variance for white students, 10 percent for Filipinos, 21 percent for Southeast Asians, and 8 percent each for Latino and black students. The cognitive variables explain a smaller percentage of the variance in time to degree: 3 percent for white students, 5 percent for Filipinos, 7 percent for Southeast Asians, 1 percent for Latinos, and 6 percent for black students. Thus, the results show that the cognitive variables play an important role in predicting senior year GPA, but they are substantially weaker predictors of degree attainment and time to degree.

In the second stage of our analyses, we compute partial correlations between each of the noncognitive predictors and each of the three dependent measures of academic performance, controlling for the four cognitive variables. In these analyses, we are interested in examining whether each of the noncognitive variables predicts academic performance at the end of college relative to the academic potential with which students began college. Again, we conduct the analyses separately for each of the ethnic groups. In the third and final stage, we conduct regression analyses to determine which of the noncognitive variables uniquely predicts subsequent academic performance when they are all examined together. Unfortunately, the few Filipino (n = 92) and Southeast Asian (n = 83) participants in the study does not allow us to examine the unique impact of noncognitive variables for the two Asian subgroups.

We thus examine the unique influence of the noncognitive predictor variables for whites, Latinos, and blacks, whose numbers are large enough to allow an acceptable number of cases per predictor variable in the equation.

To reduce the number of predictors in each of these regression analyses, we conduct these analyses in several steps. In the first step, we control for the cognitive variables. We then enter the noncognitive predictors (averaged over freshman through junior years) whose partial correlations are significant for any of the five groups in the subsample for any one of the three dependent variables. In a series of steps, we then eliminate nonsignificant predictors to generate a list of noncognitive predictors that show significant relationships with academic performance relative to cognitive potential for at least one of the subgroups on one of the three dependent variables.[17]

The results show that the noncognitive variables explain unique variance beyond that explained by the cognitive variables. For white students, the noncognitive variables explain another 4 percent of the variance in senior year GPA, 10 percent in whether students obtain a degree or not, and 3 percent in how long it takes them to obtain a degree. For Latino students, the extra variance accounted for is 6, 10, and 10 percent, respectively, and for black students it is 7, 8, and 16 percent, respectively.

We first discuss each of the noncognitive variables in turn, showing the means for the five ethnic groups in the subsample on the noncognitive variables and discussing the partial correlation and regression results when the noncognitive predictors show statistically significant relationships with the outcome variables. The means for the noncognitive predictors are shown in table 11.1.[18] The variables that show significant partial correlations are presented in table 11.2.

Disidentification from Academics

There is substantial evidence in the literature to suggest that academic disidentification may be a risk factor for minority students, especially for African American students. As shown earlier, black students were more disidentified from academics than other students in the subsample. To limit the number of variables used in the regression analyses in predicting the academic performance of the subgroups in the sample, we factor-analyze items related to disidentification to form a coherent

(Text continues on p. 272.)

Table 11.1 Means on the Noncognitive Variables Averaged Across Freshman, Sophomore, and Junior Years, by Ethnic Group

Noncognitive Variable	White	Filipino	Southeast Asian	Latino	Black
Disidentification factor (0 to 1 scale)	.36[b]	.34[b]	.33[b]	.37[ab]	.40[a]
Self-esteem (1 to 7 scale)	5.64[b]	5.52[bc]	5.23[c]	5.68[b]	6.13[a]
Feelings of belonging factor (1 to 7 scale)	3.68[b]	3.82[ab]	3.60[abc]	3.87[a]	3.24[c]
Number of white professors	7.12[a]	6.59[ab]	6.99[ab]	5.88[b]	5.72[b]
Number of Asian professors	1.04[b]	1.50[a]	1.30[ab]	.97[b]	.90[b]
Number of Latino professors	.60[b]	.42[b]	.49[b]	1.13[a]	.52[b]
Number of black professors	.29[b]	.30[b]	.25[b]	.30[b]	.73[a]
Number of female professors	2.89[a]	2.50[a]	2.43[a]	2.76[a]	2.62[a]
Number of ethnic studies courses taken each year (0 to 1 scale)	.29[b]	.31[ab]	.27[b]	.35[a]	.34[a]
Feelings of admission due to affirmative action (1 = definitely no, 7 = definitely yes)	1.53[c]	3.04[b]	2.85[b]	3.83[a]	3.09[b]
Membership in fraternity or sorority (0 = no, 1 = yes)	.31[a]	.06[b]	.04[b]	.09[b]	.04[b]
Membership in ethnically homogeneous fraternity or sorority (0 = no, 1 = yes)	.16[a]	.01[b]	.02[b]	.02[b]	.03[b]

Number of other student organizations to which one belongs	1.40[b]	1.51[ab]	1.48[ab]	1.38[b]	1.73[a]
Perceived ethnic discrimination (1 to 7 scale)	2.26[c]	2.89[b]	2.75[b]	2.91[b]	3.57[a]
UCLA does not promote diversity (1 to 7 scale)	3.13[c]	3.56[bc]	3.58[bc]	3.77[b]	4.51[a]
Personal identity stereotype threat (1 to 7 scale)	2.51[c]	3.03[b]	3.72[a]	2.40[c]	2.17[c]
Social identity stereotype threat (1 to 7 scale)	2.33[c]	3.73[b]	3.90[ab]	4.10[ab]	4.47[a]
Pressure from one's own group not to interact with members of other groups (1 to 7 scale)	2.10[d]	2.57[bcd]	3.10[ab]	2.52[c]	3.27[a]
Ethnic activism (0 to 1 scale)	.23[d]	.45[c]	.42[c]	.51[b]	.59[a]
Expectations of future socioeconomic status (1 to 7 scale)	4.66[a]	4.42[b]	4.36[b]	4.11[c]	4.52[ab]
Attributions for future economic life outcomes (1 = mostly internal, 7 = mostly external)	3.06[c]	3.94[ab]	3.66[b]	3.97[ab]	4.17[a]
Intergroup competence (1 to 7 scale)	6.06[a]	5.98[ab]	5.63[b]	5.85[b]	6.02[ab]
Permeability of ethnic-status hierarchy (1 to 7 scale)	5.07[a]	4.78[ab]	4.93[ab]	4.66[b]	4.04[c]
Stability of ethnic-status hierarchy (1 to 7 scale)	3.30[b]	3.63[ab]	3.74[a]	3.56[a]	3.86[a]

Source: Authors' compilation.

Note: The percentages for participation in the summer orientation program for minorities and the mean numbers of friends, dates, and roommates for each ethnic group are not in this table. For all variables, higher numbers indicate greater levels of the construct. The number-of-professors variables indicate the actual average number of professors from each of the groups per year; these numbers and the number of student organizations range from 0 to the highest number a participant may have reported. Analyses of variance examining mean differences between the groups were significant for each noncognitive variable, with the exception of ethnic differences in the number of organizations students were members of and ethnic differences in permeability. Means with different superscripts in a row differ significantly from one another, p < .05.

Table 11.2 Partial Correlations and Product-Moment Correlations Between Noncognitive Predictor Variables and Three Measures of Academic Performance Relative to Potential, by Ethnic Group

Predictor Variable	Outcome Variable	White (n = 179 to 764)		Filipino (n = 52 to 92)		Southeast Asian (n = 39 to 83)		Latino (n = 198 to 466)		Black (n = 88 to 144)	
		$r_{partial}$	r	$r_{partial}$	r	$r_{partial}$	r	$r_{partial}$	r	$r_{partial}$	r
Disidentification factor	Senior year GPA	-.26***	-.49***	-.09	-.30*	-.12	-.25*	-.28***	-.41***	-.17+	-.31***
	Degree attainment	-.19***	-.30***	-.11	-.20+	-.11	-.11	-.14**	-.20***	-.06	.02
	Time to degree	-.05	.00	.06	.05	-.07	-.07	-.08	-.06	-.09	-.07
Self-esteem	Senior year GPA	.03	.08+	-.02	.02	.43**	.31*	.11*	.13**	.14	-.01
	Degree attainment	.03	.05	.07	.10	-.18	-.20	-.02	-.01	.03	-.01
	Time to degree	-.13**	-.12**	-.02	-.02	-.04	.00	.01	.01	-.22*	-.17+
Feelings-of-belonging factor	Senior year GPA	.02	.10	-.03	.07	.24+	.16	.13*	.13**	.21*	.20*
	Degree attainment	.26***	.28***	.19	.23+	.37**	.20+	.14*	.15**	-.09	-.07
	Time to degree	-.04	-.03	-.16	-.12	-.07	.02	.08	.07	.07	.02
Number of white professors	Senior year GPA	.15**	.18***	.02	-.04	.08	.08	-.08	-.07	.19	.01
	Degree attainment	-.09	-.05	.27+	.20	-.08	-.05	.00	.00	-.26*	-.30**
	Time to degree	-.06	-.07	-.08	-.10	-.20	.18	-.08	-.07	-.20	-.19
Number of Asian professors	Senior year GPA	-.12*	-.17**	-.08	.05	.01	-.01	-.04	.00	-.08	.05
	Degree attainment	.01	-.03	-.28*	-.21	.01	-.01	-.07	-.07	.17	.21*
	Time to degree	.09+	.10*	-.04	.00	.23	.22	.02	.02	.09	.09
Number of Latino professors	Senior year GPA	-.06	-.13*	-.04	.01	-.17	-.14	.11+	.06	-.11	-.20+
	Degree attainment	.08	.05	-.02	.02	-.14	-.16	.03	.03	.02	-.01
	Time to degree	-.02	-.01	.32*	.31*	-.11	-.10	.07	.07	.16	.17

Variable	Measure										
Number of female professors	Senior year GPA	.05	.02	.29*	.19	.14	.08	.11	.12*	.09	.04
	Degree attainment	.02	.02	.23	.25+	.07	.06	-.04	-.02	.08	.07
	Time to degree	-.02	-.02	-.15	-.15	-.07	-.04	-.02	-.03	.15	.15
Number of ethnic studies courses taken each year	Senior year GPA	.07	.09*	.20	.11	.12	-.02	.16**	.12*	.05	.13
	Degree attainment	.18***	.19***	.12	.15	.17	.16	.22***	.22***	.09	.10
	Time to degree	.04	-.06	.02	-.03	-.05	-.05	-.08	-.09+	.02	-.02
Nonparticipation in summer orientation for minorities	Senior year GPA	.05	.04	.07	.16	.23+	.24+	.05	.03	.07	.09
	Degree attainment	.01	.02	.14	.17	.10	.10	.01	.00	-.02	-.01
	Time to degree	.03	.03	.11	.14	-.09	-.08	-.15*	-.14*	-.09	-.10
Feelings of admission due to affirmative action	Senior year GPA	.00	-.14***	-.06	-.19	-.17	-.38**	-.11	-.17**	.05	-.08
	Degree attainment	-.02	-.07	-.07	-.06	.03	-.01	-.13*	-.15**	.13	.09
	Time to degree	.00	.02	.02	-.03	.07	.01	-.04	-.04	.04	.05
Membership in fraternity or sorority	Senior year GPA	-.01	.02	.03	.16	.07	.08	-.02	-.04	-.08	-.13
	Degree attainment	.05	.06	.06	.10	.11	.11	.04	.02	.16	.13
	Time to degree	-.03	-.03	-.09	-.04	.00	.01	-.12*	-.11+	.07	.07
Number of other organizations to which one belongs	Senior year GPA	.09	.22**	-.26+	-.16	.23	.34*	-.02	.11	-.05	-.06
	Degree attainment	.03	.08	.06	.02	-.15	-.08	-.10	-.06	-.07	-.07
	Time to degree	.11	.09	-.18	-.14	.02	.03	.12	.11	.38**	.37**
Number of white friends and dates	Senior year GPA	.04	.02	.08	.16	.33*	.25*	.03	.07	.10	.18*
	Degree attainment	.06	.06	.06	.05	.24+	.22+	-.06	-.05	-.07	-.02
	Time to degree	-.07	-.07	.13	-.10	-.28*	-.24+	-.14*	.12*	.00	-.01

Table 11.2 Continued

Predictor Variable	Outcome Variable	White (n = 179 to 764)		Filipino (n = 52 to 92)		Southeast Asian (n = 39 to 83)		Latino (n = 198 to 466)		Black (n = 88 to 144)	
		$r_{partial}$	r	$r_{partial}$	r	$r_{partial}$	r	$r_{partial}$	r	$r_{partial}$	r
Number of Latino friends and dates	Senior year GPA	-.05	-.11*	-.14	-.16	.00	-.02	.00	-.04	-.01	.00
	Degree attainment	-.03	-.06	-.04	-.03	.07	.08	-.02	-.03	-.19*	-.18*
	Time to degree	.02	.03	.02	.00	-.17	-.18	.11+	.10+	.02	.02
Number of black friends and dates	Senior year GPA	-.10*	-.12**	-.01	.01	.04	.05	.12*	.15**	.02	.10
	Degree attainment	.00	-.02	.08	.10	.02	.03	.00	.02	-.13	-.11
	Time to degree	-.10*	-.09*	-.10	-.08	-.11	-.11	.03	.02	-.03	-.06
Number of white roommates	Senior year GPA	.09*	.02	-.05	.11	.24+	.25+	-.02	.07	-.07	-.14
	Degree attainment	.11*	.10*	-.03	.09	.10	.12	-.03	.00	.08	.04
	Time to degree	.01	.02	-.11	-.12	-.06	-.04	-.12+	-.12*	.04	.03
Number of Latino roommates	Senior year GPA	-.07	-.06	.11	.14	.03	.02	-.03	-.13*	.11	.05
	Degree attainment	.02	.01	.06	.01	-.17	-.15	-.04	-.07	.00	.00
	Time to degree	.03	.03	.02	.02	-.08	-.11	.20***	.19***	-.03	-.03
Number of black roommates	Senior year GPA	.04	-.11*	.11	.16	.07	-.02	.02	.06	.21*	.08
	Degree attainment	.02	-.03	.02	.10	.16	.14	-.03	-.01	.04	.02
	Time to degree	-.01	.00	-.03	.00	-.12	-.12	-.14	-.14	.01	.03
Perceived ethnic discrimination	Senior year GPA	.02	.03	.05	.11	-.04	-.16	-.03	.00	.03	.15+
	Degree attainment	.04	.05	.11	.09	.17	.08	.11*	.12*	-.01	.02
	Time to degree	-.02	-.03	.06	.04	.26+	.29*	.02	.02	-.01	-.03

UCLA does not promote diversity											
Senior year GPA	.05	−.01	.09	.25*	−.13	−.11	.00	−.03	−.06	.02
Degree attainment	.08+	.06	.12	.18	−.10	−.14	.10+	.04	.02	.03
Time to degree	.06	.06	.39**	.41**	−.04	.00	.05	.05	.19+	.17+
Social identity stereotype threat											
Senior year GPA	−.01	−.06	−.01	.00	.07	.10	.03	.03	.13	.21*
Degree attainment	−.04	−.06	.10	.07	.09	.12	.07	.07	.17+	.20*
Time to degree	.05	.06	.21	.20	.33*	.28*	.02	.02	.02	.02
Expectations about future socioeconomic status											
Senior year GPA	.00	.01	.00	.10	.30*	.21+	.02	.07	.12	.07
Degree attainment	.00	.00	−.10	−.01	.20	.19	−.07	−.05	−.14	−.14
Time to degree	.00	.00	−.25+	−.20	−.10	−.10	.04	.04	−.09	−.09
Intergroup competence											
Senior year GPA	−.01	−.01	−.08	−.08	.26*	.15	.03	.08	.08	.10
Degree attainment	−.03	−.03	−.07	−.04	−.16	−.16	−.03	−.02	.11	.13
Time to degree	−.04	−.04	−.17	−.18	−.21	−.19	−.11+	−.10+	−.09	−.08
Stability of ethnic-status hierarchy											
Senior year GPA	.03	.01	−.02	−.05	.10	.22+	.03	.03	−.21*	−.04
Degree attainment	.00	−.01	.03	−.07	−.17	−.18	.05	.05	.01	.04
Time to degree	−.02	.00	.02	.00	.07	.11	−.06	−.06	−.02	−.05

Source: Authors' compilation.

Note: $r_{partial}$ are the partial correlations between the noncognitive predictor variable (the perception or experience) and each of the outcome variables (GPA, degree attainment, or time to degree), controlling for the cognitive variables (SAT verbal, SAT math, GPA at end of freshman year, and average major GPA). The following noncognitive predictor variables were excluded from this table because their partial correlations with the outcome variables did not reach statistical significance for any ethnic group: number of black professors, membership in ethnically homogeneous fraternity or sorority, number of Asian friends and dates, number of Asian roommates, personal identity stereotype threat, pressure from one's own ethnic group not to interact with members of other groups, ethnic activism, attributions for future economic life outcomes, and permeability of the ethnic-status hierarchy. The variables assessing number of professors of a certain group are residualized for number of classes taken.

+ p < .10; * p < .05; ** p < .01; *** p < .001

factor assessing this concept. We combine items measuring self-reported disidentification from academics with items measuring dropout considerations, importance of getting a high GPA and hours devoted to studying or doing homework (both reverse-coded), and the discounting of academic feedback as valid.[19] The means for each of the ethnic groups on this disidentification factor across freshman through junior years are shown in table 11.1. The partial correlations reported in table 11.2 show that for white and Latino students, academic disidentification explains the senior year GPA and the likelihood that students obtained a degree, with more disidentification being associated with lower academic performance relative to potential. Southeast Asian, Filipino, and black students show no statistically significant relationships between disidentification and academic performance. Disidentification also had no influence on the time it took to obtain a degree for any of the groups. Disidentification emerges as a unique predictor in the regression analyses, with white and Latino students obtaining a higher GPA and white students being more likely to graduate when they are lower in academic disidentification.[20]

Self-Esteem

As shown earlier, and consistent with most other literature in the field (for reviews, see Crocker and Major 1989), across the freshman through junior years we find African American students in the sample to have higher self-esteem than the other ethnic groups in the subsample. In addition, Southeast Asian students had lower self-esteem than any other group, and white, Filipino, and Latino students fell in between (see table 11.1). The high self-esteem of black students could thus have provided a protective factor in maintaining high academic performance. Similarly, the somewhat lower self-esteem among the other groups in the subsample, especially Southeast Asian students, could have made them more vulnerable to the negative effects of low self-esteem on achievement. To the degree that the high average self-esteem of the black students in the sample was not responsive to negative feedback, it could have provided a risk factor for achievement (see Baumeister, Heatherton, and Tice 1993; McFarlin, Baumeister, and Blascovich 1984). The partial correlation analyses show, however, that self-esteem played a role in explaining senior year GPA only for Southeast Asian and Latino students, with higher self-esteem protecting performance relative to potential. Self-esteem had no influence on the likelihood of obtaining a degree for any of the ethnic groups, but the more positive the self-esteem of white and black students, the less time it took them to obtain a degree. Self-esteem did not emerge as a unique predictor in the regression analyses.

Feelings of Belonging in College

One of the most robust findings in the literature with regard to the achievement of ethnic minority students is the importance that feelings of belonging play in the academic achievement of minority students, and of African American students in particular (Jackson and Swan 1991; Smedley, Myers, and Harrell 1993; Tinto 1993; Tracey and Sedlacek 1985).[21] We combined three items into a feelings-of-belonging factor: perceptions that students at UCLA are all part of one group, perceptions that students at UCLA belong to different groups (reverse-coded), and perceptions that UCLA promotes positive interaction between groups.[22] As table 11.1 shows, African American students felt a significantly lower sense of belonging at UCLA, and Latinos a significantly higher sense, than other students in the subsample, with the other groups falling in between. High feelings of belonging on campus among Latino students have also been found in other research (Oliver, Rodriguez, and Mickelson 1985). These results suggest that a low feeling of belonging may well provide a risk factor for black students. Indeed, the results of the partial correlation analyses show that feelings of belonging play a role in explaining academic performance relative to potential for white, Southeast Asian, Latino, and black students. Specifically, higher feelings of belonging increased the senior year GPA of Latino and black students and increased the likelihood that white, Southeast Asian, and Latino students obtained a degree. Feelings of belonging did not influence the time it took students of any group to obtain a degree. In the regression analyses, feelings of belonging emerged as a unique and positive predictor of degree attainment for white and Latino students.[23]

Curriculum Variables

Curricular experiences on campus may indirectly affect the performance of students to the degree that they influence students' involvement and sense of belonging on campus. We examined whether students took part in the summer orientation program for minorities and the degree to which they felt that they might have been admitted to UCLA because of affirmative action, whether they were exposed to ethnic content in their classes, and whether they had classes with professors from each of the four main ethnic groups and with female professors.[24] We might expect that, for minority students, ethnic content in class materials and having professors of their own group might have been beneficial to maintain interest, uphold motivation, and provide a role model function (Hurtado et al. 1999; Marx, Brown, and Steele 1999; Marx and Roman 2002; Smith 1989). Such variables can be expected to have their impact by increasing the integration of minority students into the campus setting (Tinto 1975). We might then expect that having white professors would be less beneficial for minority students for the same reasons. It is not clear, however, what effects white professors would have for white students. There may be a similar role model effect that we see with minority students, but such an effect is rarely discussed in the literature. For students in general, the impact of female faculty is generally found to be positive, with the larger the number of women on the faculty, the less likely students are to drop out of college (Astin 1993). In his four-year study, Astin (1993) also found that the number of women faculty had a direct positive effect on the degree aspirations of students (controlling for other influences).

The results show that students in the subsample differed in the extent to which they had faculty of the various ethnic groups (see table 11.1). While all students had mostly white professors, there were significant differences between the ethnic groups, with the ethnicity of the professors matching the ethnicity of the students who took the most classes with them. Thus, African American students had significantly more black professors per year on average than did students in the other four ethnic groups. In addition, Latino students had more Latino professors, and Filipino—but not Southeast Asian—students had significantly more Asian professors compared to the other four ethnic groups combined. The number of female professors was similar for all the groups. As we see in the partial correlation analyses, the curriculum variables that explained how well students perform in college relative to their potential were the number of white, Asian, Latino, and female professors students had.[25] Specifically, the more white professors students had, the higher was the senior year GPA of white students. White professors had negative effects, however, on black students, with more white professors lowering the likelihood that black students would obtain a degree. More female professors positively affected the senior year GPA of Filipino students relative to their potential. Asian and Latino professors tended to negatively affect academic outcomes relative to potential. More Asian professors decreased the senior year GPA of white students and decreased the likelihood that Filipino students would obtain a degree. More Latino professors also increased the time it took Filipino students to obtain a degree. Having black professors did not significantly affect academic performance relative to potential for any of the ethnic groups. Only the number of white professors emerged as a unique predictor in the regression analyses, and it only affected white students, increasing their GPA as they had more white professors.[26]

As shown in table 11.1, students also differed in the degree to which they took ethnic studies classes; black and Latino students on average took more ethnic studies classes than white and Southeast Asian students. Filipino students did not differ from the other groups in the number of ethnic studies classes taken. The partial correlations show that having more ethnic content in one's courses had a positive effect on both white and Latino students' degree attainment and on Latino students' senior year GPA relative to potential. In the regression analyses, the number of ethnic studies classes taken emerged as a unique predictor for white and Latino students, who obtained a higher GPA and were more likely to graduate as they had more classes with ethnic studies content.[27]

As discussed earlier in this chapter, students in the subsample differed in their participation in the summer orientation for minorities (not shown in table 11.1). While 36 percent of black students and 30 percent of Latino students attended the orientation for minorities, only 4 percent of Filipinos, 6 percent of Southeast Asian students, and 1 percent of white students attended the minority orientation.[28] The partial correlations show that participation in the summer orientation for minority students was associated with increased time to obtain a degree for Latinos students.[29] Participation in summer orientation did not, however, emerge as a unique predictor in the regression analyses.

Students were also asked whether they felt they were admitted to UCLA because of affirmative action. As shown in table 11.1, Latino students were most likely to believe they might have been admitted through affirmative action, followed by African American, Filipino, and Southeast Asian students. White students were least likely of all groups to believe this. Examining the partial correlations shows that perceptions that one might have been admitted through affirmative action had negative effects on degree attainment for Latino students, with more such perceptions leading Latino students to be less likely to obtain their degree. The belief that one was admitted to UCLA because of affirmative action did not, however, emerge as a unique predictor in the regression analyses.

Participation in Student Organizations

In addition to these curriculum variables, we also examined participation in student organizations.[30] Again, we would expect such involvement to be beneficial for academic performance relative to potential to the degree that participation in student organizations binds students to the campus community (Tinto 1975), but potentially harmful to the degree that it distracts them from academic work. The means show that white students were more likely to be members of fraternities and sororities than any of the other groups (for further details, see chapter 10). White students were also more likely to be members of fraternities and sororities that were ethnically homogeneous, that is, that had a concentration of over 80 percent of members of their own ethnic group. The descriptive analyses also show that black students were members of significantly more organizations on average than were white and Latino students. Filipino and Southeast Asian students did not differ from the other groups. The partial correlations show that fraternity or sorority membership, but not membership in ethnically homogeneous fraternities or sororities (not shown in the table), decreased the time to degree for Latino students. However, membership in other organizations increased the time to degree for black students. The regression analyses showed that participation in student organizations emerged as a unique predictor for Latino and black students, increasing the time it took them to obtain a degree.[31]

The Ethnicity of Friends, Roommates, and Dates

Peer groups are thought to influence academic achievement through the individual's self-esteem and satisfaction, sense of competence and mastery, and stress and coping. We might expect that underrepresented minority students would show higher academic performance to the degree that they have peers on campus with whom they identify, who can provide support, and who can provide role models (Hurtado et al. 1999; Levin, van Laar, and Foote 2006; Marx, Brown, and Steele 1999; Marx and Roman 2002). We may find, then, that involvement with ingroup members is especially beneficial in protecting the academic performance of black and Latino students—the students who are most underrepresented on campus (see chapter 8). On the other hand, to the extent that involvement with peers of one's own ethnic group leads one to lower involvement in the larger campus or provides within-group pressures that may increase stress, we might expect that too many peers of one's own ethnicity could have a negative impact on achievement (Astin 1993; Contrada et al. 2001; Fordham and Ogbu 1986). In addition, research has found that friendships with white students, who constitute the majority ethnic group on campus, might be especially important for minority students in providing a sense of belonging to the campus and access to the social and material resources of this group (Graham, Baker, and Wapner 1984; McLaughlin-Volpe 2006).

We were able to examine the influence of the ethnicity of students' close friends, dates, and roommates.[32] In terms of differences between ethnic groups on these variables, there was one clear conclusion: students in the sample tended to have mostly friends, dates, and roommates who shared their ethnicity (for further details, see chapters 8 and 9). To limit the number of predictors in the analyses, we combined the friends and dates items of each ethnic group into one scale. The partial correlation analyses showed that among African American students, having more black roommates had positive effects on senior year GPA. The number of black friends and dates also positively affected Latino students' senior year GPA and reduced the time it took white students to obtain a degree, but having more black friends and dates reduced white students' senior year GPA relative to potential. Having Latino friends and dates lowered the likelihood that black students would obtain a degree, and having more Latino roommates increased the time it took Latino students to obtain a degree. The number of white roommates generally had positive effects on students' performance relative to potential. Having more white roommates increased white students' senior year GPA and increased the likelihood that they would obtain a degree. Having more white friends and dates positively affected the senior year GPA relative to potential of Southeast Asian students and lowered the time it took to obtain a degree for Southeast Asian and Latino students. Having Asian friends, dates, and roommates did not have a significant impact on academic performance relative to potential for any of the groups (not shown in the table). In the regression analyses, the number of black roommates uniquely and positively affected the GPA of black students and decreased the time it took Latino students to obtain a degree. The number of Latino roommates was also a unique predictor, increasing the time it took Latino students to obtain a degree.[33]

Ethnic Outlook

Much of the literature on minority students in college discusses the negative expectations, stereotypes, prejudice, and discrimination that these students still experience at predominantly white colleges (Hurtado et al. 1999). Although discrimination experiences can be blatant, research indicates that the more subtle day-to-day experiences with discrimination can be as stressful, if not more so (Landrine and Klonoff 1996; Lott and Maluso 1995; Swim, Cohen, and Hyers 1998; see also Essed 1991; Swim et al. 2003). Asian American students, often perceived to be a group that is free from such negative experiences, also report personal experiences of discrimination. In fact, on campuses where Asian American enrollments have increased substantially, Asian American students report more instances of discrimination than any other group on campus (Hurtado et al. 1999; see also Lin et al. 2005). Examining the experiences of African American students at predominantly white colleges, William Sedlacek and Glenwood Brooks (1976) found that the ability to understand and deal with racism, the preference of long-term over short-term goals, and participation in community service were three of seven important noncognitive variables relevant in explaining black students' academic success. Such engagement with one's ethnic group as a response to experiences with prejudice and discrimination may buffer social identity and reduce the impact of negative climate variables (see also chapter 8). In our study, we were able to examine the importance of the following ethnic outlook variables in explaining academic performance relative to potential: campus climate variables, ethnic activism, expectations about future socioeconomic status, attributions for the future economic life outcomes of oneself and one's ethnic group, feelings of intergroup competence, and perceptions of the permeability and stability of the ethnic-status hierarchy.

Campus Climate Variables We examined several campus climate variables. The first measure, perceived discrimination, consisted of perceptions of discrimination against oneself and one's ethnic group at UCLA and the degree to which one perceived professors at UCLA as biased against one's ethnic group.[34] As shown in table 11.1, the ethnic groups differed significantly in attributions to discrimination. Black students perceived more discrimination on campus than any other group. White students perceived less discrimination than any other group, and students in the other groups fell in between. Second, we examined the degree to which students felt that UCLA did not promote diversity.[35] Black students were most likely to perceive that UCLA lacked a commitment to diversity, followed by Latino students. White, Southeast Asian, and Filipino students were most positive about UCLA's promotion of diversity.[36]

Third, we examined the degree to which students were thinking about the stereotypes about the academic performance of their ethnic group. The results show that Southeast Asian students, followed by Filipino students, were most concerned about personal identity stereotype threat (that is, they were most likely to wonder whether the stereotypes about the intelligence of their ethnic group were true of them personally), as compared to the other groups combined. Fourth, regarding social identity stereotype threat (concerns that one's own academic performance might affect how others viewed one's ethnic group), the results show that white students suffered less from such concerns than any of the other groups, followed by Filipino students. Black students suffered from such concerns more than Filipino and white students, and Latino and Southeast Asian students fell in between Filipino students, on the one hand, and black students, on the other.[37]

Examination of our fifth and final campus climate variable, pressure from one's own ethnic group not to interact with members of other groups, shows that black and Southeast Asian students felt the most pressure, followed by Filipinos and Latinos. White students perceived the least such pressure.[38]

Ethnic Activism We also asked students the degree to which they were intending to or had engaged in actions on behalf of their ethnic group, including signing petitions, participating in demonstrations, and voting in terms of what was good for their ethnic group. As shown in table 11.1, African American students showed the highest ethnic activism, followed by Latino students. The intentions of black and Latino students to engage in ethnic activism were significantly higher than those of any of the other ethnic groups in the subsample, and those of white students were significantly lower than those of all other groups.

Expectations and Attributions Regarding Future Economic Outcomes   We also asked students about their expectations for their own future socioeconomic status and that of their ethnic group. As shown in table 11.1, white students had the highest expectations for themselves individually and for their ethnic group over the freshman through junior years. Interestingly, African American students had the next-highest expectations, with Latino students having the lowest expectations. Southeast Asian students and Filipino students fell in between black and Latino students. In addition, we examined how students explained these future outcomes: did they attribute them more to internal or external causes?[39] As shown in table 11.1, white students made significantly fewer external attributions for their future economic outcomes than all other groups, followed by Southeast Asians students, who made significantly fewer external attributions than black students. Filipino and Latino students fell in between black and Southeast Asian students.

Intergroup Competence   When asked about how competent students felt interacting with people from different ethnic groups, white students exhibited significantly more interethnic competence than Southeast Asians and Latinos.[40] Filipino and black students fell in between white students, on the one hand, and Southeast Asian and Latino students, on the other.

Perceptions of the Permeability and Stability of the Social Structure   In our final descriptive analyses, we examined students' perceptions of the permeability and stability of the ethnic-status hierarchy. The analyses show that black students perceived the ethnic-status hierarchy to be significantly less permeable than did students of any of the other groups, followed by Latino students. White students considered the ethnic-status hierarchy to be significantly less stable than did blacks, Southeast Asians, and Latinos.

When we examined whether these ethnic outlook variables played any role in explaining academic performance relative to potential in the partial correlations, we found that making more attributions to discrimination against oneself and one's ethnic group increased the likelihood that Latino students would obtain a degree. We also saw that perceptions that UCLA did not promote a diverse student body increased the time it took Filipino students to obtain a degree. Greater perceptions of social identity stereotype threat increased the time it took Southeast Asians to earn a degree relative to potential, and greater perceptions of the stability of the ethnic-status hierarchy lowered senior year GPA relative to potential among black students. On a positive note, however, we found that, for Southeast Asian students, high expectations about their future socioeconomic status and feelings of intergroup competence were protective for senior year GPA. In terms of unique predictors, the regression analyses showed that black students obtained a lower GPA relative to potential as they perceived the ethnic-status hierarchy to be more stable. In addition, white students were less likely to obtain a degree if they were concerned about social identity stereotype threats.[41]

Summary of the Analyses Examining Noncognitive Predictors of Performance

We made it very hard to find any effects of noncognitive experiences and perceptions on academic performance—controlling as we did not only for the other noncognitive variables but also for SAT scores, for the student's own earlier GPA at the end of freshman year, and for whether the student was in a major with a higher or lower average GPA. Despite this, we still found significant and substantial effects of many of the noncognitive experiences and predictors on senior year GPA, on whether students obtained a degree, and, if so, on how long it took them to obtain that degree.

As found previously (Pascarella and Terenzini 1991; Tracey and Sedlacek 1985), some noncognitive variables assume an especially important role in explaining the academic performance of minority students. For white students, noncognitive predictors explain a small additional amount of the variance in academic outcomes beyond the variance explained by the cognitive variables. However, for Latino students, these percentages are higher, and for African American students even higher still. These results underscore the disturbing finding from previous research that, in addition to the academic, social, and economic stresses that can affect the academic performance of all students on college campuses, students of color also face minority status stressors. These stressors include achievement stresses compounded by negative stereotypes about their group's academic performance and interracial stresses compounded by negative campus racial climates (see Hurtado et al. 1999; Smedley, Myers, and Harrell 1993). Particularly noteworthy is the finding that, whereas the cognitive variables can explain only 6 percent of the variability in the time it took black students to earn a degree, the noncognitive variables together explain 16 percent of this variability.

The most consistent finding was the unique and negative effect of academic disidentification on senior year GPA and on whether students obtained a degree. Both white and Latino students showed these negative effects of academic disidentification. Although earlier results showed black students to be particularly high in academic disidentification, we found that this did not independently affect the academic outcomes of these African American college students. This is consistent with existing literature on disidentification in this group (Crocker, Major, and Steele 1998; Fordham and Ogbu 1986; Major 1995; Osborne 1995). Although the product-moment correlation between academic disidentification and senior year GPA was statistically significant for African American students, the partial correlation controlling for the cognitive variables was not.[42] Therefore, the cognitive variables weakened the effect of disidentification for black students, and this effect did not reemerge in the regression analyses when the other noncognitive variables were taken into account.

Another factor that has emerged in the literature is concern over the low sense of belonging that many minority students feel in predominantly white institutions. In the regression analyses, both white and Latino students showed negative effects of low feelings of belonging at UCLA. The lower their feelings of belonging, the less likely they were to obtain a degree. While we did find that black students were lowest in their sense of belonging on campus, we did not find that this low sense of belonging explained achievement relative to potential for black students once we had taken the other noncognitive variables into account.[43] Again, it appears that black students had set up other ingroup-based support systems that buffered them from negative effects of low belonging (see chapter 8).

We were especially interested in the impact that ethnic outlook variables would have on academic performance. We found that some of these variables uniquely and negatively contributed to performance once we had taken into account the other variables. For white students, more concerns about social identity stereotype threat had negative effects on academic performance, decreasing the likelihood that white students would obtain a degree. For black students, perceptions of the stability of the ethnic-status hierarchy were especially detrimental, with greater perceptions of stability decreasing the senior year GPA of black students relative to potential.

Peers also had significant effects on performance relative to potential for black and Latino students. Specifically, having more black roommates was a unique and positive influence on the senior year GPA relative to potential of black students and on the time to degree of Latino students. Meanwhile, having more Latino roommates increased the time it took Latino students to obtain a degree, as did participating in more student organizations for black and Latino students.

Another consistent finding concerns the unique effects of taking classes with ethnic studies content. For white and Latino students, taking these classes increased GPA and the likelihood that they would obtain a degree. Having more white professors was also beneficial for white students' senior year GPA. The positive effect of white professors could be explained for white students in terms of a role model function, or through identification with the professor.

Taken together, these results indicate that if we are to explain students' senior year GPA, degree attainment, and the time it takes them to earn a degree—three measures of academic performance that heavily influence students' educational, career, and socioeconomic aspirations—we should consider not only the standard cognitive variables, such as their SAT scores and freshman year GPA, but also a number of noncognitive variables, such as their academic disidentification and belonging, the ethnicity of those they associate with, the ethnic content of their classes, and their ethnic outlook.

In the final section of this chapter, we take a closer look at a potentially more complex relationship involving the concerns that black and Latino students might have about confirming the negative stereotypes about their group's academic performance. While we found in the previous section that personal and group concerns about stereotypes did not have a direct impact on black and Latino students' academic performance, the next section examines whether these two types of concerns about confirming stereotypes play a more complex role in moderating the potentially stigmatizing effects of perceived affirmative action admission on students' academic performance.

Affirmative Action and Academic Performance: The Moderating Effects of Stereotype Threat

One of the major discussions on campus during the time this study was conducted was about the issue of affirmative action. The class of students followed in this study (the class entering in the fall of 1996) was the last class admitted under affirmative action policies at the University of California.[44] Under affirmative action, ethnic and socioeconomic disadvantage could be used as "plus" factors in university admissions decisions. The affirmative action policy continues to be quite controversial, with some objecting that it is unfair to white students who wish to pursue a college education at selective universities. Of concern here is another objection that has been raised—that admission through affirmative action policies has a stigmatizing effect on beneficiaries' academic performance. That is, students' academic performance may be negatively affected simply by their having been admitted through a method that may lead to questions about their ability or skills. The existing literature on the potentially stigmatizing effects of affirmative action is quite mixed. Overall, the literature suggests that affirmative action has stigmatizing effects on students' outcomes under certain circumstances, such as when the affirmative action procedure is not clear (Truax et al. 1998; Turner and Pratkanis 1994).[45] Also, students may be more vulnerable than employed individuals to the unintended ill effects of affirmative action, since students are typically younger and live in a highly evaluative world (Truax et al. 1998).

We examined the impact of perceived affirmative action admission on academic performance for the African American and Latino students in the subsample, the groups most closely associated with the affirmative action issue. More specifically, following work on stereotype threat, we investigated whether the stigmatizing effect of perceived affirmative action admission would not occur for all students, but rather would occur only to the degree that students were worried about confirming the negative stereotypes about their group's academic performance (Steele 1997; Steele and Aronson 1995). The concept of "stereotype threat" helps explain how the burden of a negative stereotype may affect performance by diverting attention away from the task at hand to concerns about stereotype confirmation for the self or group. We examined two types of stereotype threat: a concern that the self fits the stereotype (personal identity stereotype threat) and a concern that one's behavior confirms the image others have of one's group (social identity stereotype threat). Of special interest was academic performance during the first year of college, when students make their first adjustments to the college environment.

To examine the potentially stigmatizing effect of affirmative action admission, we measured perceived affirmative action admission status by asking students prior to college entry whether they believed they were admitted through affirmative action.[46] We found that, prior to college entry, 57 percent of black students and 72 percent of Latino students believed that they might have been or definitely were admitted under affirmative action. (In comparison, only 10 percent of white students believed that they might have been or definitely were admitted through affirmative action.) Substantial numbers of black and Latino students are thus potentially at risk from the stigma of affirmative action. To examine this risk level, we split the Latinos and African Americans in our sample into two groups: those who believed that they might have been or definitely were admitted through affirmative action and those who believed that they were not admitted through affirmative action.[47] As shown in figure 11.8, perceived affirmative action recipients (those who believed at college entry that they might have been or definitely were admitted through affirmative action) showed significantly lower achievement one year later (the end of their freshman year).[48] Examining these results in terms of GPA shows that at the end of the first year of college, the average GPA was 2.9 for those who believed that they might have been or definitely were affirmative action recipients and 3.1 for those who believed that they were not.

Some of this lower academic performance is explained by lower SAT scores. Latinos and blacks who perceived themselves as affirmative action recipients entered college with significantly lower SAT math scores (541 and 516 for Latino and black affirmative action recipients, compared to 554 and 549 for Latino and black nonrecipients, respectively). In addition, Latinos (but not blacks) who perceived themselves as affirmative action recipients entered college with significantly lower SAT verbal scores (536 and 551, compared to 569 and 547 for Latino and black nonrecipients, respectively). This alone could account for their lower achievement a year later.[49] When we look at the impact of SAT math and verbal scores on first-year academic performance, however, we find that affirmative action status is still related to performance even when we control for differences in SAT scores between students.[50]

Having controlled for actual differences in SAT scores between stu-

Figure 11.8   Mean Academic Achievement One Year After
College Entry as a Function of Ethnicity and Feeling
of Being Admitted to UCLA Because of
Affirmative Action

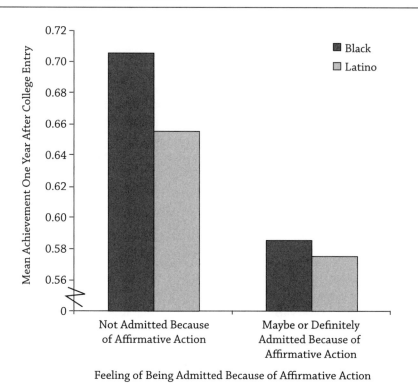

Source: Authors' compilation.

dents, we examined whether stereotype threat moderated this still existing relationship between affirmative action status and achievement in
the first year. We expected that only when students experienced stereotype threat would there be a negative relationship between the stigma of
affirmative action status and achievement. When there was no stereotype threat, we expected to find no relationship between students' perceptions of themselves as affirmative action recipients and their first-
year achievement. As the two types of stereotype threat (personal and
social identity) are only moderately correlated (r = .28, p < .001), we ex-

amined the role of both types of stereotype threat separately in moderating the relationship between affirmative action status and achievement.[51]

We first looked at personal identity stereotype threat as a moderator, regressing academic achievement on the interaction between affirmative action status and personal identity stereotype threat for black and Latino students (for the regression procedure, see Aiken and West 1991). The results show that personal identity stereotype threat was indeed a moderator of the effect of affirmative action status on achievement. As expected, simple slope analyses show that, for those who were low in personal identity stereotype threat, there was no relationship between affirmative action status and achievement. For those who were high in personal identity stereotype threat, however, there was a significant negative relationship between affirmative action status and achievement, such that those students who felt that they were admitted because of affirmative action performed less well during their first year when they experienced high personal identity stereotype threat.[52] Therefore, fears for the self, reflected in concerns that the negative stereotypes of one's group might be true of oneself, moderated the effect of affirmative action status on first-year performance.

Moving on to social identity stereotype threat, we found the same results. Social identity stereotype threat was a (marginally) significant moderator of the effect of affirmative action status on achievement. As expected, simple slope analyses show that, for those who were low in social identity stereotype threat, there was no relationship between affirmative action status and achievement. For those who were high in social identity stereotype threat, however, the stigma of affirmative action status negatively affected achievement, such that students who felt that they were admitted because of affirmative action performed less well when they experienced high social identity stereotype threat.[53] Therefore, fears for the group, reflected in concerns that one's academic performance would affect how others viewed the group, also moderated the effect of affirmative action status on first-year performance.

Summary of Analyses Examining the Moderating Effects of Stereotype Threat

The results show that black and Latino students who felt that they were admitted because of affirmative action showed negative effects of the stigma associated with this policy on academic performance. The students showed these negative effects, however, only when they were subject to stereotype threat, such as when they thought about whether the negative group stereotypes were true for themselves or whether their own performance reflected negatively on their group. The results thus show that stereotype threat concerns for the self and for one's ethnic group assume an important role in explaining when members of stigmatized groups can protect the self from stigma and when they are unable to do so. Further analyses show that students' level of ethnic identification influenced whether group or personal concerns over stereotypes were most powerful in determining the effects of affirmative action status on their academic performance. Those highly identified with their ethnic group were most susceptible to the impact of group concerns, and low identifiers were most susceptible to the impact of personal concerns (van Laar, Levin, and Sinclair in press).

Summary and Conclusions

In this chapter, we have highlighted the experiences of four ethnic minority groups—African Americans, Latinos, Southeast Asians, and Filipinos. Using whites as a comparison group, we examined mean levels of academic preparation, changes in a number of different variables over the college years, and noncognitive predictors of academic performance for these ethnic groups. We also examined factors that influenced the academic achievement of black and Latino students who felt they were admitted to UCLA because of affirmative action.

As expected, black and especially Latino students received lower anticipatory socialization for college. In addition, black and Latino students were on average less academically prepared for college in terms of SAT scores than the white students in the sample.

The analyses of changes over the college years in students' academic orientation and self-evaluation revealed the challenges facing students of all ethnic groups, and minority students in particular. All students tended to face academic challenges at the end of their freshman year, when they were most likely to have negative perceptions of their relative academic performance and to think about dropping out of college. Academic motivation also tended to decline over the college years for students of all ethnic groups. Both disidentification from academics and the tendency to discount academic feedback as valid increased over time for all students, but especially for black students. In addition, averaged over the college years, mean levels of disidentification and discounting were the highest for black students, indicating that black students were more vulnerable to the academic challenges faced by all students, but they were also protected by higher mean levels of self-esteem across the college years compared to other students. Like their Latino peers, black students' perceptions of their relative academic performance and their mean GPA across the college years were lower than those of white students. They were less likely than their white counterparts to have obtained a bachelor's degree by the end of their seventh year after college entry, and those who did obtain a degree by this time took longer to do so than their white peers.

As we attempted to explain these differences between white and ethnic minority students in academic outcomes at the end of college, we examined both cognitive and noncognitive variables that could play a role. The influence of the cognitive variables—especially students' GPA at the end of their freshman year—was as strong as we would expect. Together, SAT verbal and math scores, freshman GPA, and the average GPA of students in one's major explain 43 to 65 percent of the variance in senior year GPA. These variables explain a smaller amount (8 to 21 percent) of the variance in whether students did or did not obtain a degree within seven years after college entry, and a smaller amount yet (1 to 7 percent) in the time it took students to earn a degree.

Our main interest in this chapter was to determine whether noncognitive variables such as academic disidentification, ethnic outlook, and the ethnicity of the students' professors, friends, dates, and roommates affect subsequent academic performance when differences between students in cognitive factors are taken into account. As found previously (Pascarella and Terenzini 1991; Tracey and Sedlacek 1985), the noncognitive variables do assume an especially important role in explaining the academic performance of the minority students. For white students, the noncognitive predictors explain an additional 4 percent of the variance in senior year GPA, 10 percent of the variance in whether students obtain a degree or not, and 3 percent of the variance in time to degree. For Latino students, the additional percentage of variance explained by the noncognitive predictors is 6 percent for senior year GPA and 10 percent for degree attainment and time to degree. For African American students, these percentages are even higher at 7 percent for senior year GPA, 8 percent for degree attainment, and 16 percent for time to degree. As we suspected, these results indicate that Latino and African American students faced both achievement stresses that were compounded by negative stereotypes about their group's academic performance and additional stresses that were compounded by negative campus racial climates. These minority status stressors had a particularly strong impact on African American students, for whom the noncognitive variables together explain as much as 16 percent of the variability in the time it took them to earn a degree.

In our last set of analyses, we examined how concerns about confirming negative group stereotypes affected the academic performance of African American and Latino students who believed they were admitted to UCLA under affirmative action. These findings revealed both good and bad news. The bad news is that when black and Latino students were concerned that the negative stereotypes about their group's intellectual ability might be true of them or that their academic performance would affect how others viewed their group, the possibility that they might have been admitted to college under an affirmative action program significantly lowered their subsequent academic performance. However, the good news is that when these students were less concerned about the negative group stereotypes, there was no relationship at all between their perceptions that they were admitted through affirmative action and their subsequent academic performance. These findings should ease the concerns of those who oppose affirmative action precisely because they believe that it stigmatizes the people it is supposed to help. Students who come in under affirmative action only show such stigmatizing effects when the stereotypes of their ethnic group are a threatening element of the campus racial climate.

Taken together, these findings emphasize the important role that a positive campus racial climate can play in protecting minority students' psychological well-
being and academic achievement. Existing research shows that attempts to increase the numerical representation of minority students on college campuses (structural diversity) can have positive effects in terms of educational outcomes and changes in sociopolitical attitudes and values for many students. However, this research has shown that a focus on structural diversity alone—without addressing larger negative campus climate issues—can have negative effects on campus race relations (see Astin 1993; Gurin 1999; Hirose 1998; Pascarella et al. 2001). The results reported in this chapter support this conclusion. Specifically, a student's perception that he or she was admitted to UCLA under affirmative ac-

tion did not have harmful effects on later academic performance, unless that student was concerned about the negative stereotypes about his or her group. These stereotypes are part of a larger set of minority status stressors that can undermine minority students' psychological and academic outcomes both directly and indirectly, by exacerbating the effects of the academic, social, and economic stresses experienced by students in general. As such, we would urge institutions of higher education, as they focus on achieving greater structural diversity, to make concerted efforts to communicate to students of all ethnic groups that the institution is committed to maintaining a positive campus racial climate (Hurtado 1992; Hurtado et al. 1999).

PART IV

CONCLUSIONS

Chapter 12

Summary and Theoretical Integration

This volume began with the observation that a strikingly rapid process of ethnic diversification has been unfolding in the United States over the last forty years. Indeed, the United States, as well as most First World nations, is now home to a vibrant mix of bloodlines, skin tones, languages, and cultural practices. In the United States, this diversification has been driven by a coalescence of forces, including dramatically increased levels of both legal and illegal immigration since 1965, when a series of immigration reform measures was set into motion, and relatively high birthrates among these immigrant groups at a time when birthrates among Americans of European ancestry are on a visible downswing.

In many nations other than the United States, similar processes of ethnic diversification are under way and sometimes ethnic relations are playing out in similar ways. The United States differs from other Western nations, however, in one very important respect: until 1965, this country had a legalized system of segregation and discrimination that applied specifically to blacks, who at the time made up roughly 10 percent of the population. Under this "Jim Crow" system, blacks were classified as second-class citizens—that is, as a separate, inferior "racial" caste. Notably, because this system and its antecedents in slavery had been in place since the founding years of the nation, virtually no other minority group in the United States (Native Americans excepted) was treated in quite the same way. In virtually no other Western nations have similar systems of this scale been put in place.

The Diversity Challenge

The Jim Crow system in the United States officially ended in 1965 (though its formal and informal dissolution has been slow). This was just at the time when immigration rates exploded. Thus, Americans began to attend to issues arising from the resulting ethnic diversification at the same time as they began to grapple with the official reversal of four-hundred-year-old laws permitting the oppression of black Americans. This is the political and social context in which ethnic diversification, and many of the steps taken to respond to it, has occurred in the United States.

An early application of the American multicultural agenda was the effort to integrate African Americans into the almost-all-white higher education system. Various practices were put in place to facilitate this integration. Ironically, these practices were soon applied not just to African Americans but also to many of the new immigrants, largely from Asian and Latin American countries, who were flooding into the United States. These immigrants have been incorporated relatively quickly into the higher education system. However, the integration of African Americans has been, and continues to be, a slower process. Against this backdrop, our story in this volume has taken a keen interest in understanding the particular issues faced by different ethnic groups and the distinctive paths taken by each.

The particular locale of our research within the larger American context also deserves comment. This research was conducted with students at UCLA in the late 1990s. It is well known that the college experience can be pivotal in sculpting social and political attitudes. These attitudes are formed and reformed throughout the life span, but the college years are believed to provide people with a relatively extensive exposure to novel ideas and information. Just as importantly, these years provide students with what are sometimes their first experiences interacting with members of various social, economic, and ethnic groups on approximately equal footing. As a result, important social and political views are thought to "take hold" in college. If the underpinnings of people's diversity-related attitudes—their causes, correlates, and consequences—are to be better understood, then college students seem to be an ideal population to study.

In what ways is UCLA itself a unique research site? To begin with, relative to many other universities, UCLA has long shown a particularly deep concern about diversity-related issues, and the university has an extensive system of diversity-related initiatives in place. UCLA is also considered the premier public university in the second-largest metropolitan area of the United States and is thus a training ground for the future elites of all ethnic communities. Furthermore, amid the diversification of the United States as a whole, California has become one of the most diverse states and serves as a beacon of both the benefits and perils of an ethnically diverse society. For example, in colleges and universities across California, whites, Latinos, Asian/Pacific Islanders, and blacks make up 49 percent, 21 percent, 18 percent, and 8 percent of the student population, respectively. At UCLA, the ethnic demography shows even more of a shift, with no one group in a clear numerical majority. The proportion of Asian/Pacific Islanders at UCLA has climbed to 38 percent, while the proportions of whites, Latinos, and blacks are 34 percent, 15 percent, and 3 percent, respectively.

Therefore, this volume has sought to tell the story of how ethnic diversity is working in an extraordinarily diverse university setting. For several decades, the university has been committed to addressing diversity-related problems with "multicultural solutions." Like many of its counterparts across the nation, it has taken a variety of measures to address these problems (Association of American Colleges and Universities 2000). For example, the university has introduced ethnic studies majors, implemented ethnic studies research and teaching initiatives, established affirmative action admissions policies relating to ethnicity, and sponsored minority-targeted orientations, events, and tutorial programs. Further, the university has established programs that are intended to ease diversity-related tensions, and it has put into practice harsh punishments for students, staff, or faculty who violate or disrespect multicultural norms. Is this multiculturalism, in its many forms, working? Is UCLA witness to interethnic harmony and a sense of common purpose, or is there evidence of eroding interethnic relations and ethnic balkanization? These have been the core questions guiding our research, and ones that we sought to examine from a variety of viewpoints.

Our agenda in the remainder of this chapter is simply to address the question: What have we learned? More specifically, *does* multiculturalism "work," and if so, in what forms, for whom, when, and why? While there are no simple answers to these questions, there are several conclusions that can be drawn from our research. In discussing these conclusions, we return to the four overarching themes with which we began this volume: the acquisition of students' ethnic, racial, and political attitudes prior to college and their stability throughout the college years; the content and strength of ethnic identity and pan-ethnic identities and the ways in which ethnic identity intersects with students' national and university identities and their membership in ethnic student organizations; the effects of informal interethnic contact (contact with friends, dating partners, and roommates); and finally, the effects of a multicultural educational environment and the unique obstacles facing disadvantaged ethnic minority groups. Following these conclusions, we summarize our main research findings and offer a brief statement of what we see as the "bottom line" of our study.

The Acquisition of Sociopolitical Attitudes

One of the major themes we explored in this book was the acquisition of sociopolitical attitudes. What were students' attitudes like at college entry? Did their attitudes change across the college years? Were there notable differences in the attitudes of different ethnic groups, both at college entry and exit? In particular, how well and at what point were the new-immigrant groups—Asians and Latinos—incorporated into the American political and racial systems? We examined these questions in chapters 4 and 5, largely through the lens of symbolic politics theory (Sears 1983, 1993; Sears and Valentino 1997).

As will be recalled, symbolic politics theory posits that people hold attitudes of various strengths—ranging from attitudes that are unstable and functionally meaningless to those that are strong and enduring, which we call "symbolic predispositions." The symbolic politics view maintains that attitudes follow a "learning curve"—becoming progressively stronger and more crystallized until attitude acquisition is complete. We used two criteria for determining "complete socialization": conformity to the accepted norms of the individual's social groups and the crystallization of the individual's attitudes independent of content. This acquisition should proceed relatively quickly to the extent that people are exposed to intense attitude-relevant information. As a consequence, attitude acquisition should occur rapidly in some cases but not others. What happened in the present study? Was there evidence of strong preexisting sociopolitical attitudes already at college entry? Was there change across time through the college years? At what point was attitude acquisition complete? To address these questions we focused on two key attitudes: political conservatism (a composite of party identification and political ideology) and symbolic racism.

Attitudes at College Entry

We examined the students' attitudes at college entry in chapter 4. We began with white students, since they have been the focus of most of the previous literature. Upon entering college, the white students in our sample were a relatively liberal group: half self-identified as liberal Democrats, and one-third as conservative Republicans. Their political and racial views fell between those of the initially more conservative Asian students and those of the more liberal African American and Latino students. However, it was clear that all four ethnic groups initially tilted to the liberal side. Moreover, the white students already showed clear signs of conforming to the political and racial norms of their ethnic, gender, and religious subgroups.

Were these early, precollege attitudes meaningful and long-lasting? We approached this question in two ways. First, students' sociopolitical attitudes were not merely a reflexive imitation of their parents' attitudes or those of their social environments. Even at college entry, these white students' political orientations divided along the ideological fault lines common among white adults: liberal Democrats were more secular, less racially conservative, and more egalitarian than were conservative Republicans. In other words, the white students seemed to understand the standard conventional substantive meanings of partisanship and had adopted the political orientation appropriate to their fundamental values. The associations of symbolic racism with other relevant attitudes found among adults, such as antiblack affect, conservative outlook, and inegalitarianism, were already in place, but they were not particularly strong. White students' partisan socialization thus appeared to be nearly at typical adult levels, and their racial socialization seemed to be well along, even before they entered college.

Second, an important innovation in our study was the assessment of the crystallization of these students' early attitudes in terms of both internal consistency and stability over time. At college entry, white students' party identification and political outlook displayed levels of crystallization that were already close to typical adult levels in both respects. In addition, their acquisition of beliefs concerning symbolic racism was also near that of adults in general, though falling slightly behind political orientation. The crystallization of symbolic racism was already at typical adult levels in internal consistency, but its stability fell between the high stability of party identification, considered the gold standard for a stable political attitude, and the lesser stability of policy preferences and the components of social dominance orientation (SDO).

These sociopolitical attitudes of white students served as the benchmarks by which we assessed the socialization of the new-immigrant groups, Asians and Latinos. The major theoretical question was whether these groups' partisan and racial attitude acquisition could best be understood in terms of their relatively recent immigration. An assimilation hypothesis would lead us to expect that they would gradually become incorporated into the mainstream of American society, in much the same way the European immigrants did a century ago. However, they also might be understood in terms of their subordinate status as long-standing nonwhite minority groups treated by the broader American society as "people of color." Therefore, they might be subject to some of the same discrimination at the hands of the dominant white majority as experienced by African Americans.

What did we find? The evidence presented in chapter 4 generally supports the assimilation hypothesis. The ethnic minorities in this study were not uniformly more liberal in either their political or racial attitudes than whites at college entry. Latinos were markedly more liberal than whites at college entry, but Asians were more conservative. Especially important, ethnic minorities who had been residing in the United States for longer were no more liberal than more recent immigrants, despite greater potential exposure to color-based discrimination. In almost every case, the longer-resident Latinos and Asians were more conservative than the most recent immigrants. Second, the mainstream norms reflected in ethnic, gender, and religious cleavages among typical adults all emerged at college entry in all ethnic groups, though they were stronger among the white students. Similarly, Asians and Latinos did not show as strongly crystallized political orientations and symbolic racism as did whites at college entry. They were plainly not incorporated into the American sociopolitical system as much as whites were before they arrived at UCLA.

These differences between the new-immigrant groups and whites at college entry were partially, but not entirely, due to the presence of many recent immigrants in their ranks. The attitudes of the longer-resident Asians and Latinos were consistently more crystallized than those of the more recent immigrants. But the lesser crystallization shown by the new-immigrant groups was not wholly due to recent immigrants. Even the longer-resident Asians and Latinos showed less crystallization than did the white students. In short, the white students' socialization of key sociopolitical attitudes appeared to be close to typical adult levels at college entry, while those of Asians and Latinos were not.

The College Experience

What was the balance between continuity and change over the course of the white students' college careers? The first and perhaps most important finding is that continuity dominated change in political conservatism and symbolic racism. In terms of simple test-retest correlations, both political conservatism and symbolic racism were quite stable through the college years. However, the students' stable relative position on these attitudes was overlaid with evidence of meaningful aggregate changes. Most striking, the students became significantly more liberal over time. This liberalizing change occurred among all ethnic groups in about the same measure, appeared on almost all attitudes we measured, and emerged steadily through college rather than at any specific stage. In most cases, it reflected changes in initial attitudes, but in a few cases it reflected first-time acquisition of preferences. These changes seemed to reflect widespread responses to pervasive campus norms rather than just shifts among those most involved in campus life. In fact, immersion in the UCLA campus experience did not promote greater liberalization. Perhaps most important, ethnic differences in sociopolitical attitudes did not expand. The college experience may have provided much direct and indirect information about the victimization of minorities in American society, but it did not polarize ethnic minorities and whites. Instead, the data were more consistent with the assimilation hypothesis that a mainstream norm of liberalization through college would swing all ethnic groups to the left, regardless of immigration status.

Second, the gender gap enlarged substantially among whites, with the liberalizing effects of college being particularly dramatic for women. Partisan polarization over religion also increased among whites: the more secular gravitated to the liberal Democrat camp, and the more religious to the conservative Republican camp. In other words, the broader implications of political orientation became clearer to the white students with time. Among whites, liberal Democrats and conservative Republicans di-

301

vided even more sharply in terms of gender, symbolic racism, and religiosity by college exit; thus, all moved toward the cleavages typical of adult white Americans more generally.

Finally, we found substantial evidence that over time the college experience produced greater crystallization of whites' racial attitudes, but not their political orientations. True, the small minority of politically undecided students at college entry had virtually disappeared by college exit, but in general the white students' political orientations did not become more crystallized. The college experience helped clarify and strengthen the white students' attitudes about America's racial divide. However, regarding the political party system, crystallization had largely been accomplished by college entry.

What was the impact of college on the new-immigrant groups? By and large, the standard political cleavages among subgroups that we saw at college entry did not increase; nor did the crystallization of political conservatism increase very much. In contrast, the crystallization of symbolic racism increased substantially. In all ethnic groups, then, the college experience enhanced understanding of race in America.

The most recent immigrants showed the same pattern of liberalization as did whites and their longer-resident ethnic counterparts, suggesting that liberal campus norms had a pervasive effect across all groups of students. The initially lower levels of crystallization associated with recent immigration were less prominent after exposure to a college education, since all groups showed an increase in crystallization as they moved through college. Indeed, crystallization among native-born Asians resembled that of whites at college exit. Again, the exception was symbolic racism. By the end of college, symbolic racism played about the same role in forming partisan preferences for all groups, regardless of their immigration status. An especially noteworthy change is that, at college exit, the most recently immigrated Asians showed the same linkage between symbolic racism and political conservatism as did whites and their earlier-arriving Asian counterparts. This had not been the case at college entry. College seems to have been especially effective in socializing recent immigrants to the American racial system.

The differences between Asians and Latinos are also worth noting. Half of the Asians were immigrants and came from several different countries, while the vast majority of the Latinos were born in the United States and were of Mexican ancestry. The Latino students' largely Mexican origins and native-born status would appear to have facilitated more political solidarity. Indeed, at college entry, Latinos already seemed to be carving out a distinctive political bloc based on ethnic politics, a bloc that seemed to become more cohesive throughout the college years. By the senior year, there were few systematic individual differences among the Latino students in their political and racial attitudes, and thus few meaningful cleavages. Whether a consensual pan-ethnic political identity emerges in the future to facilitate that unity remains to be seen.

In the end, we were not fully able to distinguish the effects of college from other events that occurred at the same time in the surrounding environment. We speculated that the two presidential campaigns that book-ended the students' college experience helped increase the crystallization of political orientations at the beginning and end of college. A vigorous debate over the ending of affirmative action in UC admissions greeted the students as they entered college and may have helped to crystallize attitudes toward that issue. Simultaneously, the strenuous clashes over immigration that marked the early 1990s had waned by the end of the decade, which may explain the failure of attitudes toward immigration to become more crystallized.

Ethnic Identity

At the most general level, our study has examined whether increasing ethnic and racial diversity is producing ethnic balkanization in the United States, and particularly in institutions of higher learning. Chapter 6 considered the relevance of ethnic identity to such a process. Many contemporary universities emphasize multicultural policies to enhance equality across ethnic group lines. One possible side effect is that they may intensify students' identification with their own ethnic group, and that identification, in turn, may exacerbate cultural divisions.

The Content and Strength of Ethnic Identity

In chapter 6, we examined the issue of ethnic identity in light of the "people of color" and "assimilation" hypotheses offered in chapter 2. The people of color hypothesis suggests that the new-immigrant groups may be trapped behind the American color line just as African Americans have been. This might make their racial identity, and their perceptions of common fate and discrimination, more salient and powerful, perhaps generating ethnic balkanization. In contrast, the assimilation hypothesis predicts that immigrant minorities will assimilate to American society, even though it may take more than one generation and they may be exposed to prejudice and discrimination in the interim. The assimilation hypothesis emphasizes the central role of recent immigration as a determinant of strong ethnic identities. According to this hypothesis, with time, most immigrants should assimilate, weakening both ethnic identity and ethnic conflict.

We first looked at the content of the ethnic identities of the new-immigrant groups. What ethnic or racial labels do they use to describe themselves at college entry? Consistent with the assimilation hypothesis, these mainly first- and second-generation Americans tended to identify themselves in terms of their national origins rather than the pan-ethnic identities generally assigned to them in American society. To be sure, initially their ethnic identities were every bit as strong as African Americans' racial identities, as if they too were locked behind the color line. The best predictors of the strength of ethnic identification, however, were indicators of more recent family immigration, such as speaking a foreign language at home. Native-born Asians and Latinos had significantly weaker ethnic identification than did blacks. Moreover, strong ethnic identification was not rooted in Asian and Latino students' perceptions of societal ethnic discrimination against their own group. In other words, the main reason Asians and Latinos matched African Americans in the strength of their ethnic identification was that so many of them were recent immigrants, not because they felt badly discriminated against as people of color.

What about the effects of the college experience? The assimilation hypothesis would suggest that integration into a mainstream institution, such as a major university, would produce evidence of significant assimilation, such as the adoption of pan-ethnic identities and weakened ethnic identification. Symbolic politics theory, however, would caution that continuity of such attitudes might be more evident than dramatic changes, so the residual effects of recent immigration might persist through college. By contrast, the people of color hypothesis would suggest that a college education strengthens Asians' and Latinos' perceptions of societal ethnic discrimination and separate ethnic identities, just as it appears to do for African Americans.

In fact, the content of the new-immigrant groups' ethnic identities was largely unaffected by college. Asians and Latinos continued to refer back to their national origins, while whites and blacks continued to use the standard American pan-ethnic categories. The Asian students, in particular, continued to show evidence of national distinctiveness rather than adopting a uniform pan-ethnic identity that would permit political mobilization as "Asian Americans." The strength of the new immigrants' ethnic identification was also largely unaffected by college, showing high levels of stability both at the aggregate level (group means) and the individual level (test-retest correlations). Indeed, the best predictor of individual Asians' and Latinos' senior year ethnic identification was their precollege ethnic identification, which seemingly had already absorbed the effects of immigration. In contrast, African Americans developed stronger racial identities through college. While these findings are contrary to the people of color hypothesis, they also do not show any evidence of students assimilating in terms of ethnic identity within the college years. Instead, it appears as though assimilation of the new-immigrant groups is occurring across rather than within generations. This is consistent with the persistence of youthful orientations emphasized by symbolic politics theory. We saw this too in the initial chapters on partisan and ethnic-racial attitudes. Studies of the general adult population in Los Angeles County have also found that Latinos fit the assimilation model rather well (Citrin and Sears 2007; Sears and Savalei 2006). College does not seem to produce increased ethnic balkanization in terms of ethnic identity, despite the seemingly favorable conditions for it at UCLA.

This analysis treated Asians and Latinos as similar new-immigrant groups. Most of these findings held for both groups. In several respects, however, the people of color hypothesis fit the Latino students somewhat better than it fit the Asian students. Although the Latino students did not show increased ethnic identification across college, they were more likely to adopt an American pan-ethnic identity such as "Latino" or "Hispanic." Compared to Asian students, their ethnic identities were somewhat more politicized at college exit, and they were affected somewhat more by the amount of societal discrimination they experienced toward their ethnic group. That is, the Latinos seemed to show some indications of assimilation, but also some evidence of a politicized and separate ethnicity.

The treatment of blacks common in social structural theories, which view them as a self-conscious subordinate group, seems to match quite well with their subjective experience. Indeed, blacks experience stronger racial identity, common fate, and greater discrimination than do other minority groups (Sears and Savalei 2006). However, the treatment of Asian and Latino students as subordinated ethnic groups unified under the pan-ethnic identities assigned to them by American society does not seem to match their subjective experiences. Rather, they seem to be groups in transition whose resemblance to African Americans in terms of ethnic consciousness is primarily a function of the large number of new immigrants in their current ranks. Indeed, native-born Asians and Latinos seem to resemble whites more than blacks, with weaker ethnic consciousness. With rapidly increasing rates of intermarriage of Asians and Latinos with whites, it seems plausible that their distinctiveness will wane with the coming generations, as happened with the European immigrants of a century ago (see Alba and Nee 2003). If this portrait of gradual assimilation is accurate for today's Asians and Latinos, it would leave African Americans as a group uniquely and permanently ensconced behind the color line, consistent with the "black exceptionalism" hypothesis described in chapter 2.

Ethnic and Superordinate Identities

At several points in the book, we have explored the evolution of students' ethnic identity across the college years. We have paid close attention to the development and progression of ethnic identity among the new-immigrant groups (chapter 6). We have also examined how ethnic identification relates to symbolic racism, egalitarianism, and other intergroup attitudes (chapters 5 and 6), and we have explored the extent to which ethnic identification is shaped by particular extracurricular activities (chapter 10).

In chapter 7, we explored ethnic identification from yet another angle. Here we asked: How does ethnic identification intersect with students' broader American identification and, just as importantly, with their university identification? That is, how compatible is having a distinct ethnic identity with feeling oneself to be fully a part of larger national and university superordinate groups? Social scientists have long argued that intergroup tensions can be exacerbated when people cling to different subgroup identities, but that those tensions may be attenuated or even dispelled when people accept a common or superordinate ingroup identity. As a result, the compatibility of subgroup ethnic identities with broader, superordinate identities is at the heart of many multiculturalism debates.

The approach taken to this question in chapter 7 was informed by both the common ingroup identity model and social dominance theory (see Gaertner and Dovidio 2000; Sidanius and Pratto 1999). According to the common ingroup identity model, intergroup conflict is reduced to the degree that members of all ethnic groups are able to form and identify with a common, superordinate identity (that is, members of all ethnic groups in the United States strongly identifying themselves as American). According to social dominance theory, however, the degree to which members of diverse ethnic groups are able to form such a common ingroup identity (say, as Americans) depends on the "hierarchy-enhancing" versus "hierarchy attenuating" nature of the context. Broadly speaking, social dominance theory argues that dominant ethnic groups tend—as compared with subordinate ethnic groups—to have a sense of group identity that is more strongly tied to the larger national identity. And indeed, given that the most prestigious and salient roles in society are occupied by dominant rather than subordinate ethnic group members, and given that society is disproportionately organized to benefit the interests of dominant rather than subordinate ethnic groups, both dominant and subordinate ethnic groups are expected to associate the larger national image with the dominant ethnic group image. That is, dominant group members' ethnic identity should be seen by all groups as especially "fitting with" the overall national identity. Thus, given the very long history of racial apartheid in the United States (approximately the period between 1619 and 1964) and the disproportionate sociopolitical roles that continue to be played by members of subordinate and dominant ethnic groups within American society, within social dominance theory the national ("American") context can be classified as a relatively hierarchy-enhancing setting.

By contrast, in the culture of a university like UCLA, strong institutional efforts have been made to produce ethnic group equality over a substantial part of the university's history. Because of the very heavy emphasis placed on welcoming multiracial and multicultural institutional policies at UCLA (see the historical description of UCLA in chapter 3), and because racial prejudice appears to decrease with increasing exposure to the university environment (see chapter 5), there is some basis for classifying UCLA as a relatively hierarchy-attenuating institution. As a result, we expected that all ethnic groups, not just whites, would comfortably be able to lay claim to the common UCLA identity.

The Diversity Challenge

Given this line of reasoning, we expected that when dealing with a relatively hierarchy-enhancing superordinate identity, such as "American," members of dominant groups (whites) would show the highest levels of American identification, and that the levels of American identification would decrease among ethnic groups with decreasing social status within American society. Further, it was predicted that whites would show relatively more positive links between their ethnic identification and their American identification than would individuals in ethnic groups with lower social status. In contrast, both superordinate identification as a UCLA student and the relationship between identification as a UCLA student and ethnic identification were expected to be largely the same regardless of the social status of students' ethnic groups.

The data in chapter 7 were largely consistent with these predictions. The strength of American identification did tend to show a decline as the social status of the student's ethnic group declined. Furthermore, ethnic identification among whites was positively associated with American identification, but ethnic identification among minorities was either unassociated or negatively associated with American identification. On the other hand, the strength of students' university identification tended to be equal for all ethnic groups. Further, the correlation between the strength of university identification and the strength of ethnic identification tended to be equally positive for all ethnic groups. One interesting exception to these general findings was the higher level of university identification shown by Asian Americans compared with any of the other ethnic groups.

The main contribution of this chapter was to demonstrate that ethnic identification does not have to be incompatible with a larger community identity, such as a UCLA identity. To the extent that a larger community or society is relatively egalitarian, ethnic and superordinate identities can be compatible, and compatible to the same degree, across different ethnic groups. That said, the relatively strong attachment of Asian American students to the larger university identity was a curious finding. The proportion of Asian students on the UCLA campus has dramatically increased over the past two decades, with Asians now representing a plurality of the freshman class. This may explain why they feel a closer bond to the university identity than do students from other ethnic groups.

Ethnic Identification and Membership in Ethnically Oriented Student Organizations

Within this book, we also addressed the debate about ethnicity-centered social organizations. Some proponents insist that ethnic organizations on campus provide students with a "safe harbor" from which to engage in the larger university. Opponents maintain that these organizations simply encourage ethnic separatism. Based on social identity theory, a leading theory in the intergroup relations literature (see chapter 2), there is reason to believe that the opponents of ethnically based organizations are right at least in part. Social identity theory maintains, among other things, that ingroup identification contributes to ingroup bias. That is, the more people focus on their attachment to their particular ethnic group, the more they tend to favor that group relative to other groups. The research literature implies that ethnically oriented organizations, by cultivating students' sense of ethnic identification, are likely to increase ethnic biases and in turn to exacerbate interethnic relations. What did we find in this study concerning the effects of ethnic clubs and organizations on ethnic identification? Was there any support for a "pluralist" perspective, or were the opponents and social identity theorists more correct?

In chapter 10, we turned our attention to student involvement in ethnic clubs and organizations. We demonstrated that there are clear functional similarities between minority ethnic organizations and Greek organizations, and we argued that the latter serve as ethnic enclaves for white students. In our sample, substantial proportions of Latinos (29 percent), Asians (42 percent), and African Americans (60 percent), but virtually no whites (1 percent), were members of minority ethnic organizations. At the same time, 60 percent of the Greek system's members were white, making them substantially overrepresented in fraternities and sororities relative to their numbers in the general student body. Furthermore, minority ethnic organizations and Greek organizations showed some key parallels. For example, minority organizations attracted students with high levels of ethnic identification, and the ethnic identification of minority organizations' members tended to increase across time. Similarly, Greek organizations tended to attract white students with high levels of white ethnic identification, and the white identification of the Greek organizations' members also increased across time.

Of critical interest, and in line with social identity theory, we found that, for both minorities and whites, this growing ethnic identification partially mediated a host of relatively pernicious outcomes. For minorities, involvement with ethnic organizations failed to enhance a sense of common ingroup identity with other ethnic groups or to foster a sense of oneness with the university community at large. Rather, it actually served to sharpen perceptions of ethnic conflict and to heighten perception of ethnic discrimination. Earlier (in chapter 6) we found that four years of college did not strengthen students' ethnic identification and, in that sense, did not contribute to ethnic balkanization. However, ethnically based organizations do provide a location in which the process of ethnic balkanization takes place. Over time their members show more politicized ethnic identification, which in turn contributes to growing perceptions of zero-sum competition between ethnic groups, a core symptom of ethnic balkanization.

In parallel fashion, although whites' involvement with Greek organizations tended to increase their attachment to the university as a whole, it also increased a number of negative intergroup attitudes. Specifically, white students showed increases in their opposition to a diverse campus, their belief that ethnic organizations promote separatism, their opposition to miscegenation, their levels of symbolic racism, and their perception of ethnic discrimination. In other words, among both ethnic minorities and whites, membership in ethnic organizations and Greek organizations, respectively, resulted in ethnic identification enhancement, and this ethnic identification enhanced in turn helped to set into motion a wide variety of ethnocentric, conflict-inducing psychological and attitudinal outcomes. Notably, these processes were every bit as evident for whites as they were for minorities.

In contrast to the findings from most other chapters of this book, those uncovered in chapter 10 sound an alarm and point to a possible locus for institutional change. Socialization effects in the very well-populated, ethnically oriented minority and Greek organizations at UCLA were quite negative. Such effects conformed quite well to the expectations of social identity theory. Specifically, increasing the salience of people's ethnic ingroups can serve to raise walls between groups rather than to tear such walls down. Future multicultural efforts would therefore be wise to consider, and take to task, the value of organizations that focus attention on ethnic differences as opposed to ethnic similarities.

Ethnic Identities: On Defining "Diversity"

Finally, this discussion of ethnic identity would not be complete without recognizing the particular ways in which we have defined "diversity" and acknowledging the limitations of such an approach. Throughout the book, we have repeatedly made comparisons across ethnic groups. In many cases, in order to do so, we have herded our students into the standard four American pan-ethnic categories, which we have treated as mutually exclusive: whites, blacks, Asians, and Latinos. In doing so, we have implicitly taken the term "diversity" to mean interaction across these four major groups. This four-group scheme has some obvious shortcomings, however. Chief among them are the following concerns: biracial students, Native American students, and in some instances Middle Eastern students do not have a natural place among these four groups; the four-group scheme obscures important differences within pan-ethnic groups, such as between Koreans and Chinese or between Mexicans and Salvadorans; and subjective group identities are implied that may not in fact exist, such as the existence of "Asians" as a meaningful subjective in-group. Indeed, in chapter 6, when we looked at subjective identity, we found that about half of the putative "Asians" and "Latinos" in our sample preferred to self-identify with their specific national identities than with American pan-ethnic labels. In other cases, we looked at diversity in different ways. For example, in several sets of analyses we divided students into the categories of dominant (white) versus subordinate (minority). In chapter 11, we singled out Southeast Asian and Filipino students and studied them alongside Latinos and blacks. For the most part, however, our working definition of "diversity" followed the four-group pan-ethnic model.

In this final chapter, it is important to recognize the particularity of this working definition. We found important differences, not just among the four major groups, but also between immigrant students and native-born students. Immigrant status systematically varies across ethnicity. Thus, our research suggests a need to account for immigrant status or to incorporate it into the four-group model (see chapters 4, 5, and 6). Similarly, as suggested by social dominance theory (Sidanius and Pratto 1999), it very often does not make sense to draw conclusions about "minorities" as opposed to whites. In our research, Asians' frequent deviations from the patterns of both whites, on the one hand, and Latinos and blacks, on the other, underscored the difficulty of the simple white-

311

minority division. In a number of respects, African Americans in particular differ from other students, as in the notion of "black exceptionalism." To be sure, there are circumstances that fit the simple white-minority dichotomy or the four-group model. Nonetheless, our research suggests that different interpretations of the term "diversity" are likely to reap different results. Some of the potential problems with the two-group and four-group models should be kept in mind when considering this and other research.

Informal Contact: Friends, Dates, and Roommates

Another important question addressed throughout the volume is whether intergroup contact with roommates, fellow classmates, friends, and romantic partners tends to increase cooperation between different ethnic and racial groups or whether such contact creates intergroup tension and conflict. Earlier, we cited Allport's (1954) contact theory as one of the reigning viewpoints in social psychology about the effects of contact. In his theory, acquaintance potential is a key factor for intergroup contact to affect attitudes favorably. As a result, contact is more likely to have a positive effect in relatively intimate situations, such as between roommates, as opposed to more impersonal situations, such as in large classrooms. By contrast, other theories suggest that contact sometimes increases intergroup conflict. For example, realistic group conflict theory suggests that real conflicts of interest may well be exacerbated by direct, close, and sustained interaction.

The relationship between attitudes and contact, however, is not necessarily a one-way street. Chapter 8 examined the reciprocal effects of racial attitudes and close interpersonal contact with friends and romantic partners of different ethnicities. Not surprisingly, there were clear correlations between favorable precollege racial and ethnic attitudes, on the one hand, and more frequent interethnic friendships and dating, on the other. Nevertheless, the key questions were whether or not reciprocal causal relationships could be documented between racial attitudes and friendship or dating with members of racial outgroups. Did tolerance promote intergroup contact? Did intergroup contact promote tolerance?

First, precollege ethnic attitudes did have significant effects on the students' friendship and dating choices once in college. In this case, the prior causal role of attitudes over friendships and dating seems clear because the attitudes were measured before the students had a chance to get to know people on the campus. The reciprocal effect also held. Intimate intergroup contact, in the form of early college interethnic friendships and dating relationships, was associated with more favorable attitudes toward those groups later on. In this case, early interethnic friendships and dating were measured at the end of the freshman through junior years, and later racial and ethnic attitudes were measured at the end of the senior year. The risk with interpreting such correlations as reflecting the positive causal effect of contact is that this liberalization could just reflect self-selection of outgroup friends and dates by liberal students and avoidance of them by prejudiced students. The liberalizing effects of early close relationships with outgroup members in college were evident even with controls for precollege racial attitudes. Still, the inference of a causal effect of contact was not as secure as it would be if an experimental test had been used.

Chapter 9 extended this analysis to the effects of contact with ethnically diverse roommates in two ways. The first capitalized on a natural experiment involving roommate assignments in the freshman year. During their freshman year, the great majority of students lived in the dormitories and were assigned roommates at random; that is, whether they received an ethnic ingroup or outgroup roommate was a matter of random assignment rather than self-selection. How did interethnic residential contact affect racial and ethnic attitudes? Generally speaking, rooming with members of ethnic outgroups produced more favorable attitudes toward those outgroups. The effects were small, and not significant on all measures, but the direction of the effects was fairly consistent. Perhaps most important, white and Asian students showed positive effects of being assigned to roommates from the most disadvantaged groups, namely, African Americans and Latinos.

We also looked at the effects of voluntary choice of outgroup roommates in the later college years, using the same basic method as that employed in chapter 8 to test the effects of college friendships and dating. Having outgroup roommates was also consistently associated with improved attitudes toward outgroups, although, again, the effects were small. There were two important specific effects: contact particularly improved attitudes toward the specific outgroup represented by the roommate, and there was evidence of generalization of improved ethnic and racial attitudes from African American roommates to Latinos as a group, and Latino roommates to African Americans as a group.

In short, by all four tests—contact with outgroup members as college friends, dating partners, randomly assigned roommates, and voluntarily selected roommates—close interpersonal contact with ethnic and racial outgroup members tended to liberalize students' racial and ethnic attitudes. Although these effects of contact were quite consistent (even if generally small in absolute terms), some exceptions bear mentioning. Living with Asian roommates, whether assigned or chosen, had a tendency to shift students' ethnic and racial attitudes toward the conservative end of the spectrum. These effects were ascribed to Asians' initially relatively conservative attitudes about ethnic outgroups. As seen in chapters 4 and 5, Asian students on average did have somewhat more conservative political and racial views at college entry than did other groups of students. However, their attitudes became substantially more liberal as they moved through college. Their close contact with non-Asian students may have tended to liberalize the Asian students, while having the opposite effect on the non-Asian students.

If intergroup contact generally has beneficial effects, then ingroup contact may have harmful effects. In chapter 8, we explored this possibility with regard to ingroup friendships. We found that more ingroup contact did indeed increase ingroup bias and intergroup anxiety among students of all ethnicities. However, we did not expect the effects of ingroup friendships to be uniformly negative. In the peer support hypothesis, we reasoned that ethnic and racial minorities who are more likely to be the targets of prejudice might tend to segregate into ethnically homogeneous friendship groups in college in an effort to gain social support. We tested this peer support hypothesis by examining the effects of freshman year perceptions of discrimination against one's own ethnic group on the tendency to select friends especially from one's own ethnic group during sophomore and junior years, controlling for the student's precollege friendship patterns. As expected, we found that students' perception of ethnic discrimination on campus increased their tendency to choose friends from their own ingroups. We then examined the reciprocal peer socialization hypothesis that freshman year ingroup friendship patterns produce greater perceptions of ethnic discrimination on campus during sophomore and junior years, controlling for precollege expectations of ethnic discrimination on campus. Consistent with the notion that ingroup contact strengthens attitudes and perceptions that are viewed as normative within a group, we found that ingroup friendship choices stimulated greater perceived ethnic discrimination on campus.

Both reciprocal paths between ingroup friendship patterns and perceived ethnic discrimination on campus were especially strong among black students. This finding is reminiscent of the "black exceptionalism" contention (see chapter 2) that African Americans are not simply another lower-status racial group in American society but rather a racial-ethnic group that is uniquely vulnerable to the effects of the traditional American color line.

Finally, we examined the effects of both perceived ethnic discrimination on campus (the hostile climate hypothesis) and ingroup friendships (the ethnic segregation hypothesis) during college on social and academic adjustment at the end of college, controlling for previous levels of adjustment. We found that Latinos who had a greater proportion of friends from their own ethnic group and perceived a more hostile racial climate on campus did show greater alienation from the institution and lower academic performance. However, black students who had a greater proportion of ingroup friends fared better: They were more committed to staying in school and more motivated to perform well academically. Making more attributions to discrimination further enhanced black students' academic motivation. These differences between blacks and Latinos may be related to the black student population being smaller than the Latino student population at UCLA.

Taken together, these findings underline the importance of examining the effects of ingroup contact in addition to outgroup contact on both intergroup and adjustment outcomes, and separately for members of different ethnic groups. These effects may well vary depending on the type of contact involved, the outcome variable assessed, and the ethnic group studied.

Multicultural Education and the Unique Obstacles Facing Disadvantaged Ethnic Minority Groups

The final question we address is whether the various opportunities, issues, and obstacles encountered in the college years are seen and experienced differently by members of different ethnic groups. Perhaps an obvious point, but one worth underlining, is that the white students, and to some extent the Asian students, entered college with several advantages over their Latino and black counterparts. First, whites and some Asian groups came from families with higher socioeconomic status. Although a high percentage of Asians were from immigrant families, both whites and some Asian groups also had more educated parents and were relatively unlikely to be the first in their family to attend college. On average, they were also more likely to be admitted to UCLA than were Latinos and blacks, both of whom are far underrepresented in relation to the California population. Academically, both whites and some Asian groups tended to have stronger records at college entry. They were more likely to do well in college and to graduate than were Latinos and African Americans. In reflecting on the findings discussed in this book, these group differences are important to remember.

Of particular interest to us are the unique obstacles faced by students in disadvantaged ethnic minority groups. We therefore highlighted such obstacles in chapter 11, focusing on Latinos, African Americans, Southeast Asians, and Filipinos, all of whom were found to be disadvantaged relative to other students in terms of their preparation for college. A central focus concerned students' perceptions of their academic performance. Some research has shown, for example, that disadvantaged groups may at times become crippled by stereotypes about their groups (a phenomenon known as stereotype threat; see Steele and Aronson 1995). Members of disadvantaged groups may at times quite reasonably suspect that they have been treated differently than other people because of their ethnicity, whether positively, as a result of affirmative action policies, or negatively, because of group discrimination, for example. Consequently, they may wonder whether their academic record accurately reflects their own efforts. To the extent that their outcomes are disappointing, they may disengage themselves from this domain. While disengagement can temporarily shield self-esteem from damaging failures, it can also insidiously reduce motivation for achievement in that domain. In the context of academics, then, disengagement can protect students from feeling bad about themselves when their grades are poor. However, it can also lead to maintenance of poor grades, enrollment in less challenging programs, or an increased likelihood of dropping out of school. Did disengagement and its various effects play out this way in the disadvantaged ethnic minority groups at UCLA?

On a discouraging note, disadvantaged ethnic minority groups were found to fare more poorly in college relative to their white counterparts, even controlling for a number of relevant factors, such as incoming SAT scores. In particular, blacks and Latinos had lower grades, longer time-to-degree averages, and higher dropout rates. Second, as might be expected, all students' success in college was predictably based on cognitive factors such as SAT scores and freshman GPA. However, relative to whites' academic performance, ethnic minorities' performance was better predicted by noncognitive psychological factors, such as disidentifying from academics, and social context factors, such as the ethnicity of students' professors, friends, dates, and roommates.

Another interesting pattern of results that we uncovered in chapter 11 concerned students' thoughts about affirmative action. Not surprisingly, disadvantaged minority groups were more likely than whites to feel that they might have been admitted to UCLA because of affirmative action. By itself, that belief did not have a negative impact on students. However, when black and Latino students were also concerned that negative stereotypes about their group's intellectual ability could be true of them, or that their academic performance would shape others' views of their ethnic group (personal and social identity stereotype threat, respectively), then their suspicions about having been admitted through affirmative action hurt their subsequent academic performance. When students were not so concerned about confirming or contributing to stereotypes, affirmative action suspicions were unrelated to academic performance. While these findings should allay concerns that affirmative action automatically jeopardizes academic self-confidence and thus handicaps its beneficiaries, they should also call attention to the significant, if subtle, role played by stereotype threat. The existence of affirmative action policies, and even the perception that one has benefited from such policies, is not as important to academic performance as is the concern that stereotypes might be a situational danger, or "threat in the air."

These were just some of the findings we discussed in chapter 11, but they clearly point to the chapter's "take-home" message: the same concrete event (receiving a particular grade, having a roommate from a particular ethnic background, or being accepted to UCLA) will be interpreted by different people in ways that predictably vary across groups. Furthermore, some groups, for various reasons, are more vulnerable to different academic-related negative experiences than others, and groups respond to the same experiences in different ways—both psychologically and behaviorally. Efforts to understand inequities in higher education can thus benefit from consideration of these differences.

Summary of Main Findings

In reviewing the major themes of the volume, a number of important findings stand out.

Continuity, Not Radical Change, Is Closer to the Norm Through College

Our central goal was to assess the trajectory of college students from before college entry to graduation and provide a portrait of the impact of diversity in college on undergraduate students. At a number of junctures, however, we saw the remarkable staying power of the individual and group differences students brought with them when they entered college. In some ways, we were more struck by the continuity of students' attitudes through college than by the changes that occurred. Most notable in this regard were whites' political and racial attitudes, which seemed to be quite crystallized at college entry and were quite stable across the college years. Immigrant minorities' ethnic identities were also quite stable through college. Although we saw various signs of assimilation of Asian and Latino students, much of the assimilation seemed to occur between generations—often between the students and their parents—rather than within generations as a result of experiences such as a college education. These students were at the life stage we described as the "impressionable years," but the continuity of their attitudes and identities through that stage was at least as striking as their impressionability.

One noteworthy exception was the growing crystallization of racial attitudes (especially symbolic racism) through college in all ethnic groups, even among the newest immigrants. The same was true, to a lesser extent, for the elements of social dominance orientation (SDO). The multicultural college experience clearly helped students of all backgrounds to think through their views on race and intergroup conflict. Most came away from that experience with more coherent perspectives on cultural diversity for better or, sometimes, worse.

Intergroup Contact Helps

Despite the absence of radical shifts in students' attitudes across the duration of the study, we did find—all things considered—reasonable evidence that interethnic contact "works." This is a key conclusion that can be drawn from our research, though it must be qualified rather carefully. Simply enrolling in a diversely populated university and sitting next to members of different ethnic groups at food courts, for example, does not constitute change-inspiring contact. Instead, consistent with the work of psychologists Thomas Pettigrew, Linda Tropp, and others, our research indicates that intergroup contact serves to reduce intergroup prejudices and other conflict-related attitudes especially when there is "acquaintance potential."

Thus, the more substantial contact effects were found when we examined interethnic friendships, dating relationships, and roommate situations. In these cases, by and large, ethnically heterogeneous pairings had the effect of reducing an array of ethnic prejudices and increasing egalitarian values. That being said, and consistent with the earlier discussion concerning differential results across different ethnic groups, there were clear differences in our analyses when we considered different pairings (such as white and black versus white and Asian). It is notable, for example, that interactions with Asians sometimes had an effect opposite to that of the general trend—increasing negative intergroup attitudes— perhaps because others were being influenced by Asians' relatively conservative views. Also notable is the fact that whites, on average, tended to benefit the most from interethnic contact—presumably to some degree because, relative to other groups, they had the least amount of prior experience interacting with other groups.

Given the generally positive effects for interethnic contact, it is not that surprising that we also found some negative effects for *ingroup* contact. Of particular note were the findings concerning ethnic and Greek organizations. These findings should raise eyebrows and concern. It has been argued that such organizations play an integral role in the college experience and that, particularly for members of minority groups, they function as "safe harbors" where students can obtain needed social support. Indeed, such organizations are sometimes credited with keeping students' academic self-concepts afloat and thus deterring dropouts. How can these arguments be balanced with the effects that were found here? Are there ways in which organizations can provide social support benefits without compromising intergroup relationships?

Our research clearly suggests that having at least some "acquaintance potential" contact with outgroup members is key. A critical caveat, however, is the simple fact that intergroup contact cannot usually be forced on people. Several decades ago, efforts to desegregate public schools often foundered on the unwillingness of white parents to support it. This produced massive "white flight," as well as political rejection of the legislators, school board members, and judges who had promoted it. Similarly, even in a multicultural and largely liberal-minded community such as UCLA, it is evident that people are more often attracted to members of their own ethnic group than to members of other ethnic groups. Indeed, across the duration of the study, we found that whites, blacks, Asians, and Latinos had more friends and dating partners from their own ethnic ingroups than they did from any other group. Thus, while our research showed intergroup contact to be beneficial, it was also evident that such contact does not always occur spontaneously. For example, randomized roommate assignments are not common in the later years in college, let alone outside of college. Should they be more common? If "acquaintance potential" contact is effective, perhaps other similar programs should be implemented to foster this kind of contact.

Lessons Learned

In closing our discussion of this large and complex panel study, our research team felt that it might be useful to address some of the "lessons learned." Specifically, we thought it might be useful to consider what we would do differently if we were to start this project again from scratch. After our initial impulse to run for the hills had subsided, a few things came to mind. First, consistent with our previous survey experience, for reasons having to do with historical mistreatment (for example, the Tuskegee experiments) and relatively high levels of alienation, Latino and especially African American respondents are especially difficult to recruit for social science research. Reminding ourselves of this fact, we should have made an even more ambitious effort than we did to recruit a very large number of these minority students during the first wave of data collection. This could have given us a sufficiently large sample of these students at later waves to enable more fine-grained analyses of the data. However, given the relatively small number of black students in particular who were initially recruited to participate in the study, the effects of normal attrition over time restricted us to the simplest sorts of analyses at later waves involving these students. While we tried to correct this problem by recruiting additional Latino and black students at the second wave, this effort introduced its own difficulties and complications.

Second, while we did conduct a number of unstructured interviews and focus groups with students during the planning stage of the study, we did not continue to use these ethnographic approaches once the main study was under way. In retrospect, we have come to realize that the lack of such ethnographic data leaves a substantial lacuna in the data set. Because of this, we were not able to connect the mountains of very useful quantitative data with the students' own subjective understandings of their lives and the challenges facing them over the college years. We think that this information would have allowed us to produce an even richer and more textured analysis of the questions inspiring our study.

Third, and finally, while the multiethnic nature of the UCLA campus made it an especially rich context to examine, the fact that ours was a single-site study naturally limits the degree to which we can generalize these findings across different types of university environments. A follow-up, multi-site panel study, employing both quantitative and qualitative data, seems to be the next logical step in both broadening and deepening our understanding of these complex phenomena.

These shortcomings aside, this study has a unique standing in the social sciences. This is the only panel study of which we are aware that has used such a comprehensive set of measures to study the intergroup attitudes and behaviors of young adults over such a long period. The information in this data set should serve as a rich resource for students of intergroup relations for some time to come.

The Diversity Challenge: Concluding Reflections

We began this study with a pilot test in 1993. Initially, we were curious about the impact of the sharply increasing cultural diversity of the nation's student bodies on postsecondary students. We were also interested in the impact of the multiculturalist ideology sweeping the nation's universities, with its focus on the explicit recognition of ethnic and racial groups.

Both developments were surprising to many intellectuals and upsetting to more than a few. One of the consequences of the civil rights revolution of the 1960s was substantial pressure to integrate African Americans into predominantly white universities. The little-noted passage of immigration reform legislation at the same time has resulted in a very different kind of cultural diversity. Asians have become far more prominent in higher education, and the Latino population has grown rapidly, now outnumbering the black population. Today at universities like UCLA, blacks play a small numerical role in the student body as a whole, which is dominated by far greater numbers of Asians and Latinos.

The multiculturalist ideology, in placing explicit emphasis on ethnic and racial group membership and celebrating such differences, takes society in quite a different direction than did the civil rights movement. Martin Luther King Jr. and his colleagues famously advocated the integration of blacks into the broader society and urged that less attention be paid to the color of their skin in favor of the content of their character. The multiculturalist ideology grew out of the later black nationalist movement that sought greater recognition and autonomy for blacks as a distinct group, not blindness to color and greater integration. In response, many intellectuals feared that such a growing recognition of race and ethnicity as central elements of students' identity would lead to heightened ethnic conflict, resulting in ethnic balkanization, and they worried that the hopes of diminished attention to racial and ethnic differences, integration of minorities into the broader society, and racial harmony would have to be abandoned.

In this climate, we embarked on an ambitious empirical study that at the largest level asked two questions about this now-changed world in American higher education: Does cultural diversity have profound effects on undergraduate students? And are the effects largely in the direction of heightened ethnic and racial conflict? In some ways the premise of our study, and what we thought we might find, was quite different from what we actually did find. We, like many intellectuals of the day, expected to find that cultural diversity and the multicultural practices that universities put in place as a response to it would have some profound effects on the students. As our laboratory we chose UCLA, a hothouse of cultural diversity and multicultural institutional response, where we expected that these effects would be at their maximum.

We found, however, that the students were changed rather little in their ethnic and racial orientations by the college experience. Without retracing our earlier summaries in detail, we would simply point to two recurrent findings. The first is the strong continuity of such attitudes as racial prejudice and ethnic identities across the several waves of our study and years at college for the students. Both in the aggregate, in terms of mean differences, and at the individual level, in terms of test-retest correlations, we found relatively little change. The second finding

322

is that diversity experiences on campus, whether in ethnic organization membership or among interethnic friends, roommates, and dating partners, have quite modest effects. We found a sufficient number of significant effects to inform us about the conditions for beneficial or harmful effects, but for the most part the absolute sizes of the changes were small. Cultural diversity and multicultural education simply are not earth-shattering experiences for university students.

Nor do cultural diversity and multicultural education have the feared effects of heightening ethnic conflict and separation. We found quite the opposite. If anything, they work together to increase ethnic and racial harmony. We found no evidence of the strengthening of attachments to ethnic and racial ingroups, nor did we observe a strengthening of prejudices and antagonisms toward ethnic and racial outgroups, implied by the fears of ethnic balkanization. Instead, we found reductions in racial prejudice. Moreover, we found considerable increases in the crystallization of racial attitudes, which we interpret as reflecting greater sophistication about America's racial situation. We found, if anything, that intergroup contact reduced prejudice and conflict, at least under most conditions. Multicultural efforts to stimulate contact rather than segregation helped. Ethnic identity did not compete with and compromise a student's ability to form an attachment to the superordinate identity of being a UCLA student. Rather, the identities tended to work together, even for the least advantaged groups. We did not find much evidence that self-segregation of racial and ethnic groups, whether in interpersonal relationships or in ethnic organizations, was beneficial to the intergroup attitudes of the students involved.

These, then, would be our "bottom line" responses to the concerns of traditionalists who are nervous about the changes in higher education triggered by cultural diversity. Diversity and multiculturalism are not having revolutionary effects. Students do not undergo radical change in college but rather build on and develop what they enter college with. Yes, students of different groups get along pretty well, and if anything, they expand their appreciation for each other in light of their differences rather than despite them.

In closing, it is worth reflecting on the extent to which UCLA might be considered representative of other American colleges and universities or thought of as a microcosm of the nation at large. As indicated in chapter 3, UCLA would appear to be a relatively optimal rather than typical model for examining whether and when multiculturalism "works." In this particularly supportive setting, it is possible to establish egalitarian and multicultural norms that most people sincerely respect. It is possible for all ethnic groups to show strong attachment to the superordinate university identity and for ethnic and university identities to be, for everyone, compatible. Furthermore, it is possible for certain types of intergroup contact to foster increasingly harmonious ethnic relations. At the same time, critical disparities across groups—for example, in ethnic identification, prejudicial attitudes, academic performance, and dropout rates—remain. There is also ample evidence that students, instead of continuously intermingling, tend to cluster themselves into ethnically homogeneous groupings. It seems clear that multiculturalism *can* work in a college environment, at least to some extent—if that environment is structured appropriately. In the postcollege, relatively inegalitarian world, however, making multiculturalism work may be a larger challenge.

Appendix A: Survey Questions, Scales, and Waves

The construct labels for all survey items and scales are shown in chapter 3. Readers may find it helpful to use the labels in chapter 3 to identify constructs of interest. This appendix displays an alphabetical list of the constructs measured in all six waves of data collection.[1] The items appear exactly as they were presented to participants, with a few slight wording changes to ease the transition from the oral to the written format. The waves in which each variable was asked are presented to the left of the items, and the response labels are presented (where applicable) after the question wording. In waves 2 to 6, the response options of "don't know" and "refused to answer" were provided in the interview protocol. Many of the demographic and background questions asked in wave 1 were asked in wave 2 only if the respondent had not participated in wave 1. Since the data for wave 1 were collected before college entry, expectations of, rather than experiences with, campus life were measured at this wave.

Scales of items are labeled using the same construct name provided in chapter 3 (for example, "self-esteem scale"), and the questions combined to form the scale are listed below the scale name. (Reliabilities for all scales across all waves can be found in appendix B.) Items that are related to one another, but not combined within a scale, are similarly grouped and listed under the name of the unifying construct provided in chapter 3 (for example, "societal ethnic discrimination items"). Single questions representing a construct are also listed under the same construct name provided in chapter 3 (for example, "perceived zero-sum group conflict"). In a few cases, related items are combined into scales in some analyses and kept as separate items in other analyses. In these cases, the items are grouped and listed under the name of the unifying construct, which is designated as both a scale and individual items (for example, "intergroup anxiety scale/items," "expectancies of future socioeconomic status scale/items," "perceived ethnic discrimination on campus scale/items").

Note

* Item was reverse-coded when combined with other items to form a scale.
** Item was measured in wave 2 only for respondents who did not participate in wave 1.
n.a. = not applicable.

Wave	Construct
	Academic performance scale
2 to 6	What is your cumulative GPA at UCLA? (open-ended)
1 to 6	How well will you do (are you doing) in school, compared to other students at UCLA? (1 = not as well as most, 7 = better than most)
	Academic term expects to earn UCLA degree
5 to 6	When do you expect to earn your degree from UCLA? (respondents could indicate any future quarter)
	Affect toward the four main ethnic groups
	How positively or negatively do you feel toward the folling groups? (1 = very negatively, 7 = very positively):
1 to 6	Caucasians/whites
1 to 6	Latinos/Hispanics
1 to 6	Asians/Asian Americans
1 to 6	African Americans/blacks
	Age
1 to 2	How old are you?** (open-ended)
	American identification
2 to 6	To what extent do you think of yourself as American? (1 = not at all, 7 = very much)

Amount of education paid for by parents or other relatives, scholarships or fellowships, or own earnings or savings

5 to 6   By the end of your college education, how much of it will have been paid for by your parents or other family members? (1 = none, 2 = some, 3 = half, 4 = most, 5 = all)

5 to 6   By the end of your college education, how much of it will have been paid for by scholarships or fellowships? (1 = none, 2 = some, 3 = half, 4 = most, 5 = all)

5 to 6   By the end of your college education, how much of it will you have paid for through your own earnings or savings? (1 = none, 2 = some, 3 = half, 4 = most, 5 = all)

Atmosphere at UCLA allows versus prevents expression of true feelings about ethnic-racial issues

4 to 6   Do you think the atmosphere at UCLA allows people or prevents people from expressing their true feelings about ethnic and racial issues? (1 = people can express their true feelings, 7 = people cannot express their true feelings)

Attitude toward bilingual education

3 to 6   How do you feel about bilingual education? (1 = strongly oppose, 7 = strongly favor)

Attitude toward English as the official language of the United States

3 to 6   How do you feel about a law making English the official language of the United States, meaning that government business would be conducted in English only? (1 = strongly oppose, 7 = strongly favor)

Attitude toward the government helping minority groups

1, 3 to 6   Should the government make every effort to improve the social and economic position of minority groups or should minority groups be responsible for helping themselves? (1 = government should help, 7 = minority groups should help themselves)

Attitude toward immigrants

1 to 6   Do you think the number of immigrants who are allowed into the United States should ... (1) be decreased a lot, (4) stay the same, or (7) be increased a lot?

Appendix A

Attitude toward solving the crime problem

1 to 6
What should we do to solve the crime problem: invest more money in schools or invest more money in prisons? (1 = more money to schools, 7 = more money to prisons)

Attitude toward welfare recipients

1 to 6
Could most people who receive money from welfare get along without it if they tried, or do you think most of them really need this help? (1 = most could get along without it, 7 = most really need this help)

Attributions for future outcomes of ethnic group in society at large scale (1 = things about them, such as their ability and the effort they have put in, 7 = factors in the environment, such as opportunities and jobs)

1 to 6
What will the economic life outcomes of members of your ethnic group in society at large be more influenced by?

1 to 6
If members of your ethnic group in society at large do not do well economically in life, what will this be more caused by?

Attributions for future outcomes of same-ethnicity UCLA students scale (1 = things about them, such as their ability and the effort they have put in, 7 = factors in the environment, such as opportunities and jobs)

1 to 6
What will the economic life outcomes of members of your ethnic group who are now UCLA students be more influenced by?

1 to 6
If members of your ethnic group who are now UCLA students do not do well economically in life, what will this be more caused by?

Attributions for future self economic life outcomes scale (1 = things about you, such as your ability and the effort you have put in, 7 = factors in the environment, such as opportunities and jobs)

1 to 6
What will your economic life outcomes be more influenced by?

1 to 6
If you do not do well economically in life, what will this be more caused by?

Average number of hours per week spent studying or doing homework

4 to 6   What is the average number of hours that you spend per week studying or doing homework? (1 = zero, 2 = one to five, 3 = six to ten, 4 = eleven to fifteen, 5 = sixteen to twenty, 6 = twenty to thirty, 7 = thirty to forty)

Belonging

1 to 6   To what degree do you (expect to) experience a sense of belonging or a sense of exclusion at UCLA? (1 = a strong sense of belonging, 7 = a strong sense of exclusion)

Best way to get ahead in society is to improve personal status versus ethnic group status

1 to 6   Some people try to get ahead in society by improving their personal status, and some try to improve the status of their ethnic group. What do you feel is the best way for you to get ahead? (1 = improve my personal status, 7 = improve the status of my ethnic group)

Chose own roommate(s) or roommate(s) randomly chosen

2 to 6   Did you choose your roommate or roommates, or were they randomly chosen for you? (1 = I chose my roommate(s), 2 = my roommate(s) was/were randomly chosen for me, 3 = both, 4 = I don't have any roommates)

Classic racism scale (1 = strongly disagree, 7 = strongly agree)

1   "Blacks are inherently inferior."
1   "Latinos are inherently inferior."

College major

1 to 6   What is your (intended) major? (open-ended; in waves 2 to 6, respondents also indicated second majors and minors, if applicable)

Consideration of dropping out of UCLA before earning a degree

1 to 6   How likely is it that you would consider dropping out of UCLA before earning a degree? (1 = not at all, 7 = very likely)

Dating members of the four main ethnic groups (1 = yes, 5 = no)

2 to 6	Have you dated anyone who is Asian American since last June?
2 to 6	Have you dated anyone who is African American since last June?
2 to 6	Have you dated anyone who is Latino since last June?
2 to 6	Have you dated anyone who is Caucasian since last June?

Degree attained by the end of the seventh year after college entry

n.a.	Information obtained from the UCLA Office of the Registrar (1 = no degree, 2 = BA/BS degree)

Discounting scale (1 = strongly disagree, 7 = strongly agree)

2 to 6	"My academic performance at UCLA accurately reflects how smart I am."*
2 to 6	"The grades I have received at UCLA are not a good measure of my intellectual ability."

Disidentification scale (1 = strongly disagree, 7 = strongly agree)

2 to 6	"My performance in school does not affect whether I feel good or bad about myself."
2 to 6	"How I feel about myself depends a lot on how well I do in school."*

Employment and hours worked

2 to 6	Have you had a job this academic year? (1 = yes, 5 = no)
2 to 6	Have you worked on campus or off campus during this academic year? (1 = on campus, 3 = off campus, 5 = both)
2 to 6	How much have you worked this academic year? (1 = three quarters, 2 = two quarters or equivalent, 3 = one quarter or equivalent, 4 = less than one quarter)
2 to 6	During this time, how many hours a week have you worked on average? (open-ended)

Ethnic activism scale

How seriously have you considered participating in the following activities on behalf of your ethnic group? (1 = not at all seriously, 7 = very seriously/have done so)

1 to 6	Voting in terms of what is good for your particular ethnic group
1 to 6	Participating in demonstrations
1 to 6	Signing petitions

Ethnic identification scale

1 to 6	How important is your ethnicity to your identity? (1 = not at all, 7 = very important)
1 to 6	How often do you think of yourself as a member of your ethnic group? (1 = not at all, 7 = very often)
1 to 6	How close do you feel to other members of your ethnic group? (1 = not at all, 7 = very close)

Ethnic organizations promote separatism (1 = strongly disagree, 7 = strongly agree)

1 to 6	"Ethnic student organizations at UCLA promote separatism."

Ethnic private collective self-esteem scale (1 = strongly disagree, 7 = strongly agree)

1	"I feel good about the ethnic group I belong to."
1	"I often regret that I belong to the ethnic group I do."*

Ethnic versus American identification

1	Do you identify more strongly with other members of your ethnic group, more strongly with Americans in general, or to the same degree with both? (1 = other members of my ethnic group, 4 = both, 7 = Americans in general)

Ethnicity-race

1 to 6	Which ethnic-racial group do you most closely identify with? (open-ended)
1 to 2	Please circle the one category that most accurately describes your ethnic-racial heritage:** 1 = biracial/mixed-race (specify) 2 = African American/black 3 = Chinese/Chinese American 4 = Korean/Korean American 5 = Japanese/Japanese American

6 = Filipino/Filipino American

7 = Pacific Islander, Hawaiian

8 = Southeast Asian (for example, Thai, Vietnamese, Laotian; specify)

9 = East Indian (for example, Indian, Pakistani; specify)

10 = Other Asian (specify)

11 = Caucasian/white

12 = Chicano/Mexican American

13 = Central American

14 = South American

15 = Other Latino (specify)

16 = Middle Eastern (specify)

17 = Native American

18 = other (specify)

n.a.   Ethnicity information was also obtained from the UCLA Office of the Registrar

Ethnicity of roommates

2 to 6   What is your first roommate's ethnicity? (1 = biracial/ mixed-race [specify], 2 = African American/black, 3 = Asian American/Pacific Islander, 4 = Caucasian/ white, 5 = Latino/Hispanic, 6 = Middle Eastern [specify], 7 = Native American, 8 = other [specify])

2 to 6   What is the ethnicity of your second roommate? (same categories as for first roommate)

2 to 6   What is the ethnicity of your third roommate? (same categories as for first roommate)

2 to 6   How many of your roommates are Asian American? (open-ended)

2 to 6   How many of your roommates are African American? (open-ended)

2 to 6   How many of your roommates are Latino? (open-ended)

2 to 6   How many of your roommates are Caucasian? (open-ended)

Ethnicity of the person respondent is currently dating

4 to 6   What ethnicity is the person you are dating right now? (1 = biracial/mixed-race [specify], 2 = African Ameri-

can/black, 3 = Asian American/Pacific Islander, 4 = Caucasian/white, 5 = Latino/Hispanic, 6 = Middle Eastern [specify], 7 = Native American, 8 = other [specify])

Expectancies of future ethnic prejudice and discrimination scale (1 = not at all, 7 = very much)

1 to 6   To what extent will prejudice and discrimination against members of your ethnic group impose barriers to their future outcomes?

1 to 6   To what extent will prejudice and discrimination against you, because of your ethnicity, impose barriers to your future outcomes?

Expectancies of future socioeconomic status scale/items (1 = poor, 2 = working class, 3 = lower-middle class, 4 = middle class, 5 = upper-middle class, 6 = lower-upper class, 7 = upper class)

1 to 6   Twenty years from now, what do you think your socioeconomic status will be?

1 to 6   Twenty years from now, what do you think will be the average socioeconomic status of members of your ethnic group who are now students at UCLA?

1 to 6   Twenty years from now, what do you think will be the average socioeconomic status of members of your ethnic group in society at large?

Extent to which curriculum allowed learning about different cultures

2 to 6   To what extent has the curriculum in your classes at UCLA allowed you to learn about many different cultures? (1 = not at all, 7 = very much)

Extent to which learned about ethnic minority groups in classes

2 to 6   To what extent have you learned about ethnic minority groups in your classes at UCLA? (1 = not at all, 7 = very much)

Father's ethnicity

1 to 2   Please circle the one category that most accurately describes your father's ethnic-racial heritage** (same

categories as for respondent's own ethnic-racial heritage)

Feeling of being admitted to UCLA because of affirmative action

1 to 6 Do you feel that you were admitted to UCLA because of affirmative action? (1 = definitely no, 4 = maybe, 7 = definitely yes, 9 = I don't know enough about affirmative action to answer this question)

Feeling of exclusion versus belonging in the dormitory

2 to 6 To what degree do you experience a sense of exclusion or a sense of belonging in the dormitory? (1 = strong sense of exclusion, 7 = strong sense of belonging)

Feeling of "having a say" about what the government does

3 to 6 To what extent do you agree or disagree with the following statement: "People like me don't have any say about what the government does." (1 = strongly agree, 2 = agree, 3 = disagree, 4 = strongly disagree)

Feeling that dorm floor or suite is ethnically diverse

2 to 3 How ethnically diverse is your dorm floor or the suite you live in? (1 = not at all diverse, 7 = very diverse)

First in family to go to college

1 to 2 Are you the first person in your family to go to college?** (1 = yes, 2 = no)

Frequency of political discussions

3 to 6 How often do you discuss politics with your family or friends? (1 = every day, 2 = three or four times a week, 3 = once or twice a week, 4 = once or twice a month, 5 = less often than once or twice a month)

Friendships with members of the four main ethnic groups at UCLA (1 = none, 2 = few, 3 = many, 4 = most, 5 = all)

2 to 6 At UCLA, how many of your closest friends are Asian American?

2 to 6 At UCLA, how many of your closest friends are African American?

2 to 6 At UCLA, how many of your closest friends are Latino?

2 to 6 At UCLA, how many of your closest friends are Caucasian?

Future career or occupation
1 to 6   What do you think your future career or occupation will be? (open-ended)

Gender
1 to 2   What is your gender? (1 = female, 2 = male)

Gender activism scale
How seriously have you considered participating in the following activities on behalf of your gender? (1 = not at all seriously, 7 = very seriously/have done so)
1 to 6   Voting in terms of what is good for your gender
1 to 6   Participating in demonstrations

Gender identification scale
1 to 6   How important is your gender to your identity? (1 = not at all, 7 = very important)
1 to 6   How often do you think of yourself in terms of your gender? (1 = not at all, 7 = very often)

Graduate or professional school test achievement
5 to 6   Have you taken the GRE general test? (1 = yes, 5 = no)
5 to 6   What was your score on the verbal section? (open-ended)
5 to 6   What was your score on the quantitative section? (open-ended)
5 to 6   What was your score on the analytic section? (open-ended)
5 to 6   Have you taken the LSAT? (1 = yes, 5 = no)
5 to 6   What was your score? (open-ended)
5 to 6   Have you taken the GMAT? (1 = yes, 5 = no)
5 to 6   What was your total score? (open-ended)
5 to 6   What was your score on the verbal section? (open-ended)
5 to 6   What was your score on the quantitative section? (open-ended)
5 to 6   What was your score on the analytical writing section? (open-ended)
5 to 6   Have you taken the MCAT? (1 = yes, 5 = no)
5 to 6   What was your score on the verbal reasoning section? (open-ended)

5 to 6	What was your score on the physical sciences section? (open-ended)
5 to 6	What was your score on the writing sample section? (open-ended)
5 to 6	What was your score on the biological sciences section? (open-ended)

Groups should maintain their distinctive cultures versus change and blend

1	Is it better for America if different racial and ethnic groups maintain their distinct cultures, or is it better if groups change so that they blend into the larger society, as in the idea of a melting pot? (1 = groups should maintain their distinct cultures, 7 = groups should change and blend)

Highest degree interested in getting (and field)

4 to 6	What is the highest degree you are interested in getting? (1 = MA/MS, 2 = MBA, 3 = MSW, 4 = MFA, 5 = PhD, 6 = JD, 7 = MD)
4 to 6	In what field will you get your degree? (open-ended)

Hours per week spent at most important organization

4 to 6	How many hours per week on average do you spend participating in activities with this organization? (1 = zero to two hours, 3 = three to nine hours, 5 = more than ten hours)

Immediate plans after graduation

5 to 6	What are your immediate plans after graduation? (1 = graduate school, 2 = other study, 3 = employment, 4 = military service, 5 = other [something else, specify])

Importance of getting a high GPA

1 to 6	How important is it for you to get a high GPA at UCLA? (1 = not at all, 7 = very important)

Intention to attend graduate or professional school

4 to 6	Do you think you will attend (graduate) school or professional school (after you graduate from college)? (1 = no, 2 = maybe, 3 = yes)

Intention to vote

1, 3   Do you intend to vote in the upcoming election? (1 = yes, 2 = no)

Interest in politics

3 to 6   How interested would you say you personally are in politics? (1 = very interested, 2 = fairly interested, 3 = somewhat interested, 4 = not very interested, 5 = not at all interested)

Intergroup anxiety scale/items (1 = strongly disagree, 7 = strongly agree)

1 to 6   "I feel uneasy being around people of different ethnicities."
1 to 6   "I feel competent interacting with people from different ethnic groups."*

Involvement in a steady relationship, and its duration

4 to 6   Are you in a steady relationship right now? (1 = yes, 5 = no)
4 to 6   How long have you been in the relationship that you are in right now? (open-ended; respondents were asked to give the number of years and months)

Language spoken at home

1 to 2   What language is spoken by your family at home?** (1 = English only; 2 = primarily English, but another language also; 3 = primarily a language other than English; 4 = only a language other than English)

Last term registered

n.a.   Information obtained from the UCLA Office of the Registrar

Legitimacy of the ethnic-status hierarchy scale (1 = strongly disagree, 7 = strongly agree)

1 to 6   "Differences in status between ethnic groups are fair."
1 to 6   "It is unfair that certain ethnic groups have poorer living conditions than other ethnic groups."*

Length of time taken to earn a degree

n.a.   Information obtained from the UCLA Office of the Registrar (1 = less than four years, 2 = four years, 3 = four to

five years, 4 = five to six years, 5 = six to seven years,
6 = more than seven years, 7 = no degree yet)

Membership in fraternity or sorority

2 to 6   Are you a member of a fraternity or a sorority? (1 =
fraternity, 3 = sorority, 5 = no)

2 to 6   If so, which one? (open-ended)

Membership in student organizations

2 to 6   Are you a member of any student organizations at UCLA,
like ethnic or religious organizations? (1 = yes, 5 = no)

2 to 6   If so, which ones? (open-ended; respondents listed up to
six organizations)

Money owed for undergraduate education

5 to 6   When you receive your degree, how much money will you
owe that is directly related to your undergraduate education (that is, tuition and fees, living expenses and
supplies, transportation to and from school)? (1 = none,
2 = $5,000 or less, 3 = between $5,000 and $10,000,
4 = between $10,000 and $15,000, 5 = between $15,000
and $20,000, 6 = between $20,000 and $25,000, 7 =
between $25,000 and $30,000, 8 = over $30,000)

*The more important duty of a good citizen is to obey laws versus
vote*

3 to 6   What do you think is the more important duty of a good
citizen—to obey the laws or to be politically interested
and vote? (1 = obey the laws, 5 = be politically interested
and vote)

Most important student organization of which one is a member

4 to 6   Of all the organizations of which you are a member,
including fraternities or sororities, which one is the
most important to you? (open-ended)

Mother's ethnicity

1 to 2   Please circle the one category that most accurately
describes your mother's ethnic-racial heritage** (same
categories as for respondent's own ethnic-racial
heritage)

No attempt to befriend people from other ethnic groups
(1 = strongly disagree, 7 = strongly agree)

1   "I don't try to become friends with people from other ethnic groups."

Number of academic terms enrolled during data collection period

2 to 6   Are you currently enrolled at UCLA? (1 = yes, 5 = no)

3 to 6   Were you enrolled at UCLA during both the fall and winter quarter of this academic year, just the fall quarter, just the winter quarter, or neither quarter? (1 = both the fall and winter quarters, 2 = just the fall quarter, 3 = just the winter quarter, 4 = neither quarter)

2 to 6   Will you be enrolled at UCLA next fall?
(1 = yes, 5 = no)

n.a.   Registration information was also obtained from the UCLA Office of the Registrar

Number of Asian American, African American, Latino, and female professors had each year at UCLA

2 to 6   How many Asian American professors have you had this year at UCLA, including this quarter (if you know about any of them)? (open-ended)

2 to 6   How many African American professors have you had this year at UCLA, including this quarter (if you know about any of them)? (open-ended)

2 to 6   How many Latino professors have you had this year at UCLA, including this quarter (if you know about any of them)? (open-ended)

2 to 6   How many female professors have you had this year at UCLA, including this quarter (if you know about any of them)? (open-ended)

Number of ethnic studies courses taken each year

2 to 6   How many ethnic studies courses have you taken this year at UCLA, including this quarter? (open-ended)

Number of grandparents born in the United States

1 to 2   How many of your grandparents were born in the United States?** (zero, one, two, three, four)

Appendix A

Number of incompletes taken this year
2 to 6   How many incompletes have you taken this academic year? (open-ended)

Number of parents born in the United States
1 to 2   How many of your parents were born in the United States?** (zero, one, two)

Number of roommates
2 to 6   How many roommates do you have? (open-ended)

Opposition to affirmative action scale (1 = strongly disagree, 7 = strongly agree)
1 to 6   "Affirmative action admits too many students who have a low chance of academic success."
1 to 6   "Affirmative action is harmful to members of my ethnic group."
1 to 6   "Affirmative action stigmatizes the people it's supposed to help."

Opposition to miscegenation scale (1 = strongly disagree, 7 = strongly agree)
1 to 6   "Interethnic dating should be avoided."
1 to 6   "Interethnic marriage should be avoided."

Participation in the Academic Advancement Program
2 to 6   Did you participate in the Academic Advancement Program, or AAP? (1 = yes, 5 = no)

Participation in the summer orientation program for minorities
2   Did you participate in the summer orientation program for minorities? (1 = yes, 5 = no)

Perceived conflict between groups on campus (1 = strongly disagree, 7 = strongly agree)
1 to 6   "I expect there to be (there is) conflict between different ethnic groups on campus."

Perceived ethnic discrimination on campus scale/items (1 = strongly disagree, 7 = strongly agree)
1 to 6   "I (will) experience discrimination at UCLA because of my ethnicity."

1 to 6   "Other members of my ethnic group (will) experience discrimination on campus."

Perceived gender discrimination on campus items (1 = strongly disagree, 7 = strongly agree)

1 to 6   "I (will) experience discrimination at UCLA because of my gender."

1 to 6   "Women on campus (will) experience discrimination because of their gender."

Perceived professor bias items (1 = strongly disagree, 7 = strongly agree)

1 to 6   "Most of my professors don't have any ethnic prejudices."

2 to 6   "Many professors at UCLA are biased against people of my ethnic group."

Perceived smartness compared to other UCLA students

1, 4 to 6   Compared to other students admitted to UCLA, how smart are you? (1 = not as smart as most, 7 = smarter than most)

Perceived zero-sum group conflict (1 = strongly disagree, 7 = strongly agree)

1 to 6   "More good jobs for other groups come at the expense of fewer good jobs for members of my group."

Permeability of the ethnic-status hierarchy scale (1 = strongly disagree, 7 = strongly agree)

1 to 6   "America is an open society where individuals of any ethnicity can achieve higher personal status."

1 to 6   "Personal advancement in American society is possible for individuals of all ethnic groups."

Personal identity stereotype threat (1 = strongly disagree, 7 = strongly agree)

2 to 6   "I think about whether the stereotypes of my ethnic group's intelligence are true of me."

Place of residence

2 to 6   Where do you live? (1 = residence hall, 2 = off-campus housing, 3 = at home with parents or other relatives, 4 = some other place [specify])

Appendix A

2 to 6	Which residence hall do you live in? (all residence hall locations were given as options)

Political candidate preference and voting behavior

1	Who would you prefer to be elected in the upcoming election? (1 = Bill Clinton, 4 = undecided, 7 = Bob Dole, 9 = other [specify])
4	Did you vote in the election for governor? (1 = yes, 5 = no)
4	Did you vote for Gray Davis or for Dan Lungren as governor? (1 = Gray Davis, 5 = Dan Lungren)
4	Did you vote for Barbara Boxer or for Matt Fong as senator? (1 = Barbara Boxer, 5 = Matt Fong)
5	If all of the following candidates were running, who would you prefer to be elected in the upcoming presidential election? (1 = Alan Keyes, 2 = John McCain, 3 = Bill Bradley, 4 = George W. Bush, 5 = Al Gore)
6	For whom did you vote in the last presidential election? (1 = George W. Bush, 2 = Al Gore, 3 = Ralph Nader, 4 = Pat Buchanan, 5 = some other candidate, 6 = did not vote)

Political conservatism scale/items

1 to 6	How would you describe your own political party preference? (1 = strong Democrat, 2 = weak Democrat, 3 = independent [leaning more Democrat], 4 = independent, 5 = independent [leaning more Republican], 6= weak Republican, 7 = strong Republican)
1 to 6	How would you describe your general political outlook? (1 = very liberal, 7 = very conservative)

Precollege academic performance
SAT scale

1 to 2	What was your most recent SAT verbal test score?** (open-ended)
1 to 2	What was your most recent SAT math test score?** (open-ended)
1 to 2	What was your most recent ACT test score?** (open-ended)

Precollege contact with the four main ethnic groups (1 = none, 2 = few, 3 = many, 4 = most, 5 = all)
How many of the residents of the neighborhood where

you grew up most of the time before the age of sixteen were:**

1 to 2 Latino/Hispanic?
1 to 2 African American/black?
1 to 2 Asian/Asian American?
1 to 2 Caucasian/white?

In high school, how many of your closest friends were:**

1 to 2 Latino?
1 to 2 African American?
1 to 2 Asian American?
1 to 2 Caucasian?

In high school, how many of the people you took classes with regularly were:**

1 to 2 Latino?
1 to 2 African American?
1 to 2 Asian American?
1 to 2 Caucasian?

Preference for ingroup professors (1 = strongly disagree, 7 = strongly agree)

1 to 6 "I prefer to take classes with professors from my own ethnic background."

Preference for smaller versus larger government

1 Would you prefer a smaller government providing fewer services, or a larger government providing more services? (1 = smaller government, 7 = larger government)

Pressure from one's own ethnic group not to interact with members of other groups (1 = strongly disagree, 7 = strongly agree)

1 to 6 "I have felt pressure from members of my ethnic group not to socialize with or date members of other ethnic groups."

Registered to vote

1, 3 to 6 Are you registered to vote? (1 = yes, 2 = no)

Religion

1 to 2 What is your religious affiliation?** (1 = Protestant

[specify], 2 = Catholic, 3 = Jewish, 4 = Muslim, 5 = Buddhist, 6 = other [specify], 7 = none)

Religiosity

1 to 6   How religious are you? (1 = not at all, 7 = very religious)

Representation of the student body as one group, different groups, or individuals (1 = strongly disagree, 7 = strongly agree)

2 to 6   "Despite the different groups at UCLA, there is frequently the sense that we are all just one group."

2 to 6   "At UCLA, it usually feels as though we belong to different groups."

2 to 6   "At UCLA, it usually feels as though we are individuals and not members of a particular group."

Self-esteem scale (1 = strongly disagree, 7 = strongly agree)

1 to 6   "I feel that I have a number of good qualities."

1 to 6   "I take a positive attitude toward myself."

1 to 6   "I certainly feel useless at times."*

1 to 6   "At times I think I am no good at all."*

Self-perception as an individual American rather than as a group member (1 = strongly disagree, 7 = strongly agree)

1 to 6   "People should think of themselves first and foremost as an individual American rather than as a member of a racial, religious, or ethnic group."

Social dominance orientation (SDO) scale (1 = strongly disagree, 7 = strongly agree)

1 to 6   "It's probably a good thing that certain groups are at the top and other groups are at the bottom."

1 to 6   "Inferior groups should stay in their place."

1 to 6   "We should do what we can to equalize conditions for different groups."*

1 to 6   "We should increase social equality."*

Social identity stereotype threat (1 = strongly disagree, 7 = strongly agree)

2 to 6   "I think about whether my academic performance will affect how others evaluate my ethnic group."

Societal ethnic discrimination items (1 = strongly disagree, 7 = strongly agree)

1 to 6   "Minority groups usually don't get fair treatment in American society."

1   "American society just doesn't deal fairly with people from my ethnic background."

Socioeconomic status scale/items

1 to 2   What is the highest level of education your mother completed?** (1 = elementary school, 2 = some high school, 3 = completed high school, 4 = trade school, 5 = some college, 6 = completed college [BA/BS degree], 7 = some graduate or professional school, 8 = completed graduate or professional degree)

1 to 2   What is the highest level of education your father completed?** (same categories as for mother's education level)

1 to 2   How would you describe your family's social class position?** (1 = poor, 2 = working class, 3 = lower-middle class, 4 = middle class, 5 = upper-middle class, 6 = lower-upper class, 7 = upper class)

Stability of the ethnic-status hierarchy scale (1 = strongly disagree, 7 = strongly agree)

1 to 6   "Ethnic groups at the bottom will always be at the bottom."

1 to 6   "Over time, the social status of all ethnic groups will be equal."*

Status perceptions of the four main ethnic groups

     There are many people who believe that the different ethnic groups enjoy different amounts of social status in this society. You may not believe this for yourself, but if you had to rate each of the following groups as most people see them, how would you do so?** (1 = low status, 7 = high status)

1 to 2   Caucasians/whites?

1 to 2   Latinos/Hispanics?

1 to 2   Asians/Asian Americans?

1 to 2   African Americans/blacks?

Appendix A

Stereotypes of the four main ethnic groups
> Where would you rate the following groups in general on these scales? (1 = violent, 7 = not violent; 1 = intolerant, 7 = tolerant; 1 = unintelligent, 7 = intelligent; 1 = lazy, 7 = hardworking)

1   Caucasians?

1   Latinos?

1   Asian Americans?

1   African Americans?

Support for increasing diversity on campus (1 = strongly disagree, 7 = strongly agree)

1 to 6   "We should do what we can to increase ethnic diversity on campus."

Symbolic racism scale (1 = strongly disagree, 7 = strongly agree)

1 to 6   "Blacks are getting too demanding in their push for equal rights."

1 to 6   "Over the past few years, blacks have gotten less economically than they deserve."*

1 to 6   "The Irish, Italians, Jews, and many other minorities overcame prejudice and worked their way up. Blacks should do the same without special favors."

1 to 6   "Blacks get less attention from the government than they deserve."*

Time spent learning about ethnic ingroup (1 = strongly disagree, 7 = strongly agree)

2 to 6   "I have spent time trying to find out more about my own ethnic group, such as its history and culture."

UCLA is not at all ethnically diverse versus very ethnically diverse

4 to 6   How ethnically diverse do you think the UCLA campus is? (1 = not at all diverse, 7 = very diverse)

UCLA promotion of diversity items (1 = strongly disagree, 7 = strongly agree)

1 to 6   "UCLA promotes positive interaction between individual students of different ethnic groups."

1 to 6   "UCLA lacks strong commitment to achieving and maintaining an ethnically diverse student body."

Units passed during each academic term

n.a.   Information obtained from the UCLA Office of the Registrar

University identification

1 to 6   How often do you think of yourself as a UCLA student? (1 = not at all, 7 = very often)

U.S.-born

1 to 2   Were you born in the United States?** (1 = yes, 2 = no)

U.S. citizen

3 to 6   Are you a U.S. citizen? (1 = yes, 5 = no)

Years lived in the United States

1 to 2   If no, how long have you lived in the United States?** (open-ended; respondents were asked to give the number of years)

Appendix B: Table of Scale Reliabilities by Wave

This table indicates the reliabilities (unstandardized alpha coefficients) of all scales in the order in which they were presented in chapter 3. The reliability and number of scale items is given for each wave of data collection in which the scale was measured.

Appendix B

Scale Name	Number of Items	Reliability by Wave					
		1	2	3	4	5	6
1. Demographics and background							
SAT scale*	2	.55	—	—	—	—	—
Socioeconomic status scale*	3	.79	—	—	—	—	—
2. Group identification							
Ethnic identification scale	3	.84	.85	.85	.85	.85	.82
Ethnic private collective self-esteem scale	2	.67	—	—	—	—	—
Gender identification scale	2	.80	.81	.84	.83	.86	.84
3. Sociopolitical attitudes, orientations, and behavioral intentions							
Classical racism scale	2	.97	—	—	—	—	—
Ethnic activism scale	3	.89	.88	.88	.88	.89	.90
Gender activism scale	2	.83	.85	.84	.82	.83	.87
Intergroup anxiety scale	2	.37	.44	.49	.50	.52	.58
Legitimacy of the ethnic-status hierarchy scale	2	.41	.40	.43	.48	.54	.57
Opposition to affirmative action scale	3	.81	.79	.77	.79	.75	.78
Opposition to miscegenation scale	2	.96	.95	.95	.94	.95	.97
Permeability of the ethnic-status hierarchy scale	2	.80	.81	.83	.82	.85	.82
Political conservatism scale	2	.81	.61	.61	.64	.70	.62
Social dominance orientation (SDO) scale	4	.77	.72	.71	.72	.74	.74
Stability of the ethnic-status hierarchy scale	2	.42	.29	.39	.38	.38	.47
Symbolic racism scale	4	.64	.59	.63	.68	.73	.70
4. Psychological and academic adjustment, commitment, and performance							
Academic performance scale	2	—	.81	.78	.76	.76	.71
Discounting scale	2	—	.56	.63	.64	.66	.60
Disidentification scale	2	—	.49	.58	.58	.59	.60
Self-esteem scale	4	.77	.71	.73	.73	.75	.70
5. Expectations and attributions							
Attributions for future outcomes of ethnic group in society at large scale	2	.74	.75	.78	.81	.78	.81
Attributions for future outcomes of same-ethnicity UCLA students scale	2	.59	.76	.82	.83	.80	.82
Attributions for future self economic life outcomes scale	2	.46	.64	.71	.69	.68	.74

Expectancies of future ethnic prejudice and discrimination scale	2	.85	.84	.87	.84	.84	.83
Expectancies of future socioeconomic status scale	3	.55	.60	.58	.59	.61	.57
6. Perceptions and experiences on campus							
Perceived ethnic discrimination on campus scale	2	.90	.87	.86	.88	.88	.86

Source: Authors' compilation.

Note: A dash (—) indicates that the scale was not measured during that wave. An asterisk (*) indicates that the scale was assessed during the first wave in which a respondent participated in the study (wave 1 for those who participated in this precollege wave or wave 2 for those who did not participate in wave 1). For these scales, the reliability given in the column for wave 1 is the reliability for the combined data from wave 1 (for respondents who participated in this wave) and wave 2 (for wave 2 respondents who did not participate in wave 1).

Appendix C:

Attrition Analyses

This appendix contains the results of the attrition analyses we conducted to examine whether respondents who participated in all waves of the study differed from those who dropped out of the study at earlier stages. Our main objective was to determine whether attrition was selective with respect to our core variables. Differential attrition might have introduced various kinds of biases into our findings. We were particularly concerned about three potential biases. One was the possibility that the most prejudiced or most conservative students might have dropped out of the study out of reluctance to expose attitudes that were counternormative on the campus. This would have led us to overestimate the liberalizing effects of the college experience. A second potential bias was the possibility that the ethnic minority students who least identified with their own ethnic groups might have selectively dropped out because they were reluctant to expose attitudes that were counternormative within those groups. A third potential bias was the possibility that students whose attitudes about ethnic diversity were the least well formulated and least crystallized might have selectively dropped out to avoid exposing their poorly thought-out attitudes. This would have left us generalizing from a subset of students who were unusually interested in and knowledgeable and passionate about issues concerning ethnic diversity.

In the following analyses, we compared four groups of respondents. The "persisters" were those who participated throughout the study (n = 831). This group included those who participated in waves 1 to 5 inclusive (as well as those who spent an additional year at UCLA and participated in wave 6 in addition to waves 1 to 5). It also included the black and Latino oversample added at wave 2 if they participated in waves 2 to 5 inclusive (or waves 2 to 6 inclusive). These persisters were compared to three attrition groups. The "partway persisters" were those who participated in only the first few waves, completing wave 1 and wave 2 only or waves 1 to 3 only (n = 317). This group also included those in the black and Latino oversample added at wave 2 who participated in waves 2 and 3 only. The "voluntary early dropouts" were those who dropped out early in the study (n = 346), having completed wave 1 only, or wave 2 only if they were in the black and Latino oversample added at wave 2. Finally, the "involuntary early dropouts" (n = 175) consisted of the white or Asian students we decided not to recontact after wave 1 either because they had failed to complete much of the wave 1 questionnaire (having at least thirty missing values) or because they had not provided contact information. Since this last group was composed only of whites and Asians, and since most of our key variables were strongly correlated with ethnicity, we decided to conduct the attrition analyses within ethnicity, to unconfound attrition from ethnicity. We compared the attrition groups in terms of five categories of variables: demographic indicators, background variables (such as SAT scores and ethnicity of high school friends), major sociopolitical attitudes at wave 1, consistency of such attitudes at wave 1, and stability of such attitudes from wave 1 to wave 2.

A limitation of performing analyses within ethnic groups was a reduction in sample size. The number of cases in the persister, partway persister, voluntary early dropout, and involuntary early dropout groups seemed adequate among whites (n = 203, 112, 129, and 84, respectively) and Asians (n = 284, 89, 91, and 64, respectively). Among Latinos, the sample sizes were smaller, but they seemed adequate if our threshold for a significant effect was not too stringent (n = 182, 57, and 56, respectively, with no involuntary dropouts, by design). Among blacks, the sample sizes were small, at best (n = 44, 16, and 20, respectively, with no involuntary dropouts). Given that there were also some missing values on each variable, these numbers occasionally became even smaller. In the case of African Americans, the sample sizes were often too small to analyze. As a result, we tried to set lenient standards for detecting attrition effects.

Demographic Indicators

The first set of analyses tested for differential attrition on the eleven key demographic variables reported in chapter 3: age, gender, ethnicity-race, birthplace of student, religion, birthplace of parents and grandparents, language spoken at home, father's and mother's education, and family social class. For the analyses of categorical variables, we used chi-square analyses followed by an examination of standardized residuals larger than ±1.96 to locate deviations that were larger than what would be expected by chance. For ordinal, interval, and ratio variables, we used one-way analyses of variance with post-hoc LSD tests.

Ethnicity-race was related to attrition. This was expected, as some Latinos and blacks were added at wave 2 and some whites and Asians were not recontacted after wave 1 (the "involuntary early dropouts"). Still, ethnic minorities were more likely than whites to persist through the entire study. Removing the involuntary dropouts from the base, 61 percent of Asians, 55 percent of blacks, and 62 percent of Latinos persisted, but only 46 percent of whites persisted. Whites had a higher percentage of both voluntary early dropouts and partway persisters than did the three minority groups. As we proceeded through the analyses, we were especially alert to variables closely associated with attrition among whites, as this would allow us to detect possible selective attrition across ethnic groups on variables central to our findings.

We also compared the attrition groups on the other demographic variables. This involved forty tests (four ethnic groups multiplied by ten demographic variables). We found differences in seven cases. In only two areas do they seem to present a potentially meaningful pattern. Among whites, men were more likely than women to be persisters (44 percent and 34 percent, respectively), and men were also less likely than women to be voluntary early dropouts (20 percent and 28 percent, respectively). Conceivably, the survey's focus on ethnic prejudice and conflict was more aversive to some female students. However, the substantial political gender gap among whites at wave 1 would suggest that white women were not initially shy about taking a strong position (see chapter 4). There was also a set of significant but trivial age differences between attrition groups. (All mean differences in age were less than 0.10.) Among whites, involuntary early dropouts were slightly but significantly less likely (88 percent) to be born in the United States than persisters (94 percent) and on average had fewer parents born in the United States (1.54 versus 1.78) and fewer grandparents born in the United States. This suggests that some immigrants might have struggled with the lengthy wave 1 questionnaire about American ethnic relations. The differences are not large, however, and relatively few whites were immigrants. Among Asians, for whom immigration was a bigger part of our story, the immigration rate was almost identical among persisters and involuntary early dropouts (approximately 2 percent higher in the former group). For completeness, we mention that the Asian attrition groups differed significantly in a confusing way in subjective family socioeconomic status.

Overall, attrition seems to have been related to demographics at approximately chance levels, given that there were only seven significant differences out of forty tests. None of the significant results reflected particularly large differences. Demographic selectivity in attrition seems to have been negligible.

Background Variables

The second set of analyses examined whether there were differences among the attrition groups on fourteen background variables: measures of math and verbal SAT scores and precollege contact with members of the four main ethnic groups as neighbors, friends, and classmates in high school. For categorical variables, we again used chi-square analyses, followed by an examination of standardized residuals larger than ±1.96 to locate deviations that were larger than what would be expected by chance. For ordinal, interval, and ratio variables, we used one-way analyses of variance with post-hoc LSD tests.

There were only four significant attrition effects on background variables in the fifty-six tests (four ethnic groups multiplied by fourteen background variables) conducted. The few differences were small and inconsistent. Specifically, white persisters had high school classes with a somewhat greater number of outgroup (Latino) students than did the early dropouts, whether voluntary or involuntary. By contrast, Asian persisters had more ingroup (Asian) friends during high school than did the early dropouts, whether voluntary or involuntary, and they had fewer white neighbors than did the involuntary dropouts. Latino persisters had more outgroup (Asian) friends in high school than did the voluntary early dropouts. These differences may reflect the different neighborhood characteristics of these students. More plausible, however, is that these few, small, and inconsistent differences reflect chance variations. In any case, they suggest negligible selectivity on background variables due to attrition.

Mean Differences in Group Identification, Attitudes, Expectations, Attributions, and Perceptions

The third set of analyses examined whether attrition was selective along attitude dimensions. Here we tested whether there were mean attitude differences among the attrition groups at wave 1. Since we analyzed mean differences at wave 1 only, the black and Latino respondents added at wave 2 were not included in these analyses. We compared the attrition groups on the twenty-two main group identification, sociopolitical attitude, attitudinal orientation, behavioral intention, expectation, attribution, and perception variables first introduced in chapter 3. The group identification variables that we assessed included the following: ethnic identification, ethnic private collective self-esteem, and gender identification. In addition, we examined the following sociopolitical attitudes, orientations, and behavioral intentions: political conservatism, classic racism, symbolic racism, social dominance orientation (SDO), intergroup anxiety, ethnic activism, gender activism, stability of the ethnic-status hierarchy, legitimacy of the ethnic-status hierarchy, permeability of the ethnic-status hierarchy, opposition to miscegenation, and opposition to affirmative action. We also assessed self-esteem, expectations about future ethnic prejudice and discrimination, expectations about future socioeconomic status, attributions for future self economic life outcomes, attributions for future outcomes of UCLA students of the same ethnicity, attributions for future outcomes of one's ethnic group in society at large, and perceived ethnic discrimination on campus. We also compared attrition groups on our index of ingroup bias, for a total of twenty-three variables.[1] We conducted ninety-two tests (four ethnic groups multiplied by twenty-three attitudes). We used one-way analyses of variance, with attrition group as the independent variable and each of the scales as the dependent variables. In each case, we set a minimum threshold of marginally significant ($p < .10$) main effects of attrition group for meaningful attrition effects, and then we explored any significant differences with post-hoc LSD tests.

Appendix C

Conducting the analyses within ethnic groups showed at least marginally significant attrition effects on twelve of the ninety-two tests. Among whites, involuntary early dropouts were lower in social dominance orientation and ingroup bias than were the other attrition groups. These findings are contrary to the possibility that whites who were more prejudiced failed to complete the wave 1 questionnaire to avoid revealing their prejudices. Among Asians, the involuntary early dropouts had higher expectations for future economic success and higher perceptions of the permeability of the ethnic-status hierarchy, but they had stronger ethnic identification and greater perceived ethnic discrimination on campus than did the other attrition groups. This is a conflicting pattern that we found difficult to interpret. In four cases (one Asian and three Latino), the persisters did not differ significantly from the early voluntary dropouts, but they did differ significantly from the partway persisters, a pattern difficult to attribute to any simple selectivity in attrition. In two cases, significant differences emerged among blacks, but with a sample size smaller than ten, these results did not seem worth pursuing.

The number of even marginally significant ($p < .10$) differences (twelve of ninety-two) did not seem to depart greatly from chance. Moreover, the differences that were found presented no obvious pattern. Perhaps most important, there was no evidence for the two biases that most concerned us—namely, the tendency for more conservative or prejudiced white students to fail to complete the wave 1 questionnaire or later drop out of the study, or for the minority students least concerned about their ethnicity to drop out of the study.

Attitude Consistency

The fourth set of analyses examined differences among the attrition groups in attitude consistency. Attitude consistency was used as one component of attitude crystallization in chapters 4 and 5. Were the students with the least crystallized attitudes likely to drop out of the study selectively, perhaps because they were not much interested in the topics of the survey? The statistics we used were the Cronbach's alpha reliabilities of the twenty-two scales enumerated in the previous section. (Appendix B presents reliabilities for the whole sample on these scales.) Ingroup bias was also used in the last section on mean differences in attitudes, but it was omitted here, since alpha reliabilities cannot be computed on a scale created as a difference score. As a threshold for identifying a meaningful difference between attrition groups, we used a difference in alpha reliabilities of .10. Attrition effects smaller than that seemed unlikely to have substantially biased the findings presented in the volume. Again, we analyzed alpha reliabilities at wave 1 only, so the black and Latino respondents added at wave 2 were not included in these analyses. That reduced the number of African American participants to fewer than fifteen cases each among the partway persisters and early dropouts, so we present results only for whites, Asians, and Latinos.

For whites and Asians, this procedure yielded sixty-six comparisons of the persisters with the other three attrition groups (three comparisons multiplied by twenty-two attitudes). For Latinos, it yielded forty-four comparisons of persisters with partway persisters and early voluntary dropouts only (two comparisons multiplied by twenty-two attitudes). Among whites, the reliabilities for persisters were higher (by at least .10) than the other attrition groups in nine cases, and the reliabilities were lower in six cases. This net difference of plus three out of sixty-six did not seem to differ materially from chance. For Asians, the persisters were higher than the other attrition groups in ten cases and lower in eight cases. Again, the net difference of plus two out of sixty-six comparisons seemed close to chance. Among Latinos, there was a little more evidence of selective consistency among the persisters. In thirteen cases the persisters showed more consistency, and in eight cases the dropouts showed more. This net difference of plus five out of forty-four comparisons was greater than that for whites or Asians, but it was still not far from chance.

Across the three ethnic groups, then, the persisters showed substantially higher reliabilities (.10 or more) than the dropouts in 32 comparisons, and lower in 22 comparisons, out of a total of 176 comparisons. This reflects a net bias of only 5 percent in the direction about which we were concerned, namely, greater consistency among the persisters. Such a small net bias does not seem to reflect a sufficiently widespread difference to have greatly affected our main findings.

The Stability of Attitudes

For the final set of analyses, we examined whether there were differences among the attrition groups in a second component of crystallization, the stability of the students' initial attitudes. Again, our principal concern was that students with uncrystallized attitudes might have been more likely to drop out of the study because of lack of information or interest, leaving us generalizing about the student population as a whole on the basis of an unusually concerned and involved subset of the population. For these analyses, we computed test-retest correlations from wave 1 to wave 2 on twenty-one of the attitude scales used in the previous section. (Ingroup bias could be included here, but ethnic private collective self-esteem and classic racism could not, as they were measured only at wave 1.) Again, the black and Latino oversample added at wave 2 could not be included, because we did not have wave 1 data for them. As a result, we did not include the black students in these analyses, because the sample size was smaller than ten for the critical black partway persister cases. In addition, the analyses could not be conducted for the early dropouts (either voluntary or involuntary), because they did not participate in wave 2. Hence, we present only comparisons of persisters to partway persisters for whites, Asians, and Latinos, yielding twenty-one comparisons for each ethnic group and sixty-three comparisons total. We again adopted the threshold for a meaningful attrition effect of a difference of .10 between test-retest correlations across attrition groups. Anything less than that seemed unlikely to have biased our results.

Among whites, we found that the persisters showed more stable attitudes than the partway persisters in six of the twenty-one cases by our standard of a .10 difference in test-retest correlations, and persisters showed less stable attitudes in two cases. This yielded a net difference of plus four. However, among Asians, the persisters did not show more stability than the partway persisters in any cases, and they showed less stability in six cases, for a net difference of minus six. Among Latinos, the persisters showed more stability than the partway persisters in twelve cases, and less stability in four cases, for a net difference of plus eight.

Overall, then, the persisters' attitudes were more stable in eighteen of the sixty-three comparisons, the partway persisters' attitudes were more stable in twelve cases, and the remaining thirty-three differences fell below the .10 threshold. This does not seem to depart greatly from a pure chance pattern, by which each attrition group might have been expected to show more stable attitudes in fifteen comparisons. The possible outcome that concerned us, selective dropping out by students with less crystallized attitudes, emerged most strongly for Latinos, whereas the reverse pattern occurred for Asians. We have no ready explanation for why there might be such an ethnic difference. As a result, chance seems to be the best explanation for the overall pattern.

Conclusions

Attrition was considerable in this multi-wave panel study, as is usually the case in longitudinal research. Attrition is especially a problem with highly mobile young adults, such as those included in our study. Our concern was that attrition might be selective rather than random. Therefore, the relatively more ethnocentric students, or those uninvolved in issues of ethnic diversity, might have dropped out more readily than their more egalitarian or diversity-conscious peers. To test this, we compared students who persisted throughout the five to six waves of the study with those who dropped out after participating in just one wave or who dropped out after two or three administrations. We compared them in terms of their demographic characteristics, precollege background, group identification, precollege sociopolitical attitudes, orientations, behavioral intentions, expectations, attributions, and the consistency and stability of their precollege attitudes.

We found that whites, and especially white women, were somewhat more likely to drop out than other groups. However, we found no evidence that their reduced participation rates were related in any way to their attitudes about ethnic diversity. Beyond that, we did not find any systematic pattern of differences among attrition groups that would suggest enough selective attrition to provide alternative explanations for our main findings. Throughout our analyses, the effects of attrition were essentially what we would expect from chance. As a result, we conclude that selective attrition is unlikely to have affected our results sufficiently to qualify the findings that we describe throughout the volume.

Notes

Chapter 1

This chapter was authored by Jim Sidanius, Shana Levin, Colette van Laar, and David O. Sears.

Chapter 2

This chapter was authored by Jim Sidanius, Shana Levin, Colette van Laar, David O. Sears, Jeffrey Huntsinger, Stacey Sinclair, and Winona Foote.

Chapter 3

This chapter was authored by Shana Levin, David O. Sears, Colette van Laar, and Jim Sidanius.

1. An irony is that black admissions to the UC system as a whole are actually higher than they were under affirmative action, but UCLA and UC Berkeley, which are both more selective than the other UC campuses, have substantially lower black admissions rates.

Chapter 4

This chapter was authored by David O. Sears, Hillary Haley, and P. J. Henry.

1. An earlier version of this chapter was presented at the annual meeting of the International Society of Political Psychology, Berlin, Germany, July 19, 2002.
2. Unless otherwise indicated, the exact wording of all individual and scale items can be found under their corresponding labels in appendix A. Party identification was measured through the use of the

Notes

question: "How would you describe your own political party preference?" (1 = strong Democrat, 7 = strong Republican). In addition,
political outlook was measured through the use of the question:
"How would you describe your general political outlook?" (1 = very
liberal, 7 = very conservative).

3. For simplicity, we wanted to reduce these two seven-point scales to
three-point scales—Democratic-independent-Republican and lib-
eral-moderate-conservative, respectively. Since both seven-point
scales were labeled only at their endpoints, we were forced to make
some plausible guesses about how such scales map onto the standard measures of partisanship, which label all categories (see
Campbell et al. 1960; Green, Palmquist, and Schickler 2002; Miller
and Shanks 1996). We assumed that any student falling on either
side of the absolute midpoint of 4 had a partisan preference, while
those at the midpoint had no preference. Therefore, we classified
responses of 1 to 3 on the seven-point scales measuring party
identification and general political outlook as "Democratic" or "liberal," respectively; responses of 4 as "independent" or "moderate";
and those of 5 to 7 as "Republican" or "conservative."

4. The inegalitarianism subscale contained the following two items
(reverse-coded): "We should do what we can to equalize conditions
for different groups" and "We should increase social equality." The
dominance subscale contained the items "It's probably a good
thing that certain groups are at the top and other groups are at the
bottom" and "Inferior groups should stay in their place." For each
of the four items, participants responded on a scale ranging from 1
(strongly disagree) to 7 (strongly agree). We divided social dominance orientation into these two subscales for two reasons. First,
the two subscales often have different relationships with other attitudes (Sears and Henry 2005; Sears, Henry, and Kosterman
2000). Second, factor analyses on whites in the general population
have shown that inegalitarianism and dominance form two distinctive and weakly correlated subdimensions of SDO (Sears et al.
2000; Sears and Henry 2005).

5. The two items are highly correlated in each ethnic group. The Pearson correlations between the two items at college entry, using the
full seven-point scales on which each was originally measured,
yield r = .78 for whites, .61 for Asians, and .66 for Latinos. Extensive examination of the cross-tabulations of the two items among

different ethnic groups revealed no obvious asymmetries within groups or differences among groups, so combining them seems not to distort the realities.

6. The parental education and subjective family SES items are listed in appendix A as socioeconomic status items, and the SAT scale is listed under precollege academic performance.

7. Antiblack affect was assessed through use of the question "How positively or negatively do you feel toward African Americans/ blacks?" (1 = very negatively, 7 = very positively).

8. This weak role of dominance seems not to be an artifact of special social desirability pressures on campus against expressing such politically incorrect sentiments. Rather, dominance seems to be less politically powerful than inegalitarian values in the general population as well. For example, in five general population surveys in Los Angeles, the average correlation of inegalitarianism with racial policy preferences was r = .39, whereas the correlation of dominance was r = .11. In regression equations, all five of the inegalitarianism terms were significant, while none of the dominance terms were (Sears and Henry 2005, 140). Similarly, in several general population surveys, inegalitarianism had an average correlation of r = .29 with both party identification and political outlook, while dominance had an average correlation of r = .01 (Sears, Henry, and Kosterman 2000, 105). Our analyses of the 1996 Los Angeles Social Survey also show that inegalitarianism is more closely related to symbolic racism than is dominance. On the other hand, those analyses also demonstrate that dominance is significantly related to such blatantly antiblack attitudes as the black feeling thermometer and perceptions of biological inferiority, as well as to perceptions that blacks are trying to take resources away from other groups. Dominance appears to be more closely related to "old-fashioned" or "Jim Crow" racism, then, and to perceptions of zero-sum racial conflicts, perhaps because of its specific focus on keeping inferior groups in their places.

9. The item measuring support for Bill Clinton can be found under "Political Candidate Preference and Voting Behavior" in appendix A.

10. Alpha reliabilities typically are higher with scales having more items, everything else being equal.

11. Strictly speaking, of course, such correlations measure the stability of individuals' attitudes only when the marginal frequencies (that

is, the aggregate level of opinion) remain constant over time. If the aggregate distribution changes, then a high test-retest correlation reflects only individuals' stable position relative to others. For example, the students may move to the left en masse. If their later attitudes are highly correlated with earlier attitudes, then that means that they have maintained their position relative to others despite substantial attitude change by individuals. We treat constancy of relative standing as reflecting a clear and consistent position over time, at least relative to others, and thus as reflecting high crystallization.

12. It might be noted that the stability of opposition to affirmative action ($r = .52$) may be slightly enhanced because of the use of scales rather than of individual items to measure the other policies, presumably because individual items underestimate crystallization owing to lower reliability (Sears 1983).

Chapter 5

This chapter was authored by David O. Sears and P. J. Henry.

1. These expectations would not depart much from those of a classical or canonical assimilation theory (see Alba and Nee 2003; Gordon 1964).

2. The social structural theories so far seem not to have spoken very directly to the question of attitude crystallization, though there is no doubt that such implications could be developed in the future.

3. Unless otherwise indicated, the exact wording of all individual and scale items can be found under their corresponding labels in appendix A. The two items measuring political conservatism—party identification and political outlook—were the following: "How would you describe your own political party preference?" ($1 =$ strong Democrat, $7 =$ strong Republican) and "How would you describe your general political outlook?" ($1 =$ very liberal, $7 =$ very conservative), respectively.

4. The estimates in chapter 4 were based on all students who participated in the precollege wave of data collection and who identified themselves as whites, Asians, Latinos, or blacks. Most of our further analyses require comparing students' attitudes at college entry with their responses at later stages, and so we require data on the same students across waves. As a result, the results shown in

tables 4.1 and 5.1 differ slightly. Also, given sample attrition, the number of African Americans responding to both the precollege and senior waves is too small (n = 39) to subdivide at any point in time or to provide reliable estimates in their senior year. Even fewer responded to the precollege, sophomore, and senior waves (n = 34). As a result, we restrict our analyses to whites, Asians, and Latinos.

5. As noted in chapter 4, the inegalitarianism subscale contained the following two items (reverse-coded): "We should do what we can to equalize conditions for different groups" and "We should increase social equality." The dominance subscale contained the items "It's probably a good thing that certain groups are at the top and other groups are at the bottom" and "Inferior groups should stay in their place." For all four items, participants responded on a scale ranging from 1 (strongly disagree) to 7 (strongly agree).

6. We averaged the values of these variables across the freshman to junior waves. The precollege wave, of course, was conducted prior to enrollment, and using senior-wave responses would have left some causal ambiguity, given that they were collected simultaneously with the dependent variables.

7. The liberal majors included all those in the Divisions of Social Sciences (except for economics) and Humanities, all psychology majors, and all arts and theater majors. The conservative majors included all those in the Divisions of Physical Sciences and Life Sciences (except psychology), all economics majors, and those in the School of Engineering.

8. Once again, we do not present data for African American students in this chapter because of their small numbers.

9. As seen earlier, the gender gap among Asian students did not increase through college. Nevertheless, we checked whether there was differential change of men and women across majors. There was not—all groups became more liberal. The greatest liberalizing shift was among Asian men in conservative majors (+20 percent) and the smallest among Asian women in conservative majors (+9 percent). This finding again emphasizes the broad and general political liberalization of students through college rather than changes in limited subsets of students.

10. We also expected that greater parental education would be associated with the precollege socialization of racial tolerance, which

might then persist through college. However, it did not correlate significantly with symbolic racism at either college entry or college exit among whites ($r = -.05$ and $-.02$, respectively). Indeed, only one of twelve correlations with our two central dependent variables was significant (Latinos, with political orientation, in wave 5, $r = .16$, $p < .05$, up just slightly from wave 1: $r = .10$, not significant). The precollege percentages presented here differ slightly from those presented in chapter 4 because here we exclude students who did not respond to the senior year wave.

11. As noted in chapter 4, antiblack affect consisted of the single item regarding affect toward African Americans/blacks: "How positively or negatively do you feel toward African Americans/blacks?" ($1 =$ very negatively, $7 =$ very positively). The precollege correlations differ slightly from those presented in chapter 4 because here we exclude students who did not respond in the senior year.

12. This mixed picture is not unique to these two attitudes. For example, the white students' attitudes toward affirmative action did not become more internally consistent through college. The internal consistency of our three-item affirmative action scale at college entry ($\alpha = .78$) was actually a little higher than that at the end of the senior year ($\alpha = .73$).

13. Its internal consistency ($\alpha = .74$ at the end of the senior year) and its stability over the senior year ($r = .72$) rival the consistency and stability of symbolic racism held by white adults in the general population, which average around $\alpha = .70$ and $r = .68$, respectively, as noted in the previous chapter.

14. By college exit, students' symbolic racism was quite highly crystallized relative to other political attitudes and values held by white adults in the broader electorate. Its internal consistency ($\alpha = .74$) compares favorably to that of the values scales measured in two NES panel studies conducted in the early 1990s, including the four-item morality scale (alphas ranging from .62 to .70 over four surveys) and the six-item equality scale (alphas ranging from .62 to .72). Its stability is also comparable. In the two NES panels in the 1990s, the stability of the morality scale averaged $r = .65$, and the equality scale $r = .53$ (Henry and Sears 2002).

15. Among the four policy issues, attitudes toward affirmative action stand out as the most crystallized both at college entry and throughout college. As a result, we would not expect much increase

through college. Indeed, attitudes toward affirmative action did not become more internally consistent or more stable through college; the alpha for our three-item scale at the end of the senior year was similar ($\alpha = .73$) to that at college entry ($\alpha = .78$). Its stability was .85 across the freshman year and .77 across the senior year. It had already been an extremely controversial issue when these students entered college because of the dramatic changes in university policy described earlier and the issue's tangible impact on the students' lives.

16. As indicated in chapter 4, of the Asians at college entry, 64 percent were classified as "new," as were 49 percent of the Latinos. By comparison, only 7 percent of the whites and African Americans were classified as "new" in those terms.

17. The change was statistically significant except for the "new Latinos" regarding political conservatism, who had a smaller sample size (n = 70).

Chapter 6

This chapter was authored by David O. Sears, Ming-Ying Fu, P. J. Henry, and Kerra Bui.

1. One caveat: we have less confidence in the adequacy of our black subsample than in the other ethnic subsamples. Blacks were a small minority on the campus to begin with, they were undersampled at the beginning of the study, and it is possible that this subsample was not representative of all blacks in the freshman class. As a result, we place more stock on comparisons of our Asian and Latino subsamples with each other and with whites; for comparisons with blacks, we mostly rely on other published studies (for example, Bobo and Johnson 2001; Dawson 1994; Hochschild 1995).

2. For explication of these theories, see chapter 2.

3. Some theories, however, privilege race and ethnicity as essentialist dimensions of categorization, such as in the notion of "primordial attachments" or the competition between national identity and "communal," "tribal," or other subnational groupings (Geertz 1964; Horowitz 1985). Still, such essentialist assumptions are not required in order to view ethnicity and race as central dimensions of group categorization in contemporary American society, since

the prevailing sociopolitical context has long given them ample attention.

4. We make no hard distinction between race and ethnicity here in light of the many and fluctuating applications of these terms to both European and non-European minority groups over the years, in both common and intellectual discourse.

5. For earlier studies of ethnic identities in the broader population, see, for example, Rumbaut and Portes (2001), a volume that examines the social identities of immigrant schoolchildren, many of them quite poor. Lawrence Bobo and Devon Johnson (2001), Jack Citrin and David O. Sears (2007), Sears and Victoria Savalei (2006), and the Pew Hispanic Center (2002) have analyzed surveys of general population samples of blacks, Asians, and Latinos.

6. Unless otherwise noted, the exact wording of all individual and scale items can be found under their corresponding labels in appendix A.

7. In table 6.1, we use all the respondents who were available to maximize the reliability of the results. If we use only the students who responded to the three waves compared later in this chapter, however, the results are much the same.

8. Each major Asian national group showed this preference for national origins, including Filipinos (93 percent), East Indians (82 percent), Koreans (65 percent), Japanese (60 percent), Southeast Asians (59 percent), and Chinese (55 percent). All the Latinos of Central or Southern American origins used pan-ethnic identities, probably reflecting the dominance of Mexican Americans in this sample.

9. As already indicated, an open-ended ethnicity item came at the beginning of the questionnaire. It was followed a few items later by the standard closed-ended question about the student's and parents' ethnicities. Ethnic identification items followed twenty-eight items later. The referents for these ethnic identification items were unspecified. The reliability (Cronbach's alpha) of the ethnic identification scale was, at the college entry and senior waves, respectively, .74 and .76 for Asians; .86 and .85 for Latinos; .87 and .88 for blacks; and .87 and .77 for whites.

10. The respondent's generation in the United States was assessed through the following items: "Were you born in the United States?" "How many of your parents were born in the United

States?" and "How many of your grandparents were born in the United States?" The ethnicities of the respondent's closest friends in high school were assessed through these questions: In high school, how many of your closest friends were Latino/Hispanic? African American/black? Asian/Asian American? Caucasian/white? (1 = none, 2 = few, 3 = many, 4 = most, 5 = all). The following societal ethnic discrimination item was used: "American society just doesn't deal fairly with people from my ethnic background."

11. Among adults, the reverse of this people of color expectation holds: foreign-born Latinos actually perceive considerably more discrimination against their group than do U.S.-born Latinos (Sears and Savalei 2006).

12. The people of color idea here is that as the point of immigration recedes, according to our main indicators (language spoken at home, ethnicity of high school friends), the effects of societal discrimination should expand in later generations. But none of the interactions of generation by these variables was significantly correlated with societal ethnic discrimination, and none of the interactions of societal ethnic discrimination by these variables had significant effects on strength of ethnic identification, among either Asians or Latinos, when added as separate terms to the equations shown in table 6.3.

13. In the senior year wave, the open-ended self-categorization item was placed, as in the college entry wave, virtually at the beginning of the interview. In the sophomore year wave, it followed a number of other items. Though none of them focused on race or ethnicity, there was a slight rise in the frequency of pan-ethnic identity labels.

14. The referents for ethnic identification items were not specified in any wave. They came immediately after the open-ended ethnic self-categorization item at the end of the sophomore year, and twenty-five items after the open-ended item at the end of the senior year. The closed-ended ethnic self-categorization item was not used in either the sophomore or senior wave.

It is possible that the somewhat variable placement of these ethnic identification items across waves in some way produced artifactual differences across waves. In addition, the open-ended self-categorization item might have evoked the "true" ethnic identity, while the closed-ended item falsely forced students to choose pan-ethnic labels. If so, ethnic identification would have been greatest when measured immediately after the open-ended self-categorization item, as in the sophomore year wave. However, ethnic identification was strongest at college entry for both Asians and Latinos, as shown in table 6.2. As a result, we do not believe that item order affected these results.

15. Taken literally, of course, such correlations merely assess the stability over time of relative individual differences. However, given the absence of major aggregate-level shifts of attitude for Asians and Latinos shown in table 6.2, they can be interpreted as reflecting the extent to which individuals retain the same attitude over time.

16. See appendix A for the exact wording of all items. The item labeled "prejudice against group imposes barriers" was measured through the use of the following question: "To what extent will prejudice and discrimination against members of your ethnic group impose barriers to their future outcomes?" (1 = not at all, 7 = very much). The item labeled "minorities get unfair treatment" was measured through the use of the following item: "Minority groups usually don't get fair treatment in American society" (1 = strongly disagree, 7 = strongly agree).

17. We also examined changes in the correlations of strength of ethnic identity with evaluations of the ingroup and ethnic outgroups, using feeling thermometers (that is, measures of affect toward the four main ethnic groups; see appendix A). The changes were small and inconsistent. We are not inclined to make much of such null findings, however. The ingroup evaluations were extremely highly and positively correlated with averaged outgroup evaluations ($r = .81$ for Asians and $r = .75$ for Latinos). This is a common finding with ethnic group thermometers, on which the method variance shared across items usually far exceeds the variance uniquely attributable to evaluations of any given target group.

18. Negative kurtosis reflects flatter distributions—and positive kurtosis more peaked distributions—than the normal curve. For Asians, two of the eight indicators showed increased variance, and two showed reduced kurtosis; for Latinos, three showed increased variance, and one showed reduced kurtosis.

19. The balance of pan-ethnic and national identities did not differ

significantly across generations in the United States for either Asian or Latino students at any wave.

20. Note that we try to clarify the direction of causal flow by using friends at the end of the sophomore year as a predictor for ethnic identity at the end of the senior year.

21. Japanese Americans represented 7 percent of Asian students and were only the sixth-largest nationality group among them.

22. Latinos' own subjective racial identities tend only rarely to reflect some "black" identity, as well. In the 2000 census, 48 percent of those with Hispanic background described themselves on the race question as "white"; only 2 percent identified as "black," and 42 percent as "some other race" (U.S. Census Bureau 2001; see also Pew Hispanic Center 2002). Portes and Rumbaut (2001) found that 1 percent of the immigrant children and parents from Cuba, Mexico, and Nicaragua described themselves as "black." Most preferred to describe themselves as "white," "Hispanic," "Latino," or "Mexican."

Chapter 7

This chapter was authored by Shana Levin, Stacey Sinclair, Jim Sidanius, and Colette van Laar.

1. Given the status differences between members of different ethnic groups in American society—with whites as the dominant group, Asian Americans the intermediate-status group, and Latinos and African Americans the lower-status groups—social dominance theory would expect the greatest opposition to the ethnic status hierarchy to be shown by those most disadvantaged by it: blacks and Latinos. In this way, the social dominance model differs from the people of color model discussed in previous chapters in that it expects differences between minority ethnic groups as a function of their group status, while the people of color model does not.

2. For a multinational example of this process, see research by Christian Staerklé, Jim Sidanius, Eva Green, and Ludwin Molina (2005). However, for a counterexample, see research by Jim Sidanius, Yesilernis Peña, and Mark Sawyer (2001).

3. The exact wording of all individual and scale items can be found

Notes

under their corresponding labels in appendix A, and the scale reliabilities are shown in appendix B.

4. To test this hypothesis we conducted a one-way ANOVA for each
   year in college, with ethnicity as the independent variable and
   American identification as the dependent variable.

5. Overall ethnicity effect for freshman year: $F(3, 1,281) = 22.26$, $p <$
   $.001$; sophomore year: $F(3, 1,032) = 9.68$, $p < .001$; junior year:
   $F(3, 849) = 5.30$, $p = .001$; senior year: $F(3, 744) = 7.85$, $p < .001$.

6. This technique is preferable to repeated-measures ANOVA because
   it does not require the listwise deletion of cases. In our sample, we
   did not want to use listwise deletion because there were very few
   African American respondents who participated in all four waves
   of data collection ($n = 40$).

7. With whites dummy-coded as the reference group, the HLM results give the slopes for each group *compared to* whites, not the
   slopes in absolute terms. The slope for Latinos compared to whites
   was $b = .05$, $p > .10$, indicating a nonsignificant, less negative
   slope for Latinos compared to whites. The slope for blacks compared to whites was $b = .09$, $p > .10$, also indicating a nonsignificant, less negative slope for blacks compared to whites. In contrast, the slope for Asian Americans compared to whites was $b =$
   $.13$, $p < .001$, indicating a significantly less negative slope for
   Asian Americans compared to whites.

8. We examined these relationships in two stages. The first stage of
   the analysis used simple regression to determine the various
   slopes, among each of the different ethnic groups, for the regressions of American identification on ethnic identification. Then, in
   the second stage, slope differences between the four ethnic groups
   were tested using a two-step, hierarchical multiple regression
   analysis. In this analysis, American identification was regressed on
   the main effect terms for ethnic identification and ethnicity (ethnicity being represented by three dummy-coded variables) at the
   first step, and then the product terms for the interaction between
   ethnic identification and ethnicity were entered at a second step.
   This same two-step procedure was conducted for each of the four
   years in college.

9. For each year in college, the R^2 change associated with the entry of
   the Ethnic Identification X Ethnicity interaction terms was statistically significant, as were the overall regression models. (Fresh-

374

man year: R^2 change for the interaction effect = .05, $F(3, 1,277)$ = 22.81, $p < .001$; overall model: $F(7, 1,277) = 20.39$, $p < .001$, R^2 = .10. Sophomore year: R^2 change for the interaction effect = .05, $F(3, 1,027) = 18.30$, $p < .001$; overall model: $F(7, 1,027) = 12.40$, $p < .001$, $R^2 = .08$. Junior year: R^2 change for the interaction effect = .05, $F(3, 844) = 14.62$, $p < .001$; overall model: $F(7, 844) = 8.71$, $p < .001$, $R^2 = .07$. Senior year: R^2 change for the interaction effect = .05, $F(3, 739) = 13.50$, $p < .001$; overall model: $F(7, 739) = 9.70$, $p < .001$, $R^2 = .08$.)

10. To test this idea, for each ethnic group we performed two LISREL structural equation analyses. In the first stage of these analyses, the regression of American identification upon ethnic identification was allowed to vary across the four years of college. If this model fit the data well, it would indicate that the relationships between ethnic identification and American identification changed over the college years. In the second stage of the analyses, the regression was constrained to equality across the four college years. If this constrained model showed a significant decrease in the degree of model fit, it would indicate that the relationship between ethnic identification and American identification could not be considered homogeneous over the college years. Using a chi-square difference test, we found no significant deterioration in model fit when moving from the unconstrained to the constrained models. In other words, the relationships between ethnic identification and American identification remained essentially stable over time for all four ethnic groups.

11. Results for the series of one-way ANOVAs for each year in college (with ethnicity as the independent variable and university identification as the dependent variable) were as follows: overall ethnicity effect for freshman year: $F(3, 1,286) = 2.64$, $p < .05$; sophomore year: $F(3, 1,041) = 1.30$, $p > .10$; junior year: $F(3, 854) = 4.93$, $p < .01$; senior year: $F(3, 742) = 3.67$, $p = .01$.

12. Results for the comparisons between Asian Americans and whites were as follows: freshman year ($M = 5.92$ versus $M = 5.66$, $p < .10$), junior year ($M = 5.96$ versus $M = 5.55$, $p < .01$), and senior year ($M = 5.83$ versus $M = 5.41$, $p = .01$). Additional analyses using the HLM technique (with whites dummy-coded as the comparison group) revealed that university identification significantly declined among whites across the college

years (b = −.10, p < .001). The slopes for Asian Americans, Latinos, and blacks were not found to differ significantly from the slope for whites (slope for Asian Americans compared to whites: b = .07, p > .10; Latinos compared to whites: b = .06, p > .10; blacks compared to whites: b = .04, p > .10). In other words, university identification among whites, Asian Americans, Latinos, and blacks declined across the college years to a similar extent.

13. Inspection of table 7.4 also suggests that, if anything, the relationship between ethnic and university identification appears to become slightly larger rather than smaller over time. Despite this apparent trend, however, use of LISREL analyses showed that it was generally not statistically significant. The only exception was found among Asian American students, for whom the relationship between ethnic and university identification appeared to be stronger in the sophomore, junior, and senior years than in the freshman year.

14. For each year in college, the R^2 change associated with the entry of the Ethnic Identification X Ethnicity interaction terms was not statistically significant, and the overall regression models were significant. For freshman year: R^2 change for the interaction effect = .003, $F(3, 1,281) = 1.50$, $p > .10$; overall model: $F(7, 1,281) = 4.51$, $p < .001$, $R^2 = .02$. For sophomore year: R^2 change for the interaction effect = .004, $F(3, 1,031) = 1.29$, $p > .10$; overall model: $F(7, 1,031) = 5.66$, $p < .001$, $R^2 = .04$. For junior year: R^2 change for the interaction effect = .005, $F(3, 848) = 1.59$, $p > .10$; overall model: $F(7, 848) = 10.24$, $p < .001$, $R^2 = .08$. For senior year: R^2 change for the interaction effect = .004, $F(3, 738) < 1$; overall model: $F(7, 738) = 7.31$, $p < .001$, $R^2 = .07$.

15. We also examined possible differences within the Asian American and Latino subgroups. We conducted separate analyses comparing the effects of ethnic identification on both American identification and university identification among Asian American students who indicated that they most closely identified with an Asian subgroup (Chinese, Korean, Japanese, and Filipino) and those who indicated that they most closely identified with the Asian American superordinate group. These analyses demonstrated that American identification related to ethnic identification in similar ways for those who identified themselves as Chinese, Korean, Japanese, Filipino,

and Asian (R^2 change when the interaction between ethnic identi-fication and Asian group was entered into the regression equation after the main effect terms = .04, $F(4, 162) = 1.97$, $p > .10$), as did university identification (R^2 change for the interaction effect = .04, $F(4, 162) = 1.87$, $p > .10$). All Asian Americans were therefore grouped together in the main analyses.

Among Latinos, Chicano/Mexican American was the only sizable subgroup indicated. Nearly everyone else indicated that they most closely identified with the larger "Latino/Hispanic" category. We therefore conducted separate analyses comparing the effects of ethnic identification on both American and university identifica-tion among Latino students who indicated that they most closely identified with a Latino subgroup (Chicanos/Mexican Americans) and those who indicated that they most closely identified with the Latino/Hispanic superordinate group. These analyses demon-strated that American identification related to ethnic identification in similar ways for those who identified themselves as Chicano/Mexican American and Latino/Hispanic (R^2 change for the interac-tion effect = .000, $F(1, 207) = .11$, $p > .10$), as did university identi-fication (R^2 change for the interaction effect = .01, $F(1, 207) = 1.23$, $p > .10$). All Latinos were therefore grouped together in the main analyses.

We did not conduct these separate analyses for whites or African Americans because they overwhelmingly indicated that they most closely identified with the white or African American superordinate group rather than with an ethnic subgroup.

16. The vast majority of African Americans are descendants of Africans who arrived in the United States before 1808, while most white Americans are descendants of German, Irish, Polish, Rus-sian, Jewish, and Scandinavian immigrants who entered the United States between 1840 and 1920.

Chapter 8

This chapter was authored by Shana Levin, Colette van Laar, and Jim Sidanius.

1. At the same time, however, those arguing from a contact theory perspective also recognize that when minority students are choos-ing to form segregated friendship groups and join segregated or-

ganizations on campus, their choices may reflect the failure of the institution to establish a positive campus racial climate rather than a failure of the students to integrate themselves into an open, multicultural environment.

2. Unless otherwise noted, the exact wording of all individual and scale items can be found under their corresponding labels in appendix A. Ingroup bias was assessed by first asking the students: "How positively or negatively do you feel toward the following groups?" The individual items were: "Caucasians/whites," "Latinos/ Hispanics," "Asians/Asian Americans," and "African Americans/ blacks" (1 = very negatively, 7 = very positively). In each year, ingroup bias was computed as the item measuring ingroup affect minus the average of the three items measuring outgroup affect.

3. In each year, the measure of ingroup friends is the single item for friends of one's own ethnic group and the measure of outgroup friends is the average of the three items for friends of the other ethnic groups. The composite measure of contact with ingroup friends is the average of the ingroup friends items measured in the sophomore and junior years, and the composite measure of contact with outgroup friends is the average of the outgroup friends scales measured in the sophomore and junior years.

4. In the first block of hierarchical regression analyses, we used the composite measure of outgroup friends in the sophomore and junior years as our dependent variable. At the first step we entered the background variables we controlled for in the analyses—precollege friendships, gender, religion, foreign cultural closeness, socioeconomic status, and political conservatism—along with freshman ingroup bias and intergroup anxiety. *Precollege friendships* were assessed in terms of close friendships in high school with members of each of the four major ethnic groups. Specifically, students were asked: "In high school, how many of your closest friends were: African American? Latino? Asian American? Caucasian?" (1 = none, 2 = few, 3 = many, 4 = most, 5 = all). *Foreign cultural closeness* was computed as the average of four items that were standardized on a 0-to-1 scale ($\alpha = .87$): whether the respondent, his or her parents, or his or her grandparents were born in the United States; and language spoken at home. Higher numbers indicate that a person was not born in the United States, had fewer parents and grandparents born in the United States, and was less likely to

speak English at home. The *Socioeconomic status* and *political conservatism scales* were also used as controls in these analyses. (See appendix A for the exact wording of all items.) In the next step we entered the main effects of ethnicity into the equation, and in the last step we entered the interactions between ethnicity and the freshman ethnic attitudes to see if the effects of freshman ingroup bias and intergroup anxiety on outgroup friendships vary by ethnic group. Then we conducted the same set of analyses for ingroup friendships.

5. There were significant negative associations between ingroup bias and proportion of outgroup friends ($\beta = -.12$, p < .001) and between intergroup anxiety and proportion of outgroup friends ($\beta = -.11$, p < .001). There were significant positive associations between ingroup bias and proportion of ingroup friends ($\beta = .17$, p < .001) and between intergroup anxiety and proportion of ingroup friends ($\beta = .15$, p < .001).

6. In this series of hierarchical regression analyses, we use ingroup bias and intergroup anxiety measured in the senior year as our dependent variables (one in each analysis). At the first step, we enter the composite measure of outgroup friends in the sophomore and junior years into the equation, along with both ethnic attitudes measured in the freshman year and the background variables. In the next step, we enter the main effects of ethnicity, and in the last step we enter the interaction between ethnicity and the measure of outgroup friends to see if the effect of outgroup friendships on each ethnic attitude varies by ethnic group. We then repeat the series of analyses for ingroup friendships. Because the proportions of ingroup and outgroup friendships were negatively correlated with one another and therefore could mask the effects of one another when entered simultaneously into a regression analysis, we conduct these analyses separately for each friendship variable.

7. Results show significant negative associations between proportion of outgroup friends and ingroup bias ($\beta = -.11$, p = .001), and between proportion of outgroup friends and intergroup anxiety ($\beta = -.14$, p < .001).

8. Results show significant positive associations between proportion of ingroup friends and ingroup bias and between proportion of ingroup friends and intergroup anxiety: $\beta = .07$, p < .05, and $\beta = .12$, p < .001, respectively.

9. Although we were not able to run the same longitudinal analyses for blacks that we ran for whites, Asians, and Latinos, we were able to run analyses for blacks of the effects of ethnic attitudes during the sophomore year on interethnic dating during the junior year (controlling for gender, foreign cultural closeness, socioeconomic status, and precollege friendships) and for the effects of interethnic dating during junior year on ethnic attitudes during senior year (controlling for the sophomore year ethnic attitude and demographic variables). Results for the first analysis indicate that neither ingroup bias ($\beta = .01$, $p = .90$) nor intergroup anxiety ($\beta = .10$, $p = .39$) during the sophomore year affected the degree to which blacks dated outside their ethnic group during their junior year of college. Furthermore, results for the second analysis demonstrate that interethnic dating during their junior year of college did not affect the amount of ingroup bias ($\beta = -.20$, $p = .21$) or intergroup anxiety ($\beta = .11$, $p = .56$) that these black students exhibited at the end of college. However, because of the small sample sizes of black students ($n = 62$ for the first analysis and $n = 41$ for the second), these findings must be interpreted with caution.

10. The dating of members of the four main ethnic groups was measured by the same four items at the end of students' sophomore and junior years of college. At the end of the sophomore year, the stem question read, "Since you've been in college, have you dated anyone who is . . . ," and the individual items were: "Asian American?" "African American?" "Latino?" and "Caucasian?" (0 = no, 1 = yes). As such, these variables measure dating during the freshman and sophomore years of college. At the end of the junior year, the stem question read, "Since last June, have you dated anyone who is . . . ," and the individual items once again were: "Asian American?" "African American?" "Latino?" and "Caucasian?" (0 = no, 1 = yes). As such, these variables measure dating during the junior year of college only. Because the dating variables measured at the end of the sophomore year measured dating during the freshman year as well, we could not separate freshman and sophomore year dating. These variables were further combined with the variables measuring dating during the junior year to form composites of freshman through junior year dating.

Four composite variables of freshman through junior year dating were computed, one each for having dated whites, Asians, African

Americans, and Latinos during the first three years of college. Each of these freshman through junior year dating variables reflects the sum of two variables for each target ethnic group, one measured at the end of sophomore year (for dating a member of that ethnic group during freshman and sophomore years) and the other at the end of junior year (for dating a member of that ethnic group during junior year). Therefore, for these composite measures, 0 = have not dated a member of this group by the end of sophomore year or during junior year, 1 = have dated a member of this group either by the end of sophomore year or during junior year, and 2 = have dated a member of this group both by the end of sophomore year and during junior year. The means of these four composite measures of freshman through junior year dating are shown in figure 8.3. These measures were also combined into a composite measure of freshman through junior year interethnic dating by taking the average of the three variables for the three ethnic outgroups.

11. In the first set of analyses, the composite measure of freshman through junior year interethnic dating is the dependent variable. At the first step, we enter the demographic variables (gender, foreign cultural closeness, socioeconomic status, and precollege friendships) into the equation, along with precollege ingroup bias and intergroup anxiety. In the next two steps, we enter the main effect of ethnicity into the equation, followed by the interactions between ethnicity and the precollege ethnic attitudes.

12. There were significant negative relationships between precollege ingroup bias and interethnic dating during the first three years of college ($\beta = -.11$, $p = .001$) and between precollege intergroup anxiety and interethnic dating ($\beta = -.14$, $p < .001$).

13. In this set of hierarchical regression analyses, ingroup bias and intergroup anxiety measured at the end of senior year were the dependent variables (one in each analysis). At the first step, we entered the composite measure of freshman through junior year interethnic dating into the equation, along with the precollege ethnic attitude and demographic variables. In the next step, we entered the main effect of ethnicity, and then the interaction between ethnicity and interethnic dating to see if the effect of interethnic dating on each ethnic attitude varied by ethnic group.

14. There were significant negative relationships between interethnic dating and ingroup bias and between interethnic dating and inter-

group anxiety: $\beta = -.08$, $p < .05$, and $\beta = -.08$, $p < .05$, respectively.

15. The interaction between ethnicity and interethnic dating was significant for intergroup anxiety, $p < .01$. Separate regressions for each ethnic group showed significant negative relationships between interethnic dating and intergroup anxiety among Asians and Latinos: $b = -.16$, $p < .05$, and $b = -.19$, $p < .05$, respectively.

16. Perceived discrimination is measured by the perceived ethnic discrimination on campus scale, academic commitment by the single item of consideration of dropping out of UCLA before earning a degree (reverse-coded), motivation by the single item of importance of getting a high GPA, and performance by the academic performance scale; see appendix A for all measures.

17. In this analysis, we control for precollege friendships to take into account students' predispositions to form more ingroup friendships during college when they have had more ingroup friendships before college. We also examine the interaction between ethnicity and perceived ethnic discrimination on campus. In addition, we conduct separate regression analyses for each group to see if the effect of the campus climate variable on ingroup friendship varies by ethnic group.

18. There was a significant positive association between perceptions of discrimination at the end of students' freshman year and proportion of ingroup friends during their sophomore and junior years: $\beta = .13$, $p < .001$.

19. The interaction between ethnicity and perceived ethnic discrimination on campus was significant, $p < .05$. The ethnic groups showed the following associations between perceptions of ethnic discrimination on campus at the end of freshman year and proportion of ingroup friends during sophomore and junior years: blacks, $b = .17$, $p = .002$; Asians, $b = .07$, $p = .01$; Latinos, $b = .07$, $p = .01$; whites, $b = .02$, $p > .05$.

20. To test this peer socialization hypothesis we examine the effect of ingroup friendships at the end of freshman year on perceptions of ethnic discrimination on campus during sophomore and junior years, controlling for precollege expectations of perceived ethnic discrimination on campus. This allows us to see if perceptions of ethnic discrimination on campus increase during the sophomore

and junior years of college in part owing to the proportion of in-group friends students have at the end of their freshman year, even when we take into account preexisting differences between students in their expectations of perceived ethnic discrimination on campus. We also examine the interaction between ethnicity and prior ingroup friendships and conduct separate regression analyses for each group to see if prior ingroup friendships have similar effects on subsequent perceptions of ethnic discrimination on campus for all groups.

21. There was a significant positive association between proportion of ingroup friends at the end of freshman year and perceptions of ethnic discrimination on campus during sophomore and junior years: $\beta = .10$, $p < .001$.

22. The interaction between ethnicity and ingroup friendships did not reach statistical significance, $p > .05$. The separate regression analyses revealed significant positive associations between proportion of ingroup friends at the end of freshman year and perceptions of ethnic discrimination on campus during sophomore and junior years for each ethnic group: blacks, $b = .52$, $p = .005$; Latinos, $b = .21$, $p = .02$; Asians, $b = .14$, $p = .01$; whites, $b = .15$, $p = .03$.

23. In these analyses, we control for freshman year belonging, academic commitment, motivation, and performance, respectively. Again, we also examine the interactions between ethnicity and ingroup friendships and conduct separate regression analyses for each group to see if prior ingroup friendships have similar effects on subsequent feelings of belonging and academic commitment, motivation, and performance for all groups.

24. The associations for each ethnic group between the proportion of ingroup friends during sophomore and junior years and sense of belonging to the larger university at the end of senior year, controlling for freshman year belonging, were as follows: Latinos, $b = -.28$, $p = .001$; blacks, $b = -.08$, $p = .62$; Asians, $b = .05$, $p = .46$; whites, $b = .13$, $p = .15$; the interaction with ethnicity was statistically significant.

25. The relationships between proportion of ingroup friends during sophomore and junior years and academic performance at the end of senior year, controlling for freshman year performance, were as follows: Latinos, $b = -.17$, $p = .01$; blacks, $b = -.10$, $p = .31$;

Asians, $b = -.02$, $p = .74$; whites, $b = .06$, $p = .31$; the interaction with ethnicity was marginally significant, $p = .08$.

26. After controlling for freshman year commitment, there was a significant positive association between proportion of friends of students' own ethnicity during sophomore and junior years and commitment to staying in school at the end of senior year: $\beta = .08$, $p = .02$. Although the interaction with ethnicity did not reach statistical significance, the separate regression analyses for each ethnic group reveal marginally significant positive effects of having more ingroup friends during sophomore and junior years on senior year academic commitment for black and Asian students only: blacks, $b = .30$, $p = .07$; Asians, $b = .10$, $p = .06$; Latinos, $b = -.02$, $p = .82$; whites, $b = .13$, $p = .17$.

27. Although the interaction with ethnicity did not reach statistical significance, the separate regression analyses for each ethnic group indicate that black students who had a greater proportion of ingroup friends during their sophomore and junior years were the only ones to exhibit significantly stronger academic motivation at the end of their senior year: blacks, $b = .33$, $p = .04$; Latinos, $b = .08$, $p = .45$; Asians, $b = .05$, $p = .54$; whites, $b = .15$, $p = .13$.

28. As in the previous series of hierarchical regression analyses, we use belonging and academic commitment, motivation, and performance measured in the senior year as our dependent variables; we control for freshman year levels of these variables, respectively, as well as sophomore to junior year ingroup friendships; we examine the interaction between ethnicity and perceived ethnic discrimination on campus; and we conduct separate regression analyses for each group to see if prior perceptions of ethnic discrimination on campus have similar effects on subsequent levels of belonging, commitment, motivation, and performance for all groups.

29. The associations between perceptions of discrimination during sophomore and junior years and feelings of belonging on campus at the end of senior year for each ethnic group were as follows: Latinos, $b = -.18$, $p = .001$; whites, $b = -.13$, $p = .02$; Asians, $b = -.04$, $p = .39$; blacks, $b = .04$, $p = .76$; the interaction with ethnicity was marginally significant, $p = .07$.

30. Overall, there was a marginally significant negative relationship between perceptions of discrimination during sophomore and junior years and commitment to staying in school at the end of senior

year: $\beta = -.06$, p = .09. The relationships between perceptions of discrimination during sophomore and junior years and commitment to staying in school at the end of senior year were as follows: whites, b = −.01, p = .93; Asians, b = .001, p = .99; Latinos, b = −.09, p = .15; blacks, b = −.17, p = .19; the interaction with ethnicity was also not significant.

31.   The associations between perceived discrimination during sophomore and junior years and academic performance at the end of senior year were as follows: whites, b = .02, p = .65; Asians, b = .01, p = .79; Latinos, b = .02, p = .71; blacks, b = −.01, p = .93; the interaction with ethnicity was also not significant.

32.   The associations between perceived discrimination during sophomore and junior years and motivation to get a high GPA at the end of senior year were as follows: blacks, b = .24, p = .06; Latinos, b = .01, p = .92; Asians, b = −.07, p = .21; whites, b = −.02, p = .71; although the interaction with ethnicity did not reach statistical significance.

Chapter 9

This chapter was authored by Shana Levin, Colette van Laar, Stacey Sinclair, and Jim Sidanius.

1.   Unless otherwise noted, the exact wording of all individual and scale items can be found under their corresponding labels in appendix A. Intergroup comfort was measured by the item "I feel uneasy being around people of different ethnicities." Using a scale of 1 (strongly disagree) to 7 (strongly agree), this item was reverse-coded so that higher numbers indicate greater levels of intergroup comfort. Intergroup competence was measured by the item "I feel competent interacting with people from different ethnic groups," using the same scale of 1 (strongly disagree) to 7 (strongly agree).

2.   To compute the friendship heterogeneity variable, students were first asked how many of their closest friends at UCLA (or in high school for the precollege measure of this variable) were African American, Latino, Asian American, and Caucasian (response options were 1 = none, 2 = few, 3 = many, 4 = most, and 5 = all). Responses to these questions were then transformed into three-category scales such that responses of 1 and 5 were coded as 0 on the

heterogeneity scale, 2 and 4 were coded as 1 on the scale, and 3 was coded as 2 on the scale. Then each of these responses was weighted by the inverse proportion of the given ethnic group on campus (that is, by the inverse of 36 percent for Asian Americans, 32 percent for whites, 18 percent for Latinos, and 6 percent for blacks). Thus, being friends with African American students (a relatively small ethnic group on campus) was given more weight in this friendship heterogeneity index than being friends with white students (a relatively large ethnic group on campus). The final measure of friendship heterogeneity was then simply the sum of these recoded and weighted indices across the three ethnic outgroups. As such, a very high score indicates having close friends from many different ethnic outgroups, while a low score indicates having very few friends from many different ethnic outgroups (or having ingroup friends only).

To compute the interethnic dating variable, students were first asked if they had dated anyone within the last year who was Caucasian, Asian American, Latino, or African American. Response options were coded such that 0 = no and 1 = yes. The final measure of interethnic dating in any given year was simply the sum of the answers to these questions across the three ethnic outgroups. As a result, for any given year, the number of different ethnic outgroups the students had dated could range from 0 to 3. If a student did not date anyone in a given year, he or she was given a missing data code for that year. During freshman year this variable assessed interethnic dating since the students entered college, and during senior year the variable assessed interethnic dating since the end of their junior year.

3. The roommate and interethnic dating variables were measured every year except precollege, and all the other constructs were assessed in all five waves of data collection.

4. These constructs have the following labels in appendix A: place of residence, number of roommates, and chose own roommate(s) or roommate(s) randomly chosen, respectively.

5. These survey items are listed under *ethnicity of roommates* in appendix A. Not surprisingly, the more roommates one has, the more likely it is that these roommates will be ethnically heterogeneous. Specifically, each year the number of roommates students reported was significantly related to their roommate heterogeneity. The correlations between the total number of roommates and roommate

heterogeneity were $r = .23$, $p < .001$, at the end of freshman year; $r = .25$, $p = .001$, at the end of sophomore year; $r = .34$, $p < .001$, at the end of junior year; and $r = .35$, $p = .001$, at the end of senior year.

6. We were not able to run this analysis on affect toward the four main ethnic groups because doing so would have required us to run the analyses within each ethnic group separately, creating very small sample sizes. We were also unable to run this analysis on the interethnic dating variable because it was not measured during the precollege wave of data collection.

7. All dormitory residents had at least one roommate. Those residents who answered that they had both chosen and randomly assigned roommates (just 2.8 percent) were excluded from these analyses.

8. Simple slopes analyses (see Aiken and West 1991) showed that when regressing freshman year roommate heterogeneity on precollege attitudes and behaviors for those with self-selected versus randomly assigned roommates, the slopes tended to be larger in the self-selected category when comfort in intergroup interactions was the outcome variable ($b = .06$ versus $b = .01$, $t = -1.96$, $p = .05$, $R^2_{\text{change for interaction}} = .003$). In addition, the slopes were significantly larger in the self-selected category when intergroup competence and friendship heterogeneity were the outcome variables ($b = .04$ versus $b = .00$, $t = 2.22$, $p = .03$, $R^2_{\text{change for interaction}} = .004$; and $b = .01$ versus $b = .00$, $t = 2.23$, $p = .03$, $R^2_{\text{change for interaction}} = .003$, respectively).

9. This analysis was a 4-by-2 mixed effects ANOVA with year in college (freshman through senior year) as the within-subjects factor and freshman year roommate selection (self-selected versus randomly assigned) as the between-subjects factor.

10. Roommate heterogeneity among randomly assigned roommates versus self-selected roommates showed $M = .67$, $SD = .43$, and $M = .33$, $SD = .44$, respectively; $t(520) = -7.07$, $p < .001$; $\eta_p^2 = .09$—a medium-sized effect.

11. The interaction effect between freshman and sophomore years for randomly assigned versus self-selected roommates was $F(1, 520) = 13.07$, $p < .001$; $\eta_p^2 = .03$—a small effect.

12. At senior year, roommate heterogeneity between students who originally chose their roommates and those randomly assigned

roommates was $M = .40$, $SD = .46$, versus $M = .48$, $SD = .45$, respectively; $t(520) = -1.70$, $p = .09$; $\eta_p^2 = .01$—a small effect.

13. The effects of exposure to randomly assigned Asian roommates among whites on intergroup comfort, symbolic racism, SDO, and opposition to miscegenation were $\beta = -.12$, $p = .05$, semipartial $r^2 = .01$; $\beta = .15$, $p = .01$, semipartial $r^2 = .01$; $\beta = .16$, $p = .007$, semipartial $r^2 = .02$; and $\beta = .11$, $p = .08$, semipartial $r^2 = .01$; respectively.

14. The effects of exposure to randomly assigned Asian roommates among blacks on symbolic racism and affect toward blacks were $\beta = .26$, $p = .03$, semipartial $r^2 = .06$; and $\beta = -.23$, $p = .06$, semipartial $r^2 = .04$; respectively.

15. The effects of exposure to white roommates on symbolic racism among black respondents and on intergroup comfort among black and Latino respondents were $\beta = .27$, $p = .03$, semipartial $r^2 = .05$; $\beta = -.23$, $p = .08$, semipartial $r^2 = .04$; and $\beta = -.18$, $p = .009$, semipartial $r^2 = .03$; respectively.

16. The effects of exposure to white roommates on Latinos' sense of intergroup competence, opposition to miscegenation, and heterogeneity of friends were $\beta = -.12$, $p = .08$, semipartial $r^2 = .01$; $\beta = .12$, $p = .08$, semipartial $r^2 = .01$; and $\beta = -.14$, $p = .04$, semipartial $r^2 = .02$; respectively.

17. The effect of exposure to white roommates on Asian students' in-group affect was $\beta = .13$, $p = .04$, semipartial $r^2 = .01$.

18. The effects of exposure to white roommates on black students' SDO and opposition to miscegenation and on Asian students' affect toward Latinos were $\beta = -.29$, $p = .03$, semipartial $r^2 = .06$; $\beta = -.23$, $p = .07$, semipartial $r^2 = .04$; and $\beta = .18$, $p = .095$, semipartial $r^2 = .01$; respectively.

19. The effect of exposure to heterogeneous roommates among Asian students was $\beta = .26$, $p = .04$, semipartial $r^2 = .02$.

20. Among whites the effects of exposure to heterogeneous roommates on interethnic dating, opposition to miscegenation, intergroup competence, and intergroup comfort were $\beta = .17$, $p = .08$, semipartial $r^2 = .01$; $\beta = -.20$, $p = .02$, semipartial $r^2 = .01$; $\beta = .19$, $p = .02$, semipartial $r^2 = .01$; and $\beta = .14$, $p = .10$, semipartial $r^2 = .01$; respectively.

21. The effects of exposure to black roommates on Asian and white students' friendship ethnic heterogeneity were $\beta = .13$, $p = .01$,

semipartial $r^2 = .01$, and $\beta = .12$, $p = .02$, semipartial $r^2 = .01$, respectively.

22. Among Asians the effects of exposure to Latino roommates on affect toward Latinos and intergroup comfort were $\beta = .23$, $p = .09$, semipartial $r^2 = .01$, and $\beta = .09$, $p = .09$, semipartial $r^2 = .01$, respectively.

23. The effect of exposure to Latino roommates on whites' interethnic dating was $\beta = -.14$, $p = .03$, semipartial $r^2 = .02$.

24. The effect of exposure to Latino roommates on blacks' intergroup competence was $\beta = -.28$, $p = .02$, semipartial $r^2 = .06$.

25. The effects of roommate heterogeneity on black students' opposition to miscegenation and Latino students' interethnic dating were $\beta = .33$, $p = .08$, semipartial $r^2 = .03$, and $\beta = -.26$, $p = .005$, semipartial $r^2 = .05$, respectively.

26. The effect of exposure to black roommates on black students' opposition to miscegenation was $\beta = .37$, $p = .03$, semipartial $r^2 = .06$. While one could argue that this is a prejudice-inducing effect, some would counterargue that such a response among black students is more indicative of a positive orientation toward ingroup members than a negative orientation toward outgroup members per se (Boen and Vanbeselaere 1998; Burstein 1989; Swanson 1992).

27. Among blacks the effect of exposure to black roommates on symbolic racism; among whites the effect of exposure to white roommates on intergroup comfort; and among Asians the effect of exposure to Asian roommates on interethnic dating were $\beta = -.41$, $p = .01$, semipartial $r^2 = .07$; $\beta = .12$, $p = .07$, semipartial $r^2 = .01$; and $\beta = .23$, $p = .03$, semipartial $r^2 = .02$; respectively.

28. In all these analyses, the dependent variable was one of the prejudice indicators measured in the senior year, and the first predictor variable entered into the analysis was that same prejudice indicator assessed during the freshman year. At the second step of the hierarchical regression analysis, we entered the predictor variables of primary interest to us: average degree of roommate heterogeneity during the sophomore and junior years and the average number of white, Asian, Latino, and black roommates respondents had during the sophomore and junior years. These predictor variables measured during the sophomore and junior years were entered into the equation after the freshman year prejudice indicator in or-

der to see if they could account for a significant amount of change in the prejudice indicator between the freshman and senior years.

29. Among Latino students the effects of increased roommate heterogeneity on SDO and affect toward Latinos, African Americans, and Asians were $\beta = -.25$, $p = .03$, semipartial $r^2 = .03$; $\beta = .24$, $p = .03$, semipartial $r^2 = .02$; $\beta = .26$, $p = .02$, semipartial $r^2 = .03$; and $\beta = .26$, $p = .02$, semipartial $r^2 = .05$; respectively.

30. Among black students the effect of roommate heterogeneity on interethnic dating was $\beta = .58$, $p = .002$, semipartial $r^2 = .15$; among Asian students its effect on intergroup competence was $\beta = .13$, $p = .06$, semipartial $r^2 = .01$.

31. Among Asian students the effect of exposure to white roommates on symbolic racism was $\beta = -.15$, $p = .006$, semipartial $r^2 = .01$; the effects of exposure to black roommates on interethnic dating and affect toward African Americans, Latinos, and Asians were $\beta = .30$, $p < .001$, semipartial $r^2 = .08$; $\beta = .11$, $p = .03$, semipartial $r^2 = .01$; $\beta = .13$, $p = .009$, semipartial $r^2 = .02$; and $\beta = .12$, $p = .01$, semipartial $r^2 = .01$; respectively.

32. For Asians, the effect of exposure to black roommates on affect toward whites was $\beta = .09$, $p = .08$, semipartial $r^2 = .01$; the effect of exposure to Latino roommates on friendship heterogeneity was $\beta = .09$, $p = .06$, semipartial $r^2 = .01$.

33. For whites, the effect of exposure to black roommates on interethnic dating was $\beta = .15$, $p = .006$, semipartial $r^2 = .02$, and the effect of exposure to Latino roommates on opposition to miscegenation was $\beta = -.10$, $p = .07$, semipartial $r^2 = .01$.

34. Among Asian students the effect of exposure to Latino roommates on feelings of intergroup comfort was $\beta = -.12$, $p = .04$, semipartial $r^2 = .01$, and among Latino students the effect of exposure to black roommates on affect toward whites was $\beta = -.16$, $p = .02$, semipartial $r^2 = .02$.

35. For whites, the effect of exposure to Asian roommates on affect toward Latinos was $\beta = -.13$, $p = .05$, semipartial $r^2 = .01$.

36. For Latinos, the effects of exposure to Latino roommates on SDO and affect toward Latinos, Asians, and blacks were $\beta = -.22$, $p = .02$, semipartial $r^2 = .03$; $\beta = .26$, $p = .007$, semipartial $r^2 = .04$; $\beta = .22$, $p = .03$, semipartial $r^2 = .03$; and $\beta = .28$, $p = .004$, semipartial $r^2 = .04$; respectively.

37. For blacks, the effect of exposure to black roommates on affect toward Latinos was $\beta = .30$, $p = .06$, semipartial $r^2 = .06$.
38. For whites, the effect of exposure to ingroup roommates on opposition to miscegenation was $\beta = .12$, $p = .04$, semipartial $r^2 = .01$. For blacks, the effect of exposure to ingroup roommates on interethnic dating was $\beta = -.34$, $p = .03$, semipartial $r^2 = .07$.

Chapter 10

This chapter was authored by Jim Sidanius, Colette van Laar, Shana Levin, and Stacey Sinclair.

1. The disproportionate distribution of the ethnic groups across the minority ethnic organizations can be more easily appreciated by inspection of the standardized residuals for each ethnicity by ethnic-organization category. Because these standardized residuals are essentially z-scores, they show not only whether the observed frequency within each cell is above or below what one should expect by chance, but also whether that observed frequency deviates significantly from chance. Thus, we see that Asians and African Americans are significantly underrepresented among nonmembers of minority ethnic organizations (standardized residuals = -5.2 and -4.8, $p < 10^{-5}$, respectively), while being substantially overrepresented among members of minority ethnic organizations (standardized residuals = 8.8 and 8.2, $p < 10^{-10}$, respectively).

2. Unless otherwise indicated, the exact wording of all individual and scale items can be found under the corresponding construct labels in appendix A. Opposition to increasing diversity on campus was measured through the use of the following item: "We should do what we can to increase ethnic diversity on campus" (reverse-coded; 1 = strongly disagree, 7 = strongly agree). Common ingroup identity was measured through the use of two items assessing representation of the student body as one group versus different groups: "Despite the different groups at UCLA, there is frequently the sense that we are all just one group," and "At UCLA, it usually feels as though we belong to different groups" (reverse-coded; 1 = strongly disagree, 7 = strongly agree). The average reliability across waves was $\alpha_{average} = .73$. In this chapter, university attach-

ment was measured by asking two questions: "How often do you think of yourself as a UCLA student?" (1 = not at all, 7 = very often), and "To what degree do you experience a sense of belonging or a sense of exclusion at UCLA?" (1 = exclusion, 7 = belonging). The average reliability for this scale was adequate ($\alpha_{average}$ = .57). Ingroup bias was assessed by first asking the students: "How positively or negatively do you feel toward the following groups?" and the individual items were "Caucasians/whites," "Latinos/Hispanics," "Asians/Asian Americans," and "African Americans/blacks" (1 = very negatively, 7 = very positively). In each year, ingroup bias was computed as the item measuring ingroup affect minus the average of the three items measuring outgroup affect. In this chapter, perceived ethnic discrimination was defined as the composite of four questions: "I experience discrimination at UCLA because of my ethnicity," "Other members of my ethnic group experience discrimination on campus," "Most of my professors don't have any ethnic prejudices" (reverse-coded), and "Many professors at UCLA are biased against people of my ethnic group" ($\alpha_{average}$ = .73; 1 = strongly disagree, 7 = strongly agree).

3. Common ingroup identity is excluded from these analyses because it was not measured in the precollege wave.

4. Socioeconomic status was measured through the use of a single item: "How would you describe your family's social class position?" (1 = poor, 2 = working class, 3 = lower-middle class, 4 = middle class, 5 = upper-middle class, 6 = lower-upper class, 7 = upper class).

5. When an outcome variable is dichotomous, a logistic regression is often the analytic method of choice. An odds-ratio is one of the statistics generated by a logistic regression and indicates the odds of displaying some behavior (for example, being a member of a minority ethnic organization) in relation to the odds of not displaying some behavior (for example, not being a member of such an organization). An odds-ratio of 1.00 indicates that there is no difference in the odds of one behavior versus the other. An odds-ratio of less than 1.00 indicates that the odds of being in one group (a member of a minority ethnic organization) are less than the odds of being in the other group (not being a member of such an organization). An odds-ratio greater than 1.00 indicates the exact opposite. Within logistic regression analysis, when the independent variable is continuous, the odds-ratio is interpreted as how many times the odds are greater

or smaller for every unit increase in the independent variable. Thus, if we used the continuous variable of age as an independent variable, an odds-ratio of 2.0 would indicate that the odds of being a member of a minority ethnic organization are twice as high for a twenty-one-year-old student as for a twenty-year-old student.

6. These mediational tests were conducted by the use of t-tests for mediation within the LISREL 8 program. Product-moment correlations served as the input data for all the LISREL analyses.

7. See, for example, Julie Mertus (2001).

8. For additional research, see also Charles F. Longino Jr. and Cary S. Kart (1973), Donald E. Muir (1991), and David H. Wilder et al. (1978). For exceptions, see Ilsa L. Lottes and Peter J. Kuriloff (1994) and David Wilder et al. (1986).

Chapter 11

This chapter was authored by Colette van Laar, Shana Levin, and Jim Sidanius.

1. There were 764 whites, 92 Filipinos, 83 Southeast Asians, 466 Latinos, and 144 African Americans (total n = 1,549) in the subsample of students included in the analyses for this chapter. The groups in the subsample differed significantly in a number of important ways: Filipino and Southeast Asian students were more likely to be immigrants themselves and, along with Latino students, were more likely to be children and grandchildren of immigrants than were black and white students. Southeast Asian and Latino students also had the lowest mean socioeconomic status, and white students had the highest. Regarding interethnic contact prior to college entry, white students' neighbors and high school classmates were the most ethnically homogenous. Filipino and Southeast Asian students had the most heterogeneous neighborhoods and high school classes. Black and Latino students grew up with more black and Latino neighbors, respectively, and Latinos attended high schools with more Latino students than white, Asian, and black students. Students of all ethnicities were more ethnically segregated in their high school friendship patterns: even when their neighborhoods and high school classrooms were ethnically heterogeneous, their high school friends were still most likely to share their own ethnicity.

2. Unless otherwise noted, the exact wording of all individual and

scale items can be found under the corresponding construct labels in appendix A. Parental education was assessed through the use of two items: "What is the highest level of education your mother completed?" and "What is the highest level of education your father completed?" (1 = elementary school, 2 = some high school, 3 = completed high school, 4 = trade school, 5 = some college, 6 = completed college [BA/BS degree], 7 = some graduate or professional school, 8 = completed graduate or professional degree). Tests of differences between expected and observed frequencies in categorical data in this chapter were conducted using chi-square analyses and standardized residuals. Standardized residuals indicate the degree to which an observed value deviates from the expected value in terms of a z-score. A standardized residual (SR) of plus or minus 1.96 indicates a significant deviation from 0 at the $p = .05$ level. Tests of differences between means were conducted using analyses of variance, with Scheffé tests for pairwise comparisons. The r-squares reported in this chapter are the percentages of variance explained for the linear regressions and the Cox and Snell r-squares for the logistic regressions. The following symbols are used to indicate statistical significance: ns = not significantly different from zero; $^+ p < .10$; $^* p < .05$; $^{**} p < .01$; $^{***} p < .001$.

3. The likelihood of Latino, white, Filipino, African American, and Southeast Asian students being the first in their families to go to college was 48.2 percent, SR=11.6; 7.2 percent, SR = −8.9; 12.1 percent, SR = −2.1; 23.1 percent, SR = 0.1; and 29.3 percent, SR = 1.3; respectively.

4. We also examined whether there might have been more variance in SAT scores among the minority students. However, homogeneity of variance analyses indicated that only the variance in SAT scores among Southeast Asian students was significantly higher than that of the other students in the subsample.

5. Multivariate analyses of variance were used for analyses over time. Owing to the small numbers of black, Southeast Asian, and Filipino students in the sample and our concern that listwise deletion across all five waves of data collection would lower this number still further, we conducted the analyses over time for these students using all the data available for these smaller groups in each wave, and we made comparisons across ethnic groups in the subsample within each wave of data collection.

6. These items are listed under the academic performance scale in appendix A.

7. The average self-perceived performance scores for white and minority students were $M = 4.72$ and 4.58, respectively; the main effect of ethnicity across the college years is statistically significant.

8. Prior to college entry, students were asked about their expectations of their academic performance in college rather than their perceptions of their actual college academic performance.

9. The average GPAs for white and minority students were $M = 3.38$ and 3.03, respectively. These results remain the same when we conduct listwise (rather than pairwise) deletion for the African American, Filipino, and Southeast Asian students, examining only those who remained in the sample through the end of senior year. The differences in GPA between white and minority students are reduced only slightly when we control for differences in SAT scores between students. Specifically, average GPA decreases to $M = 3.33$ for white students and increases to $M = 3.06$ for minority students at the end of the senior year. However, the differences between the white and minority groups remain significant.

10. From precollege to senior year, the importance of getting a high GPA is $M = 6.24$ and 5.20, respectively.

11. Since we used pairwise deletion to examine the changes over time for black, Filipino, and Southeast Asian students, who had higher dropout rates in college, we wanted to be sure that the reduction in dropout considerations for these students following the peak at the end of freshman year was not due to students who considered dropping out actually doing so. We thus examined changes over time also for those black, Filipino, and Southeast Asian students who remained in the sample at senior year (listwise deletion); we found the same pattern, with dropout considerations peaking at the end of freshman year and then declining as students moved closer to graduation.

12. For Latino, African American, white, Southeast Asian, and Filipino students: 20.9 percent, $SR = 3.1$; 23 percent, $SR = 2.4$; 9.9 percent, $SR = -3.2$; 11.8 percent, $SR = -0.7$; and 9.6 percent, $SR = -1.2$, respectively.

13. See also Carmen G. Arroyo and Edward Zigler (1995), Philip J. Cook and Jens Ludwig (1998), Jennifer Crocker and Brenda Major (1989),

Carol Goodenow and Kathleen E. Grady (1993), Sandra Graham, April Z. Taylor, and Cynthia Hudley (1998), Bryan W. Griffin (2002), Cynthia Hudley and Sandra Graham (2001), Irwin Katz (1967), Brenda Major (1995), Brenda Major, Caroline Richards, et al. (1998), Brenda Major, Steven Spencer, et al. (1998), Brenda Major and Toni Schmader (1998), John U. Ogbu (2003), John Osborne (1995), Toni Schmader, Brenda Major, and Richard H. Gramzow (2001), Claude M. Steele (1997), and Colette van Laar and Belle Derks (2003).

14. See also Sandra Graham (1994), Jon W. Hoelter (1983), Michael Hughes and David H. Demo (1989), Judith R. Porter and Robert E. Washington (1979), Morris Rosenberg (1979), Roberta G. Simmons (1978), and Ruth C. Wylie (1979).

15. Note that the variable that measures whether students participated in summer orientation was measured only once, at the end of freshman year, and thus we use that measure as the predictor.

16. The correlations between senior year GPA, on the one hand, and degree attainment and time to degree, on the other hand, are .39*** and −.17***, respectively, for the subsample as a whole.

17. Specifically, we use linear regression analyses for senior year GPA and the time it took students to obtain a degree, and logistic regression for whether students obtained a degree. We eliminate one predictor at a time, every time choosing a nonsignificant predictor to eliminate that shows the smallest (and nonsignificant) relationship with performance relative to potential for each of the three ethnic groups. We then rerun the regression analyses for each of the groups and repeat the process to remove the next least significant predictor, and so on until we have a final list of predictors that show a significant relationship with performance relative to potential for at least one of the three subgroups; we can then examine the influence of these predictors for each of the groups.

18. The percentages of students in each ethnic group who attended the summer orientation program for minorities are reported later in the chapter, and the mean numbers of friends, dates, and roommates of each ethnic group are reported in chapters 8 and 9; these numbers are thus not included in table 11.1.

19. In the tables and remaining analyses, the disidentification factor was measured through the use of the following items: "My performance in school does not affect whether I feel good or bad about myself" (1 = strongly disagree, 7 = strongly agree); "How I feel

about myself depends a lot on how well I do in school" (reverse-coded; 1 = strongly disagree, 7 = strongly agree); "How likely is it that you would consider dropping out of UCLA before earning a degree?" (1 = not at all, 7 = very likely); "How important is it for you to get a high GPA at UCLA?" (reverse-coded; 1 = not at all, 7 = very important); "What is the average number of hours that you spend per week studying or doing homework?" (reverse-coded; 1 = zero hours, 2 = one to five hours, 3 = six to ten hours, 4 = eleven to fifteen hours, 5 = sixteen to twenty, 6 = twenty to thirty, 7 = thirty to forty); "My academic performance at UCLA accurately reflects how smart I am" (reverse-coded; 1 = strongly disagree, 7 = strongly agree); and "The grades I have received at UCLA are not a good measure of my intellectual ability" (1 = strongly disagree, 7 = strongly agree). The reliability of this disidentification factor was adequate, $\alpha = .54$.

20. Using the disidentification factor as a predictor of senior year GPA for white and Latino students: $\beta = -.18^{***}$ and $\beta = -.22^{***}$, respectively, and disidentification as a predictor of degree attainment for whites: $Exp(B) = 0.04^{***}$. The Exp(B) statistic gives odds-ratio information, with odds above 1 indicating that the odds of obtaining a degree increase by that factor for every unit increase in the students' academic disidentification. Similarly, odds below 1 indicate that the odds of obtaining a degree decline by that factor for every unit increase in the predictor variable.

21. See also Alexander Astin (1975, 1982), Marlene S. Dorsey and Anita P. Jackson (1995), Sylvia Hurtado et al. (1999), Ernest T. Pascarella and Patrick T. Terenzini (1991), William E. Sedlacek and Glenwood C. Brooks (1976), and Terence J. Tracey and William E. Sedlacek (1984, 1985).

22. In this chapter, feelings of belonging were measured through the use of three items: "Despite the different groups at UCLA, there is frequently the sense that we are all just one group" (1 = strongly disagree, 7 = strongly agree); "At UCLA, it usually feels as though we belong to different groups" (reverse-coded; 1 = strongly disagree, 7 = strongly agree); and "UCLA promotes positive interaction between individual students of different ethnic groups" (1 = strongly disagree, 7 = strongly agree). The reliability of the feelings of belonging factor was adequate, $\alpha = .71$.

23. Feelings of belonging as a predictor of degree attainment for white and Latino students: $Exp(B) = 1.90^{**}$ and 1.44^*, respectively.

Notes

24. These variables appear under the following construct labels in appendix A: participation in summer orientation program for minorities, feeling of being admitted to UCLA because of affirmative action, number of ethnic studies courses taken each year, and number of Asian American, African American, Latino, and female professors each year at UCLA.

25. In examining the partial correlations between the number of professors of a certain group students had and the academic outcome variables, we residualized the professor variables for the number of classes taken, as there is a confound between the number of professors students had of any group and the number of classes taken. (Those who took more classes overall were also likely to have more classes with professors of any one of the groups.) Taking more classes in any year was also likely to be related to the outcome variables, especially time to degree. This possible confound is greatest for white professors, who teach the majority of classes (correlation with the number of classes taken for the sample as a whole is .76*** for white professors, .04* for Asian professors, −.04 for Latino professors, .01 for black professors, and .08** for female professors), and thus not controlling for this confound would artificially strengthen the relationships between the number of white professors and the outcome variables.

26. The effect of white professors on white students' GPA: $\beta = .09^{**}$.

27. The effect of number of ethnic studies classes taken on white and Latino students' GPA: $\beta = .07^*$ and $.10^*$, respectively; and on their degree attainment: $Exp(B) = 79.28^{***}$ and 40.68^{***}, respectively.

28. Summer minority orientation attendance for black, Latino, Filipino, Southeast Asian, and white students: $SR = 6.1$, 7.9, -2.4, -1.9, and -8.4, respectively.

29. Note that in table 11.2, the variable is called "nonparticipation in summer orientation for minorities" and is coded such that high numbers indicate that the student did not participate in the summer orientation.

30. Several constructs measured participation in various student organizations (see appendix A), including membership in student organizations and membership in a fraternity or sorority.

31. The effect of participation in student organizations on the time it

took for Latino and black students to obtain a degree: $\beta = .18^*$ and .36**, respectively.

32. These variables were measured by the following constructs (see appendix A): friendships with members of the four main ethnic groups, dating members of the four main ethnic groups, and the ethnicity of roommates.

33. The effect of black roommates on black students' GPA: $\beta = .19^*$; the effect of black roommates on Latino students' time to degree: $-.16^*$; the effect of Latino roommates on Latino students' time to degree: $.20^*$.

34. In this chapter, perceived ethnic discrimination was measured through the use of the following items: "I (will) experience discrimination at UCLA because of my ethnicity," "Other members of my ethnic group (will) experience discrimination on campus," and "Most professors do not have ethnic prejudices" (reverse-coded). For each item, participants responded on a scale of 1 (strongly disagree) to 7 (strongly agree). The reliability of the perceived discrimination scale was high, $\alpha = .82$.

35. This construct was measured through the use of two UCLA-promotion-of-diversity items: "UCLA promotes positive interaction between individual students of different ethnic groups" (reverse-coded) and "UCLA lacks strong commitment to achieving and maintaining an ethnically diverse student body" (1 = strongly disagree, 7 = strongly agree).

36. Latinos did not differ significantly from Southeast Asian and Filipino students.

37. Latino and Southeast Asian students did not significantly differ from Filipino students and black students.

38. Filipinos did not differ significantly from Southeast Asians, Latinos, or whites in the pressure they perceived.

39. Attributions for future economic life outcomes was measured through the use of three items: "What will your economic life outcomes be more influenced by?" "What will the economic life outcomes of members of your ethnic group, who are now UCLA students, be more influenced by?" and "What will the economic life outcomes of members of your ethnic group in society at large be more influenced by?" (1 = things about you/them, such as your/their ability and the effort you/they have put in,

7 = factors in the environment, such as opportunities and jobs).

40. Intergroup competence was measured through the use of the item "I feel competent interacting with people from different ethnic groups" (1 = strongly disagree, 7 = strongly agree).

41. The effect of stability on black students' GPA: $\beta = -.18^*$, and the effect of group concerns about stereotypes on white students' degree attainment: $Exp(B) = 0.66^*$.

42. The association between academic disidentification and senior year GPA for black students: product-moment $r = -.31^{***}$ and partial $r = -.17^+$.

43. Although the product-moment correlation and partial correlation controlling for the cognitive variables for senior year GPA were significant for black students—$.20^*$ and $.21^*$, respectively—the regression coefficient controlling for the other noncognitive variables was not.

44. As discussed in chapter 3, the University of California Board of Regents decided in July 1995 to eliminate affirmative action programs in the University of California system, and California Proposition 209 was passed by referendum in November 1996, banning affirmative action programs statewide.

45. See also Christine Bennett and Alton M. Okinaka (1990), William G. Bowen and Derek Bok (1998), Susan D. Clayton and Faye J. Crosby (1992), David A. Kravitz et al. (1997), and Rupert W. Nacoste (1985, 1989).

46. In actuality, affirmative action admission at UCLA results from the use of a sliding scale. On the sliding scale, academic performance prior to college and several factors indicating disadvantage are balanced against each other. In practice, this means that a student has a better chance of admission with slightly lower scores than average because he or she has more factors indicating disadvantage (such as poverty and minority ethnic background). All students must, however, pass a certain cutoff point in terms of prior academic achievement, so all are qualified for college entry. There is no indicator in students' records of affirmative action variable weighting, nor can students objectively know if they benefited from this affirmative action policy or not.

47. Students answering between three and seven on the seven-point scale were classified as those who believed that they might have

been or definitely were admitted through affirmative action, and students answering one or two on the seven-point scale were classified as those who believed that they were not admitted through affirmative action.

48. The achievement scale, composed of freshman GPA and self-perceived performance, was standardized to a 0 to 1 scale ($\alpha = .77$), with higher numbers indicating better academic performance.

49. For the purposes of maintaining high statistical power, we pooled Latinos and blacks together in the analyses from here on. (We also examined the results for each group separately, but this made no difference in the results.)

50. Only SAT math scores explain differences in freshman performance ($\beta = .22^*$, $R^2 = .06^{**}$, when both SAT math and verbal scores are used to predict freshman performance in a regression equation). However, controlling for these differences in SATs, we find that affirmative action status still explains differences in achievement at the end of freshman year ($\beta = -.25^{**}$, R^2 change $= .06^{***}$). The effect of affirmative action status remains the same when we repeat these analyses controlling for differences in socioeconomic status between students in addition to SAT scores (the effect of affirmative action status on first-year performance once socioeconomic status and SAT scores are entered: $\beta = -.15^{***}$, R^2 change $= .02^{***}$).

51. Essential for moderation analyses is the condition that the moderator is not highly correlated with the predictor variable. This condition is satisfied in these analyses: the correlations between affirmative action status and social and personal identity stereotype threat are .02 and $.13^*$, respectively.

52. b for interaction $= -.18^*$; b for low personal identity stereotype threat $= -.04^{ns}$; b for high personal identity stereotype threat $= -.41^{**}$.

53. b for interaction $= -.14^+$; b for low social identity stereotype threat $= -.07^{ns}$; b for high social identity stereotype threat $= -.35^{**}$.

Chapter 12

This chapter was authored by David O. Sears, Hillary Haley, Jim Sidanius, Shana Levin, and Colette van Laar.

Appendix A

This appendix was compiled by Shana Levin, Colette van Laar, Jim Sidanius, and David O. Sears.

1. The following items were asked in wave 1 as part of scales but were then dropped in subsequent waves. Therefore, these items were not included within this appendix:

    Attributions for future outcomes of ethnic group in society at large item: "If members of your ethnic group in society at large do well economically in life, what will this be more caused by?" (1 = things about them, such as their ability and the effort they have put in, 7 = factors in the environment, such as opportunities and jobs)

    Attributions for future outcomes of same-ethnicity UCLA students of item: "If members of your ethnic group, who are now UCLA students, do well economically in life, what will this be more caused by?" (1 = things about them, such as their ability and the effort they have put in, 7 = factors in the environment, such as opportunities and jobs)

    Attributions for future self economic life outcomes item: "If you do well economically in life, what will this be more caused by?" (1 = things about you, such as your ability and the effort you have put in, 7 = factors in the environment, such as opportunities and jobs)

    Ethnic activism item: "How seriously have you considered participating in the following activities on behalf of your ethnic group?" (1 = not at all seriously, 7 = very seriously/have done so)
    Sending letters to government officials or organizations

    Ethnic identification item: "How strongly do you identify with other members of your ethnic group?" (1 = not at all, 7 = very strongly)

    Expectancies of future socioeconomic status items (1 = $10,000 or under; 2 = $10,001 to $20,000; 3 = $20,001 to $30,000; 4 = $30,001 to $40,000; 5 = $40,001 to $50,000; 6 = $50,001 to $60,000; 7 = $60,001 to $70,000; 8 = $70,001 to $80,000; 9 = $80,001 to $90,000; 10 = $90,001 to $100,000; 11 = $100,001 to $110,000; 12 = $110,001 to $120,000; 13 = $120,001 to $130,000; 14 = more than $130,000):

    > "Twenty years from now, how much do you think you will personally be earning (assuming no inflation)?"
    > "Twenty years from now, how much do you think members of

your ethnic group who are now students at UCLA will be earning on average (assuming no inflation)?"

"Twenty years from now, how much do you think members of your ethnic group in society at large will be earning on average (assuming no inflation)?"

Opposition to affirmative action item: "Affirmative action enriches the educational experience of students from all backgrounds." (1 = strongly disagree, 7 = strongly agree)

Political conservatism item: "In terms of economic issues, how would you describe your political views?" (1 = very liberal, 7 = very conservative)

Social dominance orientation items (1 = strongly disagree, 7 = strongly agree):

"If certain groups of people stayed in their place, we would have fewer problems."

"Sometimes other groups must be kept in their place."

"Group equality should be our ideal."

"We would have fewer problems if we treated different groups more equally."

Appendix C

This appendix was compiled by Colette van Laar, David O. Sears, Jim Sidanius, and Shana Levin.

1. Unless otherwise indicated, the exact wording and response options for each item can be found under the corresponding construct labels in appendix A. Ingroup bias was assessed by first asking the students: "How positively or negatively do you feel toward the following groups?" and the individual items were "Caucasians/whites," "Latinos/Hispanics," "Asians/Asian Americans," and "African Americans/blacks" (1 = very negatively, 7 = very positively). In each year, ingroup bias was computed as the item measuring ingroup affect minus the average of the three items measuring outgroup affect.

References

Aberson, Christopher L., Dale E. Berger, Michael R. Healy, and Victoria L. Romero. 2000. "Ingroup Bias and Self-Esteem: A Meta-Analysis." *Personality and Social Psychology Review* 4(2): 157–73.

Aiken, Leona S., and Stephen G. West. 1991. *Multiple Regression: Testing and Interpreting Interactions*. Newbury Park, Calif.: Sage Publications.

Alba, Richard D. 1990. *Ethnic Identity: The Transformation of White America*. New Haven, Conn.: Yale University Press.

Alba, Richard D., and Victor Nee. 2003. *Remaking the American Mainstream: Assimilation and Contemporary Immigration*. Cambridge, Mass.: Harvard University Press.

Allen, Walter R., Edgar G. Epps, and Nesha Z. Haniff, eds. 1991. *College in Black and White: African American Students in Predominantly White and in Historically Black Public Universities*. Albany, N.Y.: State University of New York Press.

Allport, Gordon W. 1954. *The Nature of Prejudice*. Reading, Mass.: Addison-Wesley.

Altemeyer, Robert A. 1998. "The Other 'Authoritarian Personality.'" In *Advances in Experimental Social Psychology*, edited by Mark P. Zanna. San Diego, Calif.: Academic Press.

Alwin, Duane F., Ronald L. Cohen, and Theodore M. Newcomb. 1991. *Political Attitudes over the Life Span: The Bennington Women After Fifty Years*. Madison, Wisc.: University of Wisconsin Press.

American Council on Education. 2002. *Minorities in Higher Education 2001–2002: Nineteenth Annual Status Report*. Washington: American Council on Education.

Antonio, Anthony Lising. 2001. "Diversity and the Influence of Friendship Groups in College." *Review of Higher Education* 25(1): 63–89.

Arroyo, Carmen G., and Edward Zigler. 1995. "Racial Identity, Academic Achievement, and the Psychological Well-Being of Economically Disadvantaged Adolescents." *Journal of Personality and Social Psychology* 69(5): 903–14.

References

Association of American Colleges and Universities. 2000. *National Survey on Diversity in the Undergraduate Curriculum*. Accessed at http://www.aacu.org/divsurvey.

Astin, Alexander W. 1975. *Preventing Students from Dropping Out*. San Francisco: Jossey-Bass.

———. 1982. *Minorities in American Higher Education: Recent Trends, Current Prospects, and Recommendations*. San Francisco: Jossey-Bass.

———. 1993. *What Matters in College: Four Critical Years Revisited*. San Francisco: Jossey-Bass.

Banks, James A. 1986. "Multicultural Education and Its Critics: Britain and the United States." In *Multicultural Education: The Interminable Debate*, edited by Sohan Modgil, Gajendra Verma, Kanka Mallick, and Celia Modgil. Philadelphia: Falmer Press.

Baumeister, Roy F., Todd F. Heatherton, and Dianne M. Tice. 1993. "When Ego Threats Lead to Self-Regulation Failure: Negative Consequences of High Self-Esteem." *Journal of Personality and Social Psychology* 64(1): 141–56.

Bennett, Christine, and Alton M. Okinaka. 1990. "Factors Related to Persistence Among Asian, Black, Hispanic, and White Undergraduates at a Predominantly White University: Comparison Between First- and Fourth-Year Cohorts." *Urban Review* 22(1): 33–60.

Berry, John W. 1984. "Cultural Relations in Plural Societies." In *Groups in Contact: The Psychology of Desegregation*, edited by Norman Miller and Marilynn B. Brewer. New York: Academic Press.

Bettencourt, B. Ann, Kelly Charlton, Nancy Dorr, and Deborah L. Hume. 2001. "Status Differences and Ingroup Bias: A Meta-Analytic Examination of the Effects of Status Stability, Status Legitimacy, and Group Permeability." *Psychological Bulletin* 127(4): 520–42.

Billson, Janet Mancini, and Margaret Brooks Terry. 1982. "In Search of the Silken Purse: Factors in Attrition Among First-Generation Students." *College and University* 58(1): 57–75.

Blanchard, Fletcher, Teri Lilly, and Leigh Ann Vaughn. 1991. "Reducing the Expression of Racial Prejudice." *Psychological Science* 2(2): 101–5.

Bobo, Lawrence D. 1999. "Prejudice as Group Position: Microfoundations of a Sociological Approach to Racism and Race Relations." *Journal of Social Issues* 55(3): 445–72.

Bobo, Lawrence D., and Devon Johnson. 2001. "Racial Attitudes in a Prismatic Metropolis: Mapping Identity, Stereotypes, Competition, and

Views on Affirmative Action." In *Prismatic Metropolis: Inequality in Los Angeles*, edited by Lawrence D. Bobo, Melvin L. Oliver, James H. Johnson Jr., and Abel Valenzuela Jr. New York: Russell Sage Foundation.

Bobo, Lawrence D., and Frederick C. Licari. 1989. "Education and Political Tolerance: Testing the Effects of Cognitive Sophistication and Target Group Affect." *Public Opinion Quarterly* 53(2): 285–308.

Bobo, Lawrence D., and Mia, Tuan. 2006. *Prejudice in Politics: Group Position, Public Opinion, and the Wisconsin Treaty Rights Dispute*. Cambridge, Mass.: Harvard University Press.

Boen, Filip, and Norbert Vanbeselaere. 1998. "Reactions upon a Failed Attempt to Enter a High-Status Group: An Experimental Test of the Five-Stage Model." *European Journal of Social Psychology* 28(5): 689–96.

Bonilla-Silva, Eduardo. 2003. *Racism Without Racists*. New York: Roman & Littlefield.

Bonilla-Silva, Eduardo, and Karen S. Glover. 2004. "'*We Are All Americans:' The Latin Americanization of Race Relations in the United States*." In *The Changing Terrain of Race and Ethnicity*, edited by Maria Krysan and Amanda E. Lewis. New York: Russell Sage.

Bowen, William G., and Derek Bok. 1998. *The Shape of the River: Long-Term Consequences of Considering Race in College and University Admissions*. Princeton, N.J.: Princeton University Press.

Branscombe, Nyla R., Michael T. Schmitt, and Richard D. Harvey. 1999. "Perceiving Pervasive Discrimination Among African Americans: Implications for Group Identification and Well-Being." *Journal of Personality and Social Psychology* 77(1): 135–49.

Branscombe, Nyla R., and Daniel L. Wann. 1994. "Collective Self-Esteem Consequences of Outgroup Derogation When a Valued Social Identity Is on Trial." *European Journal of Social Psychology* 24(6): 641–57.

Brewer, Marilynn B. 1979. "Ingroup Bias in the Minimal Intergroup Situation: A Cognitive-Motivational Analysis." *Psychological Bulletin* 86(2): 307–24.

———. 2000. "Reducing Prejudice Through Cross-Categorization: Effects of Multiple Social Identities." In *Reducing Prejudice and Discrimination*, edited by Stuart Oskamp. Mahwah, N.J.: Lawrence Erlbaum.

Brewer, Marilynn B., and Rupert J. Brown. 1998. "Intergroup Relations." In *The Handbook of Social Psychology*, edited by Daniel T. Gilbert, Susan T. Fiske, and Gardner Lindzey. New York: McGraw-Hill.

Brewer, Marilynn B., and Samuel L. Gaertner. 2000. "Toward Reduction of Prejudice: Intergroup Contact and Social Categorization." In *Black-*

References

well Handbook of Social Psychology: Intergroup Processes, edited by Rupert Brown and Samuel Gaertner. Oxford: Blackwell.

Britt, Thomas W., and Christian S. Crandall. 2000. "Acceptance of Feedback by the Stigmatized and Nonstigmatized: The Mediating Role of the Motive of the Evaluator." *Group Processes and Intergroup Relations* 3(1): 79–95.

Burstein, Paul. 1989. "Attacking Sex Discrimination in the Labor Market: A Study in Law and Politics." *Social Forces* 67(3): 641–65.

Cabrera, Alberto F., Nora Amaury, Patrick T. Terenzini, Ernest T. Pascarella, and Linda Serra Hagedorn. 1999. "Campus Racial Climate and the Adjustment of Students to College: A Comparison Between White Students and African American Students." *Journal of Higher Education* 70(2): 134–60.

Campbell, Angus. 1971. *White Attitudes Toward Black People*. Ann Arbor, Mich.: Institute for Social Science Research, University of Michigan.

Campbell, Angus, Philip E. Converse, Warren E. Miller, and Donald E. Stokes. 1960. *The American Voter*. Chicago: University of Chicago Press.

Cartwright, Dorwin. 1950. "Emotional Dimensions of Group Life." In *Feelings and Emotions*, edited by Martin L. Raymert. New York: McGraw-Hill.

Chan, Sucheng. 1991. *Asian Americans: An Interpretive History*. New York: Twayne.

Citrin, Jack, Donald P. Green, Beth Reingold, and Evelyn P. Walters. 1990. "The 'Official English' Movement and the Symbolic Politics of Language in the United States." *Western Political Quarterly* 43(3): 535–59.

Citrin, Jack, and David O. Sears. 2007. "The Politics of Multiculturalism and the Crisis of American Identity." Forthcoming.

Clayton, Susan D., and Faye J. Crosby. 1992. *Justice, Gender, and Affirmative Action*. Ann Arbor, Mich.: University of Michigan Press.

Cohen, Jacob. 1988. *Statistical Power Analysis for the Behavioral Sciences*, 2d ed. Hillsdale, N.J.: Lawrence Erlbaum.

Cohen, Nathan, ed. 1970. *The Los Angeles Riots: A Socio-Psychological Study*. New York: Praeger.

Contrada, Richard J., Richard D. Ashmore, Melvin L. Gary, Elliot Coups, Jill D. Egeth, Andrea Sewell, Kevin Ewell, Tanya M. Goyal, and Valerie Chasse. 2001. "Measures of Ethnicity-Related Stress: Psychometric Properties, Ethnic Group Differences, and Associations with Well-being." *Journal of Applied Social Psychology* 31(9): 1775–820.

Converse, Philip E. 1964. "The Nature of Belief Systems in Mass Publics." In *Ideology and Discontent*, edited by David E. Apter. New York: Free Press.

———. 1970. "Attitudes and Non-Attitudes: Continuation of a Dialogue." In *The Quantitative Analysis of Social Problems*, edited by E. R. Tufte. Reading, Mass.: Addison-Wesley.

———. 1976. *The Dynamics of Party Support: Cohort-Analyzing Party Identification*. Beverly Hills, Calif.: Sage Publications.

Converse, Philip E., and Gregory Markus. 1979. "Plus Ça Change . . . The New CPS Election Study Panel." *American Political Science Review* 73(1): 32–49.

Cook, Philip J., and Jens Ludwig. 1998. "The Burden of 'Acting White': Do Black Adolescents Disparage Academic Achievement?" In *The Black-White Test Score Gap*, edited by Christopher Jencks and Meredith Phillips. Washington: Brookings Institution Press.

Covington, Martin V. 1984a. "The Motive for Self-Worth." In *Research on Motivation in Education*. New York: Academic Press.

———. 1984b. "The Self-Worth Theory of Achievement Motivation: Findings and Implications." *Elementary School Journal* 85(1): 5–20.

Crocker, Jennifer, Beth Cornwell, and Brenda Major. 1993. "The Stigma of Overweight: Affective Consequences of Attributional Ambiguity." *Journal of Personality and Social Psychology* 64(1): 60–70.

Crocker, Jennifer, and Riia Luhtanen. 1990. "Collective Self-Esteem and Ingroup Bias." *Journal of Personality and Social Psychology* 58(1): 60–67.

Crocker, Jennifer, and Brenda Major. 1989. "Social Stigma and Self-Esteem: The Self-Protective Properties of Stigma." *Psychological Review* 96(4): 608–30.

Crocker, Jennifer, Brenda Major, and Claude Steele. 1998. "Social Stigma." In *The Handbook of Social Psychology*, edited by Daniel T. Gilbert, Susan T. Fiske, and Gardner Lindzey. New York: McGraw-Hill.

Crocker, Jennifer, Kristin Voelkl, Maria Testa, and Brenda Major. 1991. "Social Stigma: The Affective Consequences of Attributional Ambiguity." *Journal of Personality and Social Psychology* 60(2): 218–28.

Dawson, Michael C. 1994. "A Black Counterpublic? Economic Earthquakes, Racial Agenda(s), and Black Politics." *Public Culture* 7(1): 195–223.

Devos, Thierry, and Mahzarin R. Banaji. 2005. "American = White?" *Journal of Personality and Social Psychology* 88(3): 447–66.

Dorsey, Marlene S., and Anita P. Jackson. 1995. "Afro-American Students' Perceptions of Factors Affecting Academic Performance at a

References

Predominantly White School." *Western Journal of Black Studies* 19(3): 189–95.

Dovidio, John F., Samuel L. Gaertner, and Kerry Kawakami. 2003. "Intergroup Contact: The Past, Present, and the Future." *Group Processes and Intergroup Relations* 6(1): 5–20.

D'Souza, Dinesh. 1991. *Illiberal Education: The Politics of Race and Sex on Campus*. New York: Free Press.

Elfin, Mel, and Sarah Burke. 1993. "Race on Campus." *U.S. News and World Report*, April 19: 52.

Eriksen, Thomas Hylland. 2001. "Ethnic Identity, National Identity, and Intergroup Conflict: The Significance of Personal Experiences." In *Social Identity, Intergroup Conflict, and Conflict Reduction*, edited by Richard D. Ashmore, Lee Jussim, and David Wilder. New York: Oxford University Press.

Essed, Philomena. 1991. *Understanding Everyday Racism: An Interdisciplinary Theory*. Newbury Park, Calif.: Sage Publications.

Ethier, Kathleen A., and Kay Deaux. 1994. "Negotiating Social Identity When Contexts Change: Maintaining Identification and Responding to Threat." *Journal of Personality and Social Psychology* 67(2): 243–51.

Farley, Reynolds. 1996. *The New American Reality: Who We Are, How We Got Here, Where We Are Going*. New York: Russell Sage Foundation.

———. 2001. "Metropolises of the Multi-City Study of Urban Inequality: Social, Economic, Demographic, and Racial Issues in Atlanta, Boston, Detroit, and Los Angeles." In *Urban Inequality: Evidence from Four Cities*, edited by Alice O'Connor, Chris Tilly, and Lawrence Bobo. New York: Russell Sage Foundation.

Feldman, Kenneth A., and Theodore Mead Newcomb. 1969. *The Impact of College on Students*. New Brunswick, N.J.: Transaction Publishers.

Festinger, Leon, Stanley Schachter, and Kurt Back. 1950. *Social Pressures in Informal Groups: A Study of Human Factors in Housing*. New York: Harper Brothers.

Fordham, Signithia, and John U. Ogbu. 1986. "Black Students' School Success: Coping with the 'Burden of Acting White.'" *Urban Review* 18(3): 176–206.

Gaertner, Samuel L., and John F. Dovidio. 1986a. "Prejudice, Discrimination, and Racism: Problems, Progress, and Promise." In *Prejudice, Discrimination, and Racism*, edited by John F. Dovidio and Samuel L. Gaertner. Orlando, Fla.: Academic Press.

———. 1986b. "The Aversive Form of Racism." In *Prejudice, Discrimination, and Racism*, edited by John F. Dovidio and Samuel L. Gaertner. Orlando, Fla.: Academic Press.

———. 2000. *Reducing Intergroup Bias: The Common Ingroup Identity Model*. Philadelphia: Psychology Press.

Gaertner, Samuel L., John F. Dovidio, Phyllis A. Anastasio, Betty A. Bachman, and Mary C. Rust. 1993. "The Common Ingroup Identity Model: Recategorization and the Reduction of Intergroup Bias." In *European Review of Social Psychology*, edited by Wolfgang Stroebe and Miles Hewstone. New York: Wiley & Sons.

Gaertner, Samuel L., Mary C. Rust, John F. Dovidio, Betty A. Bachman, and Phyllis A. Anastasio. 1994. "The Contact Hypothesis: The Role of a Common Ingroup Identity in Reducing Intergroup Bias." *Small Group Research* 25(2): 224–49.

Gans, Herbert. 1979. "Symbolic Ethnicity: The Future of Ethnic Groups and Cultures in America." *Ethnic and Racial Studies* 2(1): 1–20.

Geertz, Clifford. 1964. "Ideology as a Cultural System." In *Ideology and Discontent*, edited by David E. Apter. New York: Free Press of Glencoe.

Gilliard, Michelle Denise. 1996. "Racial Climate and Institutional Support Factors Affecting Success in Predominantly White Institutions: An Examination of African-American and White Student Experiences." PhD diss., University of Michigan.

Glazer, Nathan. 1997. *We Are All Multiculturalists Now*. Cambridge, Mass.: Harvard University Press.

Goodenow, Carol, and Kathleen E. Grady. 1993. "The Relationship of School Belonging and Friends' Values to Academic Motivation Among Urban Adolescent Students." *Journal of Experimental Education* 62(1): 60–71.

Gordon, Milton M. 1964. *Assimilation in American Life: The Role of Race, Religion, and National Origins*. New York: Oxford University Press.

Graham, Calvin, Robert W. Baker, and Seymour Wapner. 1984. "Prior Interracial Experience and Black Student Transition into Predominantly White Colleges." *Journal of Personality and Social Psychology* 47(5): 1146–54.

Graham, Sandra. 1994. "Motivation in African Americans." *Review of Educational Research* 64(1): 55–117.

Graham, Sandra, April Z. Taylor, and Cynthia Hudley. 1998. "Exploring Achievement Values Among Ethnic Minority Early Adolescents." *Journal of Educational Psychology* 90(4): 606–20.

References

Greeley, Andrew M., and Paul B. Sheatsley. 1971. "Attitudes Toward Racial Integration." *Scientific American* 225(6): 13–19.

Green, Donald, Bradley Palmquist, and Eric Schickler. 2002. *Partisan Hearts and Minds: Political Parties and the Social Identities of Voters.* New Haven, Conn.: Yale University Press.

Griffin, Bryan W. 2002. "Academic Disidentification, Race, and High School Dropouts." *High School Journal* 85(4): 71–81.

Guiffrida, Douglas A. 2003. "African American Student Organizations as Agents of Social Integration." *Journal of College Student Development* 44(3): 304–19.

Gurin, Patricia. 1999. "Expert Report of Patricia Gurin: *Gratz et al. v. Bollinger et al., no. 97-75321(E.D. Mich.), Grutter et al. v. Bollinger et al., no. 97-75928 (E.D. Mich.)*." Accessed June 2, 2003 at http://www.vpcomm.umich.edu/admissions/legal/expert/gurintoc.html.

Gurin, Patricia, Shirley Hatchett, and James S. Jackson. 1989. *Hope and Independence: Blacks' Response to Electoral and Party Politics.* New York: Russell Sage Foundation.

Hamberger, Jurgen, and Miles Hewstone. 1997. "Interethnic Contact as a Predictor of Blatant and Subtle Prejudice: Tests of a Model in Four West European Nations." *British Journal of Social Psychology* 36(2): 173–90.

Hardin, Curtis D., and Terri D. Conley. 2001. "A Relational Approach to Cognition: Shared Experience and Relationship Affirmation in Social Cognition." In *Cognitive Social Psychology: The Princeton Symposium on the Legacy and Future of Social Cognition,* edited by Gordon B. Moskowitz. Mahwah, N.J.: Lawrence Erlbaum.

Hardin, Curtis D., and E. Tory Higgins. 1996. "Shared Reality: How Social Verification Makes the Subjective Objective." In *Handbook of Motivation and Cognition,* vol. 3, *The Interpersonal Context,* edited by Richard M. Sorrentiono and E. Tory Higgins. New York: Guilford Press.

Harter, Susan. 1986. "Processes Underlying the Construction, Maintenance, and Enhancement of the Self-Concept in Children." In *Psychological Perspectives on the Self,* edited by Jerry Suls and Anthony G. Greenwald. Hillsdale, N.J.: Lawrence Erlbaum.

Henry, P. J., and David O. Sears. 2002. "The Symbolic Racism 2000 Scale." *Political Psychology* 23(2): 253–83.

Herek, Gregory M., and John P. Capitanio. 1996. "'Some of My Best Friends': Intergroup Contact, Concealable Stigma, and Heterosexuals'

Attitudes Toward Gay Men and Lesbians." *Personality and Social Psychology Bulletin* 22(4): 412–24.

Hewstone, Miles, and Rupert Brown. 1986. "Contact Is Not Enough: An Intergroup Perspective on the 'Contact Hypothesis.'" In *Contact and Conflict in Intergroup Encounters*, edited by Miles Hewstone and Rupert Brown. Oxford: Blackwell.

Hewstone, Miles, Mark Rubin, and Hazel Willis. 2002. "Intergroup Bias." *Annual Review of Psychology* 53: 575–604.

Higgins, E. Tory, and William S. Rholes. 1978. "'Saying Is Believing': Effects of Message Modification on Memory and Liking for the Person Described." *Journal of Experimental Social Psychology* 14(4): 363–78.

Hirose, Shannon Miyuki. 1998. "Factors Influencing Race Relations on College Campuses." PhD diss., University of California at Los Angeles.

Hochschild, Jennifer L. 1995. *Facing Up to the American Dream*. Princeton, N.J.: Princeton University Press.

Hoelter, Jon W. 1983. "Factorial Invariance and Self-Esteem: Reassessing Race and Sex Differences." *Social Forces* 61(3): 834–46.

Hogg, Michael A., and Dominic Abrams. 1990. "Social Motivation, Self-Esteem, and Social Identity." In *Social Identity Theory: Constructive and Critical Advances*, edited by Dominic Abrams and Michael A. Hogg. London: Harvester Wheatsheaf.

Horowitz, Donald. L. 1985. *Ethnic Groups in Conflict*. Berkeley, Calif.: University of California Press.

Huber, Joan, and William H. Form. 1973. *Income and Ideology: An Analysis of the American Political Formula*. New York: Free Press.

Huddy, Leonie. 2001. "From Social to Political Identity: A Critical Examination of Social Identity Theory." *Political Psychology* 22(1): 127–56.

Hudley, Cynthia, and Sandra Graham. 2001. "Stereotypes of Achievement Striving Among Early Adolescents." *Social Psychology of Education* 5(2): 201–24.

Hughes, Michael, and David H. Demo. 1989. "Self-Perceptions of Black Americans: Self-Esteem and Personal Efficacy." *American Journal of Sociology* 95(1): 132–59.

Huntington, Samuel P. 1997. *Who Are We? The Challenges to America's National Identity*. New York: Simon & Schuster.

Huo, Yuen J., Heather J. Smith, Tom R. Tyler, and E. Allan Lind. 1996. "Superordinate Identification, Subgroup Identification, and Justice

Concerns: Is Separatism the Problem; Is Assimilation the Answer?" *Psychological Science* 7(1): 40–45.

Hurtado, Sylvia. 1992. "The Campus Racial Climate: Contexts of Conflict." *Journal of Higher Education* 63(5): 539–69.

Hurtado, Sylvia, Eric L. Dey, and Jesus G. Treviño. 1994. "Exclusion or Self-Segregation? Interaction Across Racial-Ethnic Groups on College Campuses." Paper presented at the annual meeting of the American Educational Research Association. New Orleans, La., (April 1994).

Hurtado, Sylvia, Jeffrey F. Milem, Alma R. Clayton-Pedersen, and Walter R. Allen. 1998. "Enhancing Campus Climates for Racial-Ethnic Diversity: Educational Policy and Practice." *Review of Higher Education* 21(3): 279–302.

———. 1999. "Enacting Diverse Learning Environments: Improving the Climate for Racial-Ethnic Diversity in Higher Education." ASHE-ERIC Higher Education Report 26(8). Washington: Graduate School of Education and Human Development, George Washington University.

Hyman, Herbert H. 1959. *Political Socialization*. Glencoe, Ill.: Free Press.

Islam, Mir R., and Miles Hewstone. 1993. "Dimensions of Contact as Predictors of Intergroup Anxiety, Perceived Outgroup Variability, and Outgroup Attitude: An Integrative Model." *Personality and Social Psychology Bulletin* 19(6): 700–710.

Jackman, Mary R. 1978. "Education and Policy Commitment to Racial Integration." *American Journal of Political Science* 22(2): 302–24.

———. 1994. *The Velvet Glove*. Berkeley, Calif.: University of California Press.

Jackman, Mary R., and Michael J. Muha. 1984. "Education and Intergroup Attitudes: Moral Enlightenment, Superficial Democratic Commitment, or Ideological Refinement?" *American Sociological Review* 49(6): 751–69.

Jackson, Kenneth W., and L. Alex Swan. 1991. "Institutional and Individual Factors Affecting Black Undergraduate Student Performance: Campus Race and Student Gender." In *College in Black and White: African American Students in Predominantly White and in Historically Black Public Universities*, edited by Walter R. Allen, Edgar G. Epps, and Nesha Z. Haniff. Albany, N.Y.: State University of New York Press.

Jennings, M. Kent, and Gregory B. Markus. 1984. "Partisan Orientations over the Long Haul: Results from the Three-Wave Political Socialization Panel Study." *American Political Science Review* 78(4): 1000–18.

Jennings, M. Kent, and Richard G. Niemi. 1974. *The Political Character of Adolescence: The Influence of Families and Schools*. Princeton, N.J.: Princeton University Press.

———. 1981. *Generations and Politics*. Princeton, N.J.: Princeton University Press.

Jennings, M. Kent, and Laura Stoker. 1999. "The Persistence of the Past: The Class of 1965 Turns Fifty." Paper presented at the annual convention of the Midwest Political Science Association. Chicago (April 1999).

Jetten, Jolanda, Russell Spears, and Anthony Manstead. 1996. "Distinctiveness Threat and Prototypicality: Combined Effects on Intergroup Discrimination and Collective Self-esteem." *European Journal of Social Psychology* 27(6): 635–57.

Johnston, Lucy, and Miles Hewstone. 1992. "Cognitive Models of Stereotype Change: Subtyping and the Perceived Typicality of Disconfirming Group Members." *Journal of Experimental Social Psychology* 28(4): 360–86.

Jost, John T., and Erik P. Thompson. 2000. "Group-Based Dominance and Opposition to Equality as Independent Predictors of Self-Esteem, Ethnocentrism, and Social Policy Attitudes Among African Americans and European Americans." *Journal of Experimental Social Psychology* 36(3): 209–32.

Katz, Irwin. 1967. "The Socialization of Academic Motivation in Minority Group Children." In *Nebraska Symposium on Motivation,* edited by David Levine. Lincoln, Neb.: University of Nebraska Press.

Kinder, Donald R., and Lynn M. Sanders. 1996. *Divided by Color: Racial Politics and Democratic Ideals*. Chicago: University of Chicago Press.

Kinder, Donald R., and David O. Sears. 1981. "Prejudice and Politics: Symbolic Racism Versus Racial Threats to the Good Life." *Journal of Personality and Social Psychology* 40(3): 414–31.

Kravitz, David A., David A. Harrison, Marlene E. Turner, Edward L. Levine, Wanda Chaves, Michael T. Brannick, Donna L. Denning, Craig J. Russell, and Maureen A. Conard. 1997. "Affirmative Action: A Review of Psychological and Behavioral Research." Bowling Green, Oh.: Society for Industrial and Organizational Psychology. Accessed March 5, 2005 at http://www.siop.org/AfirmAct/siopsaartoc.html.

Kritz, Mary M., and Douglas T. Gurak. 2005. "Immigration and a Changing America." In *The American People: Census 2000*, edited by Reynolds Farley and John Haaga. New York: Russell Sage Foundation.

References

Landrine, Hope, and Elizabeth A. Klonoff. 1996. "The Schedule of Racist Events: A Measure of Racial Discrimination and a Study of Its Negative Physical and Mental Health Consequences." *Journal of Black Psychology* 22(2): 144–68.

Lee, Alfred M. 1955a. *Fraternities Without Brotherhood: A Study of Prejudice on the American Campus.* Boston: Beacon Press.

———. 1955b. "Can Social Fraternities Be Democratic?" *Journal of Higher Education* 26(4): 173–79.

Levin, Shana, Jim Sidanius, Joshua L. Rabinowitz, and Christopher Federico. 1998. "Ethnic Identity, Legitimizing Ideologies, and Social Status: A Matter of Ideological Asymmetry." *Political Psychology* 19(2): 373–404.

Levin, Shana, Pamela L. Taylor, and Elena Caudle. 2007. "Interethnic and Interracial Dating in College: A Longitudinal Study." *Journal of Social and Personal Relationships* 24(3): 323–41.

Levin, Shana, Colette van Laar, and Winona Foote. 2006. "Ethnic Segregation and Perceived Discrimination in College: Mutual Influences and Effects on Social and Academic Life." *Journal of Applied Social Psychology* 36(6): 1471–501.

Levin, Shana, Colette van Laar, and Jim Sidanius. 2003. "The Effects of Ingroup and Outgroup Friendships on Ethnic Attitudes in College: A Longitudinal Study." *Group Processes and Intergroup Relations* 6(1): 76–92.

Lin, Monica H., Virginia S. Y. Kwan, Anna Cheung, and Susan T. Fiske. 2005. "Stereotype Content Model Explains Prejudice for an Envied Outgroup: Scale of Anti-Asian American Stereotypes." *Personality and Social Psychology Bulletin* 31(1): 34–47.

Lipset, Seymour Martin. 1982. "The Academic Mind at the Top: The Political Behavior and Values of Faculty Elites." *Public Opinion Quarterly* 46(2): 143–68.

———. 1983. *Political Man*, 2d ed. Garden City, N.Y.: Doubleday.

Long, Karen M., and Russell Spears. 1997. "The Self-Esteem Hypothesis Revisited: Differentiation and the Disaffected." In *The Social Psychology of Stereotyping and Group Life*, edited by Russell Spears, Penelope J. Oakes, Naomi Ellemers, and S. Alexander Haslam. Oxford: Blackwell.

Longino, Charles F., Jr., and Cary S. Kart. 1973. "The College Fraternity: An Assessment of Theory and Research." *Journal of College Student Personnel* 14(2): 118–25.

Loo, Chalsa M., and Garry Rolison. 1986. "Alienation of Ethnic Minority Students at a Predominantly White University." *Journal of Higher Education* 57(1): 58–77.

Lott, Bernice, and Diane Maluso, eds. 1995. *The Social Psychology of Interpersonal Discrimination.* New York: Guilford Press.

Lottes, Ilsa L., and Peter J. Kuriloff. 1994. "The Impact of College Experience on Political and Social Attitudes." *Sex Roles* 31(1–2): 31–54.

Lowery, Brian S., Curtis D. Hardin, and Stacey Sinclair. 2001. "Social Influence Effects on Automatic Racial Prejudice." *Journal of Personality and Social Psychology* 81(5): 842–55.

Major, Brenda. 1995. "Academic Performance, Self-Esteem, and Race: The Role of Disidentification." Paper presented at the annual convention of the American Psychological Association. New York (August 1995).

Major, Brenda, Jeffrey Feinstein, and Jennifer Crocker. 1994. "Attributional Ambiguity of Affirmative Action." *Basic and Applied Social Psychology* 15(1–2): 113–41.

Major, Brenda, Caroline Richards, M. Lynne Cooper, Catherine Cozzarelli, and Josephine Zubek. 1998. "Personal Resilience, Cognitive Appraisals, and Coping: An Integrative Model of Adjustment to Abortion." *Journal of Personality and Social Psychology* 74(3): 735–52.

Major, Brenda, and Toni Schmader. 1998. "Coping with Stigma Through Psychological Disengagement." In *Prejudice: The Target's Perspective,* edited by Janet K. Swim and Charles Stangor. San Diego, Calif.: Academic Press.

Major, Brenda, Steven Spencer, Toni Schmader, Connie Wolfe, and Jennifer Crocker. 1998. "Coping with Negative Stereotypes About Intellectual Performance: The Role of Psychological Disengagement." *Personality and Social Psychology Bulletin* 24(1): 34–50.

Marx, David M., Joseph L. Brown, and Claude M. Steele. 1999. "Allport's Legacy and the Situational Press of Stereotypes." *Journal of Social Issues* 55(3): 491–502.

Marx, David M., and Jasmin S. Roman. 2002. "Female Role Models: Protecting Women's Math Test Performance." *Personality and Social Psychology Bulletin* 28(9): 1183–93.

Massey, Douglas S., Camille Z. Charles, Garvey F. Lundy, and Mary J. Fischer. 2002. *The Source of the River: The Social Origins of Freshmen at America's Selective Colleges and Universities.* Princeton, N.J.: Princeton University Press.

References

Massey, Douglas S., and Nancy A. Denton. 1993. *American Apartheid: Segregation and the Making of the Underclass*. Cambridge, Mass.: Harvard University Press.

McCann, C. Douglas, and Rodney D. Hancock. 1983. "Self-Monitoring in Communicative Interactions: Social Cognitive Consequences of Goal-Directed Message Modification." *Journal of Experimental Social Psychology* 19(2): 109–21.

McClintock, Charles G., and Henry A. Turner. 1962. "The Impact of College upon Political Knowledge, Participation, and Values." *Human Relations* 15(2): 163–76.

McConahay, John B., and Joseph C. Hough Jr. 1976. "Symbolic Racism." *Journal of Social Issues* 32(2): 23–39.

McDermott, K. 2002. "Thesis Raises Troubling Questions About Race at Dartmouth." *The South End: The Official Newspaper of Wayne State University*. Accessed March 28, 2003 at http://www.southend.wayne.edu/days/may2002/5302002/news/dartmouth/dartmouth.html.

McFarland, Sam. 1999. "Personality, Values, and Latent Prejudice: A Test of a Causal Model." Paper presented at the annual conference of the International Society of Political Psychology. Amsterdam (July 1999).

McFarlin, Dean B., Roy F. Baumeister, and Jim Blascovich. 1984. "On Knowing When to Quit: Task Failure, Self-Esteem, Advice, and Non-Productive Persistence." *Journal of Personality* 52(2): 138–55.

McHugh, Barbara, Saundra M. Nethers, and Gary D. Gottfredson. 1993. *Meeting the Challenges of Multicultural Education: Third Report from the Evaluation of Pittsburgh's Multicultural Education Center*. Baltimore, Md.: Center for Research on Effective Schooling for Disadvantaged Students, Johns Hopkins University.

McLaughlin-Volpe, Tracy. 2006. "Understanding Stigma from the Perspective of the Self-Expansion Model." In *Stigma and Group Inequality: Social-Psychological Perspectives*, edited by Shana Levin and Colette van Laar. Hillsdale, N.J.: Lawrence Erlbaum.

Mertus, Julie. 2001. "The Impact of Intervention on Local Human Rights Culture: A Kosovo Case Study." *The Global Review of Ethnopolitics* 1(2): 21–36.

Miller, L. D. 1973. "Distinctive Characteristics of Fraternity Members." *Journal of College Student Personnel* 14(2): 126–28.

Miller, Norman, and Marilynn B. Brewer. 1986. "Categorization Effects on Ingroup and Outgroup Perception." In *Prejudice, Discrimination, and Racism*, edited by John F. Dovidio and Samuel L. Gaertner. San Diego, Calif.: Academic Press.

Miller, Warren E., and Merrill J. Shanks. 1996. *The New American Voter*. Cambridge, Mass.: Harvard University Press.

Modgil, Sohan, Gajendra Verma, Kanka Mallick, and Celia Modgil. 1986. "Multicultural Education: The Interminable Debate." In *Multicultural Education: The Interminable Debate*, edited by Celia Modgil. Philadelphia: Falmer Press.

Moran, Joseph J., Anne-Marie Algier, and Lisa Yengo. 1994. "Participation in Minority-Oriented Co-Curricular Organizations." *Journal of College Student Development* 35(2): 143.

Muir, Donald E. 1991. "White Fraternity and Sorority Attitudes Towards Blacks on a Deep-South Campus." *Sociological Spectrum* 11(1): 93–103.

Nacoste, Rupert W. 1985. "Selection Procedure and Responses to Affirmative Action: The Case of Favorable Treatment." *Law and Human Behavior* 9(3): 225–42.

———. 1989. "Affirmative Action and Self-Evaluations." In *Affirmative Action in Perspective*, edited by Fetcher A. Blanchard and Faye J. Crosby. New York: Springer-Verlag.

National Center for Education Statistics. 2001. "Educational Achievement and Black-White Inequality." Washington: U.S. Department of Education.

Nesdale, Drew, and Patricia Todd. 1998. "Intergroup Ratio and the Contact Hypothesis." *Journal of Applied Social Psychology* 28(13): 1196–217.

———. 2000. "Effect of Contact on Intercultural Acceptance: A Field Study." *International Journal of Intercultural Relations* 24(3): 341–60.

Nettles, Michael T. 1988. *Toward Black Undergraduate Student Equality in American Higher Education*. New York: Greenwood.

Newcomb, Theodore M. 1943. *Personality and Social Change: Attitude Formation in a Student Community*. New York: Wiley & Sons.

Nora, Amaury, Alberto Cabrera, Linda Serra Hagedorn, and Ernest T. Pascarella. 1996. "Differential Impacts of Academic and Social Experiences on College-Related Behavioral Outcomes Across Different Ethnic and Gender Groups at Four-Year Institutions." *Research in Higher Education* 37(4): 427–51.

Oakes, Penelope. 2002. "Psychological Groups and Political Psychology: A Response to Huddy's 'Critical Examination of Social Identity Theory.'" *Political Psychology* 23: 809–24.

Ogbu, John U. 2003. *Black American Students in an Affluent Suburb: A Study of Academic Disengagement*. Mahwah, N.J.: Lawrence Erlbaum.

Oliver, Melvin L., Consuelo J. Rodriguez, and Roslyn A. Mickelson.

References

1985. "Brown and Black in White: The Social Adjustment and Academic Performance of Chicano and Black Students in a Predominantly White University." *Urban Review* 17(1): 3–23.

Osborne, Jason W. 1995. "Academics, Self-Esteem, and Race: A Look at the Underlying Assumptions of the Disidentification Hypothesis." *Personality and Social Psychology Bulletin* 21(5): 449–55.

———. 1997. "Race and Academic Disidentification." *Journal of Educational Psychology* 89(4): 728–35.

Padilla, Raymond V., Jesus Treviño, Kenny Gonzalez, and Jane Treviño. 1997. "Developing Local Models of Minority Student Success in College." *Journal of College Student Development* 38(2): 125–35.

Pascarella, Ernest T., Marcia Edison, Amaury Nora, Linda Serra Hagedorn, and Patrick T. Terenzini. 1996. "Influences on Students' Openness to Diversity and Challenge in the First Year of College." *Journal of Higher Education* 67(2): 174–95.

Pascarella, Ernest T., Betsy Palmer, Melinda Moye, and Christopher T. Pierson. 2001. "Do Diversity Experiences Influence the Development of Critical Thinking?" *Journal of College Student Development* 42(3): 257–71.

Pascarella, Ernest T., and Patrick T. Terenzini. 1991. *How College Affects Students: Findings and Insights from Twenty Years of Research.* San Francisco: Jossey-Bass.

Pascarella, Ernest T., Patrick T. Terenzini, and Lee Wolfe. 1986. "Orientation to College and Freshman-Year Persistence/Withdrawal Decisions." *Journal of Higher Education* 57(2): 155–75.

Peña, Yesilernis, and Jim Sidanius. 2002. "U.S. Patriotism and Ideologies of Group Dominance: A Tale of Asymmetry." *Journal of Social Psychology* 142(6): 782–90.

Perlmann, Joel, and Roger Waldinger. 1996. "The Second Generation and the Children of the Native-Born: Comparisons and Refinements." Working paper 174. Annandale-on-Hudson, N.Y.: Levy Economics Institute.

Pettigrew, Thomas F. 1997. "Generalized Intergroup Contact Effects on Prejudice." *Personality and Social Psychology Bulletin* 23(2): 173–75.

———. 1998a. "Intergroup Contact Theory." *Annual Review of Psychology* 49: 65–85.

———. 1998b. "Prejudice and Discrimination on the College Campus." In *Confronting Racism: The Problem and the Response*, edited by Jennifer L. Eberhardt and Susan T. Fiske. Thousand Oaks, Calif.: Sage Publications.

Pettigrew, Thomas F., and Linda R. Tropp. 2000. "Does Intergroup Contact Reduce Prejudice? Recent Meta-Analytic Findings." In *Reducing Prejudice and Discrimination*, edited by Stuart Oskamp. Mahwah, N.J.: Lawrence Erlbaum.

———. 2006. "A Meta-Analytic Test of Intergroup Contact Theory." *Journal of Personality and Social Psychology* 90(5): 751–83.

Petty, Richard E., and Jon A. Krosnick. 1995. *Attitude Strength: Antecedents and Consequences*. Mahwah, N.J.: Lawrence Erlbaum.

Pew Hispanic Center/Henry J. Kaiser Family Foundation. 2002. *National Survey of Latinos*. Washington: Pew Hispanic Center/Henry J. Kaiser Family Foundation.

Phillips, Susan. 1994. "Racial Tensions in Schools." *CQ Researcher* 4(1): 1–24.

Phinney, Jean S. 1990. "Ethnic Identity in Adolescents and Adults: Review of Research." *Psychological Bulletin* 108(3): 499–514.

Porter, Judith R., and Robert E. Washington. 1979. "Black Identity and Self-Esteem: A Review of Studies of Black Self-Concept, 1968–1978." *Annual Review of Sociology* 5: 53–74.

Portes, Alejandro, and Rubén G. Rumbaut. 2001. *Legacies: The Story of the Immigrant Second Generation*. Berkeley, Calif.: University of California Press.

Powers, Daniel A., and Christopher G. Ellison. 1995. "Interracial Contact and Black Racial Attitudes: The Contact Hypothesis and Selectivity Bias." *Social Forces* 74(1): 205–26.

Pratto, Felicia. 1999. "The Puzzle of Continuing Group Inequality: Piecing Together Psychological, Social, and Cultural Forces in Social Dominance Theory." In *Advances in Experimental Social Psychology*, vol. 31, edited by Mark P. Zanna. San Diego, Calif.: Academic Press.

Pratto, Felicia, Jim Sidanius, and Shana Levin. 2006. "Social Dominance Theory and the Dynamics of Intergroup Relations: Taking Stock and Looking Forward." *European Review of Social Psychology* 17: 271–320.

Pratto, Felicia, Jim Sidanius, Lisa M. Stallworth, and Bertram F. Malle. 1994. "Social Dominance Orientation: A Personality Variable Predicting Social and Political Attitudes." *Journal of Personality and Social Psychology* 67(4): 741–63.

Ravitch, Diane. 1990. "Diversity and Democracy: Multicultural Educa-

References

tion in America." *American Educator: The Professional Journal of the American Federation of Teachers* 14(1): 16–20.

Reyes, Gabriel Allan. 1998. "Does Participation in an Ethnic Fraternity Enable Persistence in College?" PhD diss., University of Southern California. *Dissertation Abstracts International Section A: Humanities and Social Sciences* 58(11-A): 4207.

Rhea, Joseph T. 1997. *Race Pride and the American Identity*. Cambridge, Mass.: Harvard University Press.

Rooney, Glenda D. 1985. "Minority Students' Involvement in Minority Student Organizations: An Exploratory Study." *Journal of College Student Personnel* 26(5): 450–56.

Rosenberg, Morris. 1979. *Conceiving the Self*. New York: Basic Books.

Rosenberg, Morris, Carmi Schooler, Carrie Schoenbach, and Florence Rosenberg. 1995. "Global Self-Esteem and Specific Self-Esteem: Different Concepts, Different Outcomes." *American Sociological Review* 60(1): 141–56.

Rothman, Stanley, Seymour Martin Lipset, and Neil Nevitte. 2003. "Does Enrollment Diversity Improve University Education?" *International Journal of Public Opinion Research* 15(1): 8–26.

Rubin, Mark, and Miles Hewstone. 1998. "Social Identity Theory's Self-Esteem Hypothesis: A Review and Some Suggestions for Clarification." *Personality and Social Psychology Review* 2(1): 40–62.

Rudenstine, Neil L. 2001. "Student Diversity and Higher Learning." In *Diversity Challenged: Evidence on the Impact of Affirmative Action*, edited by Gary Orfield. Cambridge, Mass.: Harvard Education Publishing Group.

Rumbaut, Rubén G., and Alejandro Portes, eds. 2001. *Ethnicities: Children of Immigrants in America*. Berkeley, Calif.: University of California Press.

Schlesinger, Arthur M., Jr. 1998. *The Disuniting of America: Reflections on a Multicultural Society*, revised and enlarged ed. New York: Norton.

Schmader, Toni, Brenda Major, and Richard H. Gramzow. 2001. "Coping with Ethnic Stereotypes in the Academic Domain: Perceived Injustice and Psychological Disengagement." *Journal of Social Issues* 57(1): 93–111.

Schuman, Howard, Lawrence D. Bobo, and Maria Krysan. 1992. "Authoritarianism in the General Population: The Education Interaction Hypothesis." *Social Psychology Quarterly* 55(4): 379–87.

Schuman, Howard, Charlotte Steeh, Lawrence D. Bobo, and Maria

Krysan. 1997. *Racial Attitudes in America: Trends and Interpretations*, revised ed. Cambridge, Mass.: Harvard University Press.

Sears, David O. 1975. "Political Socialization." In *Handbook of Political Science,* vol. 2, edited by Fred Greenstein and Nelson Polsby. Reading, Mass.: Addison-Wesley.

———. 1983. "The Persistence of Early Political Predispositions: The Roles of Attitude Object and Life Stage." In *Review of Personality and Social Psychology*, vol. 4, edited by Ladd Wheeler and Phillip Shaver. Beverly Hills, Calif.: Sage Publications.

———. 1990. "Whither Political Socialization Research? The Question of Persistence." In *Political Socialization, Citizenship Education, and Democracy*, edited by Orit Ichilov. New York: Teachers College Press.

———. 1993. "Symbolic Politics: A Socio-Psychological Theory." In *Explorations in Political Psychology*, edited by Shanto Iyengar and William J. McGuire. Durham, N.C.: Duke University Press.

———. 1994. "Urban Rioting in Los Angeles: A Comparison of 1965 with 1992." In *The Los Angeles Riots: Lessons for the Urban Future*, edited by Mark Baldassare. Boulder, Colo.: Westview Press.

Sears, David O., and Harris M. Allen Jr. 1984. "The Trajectory of Local Desegregation Controversies and Whites' Opposition to Busing." In *Groups in Contact: The Psychology of Desegregation*, edited by Norman Miller and Marilynn B. Brewer. New York: Academic Press.

Sears, David O., Jack Citrin, Sharmaine V. Cheleden, and Colette van Laar. 1999. "Cultural Diversity and Multicultural Politics: Is Ethnic Balkanization Psychologically Inevitable?" In *Cultural Divides: The Social Psychology of Cultural Contact*, edited by Deborah Prentice and Dale Miller. New York: Russell Sage Foundation.

Sears, David O., Mingying Fu, P. J. Henry, and Kerra Bui. 2003. "The Origins and Persistence of Ethnic Identity Among the 'New Immigrant' Groups." *Social Psychology Quarterly* 66(4): 419–37.

Sears, David O., and Carolyn L. Funk. 1999. "Evidence of the Long-Term Persistence of Adults' Political Predispositions." *Journal of Politics* 61(1): 1–28.

Sears, David O., and P. J. Henry. 2003. "The Origins of Symbolic Racism." *Journal of Personality and Social Psychology* 85(2): 259–75.

———. 2005. "Over Thirty Years Later: A Contemporary Look at Symbolic Racism." In *Advances in Experimental Social Psychology*, vol. 37, edited by Mark P. Zanna. San Diego, Calif.: Elsevier Academic Press.

Sears, David O., P. J. Henry, and Rick Kosterman. 2000. "Egalitarian Val-

References

ues and Contemporary Racial Politics." In *Racialized Politics*, edited by David O. Sears, Jim Sidanius, and Lawrence D. Bobo. Chicago, Ill.: University of Chicago Press.

Sears, David O., Carl P. Hensler, and Leslie K. Speer. 1979. "Whites' Opposition to 'Busing': Self-Interest or Symbolic Politics?" *American Political Science Review* 73(2): 369–84.

Sears, David O., John J. Hetts, Jim Sidanius, and Lawrence D. Bobo. 2000. "Race in American Politics: Framing the Debates." In *Racialized Politics: The Debate About Racism in America*, edited by David O. Sears, Jim Sidanius, and Lawrence D. Bobo. Chicago: University of Chicago Press.

Sears, David O., and Tom Jessor. 1996. "Whites' Racial Policy Attitudes: The Role of White Racism." *Social Science Quarterly* 77(4): 751–59.

Sears, David O., and Donald R. Kinder. 1971. "Racial Tensions and Voting in Los Angeles." In *Los Angeles: Viability and Prospects for Metropolitan Leadership*, edited by Werner Z. Hirsch. New York: Praeger.

Sears, David O., and Shana Levy. 2003. "Childhood and Adult Political Development." In *Handbook of Political Psychology*, edited by David O. Sears, Leonie Huddy, and Robert Jervis. New York: Oxford University Press.

Sears, David O., and John B. McConahay. 1973. *The Politics of Violence: The New Urban Blacks and the Watts Riot*. Boston: Houghton Mifflin.

Sears, David O., and Victoria Savalei. 2006. "The Political Color Line in America: Many 'Peoples of Color' or Black Exceptionalism?" *Political Psychology* 27(6): 895–924.

Sears, David O., and Nicholas A. Valentino. 1997. "Politics Matters: Political Events as Catalysts for Pre-Adult Socialization." *American Political Science Review* 91(1): 45–65.

Sears, David O., and Colette van Laar. 1999. "Black Exceptionalism in a Culturally Diverse Society." Unpublished paper, University of California at Los Angeles.

Sears, David O., Colette van Laar, Mary Carrillo, and Rick Kosterman. 1997. "Is It Really Racism? The Origins of White Americans' Opposition to Race-Targeted Policies." *Public Opinion Quarterly* 61(1): 16–53.

Sedlacek, William E. 1989. "Noncognitive Indicators of Student Success." *Journal of College Admissions* 125(1): 2–10.

Sedlacek, William E., and Glenwood C. Brooks Jr. 1976. *Racism in American Education: A Model for Change*. Chicago: Nelson-Hall.

Segal, Bernard E. 1965. "Fraternities, Social Distance, Anti-Semitism

Among Jewish and Non-Jewish Undergraduates." *Sociology of Education* 38(3): 251–65.

Shivani, Anis. 2002. "From Redistribution to Recognition: A Left Critique of Multiculturalism" (October 24). Accessed at http://www.infoshop.org/inews/article.php?story=02/10/24/9279622.

Sidanius, Jim. 1993. "The Psychology of Group Conflict and the Dynamics of Oppression: A Social Dominance Perspective." In *Explorations in Political Psychology*, edited by Shanto Iyengar and William J. McGuire. Durham, N.C.: Duke University Press.

Sidanius, Jim, Seymour Feshbach, Shana Levin, and Felicia Pratto. 1997. "The Interface Between Ethnic and National Attachment: Ethnic Pluralism or Ethnic Dominance?" *Public Opinion Quarterly* 61(1): 102–33.

Sidanius, Jim, Yesilernis Peña, and Mark Sawyer. 2001. "Inclusionary Discrimination: Pigmentocracy and Patriotism in the Dominican Republic." *Political Psychology* 22(4): 827–51.

Sidanius, Jim, and John Petrocik. 2001. "Communal and National Identity in a Multiethnic State: A Comparison of Three Perspectives." In *Social Identity, Intergroup Conflict, and Conflict Resolution*, edited by Richard D. Ashmore, Lee Jussim, and David Wilder. New York: Oxford University Press.

Sidanius, Jim, and Felicia Pratto. 1999. *Social Dominance: An Intergroup Theory of Social Hierarchy and Oppression*. New York: Cambridge University Press.

Sidanius, Jim, Felicia Pratto, Michael Martin, and Lisa M. Stallworth. 1991. "Consensual Racism and Career Track: Some Implications of Social Dominance Theory." *Political Psychology* 12(4): 691–721.

Simmons, Roberta G. 1978. "Blacks and High Self-Esteem: A Puzzle." *Social Psychology* 41(1): 54–57.

Simon, Bernd, and Bert Klandermans. 2001. "Politicized Collective Identity: A Social Psychological Analysis." *American Psychologist* 56(4): 319–31.

Smedley, Brian D., Hector F. Myers, and S. P. Harrell. 1993. "Minority-Status Stresses and the College Adjustment of Ethnic Minority Freshmen." *Journal of Higher Education* 64(4): 434–52.

Smith, Daryl G. 1989. "The Challenge of Diversity: Involvement or Alienation in the Academy?" ASHE-ERIC Higher Education Report 5. Washington: Graduate School of Education and Human Development, George Washington University.

Smith, Tom. 1991. *What Do Americans Think About Jews?* Working Pa-

References

pers on Contemporary Anti-Semitism. New York: American Jewish Committee, Institute of Human Relations.

Sonenshein, Raphael J. 1993. *Politics in Black and White: Race and Power in Los Angeles*. Princeton, N.J.: Princeton University Press.

Staerklé, Christian, Jim Sidanius, Eva Green, and Ludwin Molina. 2005. "Ethnic Minority-Majority Asymmetry and Attitudes Towards Immigrants Across Eleven Nations." *Psicologia Polßtica* 30(May): 7–26.

Steele, Claude M. 1997. "A Threat in the Air: How Stereotypes Shape Intellectual Identity and Performance." *American Psychologist* 52(6): 613–29.

Steele, Claude M., and Joshua Aronson. 1995. "Stereotype Threat and the Intellectual Test Performance of African Americans." *Journal of Personality and Social Psychology* 69(5): 797–811.

Stephan, Cookie White, and Walter G. Stephan. 1992. "Reducing Intercultural Anxiety Through Intercultural Contact." *International Journal of Intercultural Relations* 16(1): 89–106.

Stephan, Walter G., and Cookie White Stephan. 2000. "An Integrated Threat Theory of Prejudice." In *Reducing Prejudice and Discrimination*, edited by Stuart Oskamp. Mahwah, N.J.: Lawrence Erlbaum.

Steward, Robbie J., Marshall R. Jackson, and James D. Jackson. 1990. "Alienation and Interactional Styles in a Predominantly White Environment: A Study of Successful Black Students." *Journal of College Student Development* 31(6): 509–15.

Stoll, Michael A. 2005. "African Americans and the Color Line." In *The American People: Census 2000*, edited by Reynolds Farley and John Haaga. New York: Russell Sage Foundation.

Swanson, Guy E. 1992. "Doing Things Together: Some Basic Forms of Agency and Structure in Collective Action and Some Explanations." *Social Psychology Quarterly* 55(2): 94–117.

Swim, Janet K., Laurie L. Cohen, and Lauri L. Hyers. 1998. "Experiencing Everyday Prejudice and Discrimination." In *Prejudice: The Target's Perspective*, edited by Janet K. Swim. San Diego, Calif.: Academic Press.

Swim, Janet K., Lauri L. Hyers, Laurie L. Cohen, Davita C. Fitzgerald, and Wayne H. Bylsma. 2003. "African American College Students' Experiences with Everyday Racism: Characteristics of and Responses to These Incidents." *Journal of Black Psychology* 29(1): 38–67.

Tajfel, Henri. 1972. "Experiments in a Vacuum." In *The Context of Social*

Psychology: A Critical Assessment, edited by Joachim Israel and Henri Tajfel. London: Academic Press.

Tajfel, Henri, M. G. Billig, R. P. Bundy, and Claude Flament. 1971. "Social Categorization and Intergroup Behavior." *European Journal of Social Psychology* 1(2): 149–78.

Tajfel, Henri, and John C. Turner. 1986. "The Social Identity Theory of Intergroup Behavior." In *The Psychology of Intergroup Relations*, edited by Stephen Worchel and William G. Austin. Chicago: Nelson-Hall.

Takaki, Ronald. 1993. *A Different Mirror: A History of Multicultural America*. Boston: Little, Brown.

Tarman, Christopher, and David O. Sears. 2005. "The Conceptualization and Measurement of Symbolic Racism." *Journal of Politics* 67(3): 731–61.

Taylor, Ronald D., Robin Casten, Susanne M. Flickinger, Debra Roberts, and Cecil D. Fulmore. 1994. "Explaining the School Performance of African American Adolescents." *Journal of Research on Adolescence* 4: 21–44.

Terenzini, Patrick T., Laura I. Rendon, M. Lee Upcraft, Susan B. Millar, Kevin W. Allison, Patricia L. Gregg, and Romero Jalomo. 1994. "The Transition to College: Diverse Students, Diverse Stories." *Research in Higher Education* 35(1): 57–73.

Tinto, Vincent. 1975. "Dropout from Higher Education: A Theoretical Synthesis of Recent Research." *Review of Educational Research* 45(1): 89–125.

———. 1993. *Leaving College: Rethinking the Causes and Cures of Student Attrition*, 2d ed. Chicago: University of Chicago Press.

Towles-Schwen, Tamara L. 2003. "White Students' Relationships with Their African American Roommates: Automatically Activated Racial Attitudes and Motivation to Control Prejudiced Reactions as Antecedents and Consequents." PhD diss., Indiana University.

Towles-Schwen, Tamara L., and Russell H. Fazio. 2002. "Interracial Roommate Relationships: The Role of Automatically Activated Racial Attitudes." Paper presented at the annual conference of the Society for Personality and Social Psychology. Savannah, Ga. (February 2002).

Tracey, Terence J., and William E. Sedlacek. 1984. "Noncognitive Variables in Predicting Academic Success by Race." *Measurement and Evaluation in Guidance* 16(4): 171–78.

———. 1985. "The Relationship of Noncognitive Variables to Academic

References

Success: A Longitudinal Comparison by Race." *Journal of College Student Personnel* 26(5): 405–10.

Treviño, J. G. 1992. "Participation in Ethnic/Racial Student Organizations." *Dissertation Abstracts International* 53(12): 4230A.

Triandis, H. C. 1977. "The Future of Pluralism." *Journal of Social Issues* 32(4): 179–208.

Tropp, Linda R. 2006. "Stigma and Intergroup Contact Among Members of Minority and Majority Status Groups." In *Stigma and Group Inequality: Social Psychological Perspectives*, edited by Shana Levin and Colette van Laar. Mahwah, N.J.: Lawrence Erlbaum.

Truax, Kathryn, Diana I. Cordova, Aurora Wood, Elisabeth Wright, and Faye Crosby. 1998. "Undermined? Affirmative Action from the Target's Point of View." In *Prejudice: The Target's Perspective*, edited by Janet K. Swim and Charles Stangor. San Diego, Calif.: Academic Press.

Tucker, Belinda, and Claudia Mitchell-Kernan. 1995. "Social Structural and Psychological Correlates of Interethnic Dating." *Journal of Social and Personal Relationships* 12(3): 341–61.

Turner, John C. 1975. "Social Comparison and Social Identity: Some Prospects for Intergroup Behavior." *European Journal of Social Psychology* 5(1): 5–34.

———. 1991. *Social Influence*. Pacific Grove, Calif.: Brooks/Cole.

———. 1999. "Some Current Themes in Research on Social Identity and Self-Categorization Theories." In *Social Identity: Context, Commitment, Content*, edited by Naomi Ellemers, Russell Spears, and Bertram Doosje. Oxford: Blackwell.

Turner, John C., and Katherine J. Reynolds. 2000. "The Social Identity Perspective in Intergroup Relations: Theories, Themes, and Controversies." In *Blackwell Handbook of Social Psychology: Intergroup Processes*, edited by Rupert Brown and Samuel Gaertner. Oxford: Blackwell.

Turner, Marlene E., and Anthony R. Pratkanis. 1994. "Affirmative Action as Help: A Review of Recipient Reactions to Preferential Selection and Affirmative Action." *Basic and Applied Social Psychology* 15(1–2): 43–69.

U.S. Census Bureau. 2000. Washington: U.S. Government Printing Office.

———. 2001. Washington: U.S. Government Printing Office.

Valentino, Nicholas A., and David O. Sears. 1998. "Event-Driven Political

Communication and the Pre-adult Socialization of Partisanship." *Political Behavior* 20(2): 127–54.

———. 2005. "Old Times There Are Not Forgotten: Race and Partisan Realignment in the Contemporary South." *American Journal of Political Science* 49(3): 672–88.

van Laar, Colette. 1999. "Attributional Determinants of Expectancies and Self-Esteem Among Ethnic Minority College Students." Ph.D. diss., University of California at Los Angeles.

———. 2000. "The Paradox of Low Academic Achievement but High Self-Esteem in African American Students: An Attributional Account." *Educational Psychology Review* 12(1): 33–61.

van Laar, Colette, and Belle Derks. 2003. "Managing Stigma: Disidentification from the Academic Domain." In *Learning and Motivation in a Multicultural Setting*, edited by Farideh Salili and Rumjahn Hoosain. Greenwich, Conn.: Information Age Publishing.

van Laar, Colette, Shana Levin, Stacey Sinclair. In press. "Social Identity and Personal Identity Concerns in Stereotype Threat: The Case of Affirmative Action." *Basic and Applied Social Psychology*.

van Laar, Colette, Shana Levin, Stacey Sinclair, and Jim Sidanius. 2005. "The Effect of University Roommate Contact on Ethnic Attitudes and Behavior." *Journal of Experimental Social Psychology* 41(4): 329–45.

Weil, Frederick D. 1985. "The Variable Effects of Education on Liberal Attitudes: A Comparative-Historical Analysis of Anti-Semitism Using Public Opinion Survey Data." *American Sociological Review* 50(4): 458–74.

Weiner, Bernard. 1985. "An Attributional Theory of Achievement Motivation and Emotion." *Psychological Review* 92(4): 548–73.

——— 1986. *An Attributional Theory of Motivation and Emotion*. New York: Springer-Verlag.

Wilder, David, and Andrew F. Simon. 2001. "Affect as a Cause of Intergroup Bias." In *Blackwell Handbook of Social Psychology: Intergroup Processes*, edited by Rupert Brown and Samuel L. Gaertner. Oxford: Blackwell.

Wilder, David A., and John E. Thompson. 1980. "Intergroup Contact with Independent Manipulations of Ingroup and Outgroup Interaction." *Journal of Personality and Social Psychology* 38(4): 589–603.

Wilder, David H., Arlyne E. Hoyt, Dennis M. Doren, William E. Hauck, and Robert D. Zettle. 1978. "The Impact of Fraternity and Sorority

References

Membership on Values and Attitudes." *Journal of College Student Personnel* 19(5): 445–49.

Wilder, David H., Arlyne E. Hoyt, Beth S. Surbeck, Janet C. Wilder, and P. A. Carney. 1986. "Greek Affiliation and Attitude Change in College Students." *Journal of College Student Personnel* 27(6): 510–19.

Williams, R. M., Jr. 1947. *The Reduction of Intergroup Tensions*. New York: Social Science Research Council.

Wright, Stephen C., Arthur Aron, Tracy McLaughlin-Volpe, and Stacy A. Ropp. 1997. "The Extended Contact Effect: Knowledge of Cross-Group Friendships and Prejudice." *Journal of Personality and Social Psychology* 73(1): 73–90.

Wylie, Ruth C. 1979. *The Self-Concept: Theory and Research on Selected Topics*, vol. 2. Lincoln, Neb.: University of Nebraska Press.

Zaller, John R. 1992. *The Natures and Origins of Mass Opinion*. Cambridge: Cambridge University Press.

Index

Boldface numbers refer to figures and tables.

Index

Index

Index

summary and conclusions, 157–62; theoretical considerations, 139–41, 302–12. *See also* American national vs. ethnic identification; common ingroup identity; university identification

ethnicity and sample attrition analysis, 62, 353–61

ethnic organizations. *See* organizations, student

ethnic segregation hypothesis, 187, 200, 204, 315

ethnic-status hierarchy, **267, 271,** 280–81, 283

ethnic studies centers and majors, 43–44, 275, 283

European assimilation prototype, 137, 158

expectations and attributions variables, 55, 59

extended contact effect of intergroup friendships, 18, 226

faculty ethnicity and academic outcomes, **268–69,** 274–75

Filipinos: anticipatory socialization for college, 253–54; campus climate variables in academic outcomes, **267, 270–71**; cognitive factors in academic outcomes, 255–56, **257,** 258, 264; curriculum variables in academic outcomes, **266, 268–69,** 274–75; and discrimination, **267, 270**; disidentification with academics, 258, **259, 261, 266, 268**; ethnic organization membership, **266–67, 269**; ethnic outlook and academic outcomes, 279, 280, 281; intergroup contacts, **267, 269–70, 271**; parental education factor, 252; proportion of sample, 52; self-esteem levels in college, **262, 266, 268**

first- vs. second-generation immigrant participants, 52

fraternities and sororities. *See* Greek (fraternity-sorority) organizations

friendships, inter-ethnic: and academic outcomes, **269–70,** 276–78, 283, 383–84n25–26; and belonging, 199–202, 383n24; and campus climate, 197–202; dating attitudes and behaviors, 193–97, **269–70,** 277–78, 380n9, 381–82n12–15; effects overview, 15; and ethnic attitudes, 188–92; extended contact effect, 18, 226; ingroup favoritism, 190, **191,** 192; introduction, 185–87; overview, 17–18; summary and conclusions, 203–5; theoretical considerations, 312–15

Gaertner, Samuel, 165, 179

gender: and faculty effects on academic outcomes, 274–75; and inter-ethnic dating patterns, 193; participant characteristics, 49, **50**; and political conservatism, 81, 84, 85, 117–19, 121–22, 134, 301, 367n9

generalization of contact effects, 16–17, 26–27

Gilliard, Michelle, 229

Glazer, Nathan, 138

Greek (fraternity-sorority) organizations: as ethnic organization for whites, 231–33, **234,** 235, 237, **238,** 309–10; intergroup attitude effects, 239–40, 242, **243,** 247–49; introduction, 229–30; mediational effects of ethnic identification, 244, **245,** 246

group-justifying motive, 177

Gurin, Patricia, 142